"No period in American history is more colorful or relevant to our own—for better and worse—than the Gilded Age. James Grant brings it all memorably to life: Mugwumps and Half-Breeds, congressmen of flamboyant plumage for sale, not to mention a political process frozen in partisanship. Looming above it all, literally larger than life, is Thomas B. Reed, perhaps the most fascinating politician you've never heard of. A hero to young Theodore Roosevelt, as Speaker of the House Reed singlehandedly crushed the filibuster. (One is tempted to say, Boy do we need him now). At the same time, Reed's erudition and stinging wit may well have cost him the White House. In the end, his ambition yielded to his principles, prompting him to resign the speakership rather than endorse the imperial vision of his fellow Republicans. It's taken a century, but Reed at last has a biographer equal to his story."

—**Richard Norton Smith, author of *The Colonel: The Life and Legend of Robert R. McCormick, 1880–1955* and Scholar-in-Residence of History and Public Policy at George Mason University**

MR. SPEAKER!

The Life and Times of Thomas B. Reed
The Man Who Broke the Filibuster

James Grant

Simon & Schuster Paperbacks
NEW YORK LONDON TORONTO SYDNEY NEW DELHI

Simon & Schuster
1230 Avenue of the Americas
New York, NY 10020

First Simon & Schuster trade paperback edition May 2012

SIMON & SCHUSTER and colophon are registered trademarks
of Simon & Schuster, Inc.

For information about special discounts for bulk purchases,
please contact Simon & Schuster Special Sales at
1-866-506-1949 or business@simonandschuster.com.

The Simon & Schuster Speakers Bureau can bring authors
to your live event. For more information or to book an event,
contact the Simon & Schuster Speakers Bureau at
1-866-248-3049 or visit our website at www.simonspeakers.com.

Designed by Paul Dippolito

Manufactured in the United States of America

1   3   5   7   9   10   8   6   4   2

The Library of Congress has cataloged the hardcover edition as follows:
Grant, James.
Mr. Speaker! : the life and times of Thomas B. Reed, the man who
broke the filibuster / James Grant.
p.   cm.
Includes bibliographical references and index.
1. Reed, Thomas B. (Thomas Brackett), 1839–1902. 2. Legislators—
United States—Biography. 3. United States. Congress. House—Speakers—
Biography. 4. California—Politics and government—1850–1950. I. Title.
E664.R3G73 2011
328.73'092—dc22
[B]   2011002798

ISBN 978-1-4165-4493-7
ISBN 978-1-4165-4494-4 (pbk)
ISBN 978-1-4516-1109-0 (ebook)

For Patricia, who else?

Contents

Preface

THOMAS BRACKETT REED was the rock-ribbed Maine Republican who led the U.S. House of Representatives into the modern era of big government. From the Speaker's chair early in 1890, he unilaterally stripped the legislative minority of the power to obstruct the law-making agenda of the majority. Enraged Democrats branded him a "czar," which epithet Reed seemed not to mind at all.

Modernity was Reed's cause from his first Congress in 1877 to the day he resigned in protest over America's war of choice with Spain. As society was moving forward, he contended, so must the government and the laws. That meant, for instance, the abolition of capital punishment, a cause he championed while representing Portland in the Maine legislature immediately following the Civil War. On the national stage, it meant protective tariffs, peace, women's suffrage, federally protected voting rights for African-Americans and a strong navy. He heaped ridicule on the Democrats for their Jeffersonian insistence on strictly limited federal powers. The tragedy of Reed's political life was that the government he helped to cultivate and finance turned warlike and muscular, just as his Democratic antagonists had predicted it would. His friend and onetime protégé Theodore Roosevelt rode that trend into the history books. Reed, heartsick, retired to Wall Street to practice law.

Peace and prosperity make a superior backdrop to everyday living, but they do not necessarily commend an era to the readers or writers of history. Not that either Reed's life (1839–1902) or his times were anything but eventful. Boom and bust, free trade or protection, race, the rights of subject peoples and the relationship between the individual and the state were the staple points of conflict during his quarter-century in politics.

Czar Reed had a suitably tyrannical presence, standing well over six feet tall and weighing close to 300 pounds. He married a clergyman's daughter, Susan P. Jones, who opposed women's suffrage; Katherine, their daughter, lived to advocate it. Reed's eyes beamed with intelligence but his massive face was bland enough to stump the portraitist John Singer Sargent. "Well," Reed quipped as he beheld the painter's failed likeness of himself in 1891, "I hope my enemies are satisfied."

The party labels of Reed's day may seem now as if they were stuck on backwards. At that time, the GOP was the party of active government, the Democratic party, the champion of laissez-faire. The Republicans' sage was Alexander Hamilton, the Democrats', Thomas Jefferson. The Republicans condemned the Democrats for their parsimony with public funds, the Democrats arraigned the Republicans for their waste and extravagance. And what, in those days, constituted extravagance in federal spending? Arguing in support of a bill to appropriate funds for a new building to house the overcrowded collection of the Library of Congress, Reed had to answer critics who charged that Congress should do without the books rather than raid the Treasury and raise up one more imperial structure to crowd the capital city's already grandiose thoroughfares.

The library fight was waged with words, but the politics of Reed's time were shockingly violent. It was embarrassing to Reed to have to try to explain away to his congressional colleagues the near war that erupted in his home state over the stolen 1879 Maine gubernatorial election. Reed had grown used to political bloodshed in the conquered South, but even he, worldwise as he was, had never expected the descendants of the Puritan saints to have to call out the militia to get an honest count of a New England vote. Meanwhile, in Washington, on the floor of the House of Representatives, ex-soldiers would put aside public business to hurl charges and countercharges over the wartime atrocities at Andersonville or Fort Pillow. Reed himself was not above the occasional jibe at the ex-Confederates—"waving the bloody shirt," this style of political discourse was called—but he affected not one jot of martial vainglory. A supply officer aboard a Union gunboat on the Mississippi River in the final year of the war, he drew no fire except the verbal kind from his own commanding officer.

As a professional politician, Reed could talk with the best of them. In the House, he was the acknowledged master of the impromptu five-minute speech and of the cutting, 10-second remark. He talked himself into 12 consecutive congresses, including three in which he occupied the Speaker's chair. "The gentleman needn't worry. He will never be either," he once remarked to a Democrat who was rash enough to quote Henry Clay's line about rather being right than president.

Reed's wit was his bane and glory. An acquaintance correctly observed that he would rather make an epigram than a friend. Too often, he made an epigram and an enemy. "They can do worse," he said of the Republicans who were sizing him up for the GOP presidential nomination in 1896. "And they probably will," he added prophetically. In the museless and pleasant William McKinley, the Republicans did, in fact, do much worse. Mark Hanna, McKinley's strategist and the first of the modern American political kingmakers, set his agents to mingle in the western crowds that Reed sought to charm in the 1896 campaign season. "There was nothing Lincolnian about Reed, obese, dapper and sarcastic," Hanna's biographer recorded. "He wasn't too friendly when they came up to shake hands after meetings. He was an Eastern Product."

That Reed fell short of the presidency was his contemporaries' loss, even more than his own. That he has made so small a mark in the modern historical record is a deficiency that this book intends to rectify. The Gilded Age produced no wiser, funnier or more colorful politician than Speaker Reed, and none whose interests and struggles more nearly anticipated our own. Reed, like us, debated the morality of a war that America chose to instigate. He wrestled with the efficacy of protecting American workers and their employers from foreign competition and resisted the calls of those who would cheapen the value of the dollar. He was—as it might be condescendingly said of him today—ahead of his time on issues of race and gender. Actually, in many ways, his views harkened back to those of the Founders. Too loyal a Republican to speak out against the McKinley administration's war in the Philippines, Reed would let drop the subversive remark that he believed in the principles set forth in the Declaration of Independence. Roosevelt wondered what had gotten into him.

If Reed resigned from Congress in bitterness, he served with zest. He loved the House and especially the Speakership, an office, as he liked to say, that was "without peer and with but one superior." In parliamentary finesse and imagination, he was among the greatest Speakers. Such 21st century political scientists as Randall Strahan and Rick Valelly rank him on a par with the great Henry Clay of Kentucky. Reed's signal achievement was to institute an era of activist legislation to displace the prevailing system of party stalemate. Empowered by the rules he himself imposed, the Republican majority of the 51st Congress, 1890–92, passed more bills and appropriated more money than any preceding peacetime Congress. To critics who decried the appropriations record of that Congress—a shocking $1 billion—Reed approvingly quoted someone else's witticism: "It's a billion-dollar country."

The overtaxed and -governed 21st century reader may wince at the knowledge that the hero of these pages was an architect of the modern American state—certainly, his biographer does. However, Reed did not knowingly set out to create Leviathan. He wanted not a big government but a functional one. He opposed what he took to be unwarranted federal intrusion into private matters, including big business, even though—to a degree—that business owed its bigness to the tariffs that the Republicans erected to protect it from foreign competition. In middle age, Reed found the time to teach himself French, but he stopped short at reading Frederic Bastiat, the French economist who demonstrated the compelling logic of free trade. The truth is that economics was not the czar's strongest suit—then, again, it has rarely been Congress'.

Burning bright through the full length of Reed's congressional years was the question of what to do about money. Alexander Hamilton had defined the dollar in 1792 as a weight of silver (371¼ grains) or of gold (24¾ grains). Most of Reed's contemporaries agreed that the law meant what it said. Money must be intrinsically valuable, worth its weight, or something close to its weight, in one of the two precious metals. Paper money was acceptable only so far as it was freely exchangeable into the real McCoy. Let the government just print up dollar bills, as it had done during the American Revolution and again, under Abraham Lincoln, in the Civil War, and inflationary chaos would descend.

In the final quarter of the 19th century, not a few Americans would have welcomed inflation with open arms. Falling prices were the norm; on average during Reed's political career, they fell by a little less than 2 percent a year. For debtors, the decline was a tribulation. They had borrowed dollars, and they were bound to repay dollars, but the value of the dollars they owed was rising. Thanks to material progress itself, the cost of producing goods and services was falling. Steamships had displaced sail, the automobile was gaining on the horse, and the telegraph and telephone were providing a fair preview of the wonders of the Internet. In consequence, prices fell even faster than wages did. Many Americans profited in the bargain, though a vocal minority lost, and this angry cohort did not shrink from expressing its demand for cheaper and more abundant dollars. Silver was a cheaper metal than gold, and paper was cheaper than either. Let money, therefore, argued the populists, be fashioned out of these common materials, the better to serve a growing nation and not incidentally lighten the debtor's load. For most of his public life, Reed took the opposite side of the argument. Supporting the gold standard, he contended that a stable, value-laden dollar best served the interests of all, wage-earners not least.

As pro-inflation sentiment was rife in Maine, Reed maintained his hard-money view at some political risk to himself. He hewed consistently to gold until the mid-1890s, when the monetary battle was raging hottest. And then, to some of his friends' despair, he casually indicated a preference for bimetallism, the monetary system under which gold and silver cohabitated (and in which gold was likely to be driven from circulation by the cheaper, and cheapening, alternative metal). To uncompromising gold-standard partisans, Speaker Reed suddenly seemed to go soft when he most needed to stand tall.

Reed's mordant sense of humor was oddly out of phase with his upbeat view of the human condition. Unlike his friend Mark Twain, he was prepared to contend that reason was on its way to banishing war, purifying religion and eradicating poverty. For Reed, there was no bygone Arcadia; always, the best was yet to come.

But not until he took matters into his own hands was there anything on Capitol Hill to resemble the ingenuity of Thomas Edison or Alexander Graham Bell. Until what were known as the Reed rules took force in 1890, the House was hostage to its own willful minority. If those members chose to obstruct, they would simply refuse to answer their names when the clerk called the roll. In sufficient numbers, sitting mute, they could stymie the House, which, under the Constitution, requires a quorum to function. Present bodily, they were absent procedurally.

So for weeks on end, the main order of business might consist of parliamentary fencing and the droning repetition of roll calls, each absorbing 20 or 25 unedifying minutes. The 50th Congress, either notorious or celebrated for its inactivity (depending on one's politics), contributed 13 million words to the Congressional Record on the way to no greater legislative achievement than the institution of the U.S. Department of Agriculture. By contrast, the 36th Congress, as recently as 1859–61, while debating war and peace, union and secession, freedom and slavery, had uttered just four million.

Reed, elected Speaker for the first time in the 51st Congress, transformed the House by declaring those members present who were actually in the House chamber, whether or not they chose to acknowledge that fact by opening their mouths. Democrats excoriated him for doing so, their rage compounded by Reed's seeming imperturbability under fire. Not that they were alone in their disapproval. The voters, deciding that Reed had overreached, handed the House Republicans (though not Reed himself) a lopsided defeat in the congressional elections of 1892. By and by, Reed lived to see both himself and his rules vindicated, the Democrats themselves coming grudgingly to adopt them in 1894.

Reed, a first-term congressman at the age of 37, had seen something of the world as Maine legislator, attorney general and Portland city solicitor. His political education continued in Congress with service on the commission to investigate the crooked presidential election of 1876. Each party had attempted to steal it, the Republicans finally outfilching the Democrats. Reed, as partisan a politician as they came even in that partisan age, distinguished himself in the investigation by bringing to light Democratic malfeasance while explaining away (or trying to) Republican offenses.

Reed held sacred the right of majority rule. Especially did he hold that right dear, as a journalist of the time dryly remarked, when he agreed with the majority. But the majority and Speaker Reed finally parted company in 1898 over the administration's program to add to American possessions in the Caribbean and the Pacific. From the Speaker's chair, he engaged in his rearguard actions against the war. Holding up the Hawaiian annexation measure, for instance, he refused recognition for the members' pet hometown appropriation measures on the grounds that "the money is needed for the Malays," or—concerning a proposed Philadelphia Commercial Museum—"This seems like a great waste of money. We could buy 15,000 naked Sulus with that."

Reed was as prone to error as the next mortal legislator, but he was inoculated against humbug. The language of McKinley's aggressive foreign policy brought out what may seem now, with a century's perspective, the best in him. "It is sea power which is essential to every splendid people," declaimed Henry Cabot Lodge, a close friend of Reed's—and of Roosevelt's too—in the Senate during the run-up to war. Said Reed, simply and winningly, "Empire can wait."

MR. SPEAKER!

Chapter 1

"Oh happy Portlanders"

Thomas Brackett Reed was born in Portland, Maine, on October 18, 1839, in a two-story wood frame house on Hancock Street, hard by the birthplace of Henry Wadsworth Longfellow. The Reed home bore not a trace of resemblance to Lincoln's log cabin, a fact about which Reed, Speaker of the House and presidential hopeful, was slightly defensive.

One day in Reed's Washington office, a congressional aide, Amos Allen, was examining a photograph of the place. He showed it to the boss.

"That's a pretty fair house to have been born in," Allen observed.

"Yes, Amos," said Reed. "But, you see"—pointing to a new addition—"I was not born in all that house."

"Even so," Allen persisted, "it is a pretty good house to have been born in."

"Yes, but still," Reed returned, "I was not born in more than two or three rooms of that house."

Then again, there were only three or four Reeds on the premises—mother, father, boy and girl, Harriet, born in 1846—and the father, Thomas Brackett Reed Sr., a sailor and fisherman, sometimes spent the night afloat. Each side of the family was of 17th century, Pilgrim-and-Puritan stock, though Reed, in later life, was no more inclined to talk up his bloodline than he was to pass around the picture of his birthplace. Rather, he would say that he was descended from generations of fishermen and sailors and that, in making a genealogical investigation, he was hard pressed to prove that his ancestors ever existed.[1] Still, Thomas Reade, the first in the family to make landfall in America, in 1630, settled at Salem in the Massachusetts Bay Colony, where he accumulated land and honors.[2] And interwoven among the succeeding Reades, latterly Reeds, were strong and accomplished men and women. George Cleve, the principal founder of the colony of Maine, was a forebear of Mary Brackett, who married Joseph Reed, of York, Maine. Among their children was Thomas B. Reed, the father of the future Republican Speaker.

The senior T. B. Reed was born in 1803. The consensus of Portland opinion was that, in courting and winning his second wife, Mathilda Mitchell, he had married above himself. Miss Mitchell had beauty, intelligence, piety and a *Mayflower*-company bloodline. The neighbors agreed that she was the probable source of young Thomas's brains. The boy was not yet three when the Reeds made a crosstown move to a little one-and-a-half-story house on Brackett Street. The absence of a stable in back meant that the family was only scraping by.[3]

To judge by the city statute book, overexuberance came as naturally to Portland's boys as it did to any other city's. Under the law, it was forbidden to swim naked in public places, shoot off fireworks or fire guns in the streets, frighten the horses or jump rides on the back of horse-drawn conveyances. And there was to be no irreverence on Sundays. It was the law against Sabbath-breaking that marked Portland as a New England community with a still-living connection to the faith of John Calvin. Young Tom Reed had not turned five when Aaron Burnhan, "a child," was fined 50 cents and court costs for fishing on Sunday. Not having that kind of money, the youngster went to jail.[4]

Fondly would Reed remember what fun he could have with a nickel, especially on the Fourth of July. A penny bought 10 firecrackers or two round cakes. Independence Day, Reed recollected, was the day of the boy: "All other days in the year he took a back seat, cowered in the darkness, or did his deeds of disorder behind fences or haystacks or in barns or sheds; but on the Fourth of July he came out openly and flouted the good citizens. What guns we used to use and what pistols!"[5]

And what theology! "[T]he happiness of the righteous, and the punishment of the wicked, will both be endless" was a fair sample of the Protestant doctrine still in place as Reed was growing up. Man was a fallen and sinful creature, "destitute of holiness and justly exposed to the wrath of God." Salvation there could be through Jesus Christ, but "such is the depravity of the human heart that no person will come to Christ except the Father draw him." By the same token, not just anybody could be drawn, only those so predestined. As for the young Sabbath-breakers, a Portland newspaper editorially advised the Almighty to lay them out in a sickbed.[6]

The Portland elders judged Reed's generation to be just as depraved, idle and lawless as most generations of adults have appraised their own rising young to be. In church, children giggled, riffled through books and ate candy with their mouths open. There was worse. Parties went on well beyond the sensible hour of 9 PM and February 22 was commemorated not in remembrance of the first president of the United States but by mobs moving through the unlit streets with burning pails of pitch and by gangs doing battle, the Middle-Enders against the Lower-Enders, or the Hog-Towners against the Liberty Street boys.[7] So it came to be that, in Portland, "Tarbucket Day" was a child's first association with the birth of George Washington. "There is a sad want of comity and propriety, or what was once termed good manners, among a portion of our boys, while in the street," attested the annual report of the Portland School Committee for 1841—"and, we wish we were not compelled to add, among our girls likewise."[8]

To the naked eye, Portland seemed not at all close to civic or spiritual breakdown. Set on a three-mile-long peninsula sheltering Casco Bay from the Atlantic, it was ventilated, then as now, by health-giving sea breezes. Climbers to the summit of the Portland Observatory, 210 feet above sea level, could gasp at the beauty of the glittering bay to the southeast, with its white sails and awkward-looking, newfangled steamboats and its hundreds of green islands. The White Mountains, then as now, rose to the west, Mount Washington, 68 miles distant, lording it over the rest. Fog rolled in from the east or southeast, winter gales from the east or northeast, summer storms from the west. In all kinds of weather, sea gulls wheeled and screeched.[9] Portland then had grand houses, rich merchants, rising entrepreneurs and thousands of sheltering trees. An arboreal census conducted in 1854 found 3,300 trees on 134 streets and lanes. "[N]o person builds a house on a respectable street but his first object is to plant trees about it," reported the census-taker.[10]

The English novelist Anthony Trollope visited Portland on the eve of the Civil War. "The faces of the people tell of three regular meals a day, and of digestive powers in proportion," the author of *The Way We Live Now* recorded. "Oh happy Portlanders, if they only knew their own good fortune. They get up early, and go to bed early. The women are comely and sturdy, able to take care of themselves without any fal-lal of chivalry; and the men are sedate, obliging and industrious." Trollope confirmed that young people did attend parties and that young women could be seen walking home at 10 PM. Yet, he pointed out, each reveler carried her sewing basket. What kind of dissipation was this? "Probably of all modes of life that are allotted to man by his Creator, life such as this is the most happy."[11]

Prohibition was the secret of this felicity, to hear the reformers tell it. The famous "Maine Law" of 1851 banned the sale of beer, wine and liquor by retail establishments throughout the Pine Tree State. Trollope, for one, wrote off the law as another futile experiment in government coercion, but the city fathers didn't doubt its necessity. They at least could see that Portland had a drinking problem.

The people drank because they wanted to or had to or even because their doctors advised them to. Alcohol made the long winters bearable and lightened the load of labor, especially the lumbering and fishing that the hard-bitten Maine men performed without the softening influence of women and children. Employers seemed not only to condone drinking, but almost to encourage it. Workers dropped tools at 11 AM and 4 PM when the town bell signaled grog time. No public hanging, firemen's parade, militia day, cattle show, election day, wedding day, town meeting or Fourth of July was complete without good, hard, purposeful drinking. Sailors ashore needed no town bell or festival day as a pretext to get drunk, and not a few landsmen followed their example. In 1840, temperance advocates estimated, 500 Portlanders, out of a population of 12,000, were generally under the influence; 1,000 more were episodically drunk.[12] Then too, alcohol lubricated the wheels of commerce.

Merchants sent their fish and timber to the West Indies in exchange for molasses and rum. The molasses, they turned into sugar or distilled into New England rum. The rum, they sold—or paid out in wages.[13]

Trollope insisted he saw no poor people in Thomas B. Reed's hometown, but the Reverend William Hobart Hadley, the city's minister at large, had seen plenty, a good many of them drunk. Hadley arrived in 1850, a decade before Trollope and a year before prohibition. "Unforeseen misfortunes and unavoidable casualties, produce a considerable amount of poverty and suffering," he wrote of the epidemic of alcoholism he encountered. "These cases call for our kindest sympathies and most liberal charities. But the great mass of squalid poverty we witness, is the effect of idleness, prodigality and intemperance. This last named evil is the great and terrible scourge which afflicts our community, and produces more poverty and misery than all other causes combined."[14]

The mature Reed had not one doubt that progress was the way of the world. "Far enough indeed are we from perfection," he once addressed his Portland constituents. "But whoever doubts progress doubts God." In the city of Reed's youth, dogs, pigs and cows competed with well-booted pedestrians for right-of-way on the unpaved streets. Stagecoaches from Boston or northern Maine scattered the pedestrians. Wagons loaded with cheese, lumber and butter from Vermont and New Hampshire rumbled down to the waterfront to trade for tools, cloth, sugar, molasses and liquor, the latter especially welcome for the long drive home through the White Mountain Notch.

To the city fathers, lighting these thoroughfares—snow-choked in winter, miry in springtime, dusty in summer, pungent with manure in all seasons—seemed a frivolous extravagance. Certainly, it was out of the question in the straitened years following the Panic of 1837. Moonlight was more than bright enough for the criminal class, which seemed bolder every year. Was not the immigrant element of the city's fast-growing population unusually prone to draw knives? Was it not remarkable that boys were "permitted to bellow through the streets, insult men and women, smoke in their faces, spit tobacco juice . . . and pull the bells and knockers of doors?"[15] To many, it seemed so.

In 1849, the city government moved to establish a full-time, day-and-night police force.[16] In the same year, it reconsidered its view of the utility of street lights. "[T]here is not a city in the Union of the size and importance of Portland that is not lighted," a citizens group petitioned the City Council.[17] Gas lamps appeared in the early 1850s.

Perhaps respectable Portlanders exaggerated the incidence of depravity in their midst, as respectable people sometimes do. The City Marshal's Report for the 12 months ended April 1, 1854, reveals a grand total of 240 complaints: three for larceny, four for assault and battery, four for assault on city officers (by this time Portland had its own police force), a few dozen for selling liquor (now prohibited) and one for "keeping a gaming-house." There had been one murder and one abduction. By far the largest number of offenses was for drunkenness, 202; the authorities had seized 4,027 gallons of illegal liquor.[18] Of the 415 persons incarcerated in city "watch houses" over the course of the year, 127 were American citizens; most of the rest were Irish.

The heavenly city that Trollope visited lacked indoor plumbing. An 1848 law mandated the siting of outhouses, or "necessaries," no closer than 20 feet from the house proper, a sign of refinement; 15 feet was the previous minimum lawful distance. A Portland barber pressed for the building of municipal baths by playing—unavailingly, as it turned out—to civic pride. In Boston, this advocate reported, Portlanders were mocked as the "great unwashed."[19]

But the ruling spirit of the Portland of the 1840s and 1850s was neither riot nor dirt but progress. Most of the Western world was embarked on a golden age of prosperity and invention. Steam power propelled vessels and machinery with a degree of efficiency never before imagined. Trade among nations had increased wonderfully, and the telegraph linked distant cities. The 1848 California gold strike expanded the world's wealth and imagination alike, even to distant Portland. The contagion known as "gold fever" found a carrier in the person of a jeweler's son who returned home from his California prospecting adventure in February 1850 bearing $3,000 in bullion. But there were better ways of profiting from the gold discoveries in California (and Australia too) than by setting off for distant parts to dig. Within 15 years, the Portland Shovel Company was turning out as many as 2,400 shovels a day "of the most improved patterns," to answer the demand from hopeful adventurers.[20]

A spirit of commercial optimism infused Portland during Reed's high-school years. Smoke belched from the Portland Sugar Company, with its two steam engines doing the work of no fewer than 75 horses while daily consuming 10 tons of anthracite coal. By 1849, 23 stationary steam engines were speeding the production of lumber, furniture and ships. They pounded piles, lifted grain, and powered presses, punches, planers, saws, drills and lathes. The pride and joy of the city's manufacturing economy, the Portland Company, turned out railroad locomotives and rolling stock for sale throughout New England, the Canadian Maritime Provinces and beyond.[21]

Not all bowed down before the mighty steam engine, which made human labor easier but also, to a degree, redundant. It was steam power that caused Reed's father, a man of sail, to quit the coasting fleet and take a job as mate on an oceangoing vessel—and, later, as a watchman at a sugar plant near the Portland waterfront.[22] The coming of the railroads disturbed long-established overland trade patterns and seemed, at first, to rob Portland of its commercial reason for being. But a pair of local entrepreneurs, John A. Poor and William Pitt Preble, conceived a railroad connection with Montreal. The "wilting" of Portland, a sentiment much on the lips of Portlanders in the early 1840s, now gave way to talk of boom and, at some length, to the gorgeous thing itself. "It was a revival movement—and everybody but a few croakers was converted," a historian of the times records. "The city loaned its credit in bonds to the amount of $2 million; 11 miles of the Atlantic and St. Lawrence Railroad were opened in 1848, and in 1853 it was finished to its junction with the Canada road from Montreal—a distance from Portland of 149 miles. The Grand Trunk Railway brought our city into connection not only with the towns and cities of Canada but the vast grain-growing regions of the West."[23]

Next came steam-propelled, seaborne connections to Liverpool, England, and the construction of Commercial Street, a mile-long, 100-foot-wide thoroughfare along the entire Portland waterfront. The Forest City was back in business again.[24]

A PICTURE OF the young Reed participating in Portland's Tarbucket riots or gang fights does not come easily into focus. The three-term

Speaker was a man of rare intelligence, physical restraint and unbending integrity. But that did not mean he yielded blindly to authority. He was the kind of adolescent who, in 21st century America, is the despair of learning specialists and school psychologists. The Portland High School for Boys, which he attended from 1852 to 1856, offered alternative tracks, vocational and classical. Reed, clearly college material, belonged in the academic curriculum. But he seemed to devote himself to demonstrating how little he deserved to be studying Virgil and how much his future lay in the manual arts. Though his academic marks were no worse than mediocre, he badly flunked deportment. "One" was the best grade, and the one most commonly awarded. In his first two terms, Reed somehow managed to score a "four."

If his teachers wished he would stay away from school, Reed refused to oblige them, though on any given day fully a fifth of the students were somewhere other than their assigned places on the hard and comfortless high-school benches. On the grounds of creature comforts alone, there were persuasive enough reasons to play hooky. In wintertime, a scholar froze or roasted, depending on his proximity to a single stove. In all seasons, rainfall dripped from the ceiling. Reed, however, missed only a single day, and that for an excused illness.

Because the future Speaker made a career out of his coruscating wit, one might infer that talking out of turn or disrespectfully was the cause of his failing deportment grades. However, no sooner did a certain assistant teacher, P. S. Perley, quit the faculty than Reed's deportment scores jumped to perfect. A few years later, to earn a little money between college terms, Reed was teaching at a public school in neighboring Westbrook. The official review of his classroom performance would have surprised neither Perley nor Reed's future congressional adversaries. "If Mr. Reed had made more effort to secure the love of his pupils, and had avoided some indiscreet remarks (which caused several scholars to leave) we should be well pleased with his labors," according to the town agent.[25]

In June 1854, in his 15th year, the budding cynic and wit was admitted to membership in the State Street Congregational Church. It seems he took this step on his own, as his parents did not belong. "Every candidate for admission to this Church will be expected to give satisfactory evidence of personal piety, and assent to its faith and covenant," the laws of the church provided. A female congregant recalled that Reed "got religion and was one of the best speakers they had at the evening meetings." So much religion did he get that he accepted a sum of money from the ladies of the church with which to pursue a contemplated career in the ministry. But the rising preacher changed his mind and gave back the money.

In high school, Reed was tall and pudgy. He studied arithmetic, geography and declamation in his first term, and algebra, chemistry, French and declamation in his second. Post-Perley, he studied Latin, Greek, grammar, bookkeeping and declamation. In his final term, he scored perfect grades in everything.

As well he might have, for Bowdoin College, in nearby Brunswick, to which he was bound, was exacting. "Candidates for admission," the college stipulated, "will be required to write Latin grammatically, and to be well versed in Geography, Arithmetic, six sections of Smyth's Algebra, Cicero's *Select Orations, the Bucolics,* two *Georgics,* and nine books of the *Aeneid* of Virgil, Sallust, Xenophon's *Anabasis,* five books, Homer's *Iliad,* two books, together with Latin and Greek Grammar and Prosody. They must produce certificates of their good moral character."

There was also the matter of tuition. Two hundred dollars, the cost of a year at Bowdoin, was what the Portland city physician earned. It was a third more than the annual salary of a Portland assistant engineer.[26] It very likely was as much as Reed's father could earn in a year, either at sea or on land. Fortunately, a long winter break at Bowdoin afforded needy students the opportunity to work off their tuition, which Reed did by teaching. And when, in his senior year he could earn no more, he borrowed $200 from U.S. Senator William Pitt Fessenden, himself a Bowdoin alumnus and father of Sam, Bowdoin Class of 1861. Reed and Sam were roommates.

Bowdoin, founded in 1794, was then, as it is today, an elite private college. In Reed's time, it catered very largely to the elite from the state of Maine. The distinguished alumni in whose footsteps Reed presumed to tread included Longfellow and Nathaniel Hawthorne, as well as the 14th president of the United States: Franklin Pierce, Bowdoin Class of 1824, was in the White House as Reed packed up for Brunswick.

Reed's class, the Class of 1860, numbered 58, of whom Reed, two months short of his 17th birthday, was among the youngest. One of the ten professors on the faculty was Joshua Chamberlain, the future Civil War hero. The president of the college, Leonard Woods, was a man of wide accomplishments and sturdy self-confidence. Once, upon being granted an audience with Pope Gregory XVI, Woods was asked in which language he would be most comfortable conversing. French, German or Latin, it made no difference, he replied. Whereupon, for 60 minutes, His Eminence and the very Protestant New England college president spoke in Latin.

The Bowdoin course of study was unvarying. Latin, Greek, theology and mathematics were the mainstays. That mathematics was not the average student's cup of tea might be inferred from the fact that the juniors ritually burned their calculus textbooks. In his year, 1859, Reed was the ceremonial Bearer of the Ashes. At Portland High declamation was a staple; so also at Bowdoin. And English composition too: Students took three years' worth. Theology—not yet watered with Harvard Unitarianism—accounted for as much as one-fifth of class time. In the absence of big-time intercollegiate athletics and electronic media, the students had to make their own amusements. They read books for pleasure, rowed, played chess, debated and drank.

Sometimes Reed and his friends read aloud to each other, as Reed and his friend Frank Dingley liked to do. One winter night Reed was reading to Dingley from Carlyle's *French Revolution*. Came a knock on the door and the college chaplain, Egbert Coffin Smyth, smilingly presented himself for conversation and prayer. Reed by then had put his piety well behind him, and his lacerating exposition on the shortcomings of organized Christianity sent Smyth, now unsmiling, out the door again.

As a writer, Reed showed the touch that can't be taught. He had a stylist's ear and a logician's mind. "Born in the lowest condition of life," he wrote of John Bunyan, "he received only a limited education which he speedily forgot." Speculating on what might have become of the world if the Spanish Armada had not been defeated, Reed seemed to speak for his Puritan forebears as well as himself: "Superstition and despotism might have weighed us down ever more. But Providence is the world's ally in all such crises. It pointed the guns of the English fleet as years before it had wielded the hammer of Charles Martel when he crushed the Saracens on the plains of France."

In Reed's collegiate essays, the parliamentarian and politician make their early appearance. "Eloquence is inspiration," wrote the greatest congressional debater of his generation. "It is the highest flight of genius and commands the loftiest ambitions of the human mind. Deep thought, quick wit and a steady earnestness of purpose can accomplish it. Motives do not arouse it because it comes of its own free will." As for the politician, a discerning reader of his "Excesses of the French Revolution" would have predicted, correctly, that Reed, though conservative, would be no reactionary: "The French Revolution was not the resistance of a free people to the encroachments upon their established rights; but the uprising of a nation trodden down by ages of despotism. It was not the slow growth of the wild tree forcing itself through the slight crevice and increasing in compass and might until it overthrew the firm foundations, but the sudden upheaval of the giants buried beneath the mountain. It is not wonderful that fire and smoke and molten lava should follow. Accordingly when we contemplate the excesses of the Revolution, we cannot but believe that a result like this must have had a proportional cause, that if the result was terrible the cause must have been terrible also."

Reed the young slacker was also in evidence: "For no success is permanent," this persona observed. "Every new attainment demands another. Every goal, that is past, but brings us in sight of the next." And: "A life of ambition must always be a life of toil and tension. And what is to be the reward? A place in history. Can this benefit the dead? Do not the millions on millions who have died and made no sign rest as quietly in their graves as those upon whom the world is heaping its useless honor?"

As he did in high school, Reed saved his best for last. All his life he was a late and troubled sleeper. Sitting in a chair, he could seem to be asleep, his face and body slack and his thoughts seemingly miles away from the business at hand. Then all at once, he would rouse himself and say or do something splendid. So it was in his senior year in college. His classmates sat agog as he recited page after page of Joseph Butler's 1736 treatise, *Analogy of Religion*. And they were in awe to hear his lucid analysis of the text he had perfectly committed to memory. "When Reed was called," one of these admirers attested, "I always sat a silent, wondering witness at the perfect exhibition of intellect, and its steady magnificent work. I never observed its equal in any other person." Reed made up enough academic ground with his sprint to the finish line to graduate fifth in his class. And so it was that the slacker, now a bachelor of arts, was elected to Phi Beta Kappa.

Late in life, Reed looked back on his student days with pride. He recalled arising at 6 AM, "almost dead tired, when it was necessary for me to lie down on the bed in the middle of putting on my clothing. Oh, but what a student I was in those times."[27]

Chapter 2

Acting Assistant Paymaster Reed

THE PHI BETA Kappa alumnus of Bowdoin College was not among the impetuous tens of thousands who dropped whatever they were doing to answer Abraham Lincoln's call to the colors in the aftermath of the Confederate firing on Fort Sumter on April 12, 1861. His classroom in the Boys High School in Portland was where Reed happened to be when the war began, and it was where he chose to remain—there and in the Portland law office of S. C. Strout where he began his legal studies. Somewhere along the way, he bought a steerage-class ticket to California to seek his fortune. Homesick—or, at least, heartily sick of California—he returned east in 1864, obtained a commission in Mr. Lincoln's navy and spent the final year of the Civil War as a supply officer aboard a gunboat on the Mississippi.

What drew Reed to California is unknown, but he made no secret of what he thought of the place after he arrived. Not even the weather agreed with him. There was no green to be seen, complained the visitor from the city of 3,300 trees. The ground was brown, and so, even, were the trees—dust enveloped all, except in the rainy season, when everything turned to mud. Stories of the great flood of 1861–62 greeted him upon his arrival. And he himself was a witness to the formative stages of the great drought of 1862–65.[1] Reed likened the fickle San Francisco summers to the treacherous San Francisco stockbrokers. "Nature never intended any man to live here," he wrote in 1863, "only to dig for gold and get himself out of it and in dreams shudder ever afterwards."[2]

For a time, Reed taught Latin and mathematics at a co-ed school in Stockton. The girls gave him fits. "He was," a former pupil recalled, "a big awkward fellow about 22 years of age, big head, hands and feet and homely. The girl pupils began making fun of him the first day he entered the school room." The future impertubable Speaker of the House blushed like a beet one February 14 when, sitting at the head of his class, he opened a valentine that the pranksters in his midst had sent him. He didn't teach for long.[3] Nor did he dig for gold. If nuggets ever littered the ground, the forty-niners had long since bent over to pick them up. Mining was now a serious, subsurface enterprise. It required capital, which seeded a stock market and called forth the concomitant evils of promoters and manipulators. Reed said he could count 4,000 publicly owned mining ventures in California, of which fewer than a dozen paid an honest dividend. Some, like the Daney Gold and Silver Mining Company, paid a corrupt dividend, borrowing the funds with which to dispense a little something to shareholders as the insiders quietly sold. Reed seemed inoculated against this speculative fever, as he later proved not to be against a bubbly Great Plains real estate market: "In my opinion, it would be far preferable for an honest man to embark his money in some well conducted lottery than to venture it in mining stock. He would come out of it, if he failed, with more faith in human nature and less belief in total depravity."[4]

California was a very long way from Gettysburg or Antietam, but the war could not have been far from Reed's mind. Sam Fessenden, his Bowdoin roommate, was killed at the Second Battle of Bull Run, in August 1862. Sam had begged his influential father to pull the strings to send him and his artillery outfit into action. "What I hope," young Fessenden wrote to Senator Fessenden six months before his death, "is that before the war is over we may show of what stuff we are made."[5] And even without this most personal reminder of suffering and death, Reed could not have escaped the intense local debate over slavery and the Union. California was nominally a northern state. It had abolished slavery a year before its admission to the Union in 1850, and its economic interests lay with the North and with the national government. Still, Confederate sympathizers were thick on the ground: "We question very much whether there be more enthusiastic rebels in South Carolina to-day than can be found in many places in California," a San Francisco newspaper ventured. So it was that when state judge Samuel Bell McKee came up for reelection in the autumn of 1863, 16 members of the bar signed a letter endorsing him. Not the least of his merits, the petitioners said, was his unquestioned determination to "uphold the Administration in its present efforts to suppress the rebellion and sustain the Constitution and the laws of the United States." Thomas B. Reed was one of the signatories.

The state bar exam was then not so grueling as it later became. In response to a question from the examining judge, Reed argued in support of the right of the national government to issue paper money without the customary backing of a gold reserve to lend it tangible value. The same judge, an ardent states' rights man, had asked the same question of another candidate, who had answered in the negative. "We will recommend you both favorably, as we think all young men who can answer great constitutional questions off-hand, ought to be admitted to the bar," the open-minded examiner told Reed. This was on or about September 8, 1863.[6]

Reed poured out his pro-Union thoughts in a speech at a San Jose schoolhouse some time in the same year. Here emerges the voice of the future forensic scourge of the Democratic party. Here too is the voice of the Decoration Day patriot, which voice an older Reed came to detest. It was the South that had started the war, the Maine transplant assured his small audience: "They dreamed that this Northern people over whom they [tyrannized] so long were as tamed and spiritless as the slaves they ruled." He contended that "the creed of the Democratic party has been conforming itself to slavery" for the past 40 years, that "we of the North have been bleeded without sting and murdered without mercy" and that, though "war has its horrors," it was a far sight better than a pusillanimous peace. "Better war: loud war, war by land and by sea," he said, now quoting Tennyson; "War with a thousand battles and shaking a hundred thrones." To the living, Reed declared, falls the sacred obligation to honor the fallen in this struggle, "that they should not fall in vain, that their deaths were but the prelude to brighter days, that in the storied annals of their country's life their names would not be linked with saddest disaster but . . . with noble victory."[7]

These were strong words to come from an able-bodied, six-foot, three-inch civilian of military age, and Reed perhaps saw the incongruity of his position. In March 1864, he boarded a ship for the east coast (a "Panama steamer," the *Sacramento Daily Union* reported) to accept a naval commission. Reporting for duty in Washington, D.C., next month, the aspiring officer was appointed an acting assistant paymaster in the United States Navy.

The men of Bowdoin College were ardent for the Union. Maybe they imbibed their ardor from the very bricks of Appleton Hall, where Harriet Beecher Stowe wrote much of *Uncle Tom's Cabin* (Calvin, her husband, was a Bowdoin theology professor). Out of the 55 members of the Class of 1860, 29 served in the armed forces of the United States. Three of Reed's classmates were killed in action. That Reed waited so long to enlist, and that he sought out a station that hits the ear more as a financial posting than a martial one, are facts to suggest that he lacked the heart for the fight. Reed himself was more than happy to contribute to the picture of antiheroism. Twenty years after he reported for duty on the Mississippi, in a speech before a Washington gathering of the Loyal Legion, an organization of former Union military and naval officers, the then-Republican congressman struck a note not unlike the one that Abraham Lincoln sounded in reminiscing about the terrible bloodletting he endured from enemy mosquitoes during the Blackhawk War.

"The Navy," Representative Reed told the assembled veterans, "means different things than to many here before me. To the distinguished admiral who sits beside me, and to the distinguished admiral who sits opposite, it means the shriek of shot and shell, the horrors of the blockade. To me it meant no roaring wind, no shriek of shot or shell, but level water and the most delightful time of my life. For I was on a gunboat on the Mississippi River after the valor and courage of you gentlemen had driven the enemy off."

The USS *Sybil*, the gunboat to which Reed was assigned, was attached to the 200-vessel Mississippi Squadron under the command of Admiral David D. Porter, hero of the Battle of Vicksburg. *Sybil* was unsightly and slow, and she presented as mortal a threat to her crew as she did to the Confederate guerrillas who skulked in wait in hidden positions along the riverbank. Reed reported aboard in July 1864, a full year after the fall of Vicksburg made the Mississippi River the Union's own. But that did not make the *Sybil's* engine room any safer. In August, the captain mustered the crew to listen to a reading of the coroner's verdict concerning the bursting of a boiler aboard the USS *Chanango*; 28 officers and men had perished in that disaster. Steam power was nothing new on the water, but it was an evolving technology.

"It was a delightful life," Reed reminisced of his navy days. "Thirteen hundred dollars a year and one ration, and nothing to do. My sad heart hath often panted for it since. . . . What a charming life that was, that dear old life in the Navy! I knew all the regulations and the rest of them didn't. I had all my rights and most of theirs."

Life aboard the *Sybil* consisted of a daily round of drills, watch-standing and maintenance work, from much of which Reed, in his capacity as a supply officer, would likely have been exempted. The men drilled at the guns and practiced buttoning up the ship for battle. They swept, swabbed and holystoned the decks, scrubbed the paintwork, mended clothes (and made them too), stood inspection and took aboard stores. They coaled the ship, measuring out the fuel in bushels, and took turns standing watch. On Sundays they listened to an ever-so-familiar reading of navy regulations ("Articles for the Better Government of the Navy"). From time to time it fell to Reed to pay the men, to issue clothing to new arrivals or to supervise the taking aboard of miscellaneous stores: for instance, on August 5, 1864, three oil cans, a dozen oak buckets, 74¼ pounds of canvas duck, a speaking trumpet, five pounds of lamp wick and two dozen corn brooms. However his body might be summoned to duty, Reed's formidable intellect was usually at rest.

The *Sybil* was armed with 24-pound cannons and 30-pound Parrott riles.[8] When not chugging up and down the Mississippi she lay at anchor, sometimes for weeks on end, at her home port in the southern Illinois town of Mound City. But when she did get up a head of steam and take up her post on the river, her mission, like that of the rest of the Mississippi Squadron, was to assist in the work of starving the Confederacy. To the blue-water navy fell the assignment of blockading the enemy's vast stretch of coastline. To the brown-water service went the work of preventing Texas beef, and every other kind of contraband, from reaching the rebellious states from the west. It was a close-drawn thing who had the more miserable time of it, the river sailors or their saltwater brethren. A sailor on the blockade advised his mother that if she wanted to know what his life was like, she should "go to the roof on a hot summer day, talk with a half-dozen degenerates, descend to the basement, drink tepid water full of iron rust and repeat the process at intervals until [you are] fagged out, then go to bed with everything shut tight."[9]

"Degenerate," however, was a relative term. The human scrapings judged unfit even for blockade duty went to the brown-water fleet. At least the Union's post-Vicksburg dominance of the Mississippi assured that Reed's tour of duty would be a mostly peaceful one. "Thereafter, an occasional enemy battery or party of irregulars might fire on passing Federal commerce, but the Confederacy had lost river superiority forever," naval historian John D. Milligan records. "All tactical and strategic advantages conferred by the Mississippi henceforth belonged to the Union."[10]

While underway, the *Sybil* spent most of her time between Mound City and Memphis—as it happened, one of the safer stretches of the Mississippi. Twice, though, she ventured deep into Louisiana, once all the way to Donaldson, and on other occasions into Arkansas on the still-contested White River. The seagoing service presented one set of risks, river duty another. In a gale, the Mississippi was the place to be. However, it was not so clear that the river sailors had an easier time of it in combat. The blue Atlantic hid no snipers, as did the banks of the Mississippi. A Union blockade vessel could at least see the enemy's approach. There was no such warning on the narrow river passages.

Action, for the *Sybil*, meant blasting away at suspected enemy positions and putting a dozen or so men ashore to give chase to fleeing rebels. Reed once helped to lead such a landing party. His detachment drew no fire, encountered no guerrillas and had nothing more to show for its few hours ashore than the destruction of a pair of small boats. In fact, the ship's log records not one round of incoming fire during Reed's time aboard. It is recorded, however, that, on December 10, 1864, at Hickman, Kentucky, the men of the *Sybil* "destroyed [a] barrel of whiskey."

As the enemy was small in number and fleet afoot, the *Sybil* was usually engaged in noncombatant pursuits. She hauled cotton (a most precious commodity in wartime), prisoners of war, mail, coal, Union soldiers and southern refugees. Elements of the Mississippi Squadron were notorious for subordinating the hunt for the enemy to the gathering up of cotton for sale on the black market. If the *Sybil* partook in that nefarious trade, Reed never mentioned it.

The logbook bulges with disciplinary infractions by sailors who wished they were anywhere else. Fighting, sleeping on watch, refusal to obey a lawful order and desertion were common offenses. If, through the gauze of middle-aged memory, Reed cherished his days on the river, not many seemed to share his view during the war. "Unable to attract recruits," a history of the service relates, "the navy scoured men from every possible source. It lowered standards . . . sought castoffs from the army and accepted men deemed unfit for blockade duty. In fact, the core group of these 'brown-water' sailors consisted of two groups: sailor rejects from the blockade and soldier transfers from the army."[11] Nor was the service too proud to accept escaped slaves and Confederate prisoners of war. Indeed, in one especially desperate 60-day stretch in 1863, former Confederate prisoners constituted no less than 11.5 percent of the brown-water navy's recruits.

Enlisted men might veer from the straight and narrow—and, when they did, expect to be punished in a manner to fit the crime: for an apprehended deserter, to be broken in rating and to forfeit all pay; or for the parties to a fistfight, to be clapped together in irons. Of course, a higher standard of conduct was expected of commissioned officers, and the *Sybil*'s logbook records only one disciplinary crisis of the wardroom during Reed's service aboard the ship. And whom should that event involve but our hero himself.

The *Sybil* was steaming down the Mississippi under a clear blue sky on January 5, 1865, when Reed and another junior officer, Acting First Ensign Samuel Tubbs, "were arrested and sent to their rooms & sentinel placed over them, by order of the Commanding Officer." Beyond those tantalizing facts, the record is silent.

In Reed's cruise aboard the *Sybil*, only one casualty is recorded: On December 14, 1864, Seaman John Boke accidentally shot himself while on picket duty.[12] But that is not to say that Reed saw nothing of war. Mound City, besides being the *Sybil*'s home port, was the site of a Union cemetery and a large military hospital. Nearby Cairo, Illinois, was a col-

lection point for southern refugees. Shortly before Reed entered the service, the Cairo Relief Association issued an urgent appeal on behalf of
indigent southern whites who were pouring in by the thousands. "They
are sent here by the military authorities," the circular related, "on government transports and steamers and landed on our levee at all hours of
the night and day. There they are left, shelterless, and penniless, their
future an aimless blank." Ninety percent were women and children. The
children were often "without hats, shoes, stockings and hundreds without a change of clothing. Those who have lived in affluence are reduced
to equal extremities of want with the poor. Of course, cleanliness is
impossible in their condition. The health of most is reduced by exposure
and by bad and scanty food. Many are sick requiring immediate medical
attention and tenderest nursing care. A mother and her four daughters
have died of exposure within the space of one week."[13]

For the officers and men of the *Sybil*, peace was every bit as anti-
climactic as war. Not until April 12, three days after Lee's surrender
at Appomattox, does the log record the end of hostilities: "A salute of
200 rounds was fired from Fort Curtis." Life for the *Sybil*'s crew hereafter
proceeded much as it had before. On May 28, Seaman Luke Burns, a
chronic troublemaker, was bound in irons and chained to a stanchion
for refusing to obey a lawful order. On June 12, Samuel Tubbs, Reed's
partner in crime, was again arrested, this time for using insolent language in speaking to the executive officer. Two days later, on the White
River, gunners loaded the battery with shrapnel in response to the sound
of nearby firing. Sick call never failed to entice a decent-size quorum of
invalids—sometimes a dozen or more. But the *Sybil*'s time under the colors was running out. On July 31, 45 crewmen left for good. On August
17, at Mound City, the *Sybil* left the service. She fetched just $10,000 at
public auction, one-third the price that Admiral Porter had paid to buy
her in April 1864.[14] Assistant Paymaster Reed was on his way home.

"The brave faces I see before me," said Congressman Reed to his
audience at the Loyal Legion so many years later, "have been bared to
the shock of battle and of storm. You have seen on a hundred battle
fields the living and the dead. It would be a shame for me to talk seriously of service to men like you. This button—insignia of the order—
you wear because *you* honor it. *I* wear it because *it* honors *me*."

Chapter 3

"The atrocious crime
of being a young man"

WANDERLUST WAS EVIDENTLY not among the emotions that washed over Assistant Paymaster Reed as he walked down the gangway of the USS *Sybil* for the last time. His wartime service honorably concluded, he returned to his hometown and to his prewar career. The learned Nathan Webb was among the satisfied lawyers on the committee that probed his professional qualifications. In October 1865, Thomas B. Reed, age 26, was admitted to the bar of Cumberland County, Maine.[1]

Now he hung out his shingle and waited, as newly minted lawyers do, for clients, income and recognition. Recognition, at least, was not long in coming. In 1867, the Cumberland County Republican party put him on the ballot for a seat in the state legislature. As the Republican nominee was invariably the victor in Portland in those days, Reed took his place at Augusta in the 47th session of the Maine House of Representatives. He was returned to the House in 1869 and elected to the state Senate in 1870. Retiring from the Senate, he became the youngest attorney general in the history of the Pine Tree State. Prosecuting an especially lurid and salacious murder trial, he added celebrity to his substantial reputation for legal learning and electability.

The law was no certain pathway to riches in Portland in the late 1860s, even for lawyers who had clients. The Cumberland Bar Association was just two years old when Reed was admitted. Founded in 1805, it had dried up and blown away during the 1830s or 1840s, when "the members appear to have yielded in despair to the spirit of reckless innovation upon old and well established principles." Now the Portland lawyers banded together to try to raise the standards of professional conduct and to pledge one another to a system of genteel price fixing. No member should draft a deed or a mortgage for less than $2, argue before the municipal court for less than $5 or appear in U.S. District Court for less than $10. Members paid $2 in annual dues.[2]

The strapping young Reed, with his college education, war record (of a kind) and connections to the family of U.S. Senator William Pitt Fessenden, was certainly not without legal or political promise. Still in his 20s, he displayed some possibly worrying signs of idealism—a deep-rooted opposition to capital punishment, a curious attachment to women's rights, a quixotic resistance to the demands of the railroad interests for public subsidy—as well as a natural youthful impetuousness. Perhaps more worryingly, the bright young man from Bowdoin had wit and a sharp tongue. Neither was he demonstrably religious. On the contrary, the rumors were true that, in 1862, prior to his embarking for California, he was excommunicated from the State Street Church.

The official record of his expulsion does not detail the cause, though such a sudden and final parting of the ways was a drastic step infrequently taken, as shown in church documents. A ladies' group at the church had, as previously noted, presented him with a scholarship on the understanding that the recipient was bound for the ministry. While at Bowdoin, Reed had changed his mind, and he subsequently returned the ladies' donation. Plainly, he did not thereby regain their goodwill, but what provoked his expulsion is a mystery.

In private, the young lawyer's remarks on religion and on the religious mores of the day were scathing—and one can safely assume that Reed's confidences on that incendiary topic would not remain private indefinitely. All this was on the debit side of Reed's personal political balance sheet. On the other side of the ledger, he had the essential professional insight that winning elections and uplifting the human race were two separate and distinct callings. To that degree, he seemed a politician born to the trade.

Reed's proudest achievement as a state legislator was his work on the House Judiciary Committee in 1868 to establish a superior court in Portland. Before this improvement in the city's juridical apparatus, a contested suit might be three years in wending its way to trial. After Reed steered the bill to passage, waiting time dropped to three months.[3] This was a rare and gratifying achievement in the life of a junior lawmaker, even one who, like Reed, quickly rose to a position of responsibility on the Judiciary Committee, a prestigious assignment. For the most part, the lawmakers spent the brief sessions in Augusta listening to the special pleading of other politicians while champing at the bit for the opportunity to do their own. Bills of no conceivable interest to anyone except their sponsors filled the legislative hopper of the House. A fair sample of the 1868 session:

"[A]n act to authorize the commissioners of the county of York to audit, allow and pay the expense incurred in the pursuit, detection and arrest of the persons who robbed the safe of D. W. O'Brien, in the county of York; an act to repeal chapter 89 of the Public Laws of 1867, entitled an act to provide for the uniformity in the taxation of legal costs by the clerks of the courts of this State. . . ."[4]

And of the 1869 session:

"[A]n act repealing all the special laws regulating the alewife fishery in the town of Bristol; an act to incorporate the Sherman Monument Association; an act to make valid the doings of the town of Wayne; an act authorizing Mary E. Belch to construct fish weirs in the Moose river; an act to amend chapter 382 of the laws of 1867, entitled an act to incorporate the Winterport Railroad Company."[5]

Close—very close—readers of legislative dispatches could catch a fleeting glimpse of Reed's name. Once, on a bill concerning municipal war debts, he "moved to amend by striking out of the 6th section 200, and insert 100."[6] Or, on another occasion, he reported that the Judiciary Committee had judged "inexpedient" a bill that would have exempted from taxation the real estate of soldiers' and sailors' widows. In 1869 he voted against legislation to establish a state police force. In 1870, now

serving in the Senate, he opposed a sumptuary measure, on the ground
that it was "uncalled for."[7]

Sometimes the legislators turned their attention to the transcendent
issues of the day. Thus in March 1868, the House resolved to commend
the Maine congressional delegation "in unanimously voting for the
impeachment of Andrew Johnson, President of the United States, for
high crimes and misdemeanors." Reed voted with the substantial Republican majority, though his mentor, Senator Fessenden, would famously
vote to acquit the president when the case came to trial.[8] One year later,
the Maine legislators took up the matter of life and death in the shape
of a bill to outlaw capital punishment. Its author was Thomas B. Reed.[9]

Maine had executed only one prisoner since 1837, when the state
legislature, through a nuanced change to the state constitution, had virtually abolished the death penalty. Late in the 1860s, there arose a popular movement to restore it. Governor Joshua Chamberlain, the hero
of Gettysburg, supported the revival of capital punishment, as did an
evident majority of the Maine lower house.[10] Reed's bill would outlaw
executions and forbid the governor from carrying out sentences on any
prisoner who had been condemned to die before his bill became law.

Not that enactment was certain. The chief proponents of the death
penalty regarded the issue as one that the Bible had settled. Who was
Reed to question it? Representative C. J. Morris, a rail-thin, middle-
aged Republican merchant from Portland, quoted Genesis: "Who so
sheddeth man's blood, by man shall his blood be shed." Here was the
universal law. Human life is sacred because man is made in the image
of God. Murder, therefore, is a crime against God. "[A]ssailing man
made in his own image, is an assault upon that most familiar form of
his appearing here on the earth, upon that temple which is the abode of
the spirit," Morris told the House. He invoked the history of California
as proof of the practical necessity of hanging. In San Francisco, murder went unpunished until a vigilante committee plucked a handful of
known killers from the city jail, tried them and put them to death. On
such foundation was civil society established.[11] Reed was unmoved, his
jaundiced views of the Golden State notwithstanding.

A veteran of Andersonville, the infamous Confederate prisoner-of-
war camp, joined the debate in the columns of the Portland *Daily Press*.

"W," as the essayist signed himself, related that, at Andersonville, the ruthless had preyed on the helpless until the decent majority of captives formed a military government of necessity. They conducted impromptu trials and hanged the jackals, as the Confederate guards looked the other way. "The laws given by the Almighty to the Jews were laws for the government of human society and the penalties were to be inflicted by human agents," "W" wrote. "To be sure it was a society differing very much from our own but the abstract proposition is none the less clear that men had the God given right to execute the death penalty. Whether it is advisable in our own State in its present stage of civilization to maintain capital punishment is quite another question."[12]

Reed was as sure of his ground as Morris and "W" were of their Bible. It was, of course, a tricky business disputing with those who regarded their critics as blasphemers. Late in February 1869, Reed rose in the House to make his case. While not "equal [to] the theological learning" of one of his adversaries, or the "didactic eloquence" of another, he said he hoped that he would be able to "bring forward some of those sound results of human reason" that are not at all inconsistent with the "revealed will of God."[13]

Reed spoke for 45 minutes. The criminal justice system was imperfect, he pointed out, but capital punishment was irrevocable. Neither did the threat of execution effectively deter crime, because "it was a penalty uncertain of infliction." He quoted Catherine the Great: "We must punish crime without imitating it," and he demanded, "If people are safe without executions in what we are pleased to call the half-civilized country of Russia, why not here?" He refused to quote Scripture in support of his position, and he doubted the power and relevance of the theological arguments invoked by his opponents: "If his colleagues insisted on the death penalty for murder as divine," a newspaper report paraphrased him as asking, "why not for the 30 or more other crimes for which the death penalty was meted out by 'them of olden times'?"[14]

In private, Reed was elaborately sarcastic: "Mr. Messer considers any one who desires to abolish strangulation as 'trying to be wiser than God,' which remark he regards as closing the whole question. Against such inner-light it is no use to burn the farthing candles of human reason." His bill went down to defeat on March 4, 1869. Next day he told a friend, "For three hours after abolition was defeated, the other side wrangled over 'how to hang [the condemned].'"[15]

And 10 days after that, the hometown newspaper showered Reed with praise. "[It] has more than satisfied the warmest anticipations of his friends," wrote the editorialist of the Portland *Press* of Reed's work in the just-concluded legislative session. "His position has been in several respects a trying one. He is one of the youngest members of the House, and at the same time the actual though not the nominal leader of that body. Besides, his views are several decades in advance of those of the majority of the members on several of the most important topics that came before the House for consideration. But his readiness and skill in debate, his solid legal acquirements and general culture together with his strong personal influence have given him beyond controversy the leading position which we have assigned to him."[16]

Reed was, indeed, that youthful leader, skillful debater and progressive thinker. But he was no less the calculating politician. In the necessary arts of forming friendships, building alliances and picking the plums of patronage, he was showing professional promise. In the opening weeks of the 1869 legislative session, he achieved a small triumph of political diplomacy by steering his reluctant colleagues to side with Hannibal Hamlin in a bitterly contested vote for a seat in the U.S. Senate (which, under the electoral rules of that time, was decided in the state legislature, not by popular vote). Reed, personally, couldn't stand Hamlin, Lincoln's first vice president, but he saw the necessity of supporting him. "I have got out of this without personal quarrel, I think," Reed confided to his legal-mentor-turned-political-ally, Nathan Webb. "I don't know of anyone with whom I have been angry on this affair."[17] Certainly not Hamlin, who won the seat.

A year later, when Webb, then the county attorney for Cumberland County, was promoted to U.S. attorney for Maine, Reed wrote to congratulate him. That was the first paragraph. The subject of the second and subsequent paragraphs was the vacancy that Webb's rise in the world had created. "What about your successor?" Reed asked before proceeding, knowingly, to survey the alternatives.[18]

*   *   *

No SOONER HAD Reed turned 30, in October 1869, than he was elected to the state Senate. And no sooner was he elected to that office than he had the pleasure of watching himself being considered for an even higher one. The attorney general of Maine, William P. Frye, was stepping down at the end of his three-year term; who should replace him? "Mr. Reed," ventured the Augusta correspondent of the Boston *Advertiser*, "is a young man of prowmise and a good lawyer of his years, and with the exception of 'the atrocious crime of being a young man,' is eminently fit to be urged for the place."[19] The editorial page of the Portland *Daily Press* seconded the news pages of the *Advertiser*: "He would, if elected, discharge the duties of the office in a manner highly creditable to himself and be of quite as much service to the State as an older man."[20] Nominated by the state Republican caucus on January 5, 1870, Reed was as good as elected; he assumed office at the conclusion of the legislative session. The pay was $1,000 a year.

All of this honor and good fortune evidently turned the head of Mrs. Susan P. Jones, the widowed eldest daughter of the Reverend S. H. Merrill, a Portland Congregationalist divine, for Reed and she were married on February 5. Most of what little is known of Mrs. Reed comes filtered through her husband's eviscerating wit. But she seems to have coaxed forth a strain of tenderness in him that would have astonished the Maine Democrats. She was in poor health in May of the next year when he wrote to her from Auburn, Maine, where he was arguing a case before a jury:

> I hope you are doing as bravely as when I left home. If you only knew how I long to hear the best news of you, you would be well at once. I've so much to say to you that can't be written that you must be satisfied to let me leave it all to be said when you are well.
> Good By [sic] Dear, I love you,
> Tom

And two days later in a more characteristic tone:

> I ought to have written you yesterday but was too late for the mail. Besides, [illegible]'s letter says that the Dr pronounces you out of danger and of course the more you get well the more you'll be neglected.[21]

Reed sat down to write a letter to his friend George Gifford, a kindred spirit who was making a career in newspapers and politics. A supporter of female suffrage and critic of the Maine Republican machine, Gifford was a polemicist fierce even by the incendiary standards of Reconstruction-era journalism. "Dear George," the impious attorney general began,

> It being the evening of the Lord's Day the melancholy fact that we have nowhere to go dawns upon us again, and I see no other way to salvation than to write to you. Your virtues loom up through the mists of the distance and even Mrs. Reed is willing to admit that you might have been a good man if you had been brought up right.[22]

By the early autumn of 1872, the Reeds had an infant son. To his father, the tiny creature "looks like ex-Gov. Robinson." Reed mused to Gifford that, "[A]s I look at him and think what a tight squeak it was . . . I wonder that we all of us got all the way down here from Adam. For my part, if the matter had been left to me in Chaos, I should have thrown up the sponge without one single round." The baby died 18 days after his birth, on September 22. A daughter, Katherine, was born on January 23, 1875.[23]

As LUCK WOULD have it, a sensational murder was Reed's to prosecute not long after he moved into the attorney general's office. On the evening of September 19, 1870, a jealous railcar painter, Edward H. Hoswell, hid himself under his wife's bed to pounce on the man whom he believed to be her lover. Hoswell saw his shoes, heard his voice, then slithered out from under his hiding place and, with a lunge, cut his throat. "I have got you now, you son of a bitch," he screamed. He slashed at his wife too, who darted out of the room streaming blood. The desperate voices froze passersby. Someone burst upon the scene and handcuffed Hoswell, saying, "See your hellish work," to which the assailant shot back, "What would you have done if you had caught a man in bed with your wife?" The suspected interloper, John B. Laflin, a 40-year-old barber, Sunday school teacher and father of three, lay dead.

The murder lacked no essential journalistic element except for novelty. The story of the avenging husband was a 19th century American set piece. It was a quirk of the law that juries dependably exonerated a husband of the charge of murder if his victim had invaded the sanctity of the marriage bed. Sensational trials of such killers—in 1859, 1867 and 1869–70—had transfixed the country and showered celebrity on the counsel of the exonerated defendants. One such lawyer, John Graham, explained the theory of the matter in these words: "The person or body of the wife is the property of her husband and the wife cannot consent away her own purity . . . where the wife's virtue does not keep off the adulterer, let her interpose the fear of her husband."[24]

Such was the state of the law—"a complex of self-defense rights," in the legal phrase—that a wronged husband virtually had a hunting license. One might suppose that a husband, catching his wife and another man in *flagrante delicto*, would receive the sympathy of an all-male jury if the defendant had struck in unpremeditated rage. But the juries of the day refused to convict the killer even if he had had time to plot and brood. In one notorious instance, the elapsed time between provocation and killing was measured in years.

What led juries to condone acts of violence that had every appearance of coldblooded murder? Defense lawyers harped on precedent. Not for 200 years, they harangued, had a man in the United States or Great Britain been punished for doing what you, the gentlemen of the jury, would assuredly do if you were ever so unfortunate as to be in the defendant's shoes. Scripture provided a second line of defense. In 1870 Graham spent hours reading biblical passages to a jury in evident support of private vengeance and women's subjugation. In closing, he coined what he was pleased to call "the law of the Bible," as follows: "That man was made for God, and woman for man; and that the woman was the weaker vessel, is meant to be under the protection of the stronger vessel, man." A reporter in the audience heard a "distinct hiss from some of the strong minded ladies present."[25]

Graham and his ilk had never done business in Maine, where adultery was a crime. At about the time that Hoswell murdered Laflin, James

E. Fallon of Portland encountered Mary B. Broad of Port Elizabeth on the road, he in his conveyance, she in hers. Both were married but not to the other. They stopped to talk—and much more, according to the witness who led a grand jury to indict them for adultery, "contrary to the peace" of the state of Maine.[26] The husband of Mary Broad had no justifiable reason to take the law into his own hands, even if he were so inclined; the laws of the state were his shield and defense.

Reed had two additional advantages over other prosecutors of avenging husbands. First, Hoswell's weapon of choice was a knife, a tool of vengeance even more gruesome than a gun. Second, Hoswell apparently attempted to kill his wife too. Nineteenth century views of adultery were laced with what a modern observer would call misogyny, but the same logic that justified a husband killing his wife's lover also forbade him from visiting any harm on his wife. She was assumed to be a passive victim of wanton advances, not a conspirator.

Working against Reed was the case, and persona, of Daniel Sickles. Twenty-one years before Hoswell killed Laflin, Sickles had been acquitted of fatally shooting his wife's lover, Philip Barton Key, the son of the author of the Star Spangled Banner, in Washington, D.C., on the grounds that learning of the affair had left him temporarily insane. A few years later, Sickles lost his leg and earned a Medal of Honor at the Battle of Gettysburg. Wary that Hoswell's actions might be equated with those of Sickles, a national hero, Reed made a point to distinguish the two cases in his closing arguments.

No CELEBRITY DEFENSE team rushed to the aid of the indigent Edward Hoswell, but that did not deter the crowds that descended on the Hallowell courthouse in early December. They filled the chamber to capacity, "yet, as the morning hour passed by, score after score of persons arrived and in some unaccountable manner, compressed themselves into the interstices invisible to mortal eye," the Kennebec *Journal* reported. (In news that the trial had shoved aside, Prussia was getting the better of Napoleon III in the Franco-Prussian War.)[27]

The facts of the case were not in dispute. The Hoswells had been married for nine years and had frequently fought. They lived in a boardinghouse in Hallowell, until he moved out following an especially bitter row in July preceding the killing. After which he bought an ad in the newspaper:

> To Whom it May Concern.
>   This is to forbid all persons harboring or trusting my wife, Jane L. Hoswell, after this date, as I shall pay no debts of her contracting.

She was flirtatious, he was violent. In moments of extreme jealousy, he would lock her out of the house. Once he burned her clothes. On another occasion, he caught her with a $5 gold piece, which he claimed she stole. She replied by swallowing it. He was 47 years old, she was 34.

That Hoswell killed Laflin, nobody denied. But the centerpiece of Hoswell's defense, the prosecution did deny. Laflin and Jane Hoswell were not, in fact, lovers, the state contended. Nobody had caught them in the act, although an apparently credible witness described a scene in which the wife and Laflin exchanged chewing gum without using their hands (the tittering that this story induced in the galleries brought a stern rebuke from the bench). What did the lady herself have to say? She was permitted to say nothing, as her husband refused to allow her to testify. Reed, the lead attorney for the prosecution, chafed at this bit of statutory misogyny. "By the law of this state, the wife is admissible as a witness with the consent of her husband," he remarked in court; "without that consent, she is not admissible. I have deemed it my duty to present to the jury in this case all the evidence in my power to establish the fact of Mr. Laflin's entire and complete innocence of any charge that could be brought against him." The prosecutor now rounded on a member of Hoswell's defense team who had branded Mrs. Hoswell an "adulteress." "I do not deem it entirely decorous on the part of my learned brother," said Reed, "at the same moment when he closes the mouth of this witness, to stigmatize her as an adulteress."[28]

If Laflin was innocent of adultery, and if extramarital sex was, in any case, a crime under the laws of Maine, Hoswell had no claim on the unwritten law of permissible vengeance. Reed, indeed, asked for a conviction of murder in the first degree.

In his charge to the jury, Reed took dead aim at the scriptural defense that Hoswell's lawyers had lifted from earlier trials. "Now, gentlemen," he addressed the twelve,

> I desire your consideration upon this subject. I ask you whether your better feelings—whether your nobler instincts—believe that the revealed will of God should be used to justify and sanctify murder? This thing is presented to you, not upon the facts of this case, but upon facts of cases widely different; and you are asked to stretch your minds, to turn your consciences, until you make the defense which is set up in the case—even a case like this. Where is this matter to end? Is this court to be under a reign of violence? Have we no laws? Are they not to protect men? By their own statements, and by the facts of the cases in every state where these things have occurred, there has been no law against adultery. I thank God that that reproach does not exist in New England![29]

Reed derided the chewing gum tale and any suggestion that the defendant was out of his mind when he pulled his knife. He banged away at Hoswell's refusal to allow his wife to take the stand. "You are not to be merciful toward the prisoner—you are to be just," he implored the jurors, and he invited them to make their mark in this world, if in no other way, than by exercising "that calm and deliberate judgment which God and your country requires of you."[30] The case went to the jury just before 3 PM, and they pronounced their verdict at 10:30 PM. Hoswell was guilty of manslaughter, though not of murder. Reed had won his case—and lost, with the jury's help, his perhaps not so earnestly sought verdict of first degree murder, a crime punishable, after all, by death. Hoswell, instead, was sentenced to nine years at hard labor at the state prison at Thomaston.

It was a rare attorney general who could entertain the public even as he served it, and Reed did not repeat his dual success in the Hoswell-Laflin trial. He did, however, pursue a seemingly dormant suit against some politically powerful people who never forgot his effrontery. In 1858, a certain Benjamin D. Peck was elected state treasurer. In keeping with the custom of the time, half a dozen citizens pledged to post bond on his behalf. If the treasurer misplaced or misappropriated the public funds with which he was entrusted, the bondsmen, or "sureties," would make good the loss, up to $150,000. Sure enough, Peck proved light-fingered, but the sureties denied ever committing to do what they had so solemnly promised to do. The state sued the vanishing sureties, including the politically well-connected Neal Dow, but the suit seemed to languish until Reed became attorney general. By the time he left office, at least two of the reluctant bondsmen, including Dow, had paid what they owed the state treasury.[31] Dow's son Frederick later took his place as a personal enemy of Reed's, a rare distinction, as Reed could name only two such people in the world.*

And neither one was a railroad man, though Reed was fast becoming a thorn in the side of the Maine rail interests. In his final report as attorney general, he urged the legislature to do something to empower the survivors of lethal railroad accidents to collect judgments from the responsible corporation. "With damages for loss of life limited to five thousand dollars," Reed dryly noted, "it will be frequently cheaper for the railroad company to kill a man than to hurt him."[32]

No attorney general in Reed's day had served two consecutive terms as attorney general, and Reed stepped down in 1872. Now his letterhead was emblazoned:

THOMAS B. REED
ATTORNEY AND COUNSELOR AT LAW
CASCO BANK BUILDING
91 MIDDLE STREET
PORTLAND, MAINE

In 1875, the private citizen again reentered public life, this time in the capacity of Portland city solicitor. At the end of his stint in 1877, he

---

* Reed's determination to do his duty seemed to puzzle the elder Dow, who sought to enlist the help of the Portland *Daily Press* in making Reed and his case go away. Inconveniently for Dow, however, George Gifford, Reed's friend, was then the paper's editor. Dow lamented Reed's persistence: "All his predecessors were most kind and friendly," he wrote to John Lynch, a Maine Republican congressman. See Neal Dow to John Lynch, undated, George Gifford Collection, Duke University Library.

was able to point to a succession of legal victories on behalf of the city as well as to the smallest backlog of cases on the city docket "for very many years." It was perhaps a distracted city solicitor who wrote those words, however. Reed was on his way to Washington, D.C.

Chapter 4

With a Flap of the "bloody shirt"

T HE CITY OF Portland had only so much time for electoral politics during the long summer days and short summer nights of June 1876. To be sure, a Republican caucus would decide the Republicans' nominee to represent the First District of Maine in the U.S. House of Representatives. And, come September, a presidential election would be overlaid on the congressional one, with Maine rendering its accustomed early verdict. Vital issues would be laid before the people. The American economy was slumping, and federal troops, 11 years after Appomattox, still occupied the South. The dollar was a mere piece of paper—no gold stood behind it, as it had before the war—and Washington, D.C., in the final year of the administration of U. S. Grant, stank of corruption.

Yet, as Portlanders must have also reflected, there would always be another election. What would never come around again was the 100th anniversary of the signing of the Declaration of Independence. To mark the nation's centennial, Portland planned a day-long patriotic celebration. Dawn of July 4 would break to the roar of cannon. The guns would boom again at noon, which blast would cue the church bells; they would peal till one o'clock. Parades (the first one stepping off before breakfast), concerts, baseball games, a sailing regatta and a procession of historically themed horse-drawn tableaux would round out the agenda. A leading citizen of precise elocution, General S. J. Anderson, would read the Declaration of Independence. The Portland Mechanic Blues would turn out, as would the Portland Cadets, the Portland Light Infantry, the Androscoggin Artillery and innumerable veterans of the Union army organized into posts of the Grand Army of the Republic; also the Masons, Knights of Pythias and Odd Fellows, the Irish-American Relief Association, the Portland Catholic Union and the Temperance Cadets. There would be bands, drum corps, a horse whisperer (Professor Magner would try to keep his seat on a notoriously unmanageable stallion), advocates of women's rights and a certain number of politicians, including John H. Burleigh, the two-term Republican incumbent from the First District whom Reed intended to send back to the woolen manufacturing field, from whence he had come.[1]

In these loving and intricate preparations, Portland was only doing what other American towns and cities were also busily doing. In the northern suburbs of New York City, a great-great nephew of Roger Sherman, Chauncey M. Depew, was putting the finishing touches on the draft of his Fourth of July oration. Ignoring the brutal business depression that had been in progress since 1873, Depew instead emphasized the wonders of the age in which his constituents were privileged to live. "We stand today," the orator was preparing to say, "in the presence of the most important hundred years in history. In everything which adds to the comfort and happiness of man; in achievements which ennoble and adorn our common human nature; in discoveries which alleviate suffering, annihilate space; and increase the sources of wealth and prosperity; in the extension of Christian and philanthropic efforts; in scientific research, in activity of thought, in freedom of discussion, and in the spread and growth of liberty, this century has no equal. It has given us the steamship, the railroad, the telegraph. It has bridged oceans, wedded seas, and belted the globe with lightning. It has overturned the despotism of ages, established widely representative government and a recognition of the individual man. It has enfranchised the slave, and given to humanity and the world the American Republic."[2]

In this very spirit of internationalism, America had invited the world to her birthday party. The Centennial Exhibition opened in May on a

285-acre tract overlooking the Schuylkill River in Philadelphia. "The Oldest People in the World Sends its Morning Greeting to the Youngest Nation," read the sign hung on the reconstructed temple in the Main Exhibition Building, a gift from Egypt. Thirty-six other nations contributed a structure, an exhibit or a display of indigenous products. Mexico sent a 4,000 pound block of silver; Peru, Inca relics; Liberia, coffee; Canada, a log house; Germany, chemicals, and weapons too. From the Japanese commissioner, Fukui Makoto, came this report of the sights and sounds: "The first day crowd come like sheep, run here, run there, run everywhere. One man start, one thousand follow. Nobody can see anything, nobody can do anything. All rush, push, tear, shout, make plenty noise, say damn great many times, get very tired and go home."

Two months later, at the Portland centennial celebration, there were also great crowds, a certain amount of running and pushing and a culminating, happy fatigue (though a late-day downpour washed out the second baseball game and the evening's parade of illuminated floats). Reed's fatigue was especially happy, for he won the June 29th caucus. It was his first Fourth of July in the capacity of aspirant to national public office.

The congressional contest had hinged, to start, on an issue of local geography. Burleigh, the incumbent, was a York County man, Reed a resident of neighboring Cumberland County, encompassing Portland. The Burleigh faction insisted that the seat should remain in York's possession; the Cumberlanders demurred. Then there was the matter of character. Burleigh, who had gone to sea at 16 and, in his 20s, commanded a deep-water vessel, had exposed corruption at the Kittery, (Maine), navy yard; corruption was, indeed, rampant at Kittery and at nearly every other navy yard in the United States. Now, Burleigh contended, the Maine Republican establishment was punishing him for exposing the rot. Reed was a tool of this very establishment, the Burleigh camp's indictment continued. Moreover, the newcomer was a professional nonentity, an upstart and a self-promoter (it was a graceless and sorrowful thing when the man sought a political office and not the other way around). "A Fessenden" he would never be, the enemy cried, an allusion to Reed's political hero and financial benefactor. And there was this alleged stain of turpitude: While pretending to serve the people as Maine's attorney general, Reed had misappropriated $112.69. A fine "reformer" he would make, the Burleigh faction jeered, when "Clarence Hale, Reed's 'little corporal,' was here, there and everywhere," encouraging "every stray delegate who did not feel confident. If he was very hard to please, he was taken by the arm and led into the barroom."[3]

Reed seems to have had nothing to say to the allegation that he was prepared to throw away his career and reputation for a sum slightly smaller than a congressman's newspaper and stationery budget. Rather, he presented himself to the voters as an unbankrolled idealist contending against his opponent's money and "control of federal offices." It was he who carried the banner of good government. In truth, Reed was the Republican organization's man, a candidate in the good graces of Maine's foremost national politician, a former Speaker of the House, James G. Blaine. But while Blaine was only too happy to conflate the public interest with his own, Reed was another kind of politician. He would not have stolen even if he knew that nobody was looking.

As late as the eve of the balloting, Reed's friends feared that Burleigh would win, but it was Reed, 134 to 113. "No man in the Convention opposed Mr. Reed more strenuously than did Col. Burbank of Saco," reported the pro-Reed Portland *Press*, on the aftermath of the primary battle, "yet that gentleman took occasion to declare that he had known Thomas B. Reed for twenty years and he could cheerfully bear testimony to his high character, his superior abilities and his eminent fitness for the position."[4] Certainly Stephen Berry, a Portland printer and sometime journalist, was prepared to second that judgment: A stillborn infant, delivered to Berry's wife on June 29, would have borne the name Thomas Reed Berry, in honor of Reed's victory, had it lived.[5]

Reed addressed his public, 6,000 strong, at a rally on July 3. "Twenty years ago, they came before us disguised as friends of the Constitution," he said of the Democrats. "Sixteen years ago they came before us as faithful friends of law and proved to be the friends of secession. . . . Eight years ago, they came before us as friends of the poor and enemies of the bloated bondholder, and they turned out to be the friends of repudiation. . . . Now they say they are friends of reform and honest government, and before you get through you will find that they are the same men who, in 1864, turned their backs upon their country."[6]

Once in Congress, Reed would rapidly lose patience with the charged political rhetoric of Reconstruction. But the Republicans in 1876, having to answer for hard times and the corruption of the Grant administration, campaigned on the defensive; Reed gave the "bloody shirt" a good, snappy wave. "We will not refer to the past," he archly assured the crowd. "Our Democratic folks don't like to hear it, and I don't blame them. They gained no laurels in war except what Eben F. Pillsbury gained in the fields of Kingfield.* Now, gentlemen, we will pass that all by. They don't like to hear about the 'bloody shirt,' although many of you have worn this bloody shirt on the battle ground. But there is no need to revive all these memories, and we will pass them by and let us come to the present. They now say they are for 'Democracy and Reform.' What a collection of words! Why, don't it make you think of Satan and the piety of the devil and the ten commandments?"[7]

And how long, Reed rhetorically demanded, would the party of Lincoln have to struggle against the party of the sublimely literate Jefferson? "Just so long," he answered himself, "as there are men who don't know how to write and read, just so long there will be a Democratic Party, and just so long as we have got to come together and fight them, and just so long we have got to beat them."[8]

The national campaign was by then in full force—such force, that is, as presidential candidates committed to a policy of dignified silence could muster. Rutherford B. Hayes, the governor of Ohio, was the Republican nominee; Samuel J. Tilden, the governor of New York, his Democratic opponent. An unbriefed 21st century observer might wonder how a Democrat could possibly lose. Maine would go to the polls on September 11, a week short of the third anniversary of the failure of the banking house of Jay Cooke & Company. What had followed the Cooke suspension was a financial panic desperate enough to force the closing of the New York Stock Exchange for 10 days. And what had followed the panic was a depression for which no end was in sight (it would not run its course until 1879). "The Great Depression," contemporaries

---

* A reference to the anti-Unionist, or "copperhead," Maine journalist who incited a Kingfield audience with an incendiary speech days before that city produced Maine's only wartime draft riot.

called the 1873–79 slump; and, indeed, an economist, appraising it from the middle of the 20th century, would rank it second in severity only to the Great Depression of Herbert Hoover.

Capitalism had had its chance and botched it, a certain number of Americans had come to believe. Adherents of alternative economic systems made their way to Philadelphia in 1876 to found the Workingmen's Party, the next year renamed the Socialist Labor Party. It was the first avowedly collectivist political party in the United States. In the second winter of the depression, 1875–76, the New York Association for Improving the Condition of the Poor estimated that as much as one-third of the city's labor force was idle. As there was no official count, the claim was contested. Whatever the correct statistics, joblessness was high enough to drive some to socialism, others to militant trade unionism and uncounted thousands to soup kitchens. That the soup was free rankled some traditional sensibilities; the *Nation*, for one, insisted that "all classes must learn that soup of any kind, beef or turtle, can be had only by being paid for."[9]

A symptom of the troubles was falling prices. As technology advanced, so the cost of production fell. And as costs declined, so did prices. Keynsian deficit spending and computer-enhanced credit creation were, of course, innovations for a later age. In the United States, the cost of living soared from 1862 to 1865, then, with the peace, deflated. The rate of decline accelerated in the aftermath of the Panic of 1873. By 1877, when an average of retail prices had fallen by 20 percent from the 1873 peak, debtors were groaning. The dollars they were pledged to repay were much scarcer than the ones they had borrowed. Panics and depressions were nothing new. They rolled around every 10 years or so, after which a new upswing began. The depression of the 1870s was different, however. Prices fell and kept falling.

That everyday low, and lower, prices are an unmitigated evil is the verdict of the modern economics profession. There was no such consensus of opinion in the 19th century. In Reed's day, many thinkers on economic subjects saw human invention as the not unpleasing cause of falling prices—and falling prices as a not unwelcome marker of progress. Sounding a little like Reed, or Chauncey Depew on the Fourth of July, theorists of this ilk pointed to the wonders of the age. The steam engine, the telegraph and railroad, among other countless labor-saving and productivity-enhancing devices, had reduced the cost of commodities and manufactured goods. Was that so terrible?

Was the working man or woman better or worse off as a result of this outpouring of invention? Better off, of course, most agreed. There was no going back, no filling in the Suez Canal, no tearing up railroad track or pulling down telegraph poles. Yet, as the congressmen also heard, workers suffered when wages fell faster than prices—as they did, for example, in the New York City masonry trades after the Civil War. What could, or should, the government do to alleviate the resulting distress? The Republican solution was a tariff wall high enough to protect American labor from low-price foreign competition. But much beyond that controversial nostrum the party was not inclined to go. With the very large exceptions of the tariff and of federal subsidies of the railroads, its doctrine was noninterference in the free market. Certainly it had no truck with schemes to reverse the fall in prices by directing the government to print more dollars. Quite the contrary: It was the Republican position to restore the gold standard.

The Constitution stipulates that money should be "coined," not printed. To finance the Civil War, Abraham Lincoln himself had overridden the Founders. But the necessity of wartime expedients had long since disappeared. In the late 1860s, Congress had put the country back on the road to metallic money. To return to a prewar level of prices—i.e., to erase the last vestiges of the wartime inflation—would be no easy thing. But, in formulating sound public policy, honor trumped ease. "[T]he faith of the United States is solemnly pledged to the payment in coin [i.e., gold coin], or its equivalent, of all the obligations of the United States . . . and of all the interest-bearing obligations," the Resumption Act of 1869 stipulated. It set the clock ticking on the era of the unballasted, paper-light greenback. Come January 1, 1879, the greenback would once more take its place among the world's respectable currencies. A dollar bill would feel no different in the hand. But anyone holding $20.67 in paper or silver coin could exchange it for an ounce of gold. At that fixed and immutable rate, evermore, dollars would be convertible into gold and gold into dollars.

President Grant, in an 1874 veto message, had crystallized the Republican party's position on the gold question. Congress had presented him with a bill to authorize the printing of up to $100 million in new greenbacks. The post-1873 depression was in full swing. Could not the federal government take a slight detour on the road to resumption for the sake of economic recovery? Grant was adamant in his refusal. He reminded Congress of the government's oft-repeated pledge to restore the dollar to prewar soundness. The 1874 Currency Bill represented not only an inflationary departure from the "true principles of finance," said the president, but also a turning away from "national obligation to creditors, Congressional promises, party pledges on the part of both political parties and of the personal views and promises made by me in every annual message sent to Congress, and in each inaugural address." In short, the bill was dishonorable.[10]

Was there ever a simpler, more objective or more elegant monetary system than the international gold standard? Republicans, and not a few Democrats, doubted it. Solon Chase, a pixyish Maine farmer, however, knew otherwise, and he took it up as his mission in life to make money more plentiful. Currency unbacked by anything except the government's imprimatur was good enough for the Union soldier when the lead was flying. It ought to be good enough for the overstuffed creditor class now that the soldiers had won the peace. "Uncle Solon," the people called him, and they listened to him lambaste the bankers and the bondholders on his proselytizing travels around the Pine Tree State. He got around by ox team, and "them steers," as he called them, doubled as his monetary teaching aid. Big, strong animals they were, he would say—why, look at the size of them. But as they had grown in stature, they had shrunk in value. He had paid $100 for the pair, but he would gladly take $50 now. Where was the justice in that? Why make dollars even scarcer and costlier for the sake of the people who already had more than enough of them? Many within the sound of his Down East voice had been wondering the same thing.

Hayes, the Republican presidential nominee, would have reminded Uncle Solon, had he had the chance to dispute with him, that prosperous societies weren't rich because their governments printed money. Work and thrift had raised them up. Societies unlucky enough to be governed by monetary ignoramuses could scarcely get ahead no matter how hard they worked. Their inflated currency discouraged enterprise and punished savings. Who would ever invest for the long term if there were no certain standard of value? A sound currency was a prerequisite to a growing economy.

Hayes believed devoutly in an economy organized along the lines of individual enterprise. He treasured it as much, in fact, as did his Democratic opponent. Before the 1876 presidential campaign season began, Governor Tilden had spoken out against the blight of federal activism. What was wanted, he told the people of New York, was a government simple and frugal, "meddling little with the private concerns of individuals—aiming at fraternity among ourselves and peace abroad—and trusting to the people to work out their own prosperity and happiness." It went without saying that Tilden was a gold-standard man. He hated "rag money" as much as Hayes did.[11]

Agree though they might on the philosophical foundations of a free economy, the major parties would gladly have slit each other's throats. The Republicans hated the Democrats for obstructing the conduct of the Civil War. The Democrats hated the Republicans for having waged it—and, once having waged it, for keeping the South in federal bondage. No partisan of that time spoke with more wit, fire or rancor than Robert G. Ingersoll. A Democrat turned Republican, Ingersoll was a minister's son turned agnostic. It was risky enough, at that time, to express public doubt as to the existence of God—to do so virtually disqualified the agnostic from elective office. Ingersoll compounded his indiscretion by writing a book about it. So he practiced law and pursued his political interests as a kingmaker from the lectern.

That Ingersoll—or "Colonel Ingersoll," as he liked to be addressed, for he had seen hard fighting with the Union army—failed to crown Blaine the 1876 Republican presidential candidate was certainly no fault of Ingersoll's. "Words can do but meager justice to the wizard power of this extraordinary man," the Chicago *Times* correspondent reported on the Ingersoll nominating speech at the Republican national convention in Cincinnati. "He swayed and moved and impelled and restrained and worked in all ways with the mass before him as if possessed by some key to the innermost mechanism that moves the human heart, and when he finished, his fine, frank face as calm as when he began, the overwrought thousands sank back in an exhaustion of unspeakable wonder and delight." There was less wonder and less delight as the delegates considered the electoral baggage presented by Blaine's evidently corrupt dealings with the Little Rock and Fort Smith Railroad. So they nominated the stolid Hayes of Ohio instead of the "Plumed Knight," as Ingersoll had famously described his Maine hero.

On August 24 Ingersoll again delighted a Republican audience, this time in Bangor. Thousands sat in the late summer sunshine to hear the famous orator say exactly what they expected him to say. "I am going to give you a few reasons for voting the Republican ticket," Ingersoll said, in fact citing many. "The Republican party of the United States is the conscience of the nineteenth century. It is the justice of this age, the embodiment of social progress and honor." This party—this "grand" party—was born opposing slavery, "an institution that made white men devils and black men beasts." Only consider, he invited them, how much their party had accomplished in its brief existence: "[I]t struck the cruel shackles from four million human beings; it put down the most gigantic rebellion in the history of the world; it expunged from the statute books of every State, and of the Nation, all the cruel and savage laws that Slavery had enacted; it took whips from backs and chains from the limbs of men; it dispensed with bloodhounds as the instruments of civilization; it banished to the memory of barbarism the slave pen, the auction block and the whipping-post; it purified a Nation; it elevated the human race." And now that the slaves were free, Ingersoll continued, the Democrats hate blacks even more than they did before the war. It was a "hatred begotten of a well-grounded fear that the colored people are rapidly becoming their superiors in industry, intellect and character."

Reed had called the Democrats illiterate. Now Ingersoll insinuated worse. But what of the enemy's national standard-bearer, "the able, zealous and intrepid and successful Reform Governor of the Empire State," as the Maine Democrats had characterized the nominee? "Samuel J. Tilden," said Ingersoll, "is an attorney. He never gave birth to an elevated, noble sentiment in his life. He is a kind of legal spider, watching in a web of technicalities for victims. He is a compound of cunning and heartlessness—of beak and claw and fang. He is one of the few men who can grab a railroad and hide the deep cuts, tunnels and culverts in a single night.

He is a corporation wrecker. He is a demurrer filed by the Confederate congress. He waits on the shores of bankruptcy to clutch the drowning by the throat. He has never married. The Democratic party has satisfied the longings of his heart. He has looked upon love as weakness. He has courted men because women cannot vote."[12]

The mature Reed was a master of political invective; in Ingersoll, the tyro congressional candidate had a teacher and a guide. And we know he did hear him, if not on that sun-dolloped afternoon in Bangor, then in stump speeches around the First District in Portland. To Ingersoll, a friend of Blaine's, it might have seemed that Reed and Blaine were protégé and mentor. So reasoning, the orator would readily have lent his tongue and wit to the Reed campaign. If, however, the older man ever nurtured the younger, and if the younger ever allowed himself to *be* nurtured (which, from what we know of Reed, appears unlikely), that relationship was destined to be short-lived. Presently, Reed and Blaine had a bitter breach, though why and when the parting occurred is a mystery.

Such support was not entirely displeasing to Reed's opponent, John M. Goodwin, a 54-year-old lawyer, savings-bank president and father of five. "He is a very worthy gentleman," a special correspondent of the then-Republican New York *Times* wrote of this capable but retiring man, "and is chiefly noted in Portland for never having done anything. He says yes to every one, and advocates his own election on the ground that he is not a politician." In fact, Goodwin *was* a politician. At 31, he had been the youngest member of the state Senate, and there had been talk of him as the Democratic gubernatorial candidate in 1876.[13]

More to his credit, Goodwin was no atheist. Ingersoll was, and Reed, by having accepted Ingersoll's support, fell under suspicion of godlessness. Six days before the election, the *Eastern Argus*, a Democratic newspaper, demanded to know how Blaine and Reed, "knowing [Ingersoll's] character, knowing the abhorrence in which his views are held by nearly the whole people," could import the heretic into Maine. Reed couldn't feign ignorance of what Ingersoll professed to believe, the *Argus* knowingly added, because the candidate owned a copy of Ingersoll's book, *The Gods and Other Lectures*, published in 1874.[14]

Besides, the Democratic indictment of Reed's character continued, a man so deficient in religion must be unsound on alcohol as well. On the contrary, shot back the Republican *Portland Press*: Reed was "as sound a temperance man as are Mr. Goodwin and Mr. Burleigh."

So, in that year of economic depression, the congressional race in the First District of Maine was fought on questions of morals. Out of a total of 31,594 votes, Reed won a plurality of 1,020. The sprint to the finish line had been exhausting. "[T]he long strain is over," wrote a diarist, a friend and neighbor of the winning candidate, soon after the election. "He lay abed yesterday morning, I think, used up with overwork, as we did not see him."[15]

Chapter 5

"Make it out of paper"

Thomas B. Reed was elected to the 45th Congress of the United States to represent the First District of Maine. That much was fixed and irrevocable. But election night, November 7, 1876, afforded no such clarity concerning the winner of the presidential race. Was it Hayes or Tilden? Early returns favored the Democratic governor of New York. Tilden had clearly won the popular vote. But, then as now, the way to the White House was through the Electoral College. One hundred and eighty-five electoral votes out of a possible 369 meant victory, and Tilden had collected as many as 184. In New York, reciprocal moods of joy and despair filled the Democratic and Republican headquarters. By all appearances, the Democratic party was set to return to the White House for the first time since the muddled administration of James Buchanan.

So the editors of the-then very Republican New York *Times* must have lamented as they sat over their joyless election-night dinner. The managing editor, John C. Reid, was among the unhappiest of these partisans. Captured by Confederate cavalry and imprisoned at Andersonville during the war, he drew no distinction between southerners and Democrats but hated them impartially. It was Reid to whom a messenger presented a pair of election-night telegrams. Each was from a senior Democratic operative anxiously seeking news on the contested balloting in Louisiana, Florida and South Carolina, the three southern states yet "unredeemed" from federal dominion. In Reid's head, a light switched on. If the Democrats were still worried, he reasoned, the Republican cause was not yet lost. It was the time to fight, not surrender.

This insight Reid chose to deliver in person to the Hayes headquarters at the Fifth Avenue Hotel. He found it dark. Zachariah Chandler, chairman of the Republican National Committee, had gone to bed. There was, however, another Chandler on the premises. William E. Chandler, former Speaker of the New Hampshire legislature and secretary of the Republican National Committee, had just returned to the hotel from a trip home to vote. "Wearing an enormous pair of goggles, his hat drawn over his ears, a great coat with a heavy military cloak, and carrying a gripsack with a newspaper in his hand," Chandler looked nothing like an agent of political destiny. Nor did he feel like one. The front page of the newspaper he carried proclaimed a Tilden victory, and Chandler had no reason to doubt it. As Reid briefed him on the *Times*'s view of things, however, Chandler's spirits soared.[1] Now Reid and he pounded on the door of the other Chandler. Rubbing the sleep from his eyes, the Republican National Committee chairman heard out the two messengers of hope.* Hayes needed 19 more electoral votes in addition to the ones he already seemed to have. Alluringly, in Louisiana, South Carolina and Florida, there were exactly those 19 votes. Each state was under federal—therefore Republican—control. Each was a likely setting for electoral fraud. Democrats would do their all to keep newly enfranchised African-Americans away from the polling places, just as the Republican vote-counters would strain to make the numbers add up for their side. So Reid and the wide-awake Chandler asked permission to wire instructions to the contested states to hold fast for Hayes. The other Chandler gave his blessing. Next day, dressed and confident, the Republican chairman declared matter-of-factly, "Hayes has 185 electoral votes and is elected."[2]

---

* They were not the first of the night. Daniel E. Sickles, the marital avenger and Gettysburg hero, had rousted Chandler out of bed some hours earlier to tell a similar story.

Presently, money, troops and Republicans went pouring into Tallahassee, Columbia and New Orleans. They did so at the immediate behest of Secretary of War James D. Cameron but under the ultimate authority of the commander-in-chief. Behind U. S. Grant, however, lurked the enterprising William Chandler, who was bound for Tallahassee with a carpetbag loaded with $10,000 in greenbacks.[3]

It was no mean feat to enlist the president's cooperation in this political intervention. Grant believed that Tilden had won the election. Indeed, Hayes himself believed it.[4] The need to insert federal troops into the capital cities of the three contested states was not one that came to Grant independently. Rather, Chandler, working through senior Republican officials, led him to see the light. The soldiers moved out on November 9, the Thursday after Election Day. On November 10, Grant wired General W. T. Sherman, commanding general of the army, ordering local commanders in the South "to preserve peace and good order and to see that the proper and legal Boards of Canvassers are unmolested in the performance of their duties. . . . Should there be any grounds of suspicion or fraudulent counting on either side it shall be reported and denounced at once." Closing with a flourish, Grant seemed to speak over Sherman's head to the public and to posterity: "No man worthy of the office of President would be willing to hold the office if counted in, placed there by fraud; either party can afford to be disappointed in the result but the country cannot afford to have the result tainted by the suspicion of illegal or false returns."[5]

In fact, to the Democratic and Republican high commands, if not to the candidates themselves, the White House was a prize eminently worth stealing. A certain amount of fraud was only to be expected in those days (and in not a few days thereafter). Neither party was above it. But the scale of the thievery alleged by Republicans in Florida, Louisiana and South Carolina far exceeded the norm—as did the scale of corruption claimed by Democrats against Chandler and his Republican confederates. The consensus of scholarly opinion today holds that the Republicans perhaps gave greater offense to the law of the land than even the Democrats, though there is much to be said against each side. If the Republicans are to be believed, southern Democrats kept black Republican voters away from the polls by force. To credit the Democrats, Republicans bribed the returning boards of the three contested states. Julius Seelye, an independent Massachusetts congressman, held a plausibly measured view of the proceedings, which he declared on the floor of the House: "It seems to me perfectly clear that the charges made by each side against the other are in the main true. No facts were ever proved more conclusively than the fraud and corruption charged on one side and the intimidation and cruelty on the other. Which side went further it would be very hard to say."[6]

The two sides were sworn enemies in everything except their professed principles. Except for obligatory partisan swipes, their respective 1876 party platforms might have been drafted by the same committee. Each supported the return to the gold standard, the phasing out of Reconstruction, the reform of the civil service, the husbanding of public money and honest administration in Washington. Neither did the individual standard-bearers seem so very different. Each was the governor of a northern state. Each championed what he called reform. Neither was overendowed with the essence that later generations would call charisma. The quality of Hayes that Republicans found most laudable was his personal integrity, that and the four wounds he suffered in the Union's service in the 23rd Ohio Regiment. And to this short list, they could have added discretion. "Be careful not to commit me on religion, temperance or free-trade," the Ohio governor instructed his campaign biographer.[7]

Tilden, by waging and winning a courageous battle against Boss Tweed and Tammany Hall, had made a more illustrious political career than Hayes. In brains and money too, the New York corporation lawyer held the advantage, but he was every bit as cold a fish as Robert Ingersoll had made him seem from the stump in Maine. "Tilden and reform!" was the candidate's fighting slogan, and he never amended it even after the party faithful had taken up the battle cry, "Tilden or blood!"

Long-disenfranchised Democrats could only too well believe their eyes as Tilden's seemingly certain victory seeped away. The enemy was not really Hayes, but the army of federal office holders who consented to be dunned for contributions to the Republican party's campaign coffers—$250,000 for the 1876 season alone. "Throw the rascals out," Charles A. Dana, editor of the New York *Sun*, had roused his readers on the eve of the election. Only two years before, Democratic voters had thrown the rascals out of Congress, restoring the House to Democratic rule for the first time in almost 20 years. Now, in 1876, was the time to uproot "Grantism" from the American political soil, the party bosses and editorialists thundered. And, in unprecedentedly large numbers, the voters responded. Yet now the rascals, through their very rascality, were turning the tables on the people.

"[H]istory will hold that the Republicans were by fraud and violence and intimidation, by a nullification of the 15th amendment, deprived of the victory which they fairly won," Hayes wrote in his diary a few days after the election. "But we must, I now think, prepare ourselves to accept the inevitable."[8] Fatalism, however, was not the outstanding mindset in the upper tiers of the Republican party. "Visiting statesmen" from both parties boarded trains for the three contested southern states to help the local returning boards see the light and the truth. There was not a moment to lose. On December 6, electors in each of the 38 states would gather at their respective state capitals to cast their ballots for president.[9]

And the electors duly assembled, to produce—an anticlimax. For all the jockeying for position, all the sidewalk superintending and all the money in the visiting statesmen's carpetbags (and there was Democratic money too), the electoral situation at the close of business on December 6 was much as it had been on Election Day a month before. It was Tilden with 184 votes, Hayes with 165 votes and 20 votes still contested. Four states were up for grabs—Oregon, in addition to Florida, South Carolina and Louisiana—and each party was still grabbing. In each of the four, feuding election officials produced not one set of returns but two.[10]

Ideas on how to break the impasse corresponded exactly with the party affiliation of the author of the idea. The Republicans, controlling the Senate, insisted that the president of the Senate should decide which votes to count. For this position, they invoked the authority of the Constitution. The Democrats, controlling the House of Representatives, demanded that the House vote on the matter, as it had done in the election of 1824, in which John Quincy Adams edged out Andrew Jackson. They too invoked the Constitution. Tilden holed up in his law library to compose a book to argue the case for a decision by the House, *The Presidential Counts.* Hayes, the less cerebral candidate, stepped up negotiations with southern Democrats. Would they consider exchanging their Yankee candidate for the removal of federal troops from the South in a Hayes administration? He found them receptive. "The Democrats are without a policy or a leader," Ohio congressman James Garfield advised Hayes two days after the Electoral College vote. "They are full of passion and want to do something desperate but hardly know how to get at it."[11]

Not taking any chances with the faction yelling "Tilden or blood!," Grant positioned troops around the capital. On the floor of the House, certain representatives packed pistols. Especially keen for another war, some noted, were those members who had sat out the previous one. "Invincible in peace and invisible in war," one Georgia congressman sneered at these belatedly bellicose northern Democrats.[12]

Neither Hayes nor Tilden supported the compromise that created the tribunal that finally settled the matter. The panel numbered 15. There were five Democratic senators and representatives and five Republican senators and representatives. Also, two Democratic Supreme Court justices, two Republican Supreme Court justices and a fifth justice selected by the other four. The all-important fifth member of the judiciary contingent turned out to be a Grant appointee, Joseph P. Bradley. And when Bradley successively ruled that every one of the 20 contested electoral votes belonged to the Republican candidate, embittered Democrats took to calling Hayes, now the 19th president of the United States, "Old Eight to Seven."

THOMAS B. REED remembered the 45th Congress as the most acrimonious of his career, not excepting the later congresses in which he himself generated most of the acrimony.[13] Democrats and Republicans were at daggers drawn long before the contested election of Rutherford B. Hayes. After the inauguration of that winner-by-compromise, the Democrats fairly spat blood. It mollified them only a little that the new president appointed a pair of southerners to his cabinet, renewed his commitment to retire after a single term and removed the remaining federal troops from Louisiana, Florida and South Carolina. Presently, four million former slaves were living under Democratic governments in the newly solid Democratic South. For all intents and purposes, Reconstruction was over.

Americans of Reed's age had grown up on an unvaried political diet of states' rights, secession and race. By 1876, they had surely had their fill of it. What would the nation talk about next? By the time Hayes took the oath of office,* the American economy had been contracting for 3½ years. The year 1876 had set records in bank failures and railroad reorganizations. Mass unemployment was well on its way to radicalizing American labor, and records were presently set in workdays lost to violent strikes. "Owing to the depression of business throughout the country," related the 1876 annual report of the Maine state prison, "the sales of the manufactures of the prison, consisting of carriages, harnesses, boots and shoes, have been made with unusual difficulty and at prices considerably less than heretofore."

There was no settled consensus on what the government could, or should, do to speed the return of prosperity. Each major political party opposed government intervention on principle. The Constitution seemed to allow no scope for fiscal or regulatory legislation, the argument went, and—besides—it would very likely do more harm than good. In Hayes's inaugural address, the subject of the national economy did not come up until the 15th paragraph, following discussions of race relations, local government in the South, the federal government's duty to the emancipated slaves and civil service reform. Not until June 1878 did Congress vote a committee into existence to hear evidence on the causes of the slump and to solicit ideas on what the government might do, if anything, to relieve the people's suffering.

Waiters and cigar-makers, printers and tramps, bankers and intellectual luminaries, came to testify. Few spoke more persuasively than the Chicago journalist Horace White. The Panic of 1873 precipitated the

---

* As a cautionary measure, it was actually administered twice, the first time in secret, on March 3, in the White House. Because March 4, the day appointed for the inauguration, was a Sunday, President Grant decided to have his successor safely sworn in before the potentially violent Democratic crowds assembled for the formal ceremony on Monday. On March 5, Hayes repeated the oath of office, this time in public.

depression, White observed, while a period of uninhibited speculation precipitated the panic. Railroad construction in the United States had averaged less than 2,000 miles a year until 1868, whereupon it entered a growth spurt: 5,000 miles in 1869, over 6,000 miles in 1870, over 7,000 miles in 1871, between 6,000 and 7,000 miles in 1872 and between 3,000 and 4,000 miles in 1873, the year the bubble burst. And as the track was laid, he testified, so did land prices inflate. The chairman of the committee, Abram S. Hewitt, a New York Democrat, asked White if the mere building of railroads, even on this scale, could account for the subsequent chain of disaster.

The culprit wasn't the building alone but the debt that financed it, the witness replied: "[T]he obligations incurred by reason of the building of those railroads and by reason of the purchase of vast amounts of real estate at high prices, and the advanced prices of everything else consequent on the enormous demand caused by railroad building could not be sustained. They were utterly factitious; and the time was sure to come when the mass of obligations so incurred had to be resolved in money and eventually in gold; and the prices were such that they could not be resolved in that way at all. Thus a vast number of people became insolvent, and their insolvency caused a dislocation of trade and industry."[14]

The committee conducted hearings in New York, Chicago and San Francisco. Not a few witnesses told stories of acute suffering. In New York, the president of the Cigar Makers' International Union, Adolph Strasser, described a kind of sub-subsistence cigar-making conducted in stinking tenements by half-naked families. In Chicago, Van H. Higgins, a lawyer, testified that, on the authority of policemen he knew, "respectable men go to the swill-barrels at the hotels to pick out pieces of bread, or something, to eat."[15] D. R. Streeter, a Chicago trade-union official, produced figures to show that the average adult Chicago workingman earned $8.68 a week for 60 hours of work, that the average wage had fallen by 38 percent since 1872 and that in his trade, printing, unemployment ranged between one-fifth and one-sixth of the work force. In the winter of 1878–79, he said, "people died from actual starvation."[16] "[T]he people are being reduced, civilization is being destroyed, and we are returning to a nomadic state," a New York City jeweler, Hugh McGregor, said.[17] "Micawberize" was the job strategy that an unemployed Boston printer gave to the committee—"to wait for something to turn up."[18]

Economists are famously prone to disagreement even in the modern age of superabundant data. Without any such statistics, noneconomists described not one American economy but a myriad of personal, local and regional ones. Henry V. Rothschild, a New York clothing manufacturer, testified that, whereas unskilled labor was in surplus, he could not find enough workers to operate his sewing machines. There was, he agreed with Hewitt, "plenty of room at the top of the ladder." The president of the New York City Chamber of Commerce, William E. Dodge, said that, for teetotaling workers, there were jobs for the asking; beer and whiskey were the cause of unemployment. Others blamed mechanization. Though a blessing in the long run, machinery was a job-killing curse in the here and now. In 1838, testified Edward Atkinson, a Boston economist, a Lowell, Massachusetts, textile mill needed 231 workers toiling 13 hours a day to produce a certain volume of goods. In 1876, a completely refurbished and modernized mill, set on the foundation of its predecessor, required only 90 people working 10 hours a day to match the previous output. Without actually speaking Joseph Schumpeter's phrase "creative destruction," Atkinson got a jump on the idea. "[T]he law of progress is the destruction of capital through invention and discovery," he said, adding that "nothing old is useful, and nothing useful is very old; that there is nothing so fluid as fixed capital; nothing that requires such constant change in order to keep up with the discoveries and inventions of the day."[19]

In San Francisco, the committee heard complaints about wage-killing Chinese immigrants, men who lived three or four dozen to a not oversize room, undercut indigenous white labor and spent next to nothing on local products but rather remitted the bulk of their $1 or $2 a day wages to China. There were perhaps 96,000 Chinese in the United States, of whom almost a third lived in San Francisco, according to T. B. Shannon, customs collector in the port of San Francisco. Shannon said that he could foresee a future in which half a million or a million Chinese, in the course of destroying the American labor market, turned the West Coast into a kind of Chinese colony. This "peaceable, quiet, plodding, industrious people," he likened to "an Asiatic herd of grasshoppers." "Did it ever occur to your mind," one of the committeemen, Calvin Cowgill, an Indiana Republican, asked Shannon, "that every man (provided that he lives in obedience to the laws of the country where he resides) has a right to pursue his happiness in his own way, and to use his earnings as he chooses, so long as he injures no one and does not disobey the laws of the country?"

"It has been an American doctrine," the witness replied. "We have played the role of the great republican asylum for the oppressed of all the world, and I think it is about time we quit playing that role."[20]

It fell to the committee's star witness, Yale professor William Graham Sumner, to point out the radical, wonderful and confounding consequences of the completion, in 1869, of both the Suez Canal and America's transcontinental railroad. These marvels, plus the telegraph, were annihilating space and time. "Large stocks of goods are no longer necessary to be kept on hand in any country when you can telegraph for new supplies from the other side of the world," Sumner pointed out, "and can get them within a short period—not as formerly, when communications were slower and transportation much more difficult. That, I suppose, is one reason for the phenomenon which a great many people call over-production."

Here was the story of the modern age, Sumner continued: jarring and unpredictable progress that, before it showers unimaginable luxuries on ordinary people, causes the ultimate beneficiaries a certain amount of grief. "For the time being they suffer, of course, a loss of income and a loss of comfort," the professor explained. "There are plenty of people in the United States today whose fathers were displaced from their labor in some of the old countries by the introduction of machinery, and who suffered very great poverty, and who were forced to emigrate to this country by the pressure of necessity, poverty and famine. When they came to this country they entered on a new soil and a new system of industry, and their children today may look back at the temporary distress through which their families went as a great family blessing."

A congressman asked Sumner if there was any way to alleviate the suffering.

"Not at all," he replied. "There is no way on this earth to help it. The only way is to meet it bravely, to go ahead, make the best of circumstances: and if you cannot go on in the way you were going, try another way, and still another, until you work yourself out as an individual."[21]

The witnesses were of two castes: those whom the committee had invited to testify and those who just showed up. Not a few of the former hewed to the hard-money, free-market line. Beyond reestablishing a dependable gold-based monetary unit, they agreed, scope for constructive government action was limited. Many of the uncredentialed witnesses (and a few of the credentialed ones) urged an activist program of lawmaking and intervention that, taken in sum, presented a fair preview of the legislative agenda of the modern age. Let the government print its own money on its own authority without regard to gold or even silver, the union leaders, socialists, splinter-party organizers, laborers and artisans demanded. A member of the Congress of Humanity, George W. Maddox, pressed the committee members to "lift up the people." Inquired a congressman, "Where is the money coming from to lift them up?"

"Make it out of paper."

"Who is going to make it?"

"The United States," replied Maddox, the visionary.[22]

Other witnesses spoke up for national prohibition (a national imposition of the "Maine Law"), the eight-hour workday, the abolition of child labor, women's suffrage and the formation of a national bureau of labor statistics. Anticipating the Employment Act of 1946, Robert W. Hume, a teacher from Long Island City, contended that "the first duty of a government is to procure for all men willing to work, work to do."

IN REED'S TIME, great political issues put down deep roots. Race and union were the hardy perennials of the 1850s and 1860s, labor and capital (and the dollar and the tariff) the plantings that displaced them beginning in the 1870s. Americans didn't stop talking about the evils of racial injustice, but they no longer seemed willing to extend themselves very far to combat them. In the rise and fall of the Freedman's Savings and Trust Company can be seen the outlines of this shift in America's preoccupations.

If good intentions were capital, the Freedman's Bank could never have failed. In the final days of the Civil War, New York philanthropists came together to found a thrift institution to receive the small savings of emancipated slaves. The bank they envisioned would be a mutual institution owned by its depositors in proportion to the size of their deposits. It would be chartered by Congress. It would do no lending but would invest in U.S. Treasury instruments. It would keep a sizable "available fund" against a rainy day. It would pay a decent rate of interest and return its profits to its owners, the depositors. It would, in short, be a refuge for the savings of people who had never had a bank account—who, indeed, for the most part, had never learned to write their names. It was to be no charitable institution but a bastion of self-help, "a cheap, valuable and welcome boon for the freedmen for whose benefit it is designed," in the words of the New York *Times*.[23]

It was no good omen that most of the progenitors melted away before the bank's first branch, in Norfolk, Virginia, opened its doors in June 1865. It was a still less propitious sign that the philanthropists were more generous with their vision than with their capital. Still, the Freedman's Bank seemed well founded. African-Americans did have money to deposit: Union soldiers their back pay and bounty, churches their weekly collections, beneficial societies their donations. Where better to entrust these funds than in their own federally chartered savings bank? Within two years of its founding, the Freedman's Bank had 22 branches in 13 states and the District of Columbia. Rare was the bank in the postwar era with even a few branches. The Freedman's fairly sprouted them.

The Hewitt Committee would hear plenty of testimony about the boom of the late 1860s and early 1870s. Pioneers and railroad companies were pushing west, innovation was on the march and bank credit was percolating. Foreign capital was pouring into the United States.[24] Was any bank born under a luckier star?

Few seemed so favored by the government itself. Its very name, so like that of the Freedmen's Bureau, officially known as the U.S. Bureau of Refugees, Freedmen and Abandoned Lands, instilled confidence. Were the two institutions not cut from the same governmental cloth? The owner of a Freedman's passbook, decorated with an image of the bureau's commissioner, General Oliver O. Howard, along with those of Generals Grant and Sherman, Admiral Farragut, Secretary of War Stanton and of the Great Emancipator himself, might logically have supposed so. After transferring from its original home in New York City in 1867, the bank was headquartered in Washington, the seat of government. Without ever hearing the late 20th century phrase "government-sponsored enterprise," the Freedman's patrons could have easily believed that they were banking with one.[25]

So widely diffused was the prosperity of 1870 that only three banks failed in the entire calendar year.[26] The speculative spirit of the day was contagious, and the Freedman's trustees seem to have caught a full dose of it. In 1870, they amended the charter to permit a more liberal lending policy. No more was the management restricted to buying dull government bonds but could now roll the dice in real estate. Up, therefore, went a splendid new headquarters building for the bank on Pennsylvania Avenue. It was in this same year that the board fell under the spell of Henry D. Cooke, brother of the era's most bedazzling financier, Jay Cooke. Under Cooke's leadership, the Freedman's Bank finance committee ominously took to calling the reserve fund "idle money." Why bother with a rainy-day fund when the sun shone bright?[27]

The Freedman's Bank was rich in trusting depositors—at length, the auditors counted 61,155 accounts in 37 branches—but in few of the other needful attributes of the solvent depository institution. Lacking were coherent books, capable managers, honest cashiers, performing assets and a positive net worth. It is doubtful that the Freedman's turned a profit even in the boomtime year of 1870. It almost certainly operated in the red thereafter. The beginning of the end was the collapse of Jay Cooke & Company in September 1873. Such connections as the Freedman's might have had with the bank of Henry Cooke's brother had supposedly been dissolved in 1872. But the depositors were inclined to run first and ask questions later.[28]

The bank managed to weather this, its first run, but its troubles ran deeper than its exposure to Jay Cooke. "That there is fraud in it I do not know," a federal examiner later testified about the state of the Freedman's head office. "The thing simply cannot be explained. There have been so many blunders in the accounts, so many duplications, so many wrong postings in the ledgers that the books are utterly and wholly unreliable. If that be fraud, then it is fraud."[29]

Sick unto death, the bank grasped for a miracle. Would the famed black abolitionist, orator and educator Frederick Douglass consent to preside over one as the new president? Douglass did so consent, and he spent three miserable months trying to allay panic, preserve hope and yet—at the same time—face facts. He could not do all three at once, and it was the facts that prevailed. To the bigoted, sadistic glee of the southern Democratic press, the Freedman's closed its doors on July 2, 1874.

"The mission of the Freedman's Bank is to show our people the road to a share of the wealth and well being of the world."[30] So said Douglass as the bank lay dying. The auditors' reckoning was a tale of fraud, neglect and titanic bungling. The assets, in the nominal sum of just over $400,000, overwhelmingly consisted of doubtful real-estate loans. Of cash there was but $31,689; of U.S. Treasury securities—the founders' idea of the bank's bedrock investment—just $400. The depositors could walk away with as much as 93 cents on the dollar of their deposits, initial reports speculated. But the deeper the reclamation committee dug, the worse the prospects appeared. In a depression, few assets are so illiquid as real estate. Nine years after the doors closed the bank paid out its final liquidating dividend. In all, the depositors—at least the sadly small minority who had had the patience and resources to persist—got back 62 cents on the dollar.[31]

What responsibility did the federal government bear for this heart-wrenching failure? "A host of petitions asked Congress to recognize that the government had a moral, if not a legal, duty to save the freedmen from becoming the victims of a catastrophe which was not of their making," the historian of the Freedman's relates. "From Charleston, Nashville, Richmond, Baltimore, Lexington, Louisville and Wilmington came pleas for federal assumption of the Bank's debts." Fifty years later, the petitions were still coming in. Reed himself lined up with the few who contended that the government owed a moral obligation to the depositors who had not unreasonably believed that the bank was backed by the U.S. Treasury. Those arguments, however, were in vain. The government paid out not one dollar.[32]

*   *   *

IN THOSE DAYS, a new representative could wait more than a year before the Congress to which he was elected was called into session. So Thomas B. Reed monitored national events from his Portland law office. Early in 1877, he filed a motion in the Maine Supreme Court on behalf of the city seeking to throw the Portland & Rochester Railroad into receivership, one of the nearly one-fourth of American railroads to succumb to bankruptcy during the depression.[33] A receiver duly appointed, Reed became its counsel. Other local railroads teetered on bankruptcy, in one case "on account of unforeseen difficulties." The phrase stuck in Reed's craw. "Unforeseen difficulties!" he wrote to George Gifford, then working in London. "It is astonishing how much a man can fail to see who shuts his eyes."

The imminent congressman had administrative and ceremonial duties to attend to as well. He paid a short visit to Washington after the Hayes inauguration, and he organized the competition by which he made his first appointment of a candidate to West Point. In August, he attended the state Republican convention at Augusta. In September, he served on the reception committee of the 14th annual New England Agricultural Society at which one Norman Taylor ran a race against a horse, finishing second.[34]

This marking of time was ushered in with a New Year's party at the home of Reed's Portland neighbor Stephen Berry. The congressman-elect arrived at 10 PM with treasures he had picked up at the Centennial fair in Philadelphia: a sealed can of pâté de foie gras aux truffes and another of kippered herring. It is recorded that Reed was an enthusiastic participant in the ritual mixing of the annual New Year's punch.

"We first brought forth the remnant of the last New Year's punch," Berry's diary relates, "which had been bottled away for this occasion. . . . Tom refused to admit any virtues to the old sample, which he still contends was far inferior to the one which he mixed just before it. But he joined in concocting this, and cheerfully praised it. The groundwork was Guadalupe rum, three half-pints; half a bottle of brandy; something more than that of catawha wine; three oranges; sundry lemons; and five and a half very little tumblerfuls of water, not forgetting a piece of ice." Pineapples being out of season, the cook made do with canned pineapple. They added lemon peels, having "soaked out the flavor with rum," and added lemon oil, obtained from scalded lemon seeds. The sum of these parts they lovingly poured, and repoured, over a block of ice. They sipped punch till midnight, toasted the arrival of 1877 and took turns reading aloud the New Year's greetings published in the local newspapers. Reed left a little before two—"early," Berry remarked.[35]

Chapter 6

The Freshman Makes His Mark

Representative Thomas B. Reed could hardly help but gawk at the sight of his magnificent new workplace on the opening day of the 45th Congress, March 5, 1877. From its gilded ceiling to its tobacco-stained floor, the chamber of the House of Representatives measured 36 feet; it was 139 feet long and 93 feet wide. Members sat in seven concentric semicircles behind small wooden desks, Republicans to the west side of the hall and Democrats to the east. Next to each desk stood a cuspidor, at which snuff-taking and tobacco-chewing members took distracted aim. Front and center was the splendid chair and the marble desk of the Speaker of the House, raised three feet off the floor. Turning his back on the 293 politicians whom he strove to control, the Speaker, handsome Sam Randall, Democrat of Pennsylvania, could gaze upon portraits of Washington and Lafayette or, at a higher elevation, the slightly less ennobling faces of as many as 65 members of the congressional press corps. In Maine, the lower house did business in a room just 50 feet square, and no special powers of vocal projection were necessary to be heard. Thick skin was a requisite for success at any level of electoral politics. In Washington, leather lungs were also required.[1]

"There is no test of a man's ability in any department of life more severe than service in the House of Representatives," James Blaine, who also first cut his legislative teeth in Augusta, said of the proceedings under the Capitol dome. "There is . . . no place where so little consideration is shown for the feelings or the failures of beginners. What a man gains in the House he gains by sheer force of his own character; and if he loses and falls back he must expect no mercy, and will receive no sympathy. It is a field in which survival of the strongest is the recognized rule, and where no pretence can deceive, and no glamour can mislead. The real man is discovered, his worth is impartially weighed, his rank is irreversibly decreed."[2]

In Portland, there was only one Tom Reed, the lawyer of mark, ex-Maine attorney general, ex-city solicitor, political prodigy, wit, clubman, religious skeptic, orator and intellect. In Washington, as one of 142 incoming first-term congressmen, he was a man of no particular professional account and—having arrived in the city without his wife—of absolutely no social consequence. At 6'2" and 250 pounds on an empty stomach, he would never be lost in a crowd. But nothing else immediately distinguished the representative of Maine's First District.

The new congressman had had a year to anticipate the glory of taking his seat in the Capitol, and a fine spot it turned out to be. In those days, the members chose their seats when their names were drawn randomly. Reed picked a desk in the second row and slightly to the west of center. On Reed's left was James Henry Randolph of Tennessee; on his right, Lucien Bonaparte Caswell of Wisconsin. Directly in front of Caswell and very near Reed was none other than Benjamin Butler of Massachusetts, known to southerners as "Beast Butler" for the brutality of his rule of occupied New Orleans during the war. Just over Reed's left shoulder sat the gaunt and venerable William "Pig Iron" Kelley, of Pennsylvania, whose nickname alluded to the subject he never seemed to stop talking about or voting for.[3]

During the hungry 1870s, Americans had every reason to envy the lot of their comfortable congressmen. Five thousand dollars a year, not to mention travel money, free baths (no small perquisite in the days when indoor bathing was scarce) and $125 a year for newspapers and stationery, was a level of emolument outside the realm of popular imagining. The congressional chaplain earned $900 a year, a District of Columbia high school principal, $1,050.[4] In the Pennsylvania anthracite fields, miners grossed barely $1 a day and took home even less than that.[5] A wife-less congressman like Reed could rent furnished rooms for $100 a month. He could have his breakfast and dinner delivered to his door for $20 a month. He could, if he smoked, buy two cigars for a nickel. Two cents got him a ride on the Washington streetcars.

The eight-hour day, though a wan hope for most Americans in 1877, was a reality for Congress. Noon to 4 or 5 PM were the typical hours of the average session. After a prayer by the chaplain came the reading of the journal of the previous day's proceedings. Those formalities out of the way, the members could introduce bills and petitions, which the Speaker referred to the appropriate committees. This portion of the day's business, called the "morning hour," invariably occurred in the afternoon. Committees met at other times.

"The House of Representatives could hardly be called a dignified body," wrote a congressional reporter as he watched the scene from the press gallery. "As I make my notes, I see a dozen men reading newspapers with their feet on their desks. Of two Congressmen standing talking in the aisle, one has his hands in his pockets, and his head bobs to emphasize his words. Amos Townsend is sitting with his arms folded, looking into the future. And 'Pig-Iron' Kelley, of Pennsylvania, has dropped his newspaper and is paring his fingernails."[6] To summon a page, a member would clap his hands. To call the members to order, the Speaker would bang his marble desk with the gavel. To seek the recognition of the chair, a member would cry out "Mr. Speaker, Mr. Speaker." Seated at desks just in front of the Speaker were the aristocrats of the clerical trade, five official shorthand reporters who earned the same $5,000 a year as the congressmen did.[7]

A Congress lived for two years, but the people's business, in those days, did not require the presence of the representatives in Washington for much more than half of those 24 months. There were two sessions, the "long" and the "short." Each began on the first Monday in December. The long session, the opening one, ran until its business was done some time during the sweltering Washington summer; the short session closed out promptly on March 3, when a new Congress took over. From time to time, a special session was called to order. Reed's first full day on the job was a special session at which the new, 45th Congress was asked to take up with the unfinished business of the 44th. The date was October 15, 1877.

The District of Columbia that Reed proceeded to make his home away from home was just then putting on its imperial face. Alexander "Boss" Shepherd, the District's appointed governor, had put through a crash construction program yielding miles-long networks of paved roads, sidewalks, sewers, gas lamps and water mains. Washingtonians gaped at these marvels, and they would marvel the more when the bankrupting cost of Shepherd's improvements was revealed a few years later. By no means, however, was the governor's vision of a modern metropolis fully realized. The District had neither a general hospital nor a morgue, and the numerous outhouses mocked the new sewers. School rooms and fire apparatus were in short supply, as were the now-customary fringe benefits of public service (disabled firemen, earning no compensation for their injuries, had to get by as best they could). Fresh water rarely reached even the second floor of dwellings in the city's higher elevations, including Capitol Hill. Swamps, slums, alleys and shanty towns bred preventable disease. "Our legislators and opulent citizens," the annual report of the District Board of Health caustically remarked in the year of Reed's arrival, "promenading the wide and scrupulously clean streets and avenues of this city, have a very faint idea of the sources of complaint to which we refer. But if they could be induced to extend their peregrinations into the slums and alleys, inhabited mostly by colored and very poor white people, their ideas might be somewhat modified." Certainly, the report intimated, the noses of the curious rich would be overwhelmed. "Six thousand and eighty-four tons of garbage, over five hundred tons a month, have been removed from these slums and alleys during the past year, and there has been no day when they were free from abominable smells arising from evaporation of slops."[8]

Washington was in a growth spurt. In 25 years, its population had more than tripled, to 165,000, of whom almost one-third were African-American. Though the District had abolished slavery in 1862, a year before President Lincoln signed the Emancipation Proclamation, and though 30,000 freedmen had found refuge in the capital during the war, the city fathers worried that the black community was losing an evolutionary struggle with the "sturdy Irish." The fact was that the black death rate was twice as high as the white, a difference that literally started at birth, with disastrously lopsided rates of infant mortality. "Of the 119 still-births investigated by the medical sanitary inspector," health officials related, "107 were colored, 44 of which were of illegitimate issues." If the shockingly high incidence of mortality were not reversible, the board speculated, "the days of the colored race are numbered."[9]

It was bad enough that newborns died of natural causes, but the city was suffering a wave of infanticide. In 12 months, 17 babies had been murdered. For comparison, there had been just six more conventional homicides. To put an end to this "wholesale slaughter," the city's coroner, Dr. D. C. Patterson, urged that the city pay for information leading to the arrest and conviction of the "unnatural mothers." A new fund should be seeded for the purpose.[10]

Though Reed had seen little of Washington before the 45th Congress convened, he would recognize it as a place that, like Portland, observed the Christian forms. The police-court docket for the 1877 fiscal year shows 69 prosecutions for unlawfully operating an establishment on Sunday, including—separately noted—two charges against impious barbers. The police made 805 arrests for profanity, the second most common infraction, behind disorderly conduct.[11]

Also like Portland, Washington was a city of trees. Since November 1, 1876, the city fathers had planted 8,654 seedlings, at $2.50 a piece. Goats devoured these plantings and caterpillars infested them. Unattended horses chomped away at their bark. To combat such menaces, the city built tree boxes, unsightly though they admittedly were. "The damages incurred by runaway and unattended horses on trees and tree-boxes, form, in the aggregate, a very considerable item of expenses," the commissioners complained. "Could entire immunity from this source of injury be secured it would effect a savings of several thousands of dollars yearly."[12]

Each family might lawfully keep a single cow, but the commissioners pressed for legislation to make the city a little less pastoral. One such law would prohibit the driving of cattle through the city streets. A second would raise to $2 from $1 the cost of reclaiming a wandering goat.[13]

Convict labor was another feature of Washington street life. "The prisoners in the work-house who now and for some time past (such as are deemed capable for work upon the streets) have been employed in cleaning the gutters and portions of the bed of various streets are, in my judgment, not remunerative," advised E. W. Chapin, superintendent of repairs. "The class of men generally found in the prison department are not even skilled as common laborers. They are rarely turned over to the guards who work them before 9 a.m., and then are returned to prison by 4 p.m., making a very short day's labor; then it is an enforced labor, requiring constant watchfulness upon the part of the guards. It is with difficulty that shelter can be found for them in sudden rains, the aversion of the people to them is so great. It has the tendency to lower and degrade the honest-paid laborer by their exhibition upon the streets, and the amount of work performed by them hardly pays the expense incurred in its execution."[14]

Unlike Portland, Washington was a city utterly divided by race. Blacks and whites went to separate schools, and the superintendents of those schools earned different salaries: $2,700 a year for whites, $2,250 for blacks. A third-year clerk in a white school earned $800 a year; his or her black counterpart, $750. It scandalized Dr. Jonathan L. Dwyer, visiting physician at the municipal refuge, the Washington Asylum, that white and black female patients were thrown together in the same ward. It was, he said, asking too much of a white woman that she "should be compelled to submit to associations which cannot be otherwise than repugnant to her, and which will have, as in all cases where the races are obliged to mingle, a demoralizing tendency."[15]

Many were the District's needs, jobs being at the very top of the list. They were the "great want . . . which now overshadows all others," according to the city Relief Commission. But there was precious little work to be had, that crying need notwithstanding. How could the destitute keep body and soul together during the cold months of 1876–77? By making written application for assistance. The application would be sliced open by a Relief Commission clerk, of whom there were five, and handed to a Relief Commission visitor, of whom there were four. The appeals for municipal aid came thick and fast, from 100 and 600 a day. To the four visitors fell the job of verifying the applicant's circumstances and suitability for relief. If approved—and only one application per month per family was allowed—the city vouchsafed fuel and groceries in the following measure: a quarter ton of coal, 50 cents' worth of kindling, 10 pounds of flour, 20 pounds of meal, 5 pounds of rice—"and in cases of sickness a little tea and sugar." In the just-ended fiscal year, the city dispensed relief to 8,191 families at a cost of $27,206.62.[16]

REED'S FIRST UTTERANCE in the first session of his first Congress was in the service of a petition to raise the salaries of the Portland letter-carriers. He subsequently sponsored a bill to change the name of a schooner and to have that vessel—now the *Minnie*, formerly the *Captain Charles Robbins*—registered with the Secretary of the Treasury. He proceeded to request federal pensions for three of his constituents, took up duties on the Committee on Territories (he later confessed that he would not have known a territory if he "met one coming down the Avenue") and, in a brief exchange on the House floor, argued that the report of the U.S. Monetary Commission should be published in its entirety.

"Mr. Speaker," an economy-minded Democrat had objected, "it will cost about three times as much to print what is suggested by the gentleman as to print what is suggested by the committee." To which the representative from Maine parried, "But I submit it will make the report three times more valuable."[17]

Reed could hardly have imagined what he had gotten himself into. The monetary question—whether a dollar should be backed by gold or silver or nothing at all—would preoccupy much of the country, and seemingly obsess the rest of it, for the next 25 years. The freshman congressman was just two weeks at his desk when one of the members of the Monetary Commission, Representative Richard P. Bland, a Democrat from Missouri, introduced a bill to allow the unlimited coinage of silver. His legislation, the Bland-Allison bill, would cheapen the currency by creating more of it. Populists cheered—including not a few in Reed's own district—while orthodox monetary thinkers quailed. Reed, at some political risk to himself, voted against the Bland-Allison bill, one of only 34 members of the House to do so. President Hayes vetoed the measure. He called it inflationary (it did not seem to matter to

Hayes that the depression was still deepening) and morally objection-able besides. Borrowing heavily from abroad to fight the Civil War, the United States had pledged to repay its creditors in dollars of the same gold weight it had borrowed. To renege on that promise would stain not only the credit, but also the honor, of the United States. Voting to sustain Hayes's veto, Reed again found himself in a highly select losing minority, though as one with the other four Maine representatives.

He was not long in bursting the cocoon of his freshman anonymity. A purely ceremonial speech, one of the type that forgettably fills the Record in every session of Congress, revealed a nuanced and unusual mind. The occasion was the January 1878 presentation of a piece of statuary to the United States by the people of the state of Maine. A call had gone out to the states to ship to Washington sculptures of their most illustrious citizens, and the Pine Tree State had responded with a figure of General William King (1768–1852), its first governor. The Maine delegation produced two speeches for the occasion of the King installation, the first by Representative William P. Frye, who spoke at length in the conventional biographical manner. Reed followed with an extraordinary meditation on the impermanence of fame.

"He has been dead scarce 25 years," said Reed of Maine's hero, "yet all that can be found in biographies and histories is [a] few dates. . . . Certainly no one would dream of taking the fading of this narrow and local fame to teach the vanity of human reputation. More striking examples might easily be found, and the lesson itself would be too trite. We all know too sadly well that oblivion begins to devour the mightiest when dead, and has in all ages been so greedy as to overtake some men yet living.

"The lesson here," Reed continued, "is far different. General King could hope for no perpetuity of his memory. Perhaps he was great enough to be careless of distinction. Although he was a man of stately presence, with sonorous voice rich with the eloquence of conviction and command, his speeches were as short as they were vigorous. His words went straight to the mark. He preserved nothing that he said. No record remains of his seven years' struggle to form the state. He did his work and was careless who had the credit. Human fame, even of those who are at pains to preserve their memories, is as evanescent as the cloud of a summer sky. But human deeds are imperishable. Sooner or later he who has been the faithful servant of all shall be looked up to as the master."[18]

These words, splendid though they were, could not have foretold Reed's aptitude for parliamentary debate. Set pieces composed in the stillness of one's rented Washington rooms were one thing, forensic combat on the floor of the House something very different. So it must have gratified the Republican leadership to watch this bear of a freshman make his first exchange of pleasantries with the East side of the House. The Democratic majority, chafing under an allegedly corrupt presidential election and in the wake of the indisputably corrupt administration of U. S. Grant, demanded investigations far and wide. Their claim that these inquests would be conducted in secret brought Reed to his feet. Sarcasm, for some, is a rhetorical affectation, and one that is usually bungled. For Reed, it was like a native language.

"How secret all things are kept here in Washington!" Reed jested. "When the body at the other end of the Capitol has a secret session, how difficult it is for the community to become acquainted with their action therein! And when one of the committees of the last House, when all of the committees were investigating the subjects before them, how secret it was and how silent all the newspapers were upon the subject! Sir, everybody knows that the reverse of [this] idea was true. We all know that when those committees had gorged themselves with accusations against men, made by persons of no character and standing in the community, they were permitted to ooze out to newspaper correspondents, thus establishing a sort of competition with each other on the subject of the slander of men and measures."[19]

Ideological lines in the House were drawn long before Reed went to Washington. In matters touching on the federal government, Democrats stood for Jeffersonian minimalism, Republicans for Hamiltonian activism. James H. Blount, a Democrat from Macon, Georgia, would carry minimalism in the foreign service to its logical extreme by firing the diplomats. Blount argued his point during consideration over the bill making appropriations for the consular and diplomatic service for the 1879 fiscal year. A Republican colleague of Reed's from Maine, Representative Eugene Hale, had proposed an amendment that would raise the salaries of U.S. ministers plenipotentiary to Great Britain, France,

Germany, France and Russia to $17,500 a year from $15,000. Blount insisted that the advent of the transatlantic cable had rendered diplomats obsolete; America could conduct her foreign affairs from a Washington telegraph office. Besides, diplomacy itself was a vestige of kings and royal courts. "We are a republican people," the Georgian declared.[20]

"I apprehend that while we are a great people, while we are a noble and magnificent people, yet there is some wisdom outside the United States," Reed answered him. And so long as America put diplomats and consular officers in the field, the government should pay them enough to allow them to hold their heads up. Now bringing the discussion down to the common denominator of the House, Reed proceeded: "We ourselves are receiving what would be a large salary if we were otherwise situated; but in the position in which we are we know that it is not too much for the expenditures we are required to make. Upon the same principle our foreign ministers should receive such salaries as will enable them out of those salaries to maintain creditably the honorable positions which we send them to occupy; we should not curtail their salaries so that none but men of large private means can afford to fill their places."[21]

On one perennial sore subject, however, the parties seemed to switch identities. When it came to claims against the government for restitution of property damaged by Union forces during the war, Democrats were prepared to put aside petty considerations of economy. Then, or so the Republicans contended, the frugal Jeffersonians were ready to fling open the vaults of the Treasury and help themselves. That the North and the South would at last come together again as one nation was a hope often expressed on the floor of the House in those days. Just as frequently, however, the hope was mocked by bitter words, some of which were spoken by none other than the freshman from the First District of Maine.

There was one such exchange in February 1878. Before the House was the question of which candidate should prevail in one of the contested congressional elections in Louisiana. Representative E. John Ellis, who had spent the final two years of the war under lock and key in a Union prison, spoke up for the Democrat, and for the Democratic party, in the South. He spoke with considerable flourish too, declaring that southern blacks, now truly liberated, in mind as well as in body, would soon "swell the columns of that grand [D]emocratic army whose thunderous yet measured tread is at the very gates of every department of this republic. Of this fact my [R]epublican friends need have no shadow of doubt."

"We do not doubt it," interjected Reed; "we saw it achieved at the muzzle of the musket and shotgun a short time ago."

"I can understand how the gentleman would tempt me to leave the argument of this case to engage in the old strife of sectionalism," Ellis shot back. "When I shall have finished my argument, if there is any time left, I will pay my respects to the taunt of the gentleman and give it such response as will hurl it back and vindicate my slandered and patient people and section."[22]

Such was the tone of sweet conciliation 11 years after Appomattox. In April, the House was asked to authorize a $65,000 payment to the College of William and Mary to make good the cost of property burned by Union forces in 1862. The bill had bipartisan and cross-sectional support. Representative John Goode Jr., Democrat from Virginia, and Representative George B. Loring, Republican from Massachusetts, each spoke on its behalf, Loring holding forth in the Augustan manner for more than an hour. Each proponent invoked the storied history of the college, its architectural legacy, its roll call of famous alumni and its claim on the affection of a civilized people. Then too, it was an uncontested fact that the soldiers who torched the college building were drunk.

Loring, a second-term congressman, a physician and a Harvard man, had not previously addressed the House. This, his "maiden effort," the New York *Times* correspondent reported, "has placed him in the front rank of Congressional orators." He took his seat to warm bipartisan applause.[23]

Loring did not skimp on historical allusions or lofty turns of phrase, and his remarks bore the imprint of careful composition. Reed, pear-shaped and laconic, dealt with these flourishes as a judo master does an armed assailant. "Of course," the Maine freshman admitted, "this is a fair-seeming claim.

"It is always in this way that matters are presented . . ." he continued. "Always the knife is placed under garlands. It never happened that a claim like this was not advocated by the most eloquent men. It never happens that claims like this are not disguised by classical allusions and by references to history, English or ancient. I must say that it seemed to me strange when Washington and Jefferson and Sir Christopher Wren were brought in to decide the question whether we should pay $65,000 for a burned building. But when it came to the introduction of Milton, and for aught I know to Luther and Locke, I confess I was astounded. [Applause and laughter.] We heard of Sir Harry Vane and Cromwell. Why, said Cromwell, 'The Lord deliver me from Sir Harry Vane,' and I say, upon a question of this kind, the lord deliver the Congress of the United States from Sir Harry Vane and Cromwell too. [Laughter.]"[24]

Not that he could hope to prove as interesting a speaker as "the gentleman who preceded me," Reed lightly protested, "for that would transcend my utmost powers." Still, within the scope of his limited talents, he would present reason, not rhetoric.

The House was full of lawyers, and Reed played to their professional reverence for precedent. There was no precedent, as yet, for the "folly and imbecility" of the legislation now in front of the House. Sponsors from both sides of the Mason-Dixon Line had searched in vain for relevant historical examples. "The graceful learning of Massachusetts has twined itself with the rugged and interesting persistence of Virginia in its search for a parallel," Reed said, "but to no purpose whatsoever. You may bring together Bunker Hill and Yorktown, Massachusetts and Virginia, and tie them together with all the flowers of rhetoric that have ever bloomed since the Garden of Eden, but you cannot change the plain, historic fact that no nation on earth ever was so imbecile and idiotic as to establish a principle that would more nearly bankrupt its treasury after victory than after defeat."[25]

"Read them all," someone on the floor shouted encouragingly as Reed began to recite from the war claims that were already before the House. He estimated that no fewer than 10 percent of the bills on the docket of the 45th Congress sought compensation for damages allegedly caused by Union forces, a bit of research he had conducted with the help of a friendly newspaper reporter. Approve the William and Mary payment, and you would open the floodgates. "Think of all this," Reed continued, with a wink to the eloquent Loring, "in the sonorous voice of some gentleman from Massachusetts, advocating this measure, just think of it! [Laughter and applause.] . . . Think of all these claimants translated into that magnificent upper air in which Massachusetts and Virginia and possibly South Carolina alone can live! [Laughter and applause.] Just think of them in that blue empyrean, surrounded by Washington and Jefferson and dead heroes, and Milton and Sir Harry Vane and Sir Christopher Wren and the whole of our English literature, and my friend from Massachusetts here below emblazoning it all in gorgeous language! I ask you how you could meet that."[26]

There remained the perpetually tender issue of the war. It was the South in particular, and the Democrats in general, who persisted in rubbing that raw wound, Reed said. Every claim for restitution of wartime damages was a provocation. "Now I ask gentlemen on the other side," he went on, "if under all the circumstances it is too unreasonable to expect them to cease this constant, persistent attack on the United States Treasury and on the laws which grew out of the war. They want peace. Then why do they not cease to provoke controversy?"[27]

The plain fact was that the Confederacy was defeated. "Now whatever may be the question of right or wrong for any individual," Reed addressed the former Confederates, former copperheads and others on the east side of the hall, "the only justification for rebellion is success. The consequences are too fearful for men to be allowed to make it the escape of their passions. It involves death to men and destruction to property. You do not need to be told of its miseries, for you have suffered them. Any set of men who purpose to plunge their people into these horrors are bound to be successful or take the consequences. You were beaten and yet you want us to take the consequences."[28]

"YOU WERE BEATEN. . . ." In presidential politics, Democrats had not relinquished the burning conviction that Tilden had beaten Hayes. A grand compromise there might have been—Hayes to the White House, federal troops out of the South, the state houses of Louisiana and South Carolina turned over to the Democrats—but that hardly doused the flames of Democratic anger. They burned all the brighter when a Louisiana election supervisor, James E. Anderson, came forward in July

1877 to swear that he and others had stolen the election from Tilden. Anderson, 31 years old, a news editor of the Philadelphia *North American* newspaper, had served during the 1876 election as the supervisor of registration in the parish of East Feliciana, Louisiana. Putting his name to an affidavit alleging gross irregularities in the service of the Republican party, he set Washington, D.C., abuzz. Representative Clarkson N. Potter, a New York Democrat, vowed to get to the bottom of the matter. He proposed to lead a special committee to investigate.

Some Democrats, and most Republicans, wished that Anderson could be made to disappear. If his charges were true, Hayes was a fraud, the Electoral Commission that installed him in the White House office was a hoax and the already depressed economy of the United States was hostage to an unwelcome new source of political uncertainty. Besides, as one Democrat, Representative Roger Q. Mills, of Texas, told the New York *Times*, the Democratic party had had its chance. It needed no sworn statement to prove that the 1876 election was stolen. It knew it, and it had known it when it rolled over to accept the compromise that ended the electoral and constitutional crisis. "They gave up the question to avoid revolution," said Mills, "and they ought to abide in good faith by their decision now."[29]

Then again, most Democrats reasoned, the very public unmasking of the Republican fraud would likely give Tilden, should he choose to run, and the rest of the Democratic slate for federal office a clean sweep in the 1880 elections. It only remained to get on with the unmasking.

One might have supposed that Potter had free rein. There were 152 Democrats in the House, five more than the minimum necessary for a quorum. Republicans might have filibustered but chose not to. They would do nothing to facilitate the investigation but neither would they be seen to impede it. Literally, they would sit on their hands. The operative foot-dragging was rather on the Democratic side of the aisle. "No quorum, Mr. Speaker," was the familiar daily refrain in the mid-May debates over the Potter resolution. Some Democrats were out of town or indisposed, but even when the necessary 147 were physically present, a critical few refused to answer the roll call. By custom, a quorum was defined not as the minimum number of representatives on hand but the minimum number on hand and choosing to vote. Republicans refrained from voting on the Potter resolution as a parliamentary tactic. But so too did a few Democrats.

In the heat of the debate, a first-term Tennessee Democrat, William P. Caldwell, rose to direct the attention of Speaker Randall to House Rule 31. Randall directed that the rule be read. "Every member," spoke the clerk, "who shall be in the House when a question is put shall give his vote unless the House shall excuse him."

The freshman seemed to believe he had solved the problem of the disappearing quorum. "The language of that rule is imperative," he declared. "It says that every member shall vote."

"This is not a new difficulty," Randall advised the tyro. "The Chair has caused the rule to be read, which is the extent, he thinks, of his power in that direction. In other words, he knows of no physical power, even by means of the Sergeant-at-Arms, or through any persuasive power which he possesses, [Laughter.] to compel gentlemen to vote; but if the gentleman from Tennessee will indicate a way, the Chair will cause it to be followed."

"I suggest," Caldwell replied, "that the Chair can order the Sergeant-at-Arms to arrest any member who disregards this rule, and carry him between the tellers. [Derisive laughter, and cries of 'Suppose you let him try,' from the Republican side.]"[30]

Mills of Texas, who had had two congressional terms under his belt, recalled that when James G. Blaine was Speaker, he too had failed to solve the problem of dilatory tactics. In response to the Democrats' obstruction of the civil rights bill in the 41st Congress, Blaine, a Republican, had fatalistically remarked, "You could bring a horse to water, but you could not make him drink." So it was on May 15, 1878: 263 members were present on the House floor, yet there was no quorum.[31]

Two days later, Potter, still unable to form a quorum, took drastic action. "Knowing the tendency of many of his colleagues to pass from the labor of voting in the House to the bar where liquid refreshments are dispensed," the New York *Times* reported, "Mr. Potter determined to have enforced the rule requiring the doors be closed when there is not a quorum present, and moved that the Speaker issue his warrant for the arrest of absentees."

The doors were closed and the warrant was issued. Tempers flared, with an old Confederate, John Goode of Virginia, broadly threatening a former Union colonel, Omar Conger of Michigan, with an invitation to meet him on "the field of honor." Mocking laughter on the Republican side did not serve to mollify the offended Virginian.

Now it was the Democrats' turn to cheer, for a messenger entered the House with four Democratic stragglers in tow. Finally, Potter had his quorum—and, after a prompt vote, his authorization to investigate the alleged theft of the 1876 presidential election. A few days later came an announcement of the personnel of the Potter Committee. There would be seven Democrats and four Republicans, including, among the latter, Benjamin Butler of Massachusetts, who already had one foot out of the Republican party and pointed toward the easy-money movement, i.e., greenbackism; Jacob Cox, a former governor of Ohio, Secretary of the Interior and president of the Wabash Railroad; Frank Hiscock, of upstate New York, a protégé of the Republican boss Roscoe Conkling; and Thomas B. Reed. Before very long, the New York *Times* would hardly have a civil word for Reed. For now, however, it appraised the rising Republican with well-grounded generosity. "Mr. Reed, although a young man," the paper related, "has been Attorney General of Maine and has served in both branches of the legislature of that state. Those who know him intimately speak of him as a man of large abilities and great promise."[32]

Chapter 7

"Before God and my country"

S O THE POTTER Committee—officially, the Select Committee on
Alleged Frauds in the Presidential Election of 1876—got down to
cases. The first witness was the man who had started the ruckus, James
E. Anderson, supervisor of voter registration in the parish of East Feliciana, Louisiana. Anderson was prepared to swear that he falsified the parish vote count, so helping to tip Louisiana and the presidency to Rutherford B. Hayes.

By Anderson's telling, John Sherman was his seducer. If Anderson
would throw out a sufficient number of Democratic ballots, the Republican senator from Ohio allegedly promised, Hayes's gratitude would take
a pleasingly tangible form. At Anderson's insistence, Sherman supposedly conveyed this proposition in a letter.

So Anderson testified on the morning of the first day of the proceedings, June 1, 1878. What did Sherman, now Hayes's Secretary of the
Treasury, have to say for himself? Sherman was sworn that very afternoon. "I do not believe I ever wrote that letter," the alleged tempter told
the committee.[1] Here was a notable change in tone. Before testifying,
Sherman had charged Anderson and his other accusers with forging his
name to the letter he insisted he never wrote.[2] Under oath the fight
seemed to go out of him.

Then again, compared to the evasions, inconsistencies and apparent inventions of the Democrats' star witness, Sherman was the very light of literal truth. Anderson was a liar the Republicans could not have hoped to invent. As an election official, he had attested to the accuracy of the vote count, then repudiated it. As a witness, he had sworn to one set of facts before a Senate investigating committee, then another before the Potter panel. It required no seasoned prosecutor to probe the witness's dubious veracity. Reed was in the position of a professional cardsharp inserted into an amateur poker game.

Anderson had admitted to misleading the Senate investigators. Had he not, then, deceived them? Reed asked the witness. Not necessarily, Anderson replied. He had, in fact, told "the truth," or at least some of it. The senators had been free to "put a different construction on it."[3]

"What in your judgment is the difference between that and perjury?" Reed asked him.

"I think there is a vast difference."

"Will you state the difference?"

"I think the difference is this. Perjury means where you willfully deceive by telling falsehood. I confined myself to the truth."

"You did not willfully deceive the Senate committee?" Reed persisted.

"No, sir; but while I told the truth I did not state all the truth."

"You gave them an entirely wrong idea, didn't you?"

"They may have taken a wrong idea."

"Didn't you intend that they should take a wrong idea?"

"I don't know but I did."

"Don't you know?"

"I do not."

REED AND ANDERSON went on in this vein.

"Do you not recollect that you took an oath to tell the truth, and
     the whole truth?"

"Yes, I presume I did."

"Do you not know you did?"

"Yes, I know I did."

"And you did not do it?"

"I don't think I did."

"You perjured yourself, did not you?"

"No, I don't think I did."

"What is the distinction that you make?"

"I told the truth, just as it existed."

"Did you tell the whole truth?"

"No, I didn't tell the whole truth."

"Then you did not do what you said under oath you would do?"

"No, sir."

"Was, or was that not, perjury?"

"It may be in your estimation."

A Democratic committeeman interrupted: "I believe, Mr. Chairman, that we are not sitting here to get from the witness a legal definition of perjury."

"We probably could not get a moral definition of it here," Reed replied.[4]

It augured poorly for the radical Democratic agenda that, only two weeks into the committee's proceedings, the House overwhelmingly resolved that the ruling of the 1876 Electoral Commission would be final. Hayes would remain in the White House whatever the Potter inquisition turned up. The vote, 215–21, left no doubt as to the bipartisan yearning, if not for peace and quiet, then for a little less focused light on the apparatus of American elections. The Republican Chicago *Daily Tribune* advanced the theory that the investigating committee and its "insufferably tiresome" proceedings actually presented a threat to American journalism. If they went on much longer, people would stop buying newspapers. "Give us a rest!" cried the editors.[5]

But the committee—with its train of stenographers, its "force of clerks"[6] and its deputy sergeant-at-arms—was relentless within the partisan bounds of its Democratically defined remit. It surfaced evidence that Louisiana election officials—constituted as the state Returning Board—had trumped up claims of voter intimidation. It revealed that Republican officials had ordered black voters to stay home, then blamed the resulting low turnout on the Democrats. It showed that the Republicans had thrown out legitimate Democratic votes not randomly but in exact proportion to the numbers needed to deliver a majority to Hayes. And it brought to light the interesting coincidence that Republican election officials in the contested states had, almost to a man, found remunerative work in the Hayes administration after the election was won (Anderson, a turncoat, was jobless). "[T]he Fraudulent President in fulfillment of Sherman's . . . promises," in the words of the Democratic Washington *Post*, "has rewarded with office every scoundrel connected with the great crime in both Florida and Louisiana."[7]

But the Democrats had their own scoundrels, one of whom had lived under the very roof of candidate Tilden. The October 7, 1878, edition of the New York *Tribune* streamed the news that, according to encrypted telegrams that the paper itself had deciphered, Tilden's own nephew, William T. Pelton, had tried to buy the votes of the state of South Carolina for his uncle. The existence of such coded messages was not news. It was what they said that left the nation wide-eyed. The Chicago *Tribune* had worried in vain about newspaper sales.[8]

Republicans fairly hugged themselves. What had they done to deserve their opponents? It was true that their own campaign correspondence was yet undisclosed. And it was no less true that the states they won were up for sale. What did it say about them that they had won them? The *Nation*, the rare organ that could honestly lay claim to the mantle of journalistic impartiality, ventured that "if the truth were known it would be found that very few politicians on either side in their secret hearts think it any great sin to buy whatever is for sale—or, in other words, when great interests are at stake, to bribe the bribable."[9]

This was not at all the unmasking that Clarkson Potter had had in mind. By the looks of things, the very best outcome now available to the Democrats was one that established the comprehensive moral bankruptcy of American electoral politics. Fortunately, the Democrats reflected, the Potter Committee's $20,000 budget was very nearly exhausted. Perhaps the investigation could be allowed to fade away.

*   *   *

On Christmas Day, 1878, Reed, still in Washington, was out for a walk, bundled up against the cold. A *Post* reporter spotted him, shook his hand and asked him a question: Was the Potter Committee investigation going to look into the cipher messages? Reed pleaded ignorance. Alluding to the existence of encrypted Republican campaign messages, the reporter demanded, "[I]sn't it a fact that you Republicans are afraid to investigate this matter?"

The next morning, Reed picked up the paper to read his reply:

"'No, it ain't,' emphatically replied the fat man from Maine—and it's not often that men get fat in that climate. 'We've got no interest in it except to decide which of the Democratic leaders are guilty. . . .'

"Mr. Reed had on an overcoat, though he is a disciple of Hannibal Hamlin [a Maine politician famous for venturing out in nothing more than an old-fashioned swallowtail], but as he was shivering from the cold, the *Post* let up on him, and wishing him a happy Christmas, bade him good day."[10]

In fact, on January 15, 1879, it was a Democrat, and a highly partisan one at that, Representative John A. McMahon of Ohio, who moved that the Potter Committee be directed to investigate the cipher messages. The motion passed, though with no overt Republican support. Reed and his colleagues, maintaining their original principled opposition—they had contended all along that the investigation was a waste of time and money and threatened the still frail American economy—abstained from voting. They abstained too from public gloating over the happy turn of events by which the moralists who had started it all were themselves in the dock.

On February 4, Potter and his committee convened at the Fifth Avenue Hotel in New York to begin their examination of the cipher-telegram affair. The first witness was Smith W. Weed, of Plattsburg, New York, a Democratic lawyer. Yes, Weed freely admitted, he had traveled south at the direction of the acting secretary of the Democratic National Committee. He had entered into negotiations to bribe South Carolina election officials—the state Returning Board—but had failed to close the deal. He had wired Henry O. Havemeyer, a rich New York Democrat, that the state was up for sale. "Looks now as though the thing would work at 75,000 dollars," Weed wrote, in translation, in one of the telegrams, "for all seven votes. Have safe man to bring stuff on receiving telegram in morning. . . . The exact status is that two of the board have agreed and are consulting with the third, which is a majority, and will report to-night. They set stakes and I assented, but can withdraw."[11]

"You have no doubt of its substantial accuracy, have you?" Reed asked the witness about the way that message was reported in the press.

"No, sir," Weed replied; "I have no doubt of the substantial accuracy of it."[12]

Weed spoke casually, fluently and without remorse. The chairman directed another telegram to be read aloud. It too originated in South Carolina and was addressed to Havemeyer: "If Returning Board can be procured absolutely, will you deposit 30,000 dollars? May take less. Must be prompt."[13] Did Weed remember sending it?

"I have no doubt that it is substantially correctly translated, but I don't know," the witness replied; "I have no recollection that I sent it, but I take it for granted that I did."[14]

Weed was trying to buy enough electoral votes to put Tilden over the top—he made no bones about it—and he was negotiating at the behest of the acting Democratic secretary, Tilden's own nephew, William T. Pelton. It was Weed's theory that buying back the votes that the Republicans filched was the moral equivalent to bribing a thief to recover stolen property.

Attendance at the hearing was sparse, though the Republicans, at least, seemed to appreciate the political possibilities of the unfolding drama. Pelton was the man behind Weed, and Tilden—surely—was the man behind Pelton. They occupied the same house, uncle and nephew, at 15 Gramercy Park in Manhattan. How could they not have acted in concert?

Weed, however, emphatically denied that the candidate had any knowledge of what Pelton and he were doing until after they had failed to carry it off. Weed had bought no votes when the candidate got wind of it, and Tilden—in no uncertain terms—had ordered him to stop trying.

"You say," Reed questioned him, "you never spoke to Mr. Tilden about this matter until after the Returning Board of South Carolina had decided the result?"

"I do," affirmed Weed.

"When you did speak to him you opened the conversation, did you?"

"I did not."

"He opened it himself?"

"He did."

"Did he seem to agree in your view about ransoming goods from robbers?"

"He did not. Quite the reverse."[15]

Reed needled the witnesses he interrogated, as he did the politicians he debated. Weed needled right back.

"You said," Reed asked, "that Mr. Tilden's manner to you had changed?"

"I did not say quite that. You asked me if he had been as cordial as formerly, and I said that I thought that since the publication of these dispatches he had not been, quite. But I don't know but that may be imagination or a feeling on my own part."

"You have a sort of feeling that you are not worthy to associate with that good man, I suppose?" Reed asked.

"Perhaps so, or with any other good men—Congressmen, for instance," Weed replied.[16]

COLONEL WILLIAM T. Pelton had borne the death of a wife and had failed in business. He had a daughter to look after and an uncle to look after him, though Tilden had shooed him out of the house upon hearing of his escapades in South Carolina. Pelton was as adamant as Weed that the candidate himself knew nothing about the undercover operation in South Carolina. But Pelton, sworn on February 6, was as reluctant as Weed was accommodating. He could recall little about the ciphers or anything else that might interest the committee. The Republican committeemen pressed him hard.

Reed read aloud a message to Pelton from Weed, which said in part: "Am here. Things very much mixed. Intend to count us out. If a few dollars more can be placed in Returning Board, what say you?" Reed asked if Pelton had shown the message to Tilden, "importing as it does unpardonable wickedness from your uncle's point of view." Pelton said no. Nor had he shown any other such messages to him.

"You felt that you could go on and buy a State or two without consulting him?" Reed continued.

"I never consulted him about such matters at all, sir."

Moments later, Reed asked, "You consulted your uncle about innocent matters, didn't you?"

"I consulted him about general matters in the campaign."

"And you consulted him about general matters in this business of the electoral count, keeping shy all the time of anything that the outside world would call immoral or wicked?"

"The only thing I object to is the form of your question."

"On account of its being leading?"

"I don't know that it is necessary for you to pass judgment upon the matter, and that is what your question implies."

"I took great pains not to pass judgment upon it myself by saying what the outside world would call immoral or wicked."[17]

Reed was flipping through the book that the enterprising staff of the New York *Tribune* had published. It was a compendium of the cipher telegrams, and Reed quoted from it, including a wire indicating that South Carolina could be had for $30,000. He asked Pelton where he had received this interesting information.

The witness said he didn't know.

"Can't you recollect where you got a startling telegram like that?"

"No, sir."

"You had not been in the business of buying States before?"

"No; and I had not been buying any then."[18]

At length, Reed got Pelton to admit that he had "intended to call together the national Democratic committee, to furnish whatever money might be necessary," and that he did meet, on a Sunday, with Edward Cooper, the Democratic committee treasurer.[19] Reed feigned pious horror.

"What! This transaction with Cooper on Sunday?"

"Yes, sir."[20]

MANTON MARBLE WAS a witness that the Republican inquisitors looked forward to ripping to shreds. The longtime editor of the New York

World, Marble was a Democrat and, during the war, a Democrat *and* a copperhead. Under his stewardship, the *World* had editorialized against the Emancipation Proclamation. It had opposed the Lincoln administration's income tax and paper money. And when, in May 1864, the *World* was duped into printing a fraudulent defeatist presidential proclamation, Secretary of War Stanton ordered the paper suppressed and its editor arrested (though Marble had done his best to recall the edition in which the phony message was printed as soon as he realized that the paper had been tricked). "I have no occupation at present," he said in response to the first question he fielded at the Potter Committee hearing on February 7, for he had left the *World* in 1876.[21]

He did, however, have an avocation. He was a "visiting statesman" in Florida following the 1876 election. Other Democrats were keeping vigil in Louisiana and South Carolina. Marble chose Florida because there would be fewer opposing visitors on the ground (in those days, it was harder to get to). He left New York with the key to Pelton's cipher and with the unshakable conviction that Tilden, with whom he was on friendly terms, had been robbed. On station in Tallahassee, Marble kept up a brisk telegraphic correspondence with Pelton and filed the occasional dispatch to receptive New York newspapers. If "irregularities, falsehoods, and frauds" were purged from the Florida electoral tally, he wired the New York *Sun*, "the final result would be the election of the Tilden electors by from five to ten thousand majority."[22]

Whatever the true count, there would be no such purging unless the money was made available to pay for it. Florida election officials, convened as the state Canvassing Board, were for sale, Marble was informed, and he wired this intelligence, in cipher, to Pelton.

Smith Weed was forthright about his attempts to buy South Carolina, or, as he saw the situation, to buy it back from the Republicans who had stolen it. Marble made no such concession about his discussions with the intermediaries of evidently bribable Florida officials. The venality of the Canvassing Board was a political fact that he had merely reported to the Democratic hierarchy, via Pelton.

Marble managed to give the impression that he had rehearsed his testimony in the dual presence of a grammarian and drama coach. "It is not a trivial misrepresentation to which I have alluded," he said at one point in response to an assertion that the Democrats in Florida didn't really think that Tilden had won. "It is important; it is cardinal. All the misrepresentations of the *Tribune* in its broadside of October last, and later in its pamphlet, hinge upon the false representation that we were bereft of every honest hope, and therefore that we were obliged to resort to dishonest arts. The proof is conclusive all through my dispatches that I believed we had carried the State, and I also gave proofs that we had carried the State."[23]

What interested the Potter panel, however, was Marble's conduct, not his convictions. On December 2, 1876, he had wired Pelton at the home of his uncle: "Have just received a proposition to hand over at any hour required Tilden decision of Board and certificate of Governor for 200,000."[24] He had quoted other prices in other wires. From whom did these propositions originate?

"Simply because I wish to be perfectly accurate," Marble replied, "and I would not be willing to undertake to state at this long distance of time, when I well recollect receiving scores of such propositions, I might almost say—I would not undertake to say specifically whom that came from; the air was full of such things."

"This must have come from a responsible person, in your opinion, or you would not have sent the [telegram to Pelton reporting it]?" posed Representative William M. Springer, an Illinois Democrat.

"Yes," said Marble; "I thought it was a very significant fact, and I threw up a danger signal pretty quickly."[25]

It was another Democrat who asked Marble if he had spoken with Tilden about buying the Florida votes.

"Heavens and earth! No," Marble said.

"He said that with emphasis," Reed observed.

"I did, indeed," returned the witness. "I was surprised to be asked the question."[26]

If Marble was surprised, he was among the few. Tilden, who left an estate worth $5 million at his death in 1886, was rich enough to buy a great many electors. The Republicans set out to show that he had tried.

They relished their work the more because Marble would say such things as "The question is not suited to elicit the facts," trying to put the freshman Republican Frank Hiscock, a former upstate New York district attorney, in his place.[27] Later, Hiscock asked the witness a question which implied that he, Marble, had not merely transmitted an offer to bribe but also had supported it.

"What do you mean by that?" the witness demanded.

"Precisely what I say," Hiscock replied. "It is not necessary to spend time on that."

"Yes it is," Marble shot back. "I do not propose to have any language used which shall imply that any pecuniary proposition which I transmitted was any plan of mine, or that I ever had any plan to buy the board."

"Certainly not," said Hiscock.

"That is enough," said the witness, detecting sarcasm.[28]

Reed picked up where Hiscock left off. He asked Marble to explain what he meant when he said that, in passing along an invitation to buy the Florida electors, he was merely sending up a "danger signal" to Democratic headquarters.

Marble said that the phrase spoke for itself.

Reed pressed: "[E]xplain how you supposed that Pelton, instead of mistaking it, as he naturally did, for a proposition to assist in bribery, was to understand it as a 'danger-signal?'"

"I wished him to make the Democratic committee aware that the Canvassing Board was thought to be venal."

"So, instead of saying that the Canvassing Board was thought to be venal, you made the unfortunate mistake of transmitting a message from which persons not acquainted with your character would infer that you were acting as a medium to assist in bribery?"

"I have no idea that it was a mistake. I stated the specific, exact fact."

"You intended it as a 'danger signal,' but it was such a message that persons not knowing your character might have mistaken it for a proposition to assist in bribery?"

"You may state what you please about it."

"Is that so?

"It is not what I state."

"Will you state how it was not so?"

"I have said all I care to say on that subject."[29]

There was no missing the sarcasm in Reed's voice. "He quoted Marble's high-flown eulogies of Tilden," the New York *Times* reported the next day, "turned his most cherished expressions into ridicule, and succeeded in fairly angering the man whom his fellow-committeemen had failed to move in the least degree."[30]

AND THEN TILDEN himself appeared. He came voluntarily on February 8, the day before his 65th birthday. He looked every bit his age, shuffling stiffly into the examining room, now packed with spectators. He was all in black. His left hand trembled, his face was immobile and his body seemed to creak as he removed his silk-lined topcoat. "Not a muscle of his face relaxed with animation or expression as he stiffly extended his hand to Mr. Reed, of Maine, who received the salutation with something like a profound bow."[31] Grave and didactic, the disappointed candidate in the 1876 presidential ballot was no great advertisement for his own electability, though both parties counted him as the Democrats' certain choice for 1880.[32]

"There never was a time—not a moment, not an instant—in which I ever entertained any idea of seeking to obtain those certificates [of the various returning boards of the disputed states] by any venal inducements, any promise of money or of office to the men who had them to grant or dispose of." So Tilden had written to the editor of the Herald in response to the cipher-telegram revelations of the previous October. Never before in his career had he found it necessary to make a public defense of his character, and he did not look forward to repeating the exercise at the Fifth Avenue Hotel.[33]

Reed, Tilden's first inquisitor, homed in on the October letter to the editor. It had omitted the fact that Tilden had known about his nephew's intrigues long before the Herald had broken the news.

"Why did you keep that fact from the public? That would not incriminate anybody except your nephew, who, you knew, deserved to be incriminated."

"I did not know that; I knew only that he had gone to receive an offer," he replied. Tilden's voice was soft, and the hometown crowd strained to hear him.[34]

"Did you not very carefully draw these sentences so as to avoid coming in conflict with that fact after it came out, if it should come out?" Reed continued.

"No. I drew these sentences very carefully, so as to conform to the exact truth."

Had Tilden spoken to Weed before the mission to South Carolina? Perhaps a conversation at a bank, say the Third National Bank in New York (the president of that institution had publicly recollected seeing Weed and Tilden on the premises together at about that time).

"I do not think that I did."

"Can't you not put it any stronger than you don't *think* you did?"

"I do not *believe* I did."

"Don't you know whether you did or not? Be frank with us."

"I am perfectly frank with you, sir. I have no recollection or belief that I had any such interview."[35]

It was under Hiscock's interrogation that Tilden was provoked to righteous anger. Why, Hiscock pushed the witness, had he not gone to the Democratic National Committee to report Pelton's bungled bribery attempt as soon as he heard about it?

It was unnecessary, Tilden replied, not least because it was bungled. "The civil law does not recognize purposes until they embody themselves in action; the church punishes those purposes merely as sinful thoughts," he said, his face flushed and his voice suddenly strong. "And then," Tilden continued:

> without meaning in the least to excuse Pelton, which I do not, the atmosphere at that time was filled with rumors and assertions of the venality of the Returning Boards in [the disputed states] and of their offers. I declare before God and my country that it is my entire belief that the votes and certificates of Florida and Louisiana were bought, and that the Presidency was controlled by their purchase. Pelton, seeing that condition of things, committed a fault; committed an error; committed a wrong. He adopted the idea that it was justifiable to fight fire with fire. He adopted the idea, when he saw the Presidency being taken away from the man who had been elected by the people, elected according to the law and the fact, that it was legitimate to defeat the crime by the means he proposed to take. . . . I scorned to defend my righteous title by such means as were employed to acquire a felonious

possession. Pelton did not live up to that standard. He may be tried; he may be condemned; public opinion may punish him. At the same time, that fault is to be judged of according to the facts, according to the times, and according to what was being done, and what was done. His act was an inchoate offense. On the other side, the act that was done was a completed and consummated offense. It built up a possession of the Presidency of the United States in the man who was not elected; and the representatives and champions of that condition of things are the men whose consciences are troubled by the inchoate wrong-doing of Pelton, which I stopped and crushed out in the bud.[36]

The phrase "before God and my country" was arresting. Tilden had punctuated it by pounding his fist on the table, upon which the crowd applauded[37] and Hiscock made a note. When Tilden was finished the congressman asked the stenographer to read back those vivid words. Hiscock asked Tilden how he knew that the presidential ballots of Florida and Louisiana had been bought and paid for.

"I had no personal information," Tilden answered.

"I do not ask you for personal information. You have stated here, under the solemnity of your oath, appealing to high Heaven, your belief that these men were debauched by the Republicans. Now, in the face of that appeal to Heaven, and under that same Heaven, I ask you for your authority, and I ask you to give the name of the gentleman who communicated that fact to you.

"I stated my conviction—"

"I do not care for your conviction; I am now after the name of the man that told you."

"I cannot give you the name of any man."

"You cannot give me the name of any man?"

"No; I stated my belief, and I state it on evidence that, in my judgment, would convict anybody before a common jury."

"Will you give me the name of the person who conveyed that evidence to you?"

"The evidence is public."

"O, it is public!"[38]

Indeed, it was, retorted Tilden—just read the transcripts of the Pot-ter Committee.

TILDEN WAS TWO and a half hours in the chair, the committeemen to the very end demanding that he back up his charge that the Republicans had bought the 1876 election, and Tilden, to the very end, seeming at a loss. "You had information that led you to believe, and that, if true would convince you, that at least one of those [returning] boards offered itself for sale to the Democratic side," the chairman of the committee said, in an attempt to extend his former standard-bearer a helping hand. "Now, it was not sold to the Democratic side, and is not the conclusion legitimate and proper that if not purchased by one side it was by the other?"

Reed piped up: "I object to that question and ask for the ruling of the chairman on it."

Tilden: "That is a matter of logic."

The chairman (laughingly to Reed): "Do you expect the chair to rule out a question he has himself asked?"

"Yes, sir; that one, with confidence."

"Well," the chairman replied, "the witness says it is a question of logic, and as that is not a matter of investigation, I will rule out both question and answer. That is all, Governor Tilden."[39]

THE INVESTIGATORY WORK of the Potter Committee was now complete. Months of testimony, of shocking charges and emphatic denials, had come to what? Something was rotten in American politics. The Republicans either had, or had not, stolen the White House; the Democrats either had, or had not, tried to buy it back.

Presently, the Democratic members of the committee published their conclusions, the Republican members theirs—and Ben Butler his. "Beast" Butler, the heavy-handed occupying general of New Orleans, the ineffectual prosecutor at the impeachment trial of President Andrew Johnson in 1866 and the chronically unsuccessful candidate for governor of Massachusetts—Benjamin Franklin Butler, of all people, came closest to seeing the facts plain and true. "Everybody Republican was elected whom it was necessary to elect," Butler concluded about the Louisiana vote, "everybody Democratic defeated whom it was necessary to defeat, and the proximate result was that everybody that had anything to do with the election prominently, especially the counting and returning part of it, got Federal office."[40]

And the Pelton caper? Even the majority report condemned it for the bald-faced attempt at vote-buying it was. But it was Pelton's misdeed, the Democrats insisted, not that of the party's standard-bearer. "The idea," the Republicans shot back, "that this penniless man, living in the house and sitting at the very table of his wealthy uncle, Mr. Tilden, should have conducted negotiations involving such large sums without word or hint to the man most deeply interested, or to anybody else, cannot for a moment be entertained by candid men."[41]

The American people seemed almost to stifle a yawn. Release of the dueling reports, in early March 1879, elicited no outcry, certainly "no loss of life," as the *Nation* dryly noted (for not a few hotheads had talked about a new civil war in the aftermath of the 1876 election). The stock market was unperturbed. Republicans would be Republicans and Democrats, Democrats, the people seemed to say.[42]

Not that, for Reed, the Potter Committee was a wasted effort. An anonymous freshman no more, he was that big man from Maine, sharp-tongued, quick-witted and a partisan force to be reckoned with.

Chapter 8

Battling Heresies

G REAT THOMAS, THE Fat," as a Portland Democratic newspaper styled the rising star from the First District, excused himself from his Potter Commission duties long enough to run for reelection. Never had he been so confident about an upcoming canvass, Reed bravely assured the Republicans who nominated him, by acclamation, for a second term.[1] But the incumbent was too proficient a counter of noses not to harbor doubts. Come September, he would face not only the usual Democratic opposition, but also the rambunctious Greenbackers.

The National Greenback party of Maine, convened in Lewiston on June 5, 1878 demanded that the federal government print enough money to cut short the depression and restore prosperity. That is, Solon Chase and his followers insisted, the Treasury should strike off paper dollars unbacked by anything except the government's imprimatur, just as it did during the Civil War. Let enough greenbacks pass from hand to hand, and the people would be delivered from the "credit-mongers of the world." The platform denounced "the red flag of communism, imported from Europe," as well as the federal debt, "useless [government] offices" and imprisonment for indebtedness. It sought to postpone the restart of the machinery of the gold standard, fixed for January 1, 1879. Maine was, by this time, a proven breeding ground of radical ideas, from temperance to fiat currency, although Chase and the other 886 Green-back delegates did have their limits. They voted down, "almost unanimously," a resolution endorsing female suffrage.[2]

The monetary portion of the Greenback program was enough, however, to mark Chase and his followers as wild-haired revolutionaries. Most Republicans and, indeed, most Democrats held that a dollar was sound only to the degree that it was intrinsically valuable: It should itself be worth a dollar in gold or silver. A sound dollar was one that, if dropped on the counter, would literally ring. Paper was sound if it were exchangeable into one of these musical coins. Yes, the government had printed millions of dollars to save the Union, but that was a desperate measure. It was high time for the United States to rejoin the family of progressive, gold-standard nations—to revert, in fact, to the intentions of the Founders. Thus was joined "the most important question of this century, after slavery," as the *Nation* styled it.[3]

The Greenback furor is calculated to mystify most patrons of a 21st century automatic teller machine, for whom paper money is the only money they know. Not since 1971 has the dollar been even remotely backed by gold, and not since 1933 has an American citizen been able to exchange paper for gold, or gold for paper, at a fixed, statutory rate. From the millennial vantage point, therefore, the paper dollar is the modern contrivance, the gold dollar the anachronism. Not so, however, in the late 1870s. At that time, gold was the money of the future, as it had been of the past. As Reed was finishing his first congressional term and beginning his second, the gold standard was being institutionalized in Europe. Silver, now much the cheaper of the two precious metals, was the money of Mexico, China, India and other such poor and forlorn lands. Paper, held the enemies of Solon Chase, was the money of communism and anarchy.

The monetary debate, in Reed's time, was no dry and technical affair. Sometimes the partisans burst into song, as the Greenback faithful did to the strains of "America":

> *Thou Greenback, 'tis of thee,*
> *Best money for the free,*
> *Of thee we sing.*

Throughout all coming time,
Great souls in every clime
Will chant with strains sublime—
    Gold is not king.

Or to the tune of "John Brown":

The morning light is breaking, the darkness disappears,
Old parties now are shaking with penitential fears;
Republicans and Democrats, we've got you by the ears,
    As we go marching along.[4]

In Maine, there was at least one Greenback band and one Greenback baseball team.[5] Hard-money champions and inflationists did forensic battle in the language of morality, honor and the Constitution. Nowhere did the Founders, in their operating instructions to posterity, use the verb "to print," as advocates of the gold standard never tired of pointing out. It was the power "to coin money and regulate the value thereof" that the Constitution vested in Congress. The nation's basic monetary law, the Coinage Act of 1792, defined the dollar in terms of silver and gold. It was 371¼ grains of pure silver or 24¾ grains of pure gold.*

To Alexander Hamilton goes credit for the Coinage Act but to Sir Thomas Gresham is attributed a higher law. Cheap money drives dear money from circulation, observed Humphrey Holt (actually, it was not Gresham), in 1551, and so it proved in the early United States. It was a dull Yankee trader who would waste a gold coin on the tax collector when silver was available in the open market at a discount to Hamilton's stipulated value. By 1834, an ounce of gold would get you not 15 ounces of silver but 15.625 ounces. At this ratio, a lucrative career opportunity was opened to anyone who was willing to present the mint with 15 ounces of silver; to receive, in return, one ounce of gold; and

---

* One could present that much silver or that much gold to a federal assay office and receive in return one dollar; alternatively, one could exchange a unit of currency for the underlying lawful weight of metal. The law fixed the value of an ounce of gold at 15 times the value of an ounce of silver.

to exchange that gold on the open market for 15.625 ounces of silver. One might theoretically repeat these steps until the mint had run out of gold. So it was that gold coins disappeared into private hoards. For all intents and purposes between 1792 and 1834, the country was on a silver standard.[6]

PRESIDENT ANDREW JACKSON himself returned gold coins to the nation's pockets by resetting the silver-gold ratio at 16:1. All at once, gold became the cheap way to discharge a debt, and the great gold strikes of the 1840s and 1850s made it all the cheaper. Now gold coins circulated freely, while silver went into hiding. Jackson's motive was political: to cut the Second Bank of the United States down to size. The Bank circulated its notes in competition with gold coins. At the new silver-to-gold ratio, gold would give the bank an even stronger run for its money. By 1841, Jackson's nemesis was out of business.[7]

The Civil War worked another monetary transformation. The Lincoln administration, quick to spend but slow to tax, waged war on the cuff. It paid its creditors a more than generous interest rate, it judged: 7.3 percent for a three-year loan. But high yields provided only so much comfort to a creditor when the South was winning the battles. What the capitalists craved was security of principal along with the knowledge that they would be repaid in the same gold dollars as they had lent. Would there be treasure enough in the federal vaults to redeem these fast-multiplying claims at maturity?

Late in November 1861, Charles Wilkes, U.S. Navy, captain of the USS *San Jacinto*, seized a pair of Confederate operatives from the British steamer *Trent* on the high seas. Cheers died in the throats of northern patriots as Whitehall replied to this coup with an ultimatum: Return the Confederates and apologize for Wilkes's insult to the British flag—or else.

At the time, one war seemed more than enough for the Union. At the prospect of a second, northern capital scurried to safety. Moneyed people began to exchange paper currency for the gold that supposedly stood behind it. Their anxieties were, in fact, well founded, for there were more such claims than there was gold with which to redeem them.

To prevent a run, the nation's big banks stopped paying out gold in exchange for the promises to pay gold. These promises were their own notes, which constituted the paper money of the day. By common agreement, they "suspended payments" on December 30. A few days later, the Treasury too stopped exchanging gold for paper.[8]

And a few days after that, on January 7, 1862, a New York congressman, Elbridge Gerry Spaulding, stood before the House to urge passage of a bill to strike off dollars on the Treasury's printing presses. It was only by this measure, he warned, that the government could pay its bills; without it, the Treasury would be broke within 30 days. Spaulding almost apologized for the fact that his committee, the Committee on Ways and Means, had seen fit to report such a radical bill to the House. It was "a measure of *necessity* and not one of *choice*."[9]

The North was rich enough in capital: factories, farms, ships, railroads and the other means of production. Owners of taxable property admitted to the sundry taxing authorities that their holdings were worth $16 billion; heaven only knew how much more they were really worth.[10] What the loyal states lacked was money. It was a motley and ill-assorted collection of scrip, notes and coins that passed from hand to hand in the absence of the now-cowering gold and silver. In antebellum times, there was no national currency. The main source of folding money were the notes of some 1,600 state-chartered banks.[11] Gold alone being legal tender, the notes promised payment, on demand, in gold coin. Some banks' promises were better grounded than others, of course. To distinguish good money from bad was itself a vocation— some made a business out of uncovering insolvent institutions and counterfeit notes and of unmasking the pretenders. The lay depositor was typically at sea. A uniform national currency, long sought in America but never realized, would unquestionably serve a need. Would it be so bad if the government printed a dollar, with nothing behind it but good intentions, and stamped it "legal tender"?

Yes, came the high-volume answer from Congress and Wall Street. It would be unconstitutional, inflationary and dastardly, besides. It was what the Confederacy was already doing, what desperate and high-handed governments had always done. "Necessity!" sneered Representative Roscoe Conkling, Republican of New York. "[T]hat market price of principle at which every virtue has been sold for six thousand years. From the apothecary selling poison, to the lord chancellor selling justice, the plea has always been, 'My poverty, but not my will, consents.'"[12]

Opponents entered into evidence a few of the many examples of worthless government scrip in history: the unmourned Continentals of America's Revolutionary times, the French *assignats*, the paper-money experiments of colonial Rhode Island and Massachusetts, the contemporary Austrian currency. The trick never worked.[13]

"All the gentlemen who have spoken on this subject, and pretty much all who have written on this subject, except some wild speculators in currency," said Reed's friend and benefactor Senator Fessenden of Maine, "have declared that, as a policy, it would be ruinous to any people; and it has been defended . . . simply and solely upon the ground that it is to be a single measure, standing by itself and not to be repeated."[14]

Did the Constitution allow it, even in the cause of national self-preservation? Spaulding insisted it did. Granted, the power to stamp a piece of paper with the legend "legal tender" was nowhere vouchsafed to Congress. But to execute such powers as the Constitution did explicitly grant, Congress might "make all laws necessary and proper." It could, furthermore, "regulate" commerce—and therefore, by extension, regulate the medium of exchange in which commerce is transacted. J. A. Bingham of Ohio retorted that, by replacing gold with paper, Congress would regulate commerce into extinction.[15]

"It is not in the power of this Congress . . . to accomplish an impossibility by making something out of nothing," Representative Owen Lovejoy, Republican of Illinois, insisted. "The piece of paper you stamp as five dollars is not five dollars, and it never will be, unless it is convertible into a five-dollar gold piece; and to profess that it is, is simply a delusion and a fallacy."[16]

The fallacy, the Spaulding side rejoined, lay in imputing an excess of importance to the legalism of gold convertibility. Really, the proponents of the legal tender bill contended, it was the wealth of the country that would stand behind the Treasury's new money. Besides, the pending legislation authorized only a modest issuance: $150 million. In relation to the demand for money, or to the size of the country's business, it was trifling. Given the crying need for a uniform currency, one proponent made bold to predict, the appearance of greenbacks would likely drive down the price of gold, not the other way around.

The opposition presciently retorted that the government would never be content with one modest emission of paper money but would, instead, "require 60 days hence a similar issue, and then another, each one requiring a larger nominal amount to represent the same intrinsic value."[17] Spaulding's side could hardly deny the historical evidence; it was all against them. They therefore contended that the United States would prove to be the great exception to the historical rule, succeeding where other governments had failed.

Reed lived before the dawn of modern monetary economics. His contemporaries and he understood that the greater volume of currency in circulation, the higher the level of prices, other things being the same. But the plane on which they argued was typically not that of interest rates, money supply or the velocity or turnover of money. They rather contended over honor and principle. "The bill says to the world," protested Representative Valentine B. Horton, Republican of Ohio, about the Legal Tender Act, "that we are bankrupt, and we are not only weak, but we are not honest."[18] It would, said Conkling of New York, "proclaim throughout the country a saturnalia of fraud, a carnival for rogues." It would tempt every debtor to discharge his obligation in depreciated currency, for Conkling had no doubt that the government's scrip would depreciate against gold. "Think of savings' banks intrusted with enormous aggregates of the pittances of the poor, the hungry, and the homeless, the stranger, the needle-women, the widow and the orphan," he went on, "and we are arranging for a robbery of ten, if not of fifty per cent, of the entire amount, and that by a contrivance so new it has never to have been discovered under the administrations of Monroe Edwards* and James Buchanan."[19]

But it was finally expediency, or, as the sponsors of the Legal Tender Act saw the situation, necessity, that carried the day. "Surely," said Senator Charles Sumner of Massachusetts, "we must all be against paper money"—except, he quickly added, in this crisis.[20] So, on February 25,

---

* An early Texas smuggler and forger.

1862, a bill to allow Congress to print up to $150 million of legal tender notes was passed into law.[21] Duties on imports must still be paid in gold, and the Treasury would continue to pay out gold to meet the interest obligations on its bonds and notes. Otherwise, paper was the new gold. President Lincoln put the best face on this revolutionary departure from American practices. Congress, he said, "has satisfied, partially, at least, and for the time, the long-felt want of an uniform circulating medium, saving thereby to the people immense sums in discounts and exchanges."[22]

Whatever the intensity of this popular yearning, Congress worked overtime to satisfy it. The soaring cost of the war—as much as $3 million a day for the Union side, up from $1 million when the first Legal Tender Act was under consideration—elicited a second act, in 1862, and a third, in 1863. The first forbade the printing of legal tender notes in denominations of less than five dollars. Congress early relaxed that restriction. In 1863, $1 and $2 bills, as well as notes standing in for silver coins, entered circulation. Postage stamps too were drafted into service in lieu of metallic small change. At the time of Lee's surrender, $431 million of greenbacks were outstanding, in addition to $236 million in interest-bearing Treasury notes that also did duty as legal tender. Gold and silver still circulated on the West Coast—Californians shared none of Lincoln's perceived "long-felt want" for an alternative monetary asset—but only to the extent of $25 million. Before the shooting started, Americans had passed $245.3 million in gold coins and $42.2 million in silver coins from hand to hand.

In the event, the United States wrote no new chapter in the history of fiat money. Rather, the American experience was a page out of the well-thumbed, standard text. The government, having printed one batch of paper money, did, indeed, need more, and its notes did not, after all, appreciate against gold but went to a steep discount. The New York gold market became a daily straw poll of the Union's fortunes. Bad news pushed the gold price higher, good news, lower. A rising gold price (i.e., a depreciating dollar) elicited choruses of "Dixie" from the bulls in the gold room, acid chants of "John Brown" from the bears.[23]

The Lincoln administration had only so much patience with the market's daily verdict on the odds of survival of the United States. It ran out of patience late in the spring of 1864, a time when, for sheer bleakness, the financial news almost rivaled the military. A bill to outlaw the gold market came up for a vote in Congress in June. "Gold does not fluctuate in price . . . because they gamble in it," said Senator Collamer, a Vermont Republican, in opposition to the measure; "but they gamble in it because it fluctuates. . . . But the fluctuation is not in the gold; the fluctuation is in the currency, and it is a fluctuation utterly beyond the control of individuals."[24] Over Collamer's objections, the bill made its way to President Lincoln, who signed it into law on June 17. But the administration bought itself no peace. While the speculative gold market was silent, the substantial citizens who depended on that market, and who organized to demand a repeal of the ban, were anything but. Yielding, the gold-trading abolitionists prepared a second bill to reverse the first, and Lincoln signed this measure on July 2. "[T]he rampant and heartless and wicked spirit" that drove the gold bulls to bet against the currency of the United States again asserted itself. On July 11, an ounce of gold fetched $285, which, however, proved to be the highest price of the war. Since Hamilton's Coinage Act, the price had been fixed at about $20 an ounce.[25]

The rising gold price (the depreciating dollar against gold) was no anomaly. An index of 60 staple commodities more than doubled between 1860 and 1865.[26] The great debasement, though a certain net detriment to the nation, rewarded some groups even as it punished others. Creditors and wage-earners each were clear losers—the dollar depreciated faster than their money incomes rose. Business proprietors, on the other hand, tended to come out ahead—profits rose faster than the rate of inflation, or, at least, the relative paucity of bankruptcies during the war years might lead one so to infer.

In short, monetary events took their time-honored turn. War-induced emissions of paper money did what they always had done. To the nimble and crafty, wide vistas of profit-making enterprise were opened by the very changeableness of the monetary yardstick. "[L]arge numbers of our population," related David A. Wells, special commissioner of the revenue, after the war was over, "under the influence and example of high profits realized in trading during the period of monetary expansion, have abandoned employments directly productive of national wealth, and sought employments connected with commerce, trading or speculation. As a consequence we everywhere find large additions to the population of our commercial cities, an increase in the number and cost of the buildings devoted to banking, brokerage, insurance business and agencies of all kinds, the spirit of trading and speculation pervading the whole community, as distinguished from the spirit of production."[27]

All told, concludes the great historian of the greenback era, Wesley C. Mitchell, " 'business' was, in reality as well as in appearances, rendered more profitable by the greenbacks. There is therefore no error in saying that the business of the country enjoyed unwonted prosperity during the war."[28]

Opponents of the legal tender initiative were, however, as right as rain. Their every prediction was vindicated by the Union's experience during the war (and in spades by the hyperinflationary Confederate experience). The pro-greenback majority had not, in fact, denied they were voting for inflation and related monetary troubles. Their argument was, rather, that the alternative would mean much bigger trouble. Therefore, now that the war was over, did not Congress and the executive branch of government pant for the restoration of sound money?

There were fine words all around. President Andrew Johnson, citing the "increasing evils of an irredeemable currency," called for a prompt return to gold convertibility. The Treasury Secretary, Hugh McCulloch, was not content with words. By September 30, 1866, he had redeemed $43 million worth of this paper—extraconstitutional, inflationary and thoroughly repugnant, in his opinion—leaving $390.2 million in circulation.[29] Indeed, if McCulloch had had his way, the outstanding supply of greenbacks would instantly have been zero. But less orthodox heads prevailed. Indeed, a wholly different idea began to elbow its way to the fore. Most of the nation's war debt, not quite $3 billion at its peak, in August 1865, was incurred after passage of the Legal Tender Act of 1862. America's creditors had lent cheap, inflated wartime dollars. Let them be repaid in kind, some began to urge.

Congress had an answer to this heterodox murmuring. A resolution dated December 5, 1865, passed with one dissenting vote, affirmed:

as the sense of this House, the public debt created during the late rebellion was contracted upon the faith and honor of the Nation; that it is sacred and inviolate and must and ought to be paid, principal and interest; that any attempt to repudiate or in any manner to impair or scale the said debt shall be universally discountenanced, and promptly rejected by Congress if proposed.[30]

A recession was already in progress. Lee's surrender had marked the end not only of the confederacy but also of the northern economy that had been erected to destroy it. Hard times rarely foster a strong popular demand for hard money, and the late 1860s were no exception. President Johnson now began to hedge. He insisted that, although he favored the timely resumption of gold convertibility, he saw no need to reduce the supply of greenbacks. The new pragmatism (or, from a different vantage point, heresy) was bipartisan. Democrats had damned the first Legal Tender Act as unconstitutional. Now they rose up as the enemies of "contraction." Republicans joined them in passing an act in February 1868 to rescind the authority of the Treasury Secretary to retire these now rather popular green pieces of paper.[31] In his annual message in December 1868, Johnson went so far as to lecture America's creditors on the risks of biting the hand that had fed them so well: "The lessons of the past admonish the lender that it is not well to be over anxious in exacting from the borrower rigid compliance with the letter of the bond." Still, the House and the Senate each rebuked the president for this broaching of the subject of "repudiation."[32]

The presidential election of 1868 afforded the American people a clear choice on the great monetary question. The Republican plank denounced "all forms of repudiation as a national crime," meaning gold dollars for the Treasury's creditors. The Democrats, in contrast, demanded "one currency for the Government and the people, the laborer and the office-holder, the pensioner and the soldier, the producer and the bondholder"—by which was implied greenbacks for the creditors. Coupon clippers, if voting their financial interest, would, therefore, mark their ballot for U. S. Grant. Debtors, if voting their financial interest, would vote for Horatio Seymour on the Democratic ticket. Grant won in an Electoral College landslide.

The money passage of Grant's inaugural address acknowledged the interests of the "debtor class." But superior to those interests was the public interest: "To protect the national honor every dollar of government indebtedness should be paid in gold, unless otherwise stipulated in the contract. Let it be understood that no repudiator of one farthing of our public debt will be trusted in public place, and it will go far toward strengthening a credit which ought to be the best in the world, and will ultimately enable us to replace the debt with bonds bearing less interest than we now pay."[33]

The legislative fruit of this soaring language was the act "to strengthen the public credit" dated March 18, 1869. It pledged the government to discharge its obligations in gold and to prepare "at the earliest practicable period" for the redemption of greenbacks in gold.[34]

However, it soon became evident that, in the forgoing phrase, "practicable" was a more significant word than "earliest." The Grant administration was prepared to pursue monetary virtue but only at a deliberate, reasonable pace. It would not rip the greenbacks out of the hands of the people but rather allow the natural growth in the American economy to render $356 million of irredeemable currency ever less consequential. Nine months after his ringing inauguration address, President Grant returned to the dollar in a somewhat less ringing annual message: "Immediate resumption [of gold convertibility], if practicable, would not be desirable. It would compel the debtor class to pay, beyond their contracts, the premium on gold at the date of their purchase, and would bring bankruptcy and ruin to thousands."[35]

Early in 1870, the Supreme Court had its say. The case in which it spoke involved a debt that had been contracted before the 1862 passage of the Legal Tender Act and that had fallen due some time thereafter. At issue was whether Congress had the constitutional authority to cheapen the dollar and to impose that debased currency on debtors and creditors when the two contracting parties had agreed to settle up in gold. The Court ruled 5–3 (it was one justice short of full strength) that it had no such power, not even when the Union itself was thought to be in jeopardy. The majority opinion made note of the desperate circumstances in which many a congressmen had put aside his hard-money scruples to support the greenback legislation for the sake of national survival. Yet, as the Court observed, "Not a few who then insisted upon its necessity, or acquiesced in that view, have since the return of peace and under the influence of the calmer time, reconsidered their conclusions, and now concur in those which we have just announced." The author of those words was none other than Chief Justice Salmon P. Chase. It was Chase who, as Secretary of the Treasury under Lincoln, had first brought greenbacks into the world.

But there the matter did not rest. When the Legal Tender Act met with new legal challenges late in 1870, the Court had a different complexion. Two new justices now saw the matter as Chase had originally, and they voted with a 5–4 majority to uphold the government's right to preserve itself and the Union in a time of peril by printing money and calling it legal tender. There remained the question of whether the government could crank up the printing presses in times of peace. Indeed, it could, the Court finally came to decide in 1884. With only one dissent, the justices held in *Juilliard v. Greenman* that the power to print money, and to require contracting parties to accept it, was an integral part of the apparatus of sovereignty. The states could make nothing but gold and silver legal tender: The Constitution so stated. But the Founders did not expressly deny Congress that power. Indeed, by allowing Congress to borrow and issue bills of credit they had inferentially bestowed it.

"From the decision of the court I see only evil likely to follow," the minority of one, Justice Stephen Field, wrote in dissent. "There have been times within the memory of us all when the legal tender notes of the United States were not exchangeable for more than one-half of their nominal value. The possibility of such depreciation will always attend paper money. This inborn infirmity no mere legislative declaration can cure. If Congress has the power to make the notes a legal tender and to pass as money or its equivalent, why should not a sufficient amount be issued to pay the bonds of the United States as they mature? Why pay interest on the millions of dollars of bonds now due when Congress can in one day make the money to pay the principal? And why should there be any restraint upon unlimited appropriations by the government for all imaginary schemes of public improvement, if the printing press can furnish the money that is needed for them?"

There was, however, no such finality to the political struggle. It went on and on. In 1873, Congress enacted a bill to retire the silver dollar. "The Crime of '73," its opponents eventually styled this act—that is, when they got around to discovering what it said. The House vote—110 to 13, in favor—tells how little controversy it kicked up at the time. There seemed to be nothing to argue about. The silver content of dollar coins was worth $1.03.[36] Better to hoard them, or melt them and sell the silver for a small profit, than to hand them over the counter to pay the grocer or tax man. Congress was, indeed, striking the silver dollar from the registry of American coinage, but it was not so much passing a political judgment as validating a market verdict.

However, the market was even then changing its mind. American miners had dug up 9.3 million ounces of silver in 1869. By 1876, they were were on their way to producing 30 million ounces. And as the supply climbed the demand plunged. Gold was fast becoming the preferred monetary metal of the rich nations of the West. In 1871, Germany announced it was closing its mint to silver coinage. In 1874, the nations of the so-called Latin Union—France, Belgium, Greece, Italy and Switzerland—followed suit.[37] A year or two later, the Scandanavian Union— Denmark, Norway and Sweden—the Netherlands and Russia opted for gold. In 1876, the metallic value of a silver dollar fell to 90 cents.

A 21st century student of monetary affairs may stare in wonder at the nature of the monetary debate in mid-1870s America. A business depression was in progress. From the south, west and parts of the east arose a demand for a cheaper and more abundant currency. Yet such appeals were met with, and finally subdued by, a countervailing demand for a constant, objective and honest standard of value. Mark Twain facetiously blamed the Civil War on the romantic novels of Sir Walter Scott: The southerners had seemed to take them seriously, he complained. No less did a sense of fidelity to principle inform the not-so-dry discussion over the nature of the dollar.

And what was that principle? To render monetary justice. For the one side, justice entailed discharging the national debt in dollars either coined from, or exchangeable into, gold. For the other, it meant adapting the monetary standard to the needs of the American people. The creditors of Lincoln's Treasury had lent wartime "dollars"—i.e., mere pieces of paper, champions of the inflation movement observed.

Let the bondholders therefore receive pieces of paper in return. Or, alternatively, dollar bills exchangeable into silver. Here, said partisans of monetary relief, was the good old dollar of yore, the "dollar of the daddies."

Of course, high honor was not the only consideration on the minds of the monetary contestants of the 1870s. Silver producers bemoaned the sinking price of their favorite metal. Encumbered farmers yearned for inflation to lighten the burden of their debts (and to lift up the prices of their crops). Then too it was not the best press for a new American gold standard that Britain was the world's financial leader. For a certain portion of the American electorate the golden pound was reason enough to embrace silver.

These objections, however, fell before the Resumption Act of 1875, which fixed a date certain for America's return to the gold standard; the date was January 1, 1879 (actually it was January 2; the lawmakers had forgotten that New Year's Day was a bank holiday). A compromise measure, the Resumption Act dismayed the true-blue gold partisans as it did the silverites and greenbackers. The former regretted that there were four more years to wait until deliverance from paper money; the latter regretted that the interval wasn't a hundred years. A sign of things to come was that the opponents of the restoration of the gold dollar viewed the Resumption Act not as a final defeat but a reversible error. Why, the 1873 Coinage Act was the work of a creditors' conspiracy to bleed the American debtor, George M. Weston, a one-time Maine newspaper editor, charged in a letter published in the Boston *Globe* in March 1876. It was, he contended, "the most flagrant and audacious of the manifestations of the control exercised by foreign and domestic bankers over national legislation in these recent and evil days."[38] Bills to restore silver to the American monetary menu began to appear in 1876, including one by none other than "Pig Iron" Kelley, who, as floor manager of the Coinage Act only three years earlier, had been instrumental in demonetizing silver.[39]

THE GREENBACK PARTY of Maine was on Kelley's wavelength. Why not print the money with which to redeem the public debt? the delegates had demanded at the start of the 1878 electoral season. Reed delivered a rebuttal in the speech he made on August 1 to accept the Republican nomination.

"This is to be a campaign of education, of instruction to all of us," the incumbent told the friendly Republican faces before him, "to those who speak and write as well as to those who read and hear. Ever since the war thoughtful men have been watching the course which the American people have taken with the currency called into being by the exigencies of that war. That course has been fluctuating, uncertain, a source of constant apprehension and alarm to all who are capable of looking beyond temporary interests."

But there was, Reed went on, "one steady ray of sunlight," namely, the determination of the American people to do the right thing, "no matter what it might cost." Americans had an instinctive belief in sound money: "We have a sound and righteous faith, but we have not so studied it ourselves as to be able always to give a reason for the faith that is in us.

"Why was it," he continued, "that after the war we declared with one heart and voice that one of the first duties of the Government was to return to specie [i.e., gold] payments? There was no difference of opinion then. Republicans and Democrats vied with each other and with Solon Chase in denouncing a 66-cent currency and demanding 100 honest cents to the dollar. [Applause.] Why? Had we studied the currency question? Did we know any more about it then than now? Not at all. We did it because our instincts were honest and because this was demanded by the sound principles of our forefathers, in which we had been born and nurtured and educated."

Jefferson and Hamilton, Democrats and Federalists, had had their differences, of course, Reed continued, but hard-won experience had united them on money. "They had seen emerge dishonored from the clouds of repudiated paper the confederation that fought the Revolution, and every State in it. They had seen wave after wave of paper money roll over the land at the beck of speculation, until ruin engulfed the country. In one word, they hated irredeemable paper money because they had suffered by it. Hence it was that they determined to build the foundation of finance in this country on a solid basis."

So the United States had hewed to the straight and narrow for 50 years after the Founders went to their graves. "Never till this terrible war did we violate the principles of these honored men, and then only because we thought the safety of the nation demanded it. My friends, whether this Legal Tender Act was an act of indelible disgrace, depends upon the history of the near future. The possibilities make all thoughtful men tremble. No nation on the face of the earth, Asiatic, European or American, ever issued such a paper currency and did not finally repudiate it. Nevertheless, I believe as surely as I stand here, that to the American people is reserved the proud distinction of redeeming its paper to the uttermost farthing, and the loftiest and most historic day in the life-time of any Secretary of the Treasury will be the day when that happens."

Not forgetting that he was running for office, Reed closed with a wave of the bloody shirt. It was no accident, he said, that the South demanded inflation. It was as united in its love of the greenbacks as it was in its hatred of the North. It was poor before the war and much poorer afterward. Its demands on the Treasury—millions of dollars for war claims, Mississippi levees, railroads, et cetera—were insatiable. "Now," Reed wound up, "just so long as we have an honest dollar, so long as we are on the solid basis of value, so long they know it is in vain for them to demand, and we are safe. If we are ever tempted into inflation, into printing dollars instead of coining them, by the aid of Northern speculators, the hour of the South will have come. They know this."[40]

REED HAD A fight on his hands. Ben Butler too put aside his Potter Committee duties to campaign in the First District of Maine. But the candidate with whom Butler aligned himself was not his fellow Potter committeeman but Reed's Greenback opponent, E. H. Gove. Butler invited the crowds to consider the virtues of "a dollar fixed by law, dependent on nothing, redeemable in nothing, which should be legal tender for all debts, bearing the stamp of the wealthiest nation of the earth."[41] Disciples of Solon Chase heckled Reed about the miseries of deflation. What about "them steers" they demanded, referring to Chase's famous oxen whose quoted value had curiously declined, not increased, as the animals grew taller and stronger. Reed replied with the unassailable observation that "You won't have any more potatoes if you call them 4,000 pecks than if you call them 1,000 bushels."[42] This was, in fact, the least of the wit of the outsize incumbent, and the hecklers learned to bite their tongues. Not so, however, the Democratic press, which mocked the Republican's weight and speaking voice ("the sharp, nerve-splitting notes from an unmusical Reed")[43] and heaped scorn on his crowd-pleasing recourse to the bloody shirt.

Reed brought in some of his own out-of-district campaign muscle. James A. Garfield, the nationally prominent Ohio congressman, and Galusha A. Grow, the Republican Speaker of the House in the opening years of the Civil War, stumped Portland on his behalf. Reed was fortunate not only in his friends but also in his divided opposition. The Democrat Samuel J. Anderson, the 54-year-old president of the Portland & Ogdensburg Railroad (and sometime July 4 orator), was either "General" or "Copperhead," according to party affiliation. The candidate was, indeed, a major general in the state militia, but he had sat out the Civil War.[44] On the hustings, Anderson spoke rapidly and urgently, too fast for longhand reporters to quote him verbatim. Unmistakably, however, he damned the Republicans for the swarm of federal officeholders they had created for the cynical purpose of perpetuating themselves in power, and for the hard times they had inflicted on the country. "Fifty years ago this year," Anderson reminded the Democrats who had nominated him to run against Reed, "the old Cumberland district was the first district in New England to elect a Democrat to Congress, and they called her the Star in the East—one Democratic district in New England, and following this came the election of Andrew Jackson as President." The correspondent of the *Eastern Argus* judged that the "words fell like living water from the lips of the eloquent orator."

This was the judgment of the paper's not so objective news columns. The editorial page endorsed Anderson and warned the Greenbackers that they would never elect their man; by throwing away their votes on a certain loser, they would certainly elect Reed. The total vote in the previous congressional race had been 31,581. Gove could expect to draw, at most, between 5,000 and 6,000. Subtract, say, 5,500 from that 31,581 and roughly 26,000 votes would remain. Anderson and

Reed could be expected to split them, the *Argus* speculated: "Let Democratic Greenbackers think of this carefully. Their votes cannot elect Mr. Gove. They will elect Gen. Anderson if thrown for him. They will elect Mr. Reed if thrown for Mr. Gove. And the election of Mr. Reed would be as clear a victory for the old rotten Republican party as Blaine & Co. ever achieved."

Not for the last time in American politics did the zealous adherents to a third-party cause refuse to listen to reason. The incumbent polled 13,483 votes to Anderson's 9,333 and Gove's 6,348. It was a victory sweet enough on its own terms, better still in relative ones. Greenback candidates knocked off Republicans in the state's Fourth and Fifth congressional districts. Nationally, the Greenback party picked up six seats, including the two in Maine, while the Democrats held on to slim majorities in both the House and Senate. As for the Maine gubernatorial race, the popular vote produced no winner, so the choice fell to the Republican Senate. The choice was distasteful: the Democrat Alonzo Garcelon, or his Greenback rival, named Joseph L. Smith. Holding their noses, the Republicans elected Garcelon.

On election night Reed stood triumphant before his Republican supporters and breathed a sigh of relief over the happy outcome. "The prevalence of the heresies we have fought would do this country greater injury than either war or pestilence," said the voice that grated so on the friends of Sam Anderson.[45]

Chapter 9

Maine's Disgrace

As GARFIELD STUMPED for Reed, so Reed stumped for Garfield. It was enjoyable work, Reed reported of his tour of Ohio's 19th congressional district, "all the pleasures of campaigning and none of the anxieties."[1] Garfield was a winner in that election, as, indeed, he was a winner in most everything he did: Williams College alumnus, Ohio state senator, major general in the Union army, hero of the Battle of Big Sandy and wartime congressman, all before the age of 33.

Reed's anxieties were waiting for him upon his return home. His Portland law practice was sadly neglected—it had not, after all, looked after itself during his lengthy absences. Nor was his political position secure. Though he had won his election, the divided opposition deserved as much credit as did he himself. If the Democrat Anderson's 9,333 votes had been added to the Greenbacker Gove's 6,348 votes, Reed would have fallen short by 2,198. Fellow Republicans Eugene Hale from the Fifth District and Llewellyn Powers of the Fourth District did, in fact, come up short.[2] The people of Maine had a bone to pick with their government.

On January 2, 1879, the United States at last returned to the gold standard. Argue, threaten and cajole as they might, Solon Chase and the Greenback faithful could not prevent the dawning of Resumption Day.

No longer did the dollar derive its value from the promises of the government. The government, rather, was once more a party to a contract with the people. The Treasury would exchange gold for paper currency, and paper currency for gold, at a fixed and certain rate. Present an ounce of gold to the Treasury, and the Treasury would pay you $20.67. Alternatively, present that sum to the Treasury in bills and small change, and the Treasury would hand over an ounce of gold.* For the first time since 1861, legal tender was that thing that could be coined but not printed. Uncertainty is inherent in commercial and financial life. Resumption Day at least lifted the monetary doubts.

The nation was, in fact, launched on a mighty boom, though only the most faithful Republican could have expected it. Treasury Secretary Sherman had no way of knowing what pent-up demands for gold resumption might release. Not for 18 years had Americans had the right to convert their paper money into the real McCoy at a fixed, statutory rate. Now that they could, would they? Frederick D. Tappan, president of the Gallatin National Bank in New York, had been heard to boast that he would pay $50,000 to be the first in line on January 2. So positioned, he would present the clerk behind the bars with $29 million in U.S. notes, aka greenbacks, and thereby break the government and make off with its gold.[3] Taking no chances, the authorities laid in $110 million of gold coin at the sub-Treasury office in New York to satisfy the expected crush. All told, the federal gold hoard stood at $141.9 million, against which were outstanding $346.7 million in paper dollars. Let Tappan come and bring his friends; Sherman was ready for them.

In New York it had been snowing since New Year's Day. But apart from the drifts and Hudson River ice, it felt a little like the Fourth of July. At 10 AM, a hard-money salute roared from guns at the Brooklyn Navy Yard across the snowy East River from Manhattan. "Flags were run up on the staffs surrounding nearly every bank, all the government buildings and the commercial buildings," according to the Hartford *Courant*. "The top of the Custom House was covered with flags. The Gold Room was deserted, and on the great blackboard was chalked in large letters, 'Par.'"[4]

---

* One could make the exchange at the Treasury office on Wall Street in amounts of $50 or more.

*   *   *

THE PEOPLE STAYED away in droves. Two hours into the business day, the government's $110 million was smaller by only $2,500. A man presented $5,000 worth of gold at the counter in exchange for the same value in paper. In fun, he tossed the bag of coins up in the air and let it fall to the floor. It burst, "and the coin rolled all about the room to the great amusement of the bystanders. He dropped upon his knees to gather his treasure, and after 15 minutes spent in gathering and counting it, he went again to the counter, and, asking for 'something that would not roll,' exchanged his gold for legal tenders." At the end of the day, the office had paid out $130,000 in coin while taking in $100,000: "[W]here everybody could get gold, next to nobody wanted it."[5]

Sherman breathed a sigh of relief. But wasn't it odd, he mused in victory, that so many Americans had opposed resumption? Irredeemable paper currency was a wartime expedient. To close out that desperate chapter in the nation's monetary history—to resume gold payments— Sherman said, "is to recover from illness, to escape danger, to stand sound and healthy in the financial world, with our currency based on the intrinsic value of solid coin."[6]

Resumption, however, silenced neither party to the generation's great debate. Gold-standard partisans warned that inflationists were still scratching at the door; the greenbackers fairly vowed to knock the door down. In a Resumption Day address to the Honest Money League of Chicago, Garfield asked if the gold standard would stick. "Believing that in the long run the matured and deliberate judgment of this nation is honest and intelligent," he replied, "I answer yes, it will be maintained. . . . But we must not assume all danger is past."[7]

Garfield might have been thinking of Maine. In Augusta, Democrats and Greenbackers were forging a new year's alliance against gold and the Republican party. The state was temporarily without a governor, the people having entrusted no candidate with a majority of the votes in the September 1878 election. Under the constitution, popular indecision redirected the choice to the Senate, then Republican-controlled. Alonzo Garcelon, of Lewiston, a 66-year-old surgeon and Republican-turned-Democrat, was the senators' choice. Better Garcelon, the majority reasoned, than the Greenback alternative, Joseph L. Smith, a rich Old Town lumberman.

Little did the senators anticipate how close the Pine Tree State would come to civil war under the Garcelon stewardship or how nearly the conduct of the state's high officials would come to resemble that of the ruling cliques of South Carolina, Florida and Louisiana in 1876. There were clues to the coming troubles in the 1879 convention of the Maine Greenbackers, who met in Portland on June 3.[8] Rain forced the cancellation of a planned procession from the railway station to city hall led by Solon Chase riding in a chariot behind his famous steers. But the party found other ways to engage and amuse the faithful. Charles A. White, chairman of the state committee, welcomed the delegates with a speech that featured a personal attack on the Secretary of the Treasury. "John Sherman the Jew," White called the author of resumption, charging that Sherman wouldn't rest until he had put America into bankruptcy. Inasmuch as White, in his workaday capacity, was the treasurer of Maine, the attack seemed a shocking breach of professional courtesy.[9]

The delegates were mad at the Republican administration in Washington and at the Republican establishment in Portland and Augusta. They were mad at the gold standard, at the demonetization of silver and at the institution of the national banks. But no small part of their anger was inward. They were suspicious about the platform—some urged that the money planks be made a little less conspicuous, the better to appeal to wavering Democrats. Hard-line Greenbackers were livid: "For the first time in history . . ." a witness related, "Solon Chase violated one of the commandments." Then, just as the convention seemed to slide into chaos, "Chandler's band struck up the 'Angel of Peace,' and a comparative quiet was restored"[10] For governor, the delegates again put forward Joseph Smith.

The Republicans, convened at Bangor, made Daniel F. Davis, a 30-something lawyer and state legislator, their standard-bearer. And just who was this would-be chief magistrate? An opposition newspaper ventured an answer in the form of a limerick:

> Now here's to Daniel F. Davis,
> The Hamlin-Blaine rara avis
> Only Hamlin and Blaine

In the whole State of Maine
Knew there was a Daniel F. Davis.[11]

For their part, the Democrats renominated Garcelon, though, according to one Maine historian, "There was a general understanding that Smith was the real anti-Republican candidate, and that the nomination of Garcelon was little more than a form. In many districts the Greenbackers and Democrats coalesced and a 'Fusion' ticket was nominated."[12]

Republicans, properly worried by the Fusionist threat, campaigned hard, as did the united Greenbackers and Democrats. Once more, no gubernatorial candidate took away a majority of the votes; again, therefore, the decision fell to the Senate. And because the Republicans appeared to have carried the legislature, it seemed as if the statehouse too were theirs. Daniel Davis was as good as elected.

However, in no way were the politics of the Pine Tree State to be confused with the Era of Good Feelings. In this most partisan of times, Maine was among the most partisan of states. Garcelon and his allies had no intention of moving aside for the party that, in their eyes, had stolen the 1876 presidential election. As the Republicans had connived their way to victory with Hayes, so might the Fusionists with Smith. "[Y]ou cheated us in the count for President," a Republican reported being informed by one of the enemy camp, "but we have the returning board here in Maine."[13]

Strict procedures for the lawful counting of the votes were enumerated in the state constitution. The ballots, properly tallied and checked, signed and sealed, had to be shipped to Augusta, there to come under the scrutiny of the governor and his executive council. Winners would thereupon take their respective seats.[14]

So Garcelon and his council set to work. But rather than counting the votes first and determining the results second, the conspirators worked backward. It was the desired outcome first, the counting second. In went the Fusionist votes, out came the Republican ones. For example, they adopted the rule that "where the middle initial letter of the name of a candidate was not properly stated or was omitted, the votes would not be counted, and that the defect was 'fatal'; they also declined to receive testimony when offered by Republicans to cure any defect in this particular occurring in the names of senators and representatives."[15] When there were no defects, it was necessary to invent them. In the case of George H. Wakefield, Republican candidate for the Senate in the town of Berwick, for instance, they forged ballots such that an "H" became an "A." So as Wakefield's votes were counted out, those of his Fusionist opponent, Ira S. Libby, were counted in.[16]

For the Republicans, then, an apparent victory at the polls turned into an emphatic defeat at the Returning Board. Garcelon-attested results were, in the House: Fusionists 78 (with 12 vacancies), Republicans 61; and in the Senate: Fusionists 20, Republicans 11.[17]

From Washington, Reed looked on these proceedings with embarrassment and outrage. Unaccountably, the Fusionists of his own state had adopted the larcenous political mores of the postwar South. It was worse, even, than that. "It is a performance which has no equal in the history of the Republic," he complained to a correspondent from the Chicago *Tribune*. "It was no case of close majorities or contested precincts. There was no charge that ballot boxes had been stuffed, tissue ballots used or names forged. It was a clear, open, unblushing steal."[18]

Peace on earth and goodwill toward men was the missing element in the 1879 Maine Christmas season. The clergy denounced Garcelon from the pulpit, or, in the case of the Reverend H. W. Tilden, a Baptist in Augusta, from the lectern. "Mob violence would settle nothing whatever, but open, systematic war would if it must be had," Tilden told his flock at a Saturday evening lecture in late December, according to a paraphrased report of his remarks. Senator Hannibal Hamlin was quoted as telling a Boston newspaperman that if Garcelon et al. did "usurp the laws of the State, I favor going to the State House and take the revolutionists by the nape of the neck and pitch them into the stream, and I will be one to go and assist."[19]

Garcelon admitted to no bad faith, let alone theft, but insisted that he was only following the letter of the law—as, he pointed out, the Senate Republicans had done in the Hayes-Tilden presidential election by tossing out the vote of the town of Van Buren on a piddling technicality. To discourage rash action by the Blaines and Hamlins, Garcelon ordered 120 rifles and 20,000 rounds of ball cartridges removed from the Bangor arsenal and delivered to him at the capital.[20] These weapons he put into the hands of 100 special deputies, including one ex-convict (there were others) whom the governor had personally pardoned.[21]

Under the constitution, it fell to the state Supreme Court to review the legality of disputed returns, and to the Court Garcelon now had to turn. He did so reluctantly, submitting a list of questions so narrowly drawn as to discourage broad consideration of the issue. But the justices, as the historians John Abbott and Edward Elwell relate, "did not confine themselves to these, but reviewed the whole matter, and explicitly condemned at every point the action of the Governor and Council, declaring that the returns made by municipal officers, in the hurry, bustle and confusion of an election, are not to be written with scrupulous nicety, and are not to be strangled by idle technicalities. They were unanimous in their decision, one of the justices being a Democrat." Garcelon ignored them.[22]

There was an authority even loftier in Maine at the time than the Supreme Court, and he was the hero of Little Round Top. General Joshua L. Chamberlain, congressional Medal of Honor recipient, four-term governor and, currently, president of Bowdoin College, was remobilized by Garcelon as commander of the state militia and ordered to Augusta to protect public property and keep the peace until a new governor could be lawfully installed.

And who might that governor be? Rival Republican and Fusionist legislatures each appealed to Chamberlain to recognize its favorite son, appeals that Chamberlain impartially refused; it was the Court's decision, he said. On January 16, the Court did rule, again, once more holding for the Republicans. The next day, the Republican Senate, duly installed, elected Davis the governor, and Chamberlain, declaring victory (or, at least, the restoration of civil order), withdrew.

The Fusionists, however, did not withdraw. The state seal was in their possession—Garcelon's deputy-secretary had made off with it—and there were reports of Fusionist militias forming all over the state. On the evening of January 23, 1880, the mayor of Augusta advised Governor Davis that his police could not defend the state house "against such force as the public enemies seem to be willing and able to bear against it." The Capitol Guards of the Maine militia were duly mobilized. Reinforcing the capital, next day, were, among others, the Androscoggin Light Infantry, its Gatling gun in tow. Outgunned if not shamed, the Fusionist legislature on January 28 voted to adjourn till August 1—in effect, for all time. By January 30, the last of the troops was gone. "Late in the afternoon of the 31st," records Louis Clinton Hatch, another historian of this not-so-funny opera bouffe, "P.A. Sawyer, the Fusionists' Secretary of State, appeared at the secretary's office and surrendered under protest the state seal, the election returns, the Council record and the reports on election returns for 1879."[23] The crisis was over.

PRESIDENT HAYES CALLED the new Congress into special session in mid-March 1879 to take up the unfinished business of its predecessor. This was the annual army appropriations bill for the fiscal year already in progress. That Congress should talk this annual measure to death and, finally, pass no bill that a Republican president could bring himself to sign had become a post-Reconstruction Washington ritual. The source of friction was not the appropriation itself but the amendments that a Democratic-controlled House affixed to it. The army belonged in its barracks or on the frontier, the Democrats insisted, not policing the polling places, as it had been doing since the end of the war. The Democrats objected most pointedly to the concentration of troops in polling places below the Mason-Dixon Line. So, upon Hayes's summons, the brand new 46th Congress took up where the 45th left off.*

William M. Lowe, 36, a freshman congressman from Alabama, had risen through the ranks in the Confederate army from private to lieutenant colonel. He was a greenbacker, and, scarcely a month into his first congressional session, he had lost all patience with the two established parties: "[T]he partisanship of the one side finds its sanction in the partisanship of the other," he made bold to inform the House.

---

* There were, in fact, two issues. First, the merits of the case: Should the army be prohibited from performing Election Day duties that, critics charged, served unlawfully to perpetuate Republican control of the federal government? And, second, a point of order: Should such a prohibition, if it were desirable, be enacted as an amendment to the appropriations bill or considered as a separate measure?

"No member of this body is more opposed than I am in theory and practice to the use of the Army at elections," Lowe went on. "It cannot be defended in this country upon either policy or principle. We prefer the tumults of a free people to the 'order' which results from military domination. But I do not understand that question to be the real issue before the committee [i.e., the committee of the whole, or the entire House]. It is not a question whether the objectionable legislation, which permits the political use of the Army, should be repealed, but whether the repeal shall be put as a rider upon an appropriation bill, or be passed as a distinct and independent measure."

For his part, said Lowe, he deplored the practice of government-by-rider, though he had no doubt that the rider would pass. "I know the power of the caucus," he said. "I appreciate the force of party discipline. But I would invoke, if possible, on our part, a more national and patriotic disposition." He would, but not many of his new colleagues were apparently so inclined. He marveled that "In the wide range of this discussion every . . . old grudge of the sections, and every new grievance of the races, have been flung into the muddy currents of this debate. I am sure the better sense of the country is not satisfied with it, with the evidence it affords of the character and capacity of our leadership. The Army is on a distant frontier. Peace prevails throughout the country. The war is over everywhere except in Congress. [Laughter and applause.]"[24]

Only weeks after Lowe had raised this knowing laughter from the floor, Representative James R. Chalmers, a Mississippi Democrat and former Confederate cavalry commander under General Nathan Bedford Forrest, occupied 90 minutes of the House's time with a defense of his personal conduct at the Battle of Fort Pillow, at which hundreds of African-American defenders were killed, many allegedly after they had surrendered. At length, a member protested that Chalmers was going to preempt the regular order of business, namely a debate on silver legislation. "Oh," Reed piped up, raising more knowing laughter, "the silver bill can wait."[25]

Alexander H. Stephens, onetime vice president of the Confederate States of America, was, like Lowe, in favor of letting bygones be bygones. But, unlike Lowe, Stephens favored the amendment to the appropriations bill that would turn back the clock to 1860 so far as the policing of elections was concerned. Let local civil authorities watch the polls, as they had always done. Let the army ward off Indians and the navy protect American shipping, said the Georgia Democrat. Let members of Congress be elected as they used to be. "[A]nd if any man has been deprived of his right to a seat here, then let this high constitutional court, the House of Representatives, decide that question, and not submit it to the decision of bayonets instead of ballots."[26]

These remarks Reed now rose to answer. In debate, the man from Maine kept his hands by his sides, like an Irish river dancer. He spoke in what was invariably described as a "twang." Democrats found the pitch of Reed's voice to be high and grating, the more so as it carried comfortably throughout the chamber with arguments that amused even when they failed to persuade. Reed spoke fluently, as so many of his colleagues did, in complete sentences and fully formed paragraphs. He was no doubt a favorite of the reporters and transcription clerks who compiled the Congressional Record. He was said never to touch up his remarks for publication nor to decorate the text with such self-promoting parenthetical stage directions as "Laughter" or "Applause." When the text so indicated, it was because he had genuinely succeeded in rousing the House.

Reed said it was not his purpose to take up the merits of the question but rather to address the point of order. Here was an advance look at the budding parliamentarian. The youth who had memorized long passages of Butler's *Analogy of Religion*, the regulations-savvy former naval officer, the accomplished lawyer and prosecutor, the Maine legislator—Reed had the mind and experience to make of the House rules, and the parliamentary law that underlay them, a kind of musical instrument. Listening to him on the floor in the first session of the 46th Congress, one could hear the strains of a rising virtuoso.

The point of order, in Reed's estimation, was no less important than the main question. Indeed, it trumped it. Because the proposed amendment was out of order, there should be no discussion about its merits. Unless the business of the House were conducted in an orderly fashion, no real business would ever be completed. In a sense, the form of the House was also the substance of the House, and of the present debate. The form had long since become misshapen.

Reed and Lowe, Republican and Greenbacker, saw eye to eye on the army appropriation bill. It was no place to hang an amendment concerning the use of federal resources—military or naval or, for that matter, civilian—on Election Day. Whereas Lowe dwelled mainly on the principle of the thing, Reed emphasized the parliamentary question. Legislation-by-amendment aggrandized an already overbearing and overworked Committee on Appropriations. It puffed up a similarly over-muscled House-Senate conference committee.

House Rule 120, Reed reminded his colleagues, stipulated that such amendments as those now proposed fit two criteria. They must be germane to the bill and serve to reduce federal spending. Now then, Reed demanded, how would a rider to ban armed federal agents at polling places be in any conceivable sense relevant to a bill to pay the troops? And how, exactly, would it save money? It was neither germane nor economical. The House should therefore vote it down—which, however, the House did not.[27]

WITHOUT THE RULES of parliamentary procedure, as Reed often said, the House would achieve nothing. As it was, it seemed to achieve very little, the rules being often bent to the cause of inaction. To opponents of federal intervention, this was just as it should be. "Nearly all the machinery of Congress," asserted William Graham Sumner, the laissez-faire exponent from Yale, "is an elaborate mechanism for preventing anything from being done, and although it stops many measures which a great many of us might think it very advisable to pass, we cheerfully do without them lest some of the others should get through likewise. The only fault with the mechanism is that it is not perfect enough."[28]

Reed held no such view; Congress should express the will of the majority, he held. Especially did he uphold that doctrine when the Republican party was in the majority. When, however, as in the 46th Congress, there was a Democrat in the Speaker's chair, Reed happily threw his considerable weight in the cause of obstruction.

A time-honored way to hobble the House was not to attend its proceedings. Let a critical number of members absent themselves and there would be no quorum, therefore no business. Absenteeism, however, was only as effective as the Speaker allowed it to be. At his command, the sergeant-at-arms could track down the truants, take them into custody and lead them back to the House chamber, there to face the smirking judgment of their colleagues. Reed was one of 21 such miscreants who stood awaiting justice at the bar of the House on May 23, 1879. To the first defendant, Alfred Scales, a Republican from North Carolina, was put the customary question, "What excuse have you to offer?"

"I have only this excuse, Mr. Speaker, I was hungry and I went to get my dinner, and did not expect to get caught. [Laughter.]"

From the chair: "What is the pleasure of the House in reference to the excuse submitted by the gentleman from North Carolina?"

From the floor: "I move that he be discharged from further custody without payment of costs." Now Benjamin Wilson, Democrat of West Virginia, seeming to dread the prospect of 20 more such exchanges, moved that all the absentees be discharged at once.

"Oh, no!" came cries from the floor.

"I insist on my motion," said Wilson.

"The amendment is not in order," the Speaker pro tempore replied. "The rule requires that each excuse shall be given separately and the action of the House had thereon."

Here a man born under a Democratic star, William Andrew Jackson Sparks, of Illinois, interjected, "Ought not all members be seated except for the criminals?"

Reed piped up, "I ask that the gentlemen's words be taken down," meaning struck from the Record. Reed, who raised a laugh, was chided from the chair, "No member under arrest can address the Chair except to present his excuse when his name is called."

Now the same Wilson changed tack, no longer seeking to speed things up but rather to slow them down. "I rise to a parliamentary point," he said. "Are these gentlemen [i.e., the "prisoners" of the sergeant-at-arms] allowed to vote?"

"They are not while in custody," the Speaker pro tempore answered.

"I insist," returned Wilson, "that they have the constitutional right to vote, which right cannot be taken away from them."

That not everyone was amused by this banter was evident from another motion to discharge all the absentees at once. But that motion was voted down, 97–39. Someone moved to adjourn, but neither did that motion pass. So the Speaker pro tempore quizzed the absentees, one by one. This one went to dinner, that one, to his doctor; one had no excuse, another pled advanced age.

Presently, the Speaker pro tempore addressed Reed: "What excuse have you to offer?"

"Mr. Speaker, about six o'clock I found myself suffering under temporary nervous prostration, and I left the House. On my way from the House I got into a discussion on finance with a stranger. That of course delayed me. But I got home, and when I returned to my surprise I found the door of the House barred against me, and it has been so for the last half hour, or perhaps hour. In any other assembly but this, I should expect an apology; but under the circumstances, I am willing to be released, and call it square at that."

Not many more minutes passed before Reed, now a free man, raised a mock objection to a motion that one of his former fellow absentees be discharged from custody with no fine.

"I think an example ought to be made," Reed interjected. "We have to do something in the way of punishment to put a stop to these absences." The House dissolved in laughter.[29]

REED, NEWLY PROMOTED to the House Judiciary Committee, had an immense store of legal and parliamentary knowledge as well as a fearsome wit. But he was no more expert in finance or economics than the average member of the 46th Congress. He had a lawyer's reverence for precedent and contract and a conservative's respect for tradition. He was as fatalistic toward the business cycle as he was toward the weather. Mankind, being averse to work, speculates when it can, to avoid work. It piles debt on debt, false value upon false value, till the jury-rigged structure comes crashing down. After a certain amount of penance comes the next upswing. The federal government had little to say on the subject, still less to do with it.

This was not the position of the Greenback party. Neither was it the view of all the Democrats, nor even of all the Republicans. Representative Kelley, as noted, had personally approved the legislation that wrote the silver dollar out of circulation and ushered in the gold standard. The "Crime of '73," the Greenbackers and silverites now called it, with Kelley in their indignant company. He got up on the floor in May to confess his error of six years earlier—really, he had no idea what mischief this bill perpetrated—and to demand redress. Let the Treasury continue the monetization of gold, he said. But let it equally resume the monetization of silver. He was now a bimetallist.

Kelley, an archprotectionist, had changed his mind before. Once upon a time, he was a proselytizing free-trader, but then he saw the light, just as he had come to understand the error of his ways about money. Gold was unsuitable as a single standard of value, he said. Then again, neither was silver sufficient unto itself. The country needed both. Never, Kelley said, was there an era so rich in invention and discovery as the one in which they were privileged to live, yet many lived in penury: "From New England, New York, Pennsylvania and the entire manufacturing sections of the East, working men, women and children, who, having secured their own homes or partially paid for them through building associations, were prosperous and contented, are fleeing to the remote West to endure the hardships and risks of frontier life and to make at best bad farmers. Remonstrate with them against the change as we may, they will say to us, 'there we can at least live; but here, without employment, or with partial employment at reduced wages, we cannot live.'"[30]

To Kelley, America—indeed, the world—looked like Rome before the fall or France before the Revolution. Society was on a knife's edge. Restore silver to its proper place in America's menu of coinage, he urged—restore it to the world's—and thereby avert calamity.[31]

Reed was the first to answer. It was not lost on him that, by proposing a dual or bimetallic standard, Kelley was actually proposing a single silver standard. The value of silver was falling. If the Treasury undertook to buy, and to mint, all the silver offered at a value above that falling price, as Kelley seemed to propose, Sherman's carefully husbanded collection of gold coins would vanish from the government's vaults. Anyone could present cheap silver to the Treasury in exchange for dear gold. Then they could use that gold to buy more cheap silver, and on and on. The process would end only when the government changed the rules or when the last U.S. gold coin was carried away.

Reed chose not to dwell on the technicalities: "My knowledge . . . is extremely limited."[32] Rather, he refuted the Greenbackers' claim that the demonetization of silver was a conspiracy against the common man. He quoted Kelley before his conversion arguing against his present, ardently held opinion. "Now," said Reed, "I do not find any fault with the gentleman from Pennsylvania because he has received information on these various subjects. I do find a little fault, however, that he should boast of the necessity of having received so much; that he should have stated to this House that he had changed his mind upon all economical and financial subjects and then made a merit of the change. That a man should learn is an advantage not only to him but to the world at large. But there is one thing that I do insist upon, that he shall not in any way talk about the conduct as 'fiendish' of gentlemen who have not been able to get his light. Why in the world cannot a man get credit for honesty when he is consistent as well as credit for honesty when he is inconsistent? [Laughter.] In short, does all human virtue consist in wobbling?"[33]

REED HIMSELF, MUCH later, would execute one of the most famous wobbles in the history of the House. The baseline from which the wobble was measured came in January 1880 during debate over a proposed amendment to the House rules. John Randolph Tucker, Democrat of Virginia, proposed to put a stop to the so-called vanishing quorum. His rule would allow the Speaker to count as "present" every member who was, in fact, in the chamber at the time of a vote, whether or not the member chose to vote. No more, if Tucker had his way, could the minority obstruct the work of the House by refusing to answer a roll call. A nephew of John Randolph of Roanoke and one of the ablest lawyers of his day, Tucker denied any partisan motives in proposing this radical reform. "[A]nd I mean no disrespect to anybody, and I feel no gentlemen on the other side will charge me with disrespect toward them," he told the House; "but it seems to me not in accordance with the progress of the age we live in that we should sit here in a condition of non-action under the self-delusion we are not present when we are present, and that there shall be a power on the part of gentlemen here upon any question of remaining silent and saying, 'You cannot prove I am here unless I choose to open my mouth.'"[34]

The Republicans, being out of power, cherished the vanishing quorum, just as the Democrats had done when they were in the minority. Garfield, speaking on behalf of his Republican charges, vowed to oppose the Tucker amendment "with all our might." Omar D. Conger, Republican of Michigan, condemned the proposed amendment as "wrong," "unconstitutional" and "violently partisan." "I take my position with that horse which is brought to the water, but cannot be made to drink," concurred John R. Hawley, Republican of Connecticut, alluding to James G. Blaine's procedural quip.[35]

Now Reed spoke up. "It is not the visible presence of members," he said, "but their judgments and their votes that the Constitution calls for." But, said Reed, he would prefer to address the subject from a different vantage point. The privilege of not answering the roll, therefore of contributing to the notorious vanishing quorum, was a privilege that "every minority has availed itself of since the foundation of our government. . . .

"It is," Reed continued, "a valuable privilege for the country that the minority shall have the right by this extraordinary mode of proceeding to call the attention of the country to measures which a party in a moment of madness and of party feeling is endeavoring to enforce upon the citizens of this land. And it works equally well with regard to all parties, for all parties have their times when they need to be checked, so that they may receive the opinions of the people who are their constituents and who are interested in the results of their legislation."[36] Tucker's idea went nowhere until Reed himself put it into effect over the howls of a Democrat opposition that quite clearly remembered this little speech of January 28, 1880.

THE FORMER ASSISTANT paymaster of the USS *Sybil* supported a modern navy and the funds with which to build and maintain it. The fleet that put down the rebellion was hardly recognizable in 1880. From a wartime peak of 700 vessels, it had dwindled to 48. How little naval affairs counted for in the Hayes administration was apparent in the president's choice of his Navy Secretary. Richard W. "Uncle Dick" Thompson, from the great seafaring state of Indiana, had never been aboard a ship before he was put in charge of the sea service of the United States. When he did set foot on his first man-of-war, he tapped his cane on the deck and expressed his astonishment: "Why, the durned thing's hollow."

Reed, whose constituents built and repaired naval vessels, not unnaturally favored a bigger and better fleet. The way forward, he argued on the floor, was not to continue patching up obsolete vessels (among the navy's 48 commissioned vessels were five relics from the age of sail). "People find fault because too many repairs have been made," he observed, "repairs in some cases amounting to 90 per cent of the original cost of the vessel, but that source of trouble has been largely in the House of Representatives and in the representatives of the people themselves; for singularly enough, it has been possible, if I may use a rather exaggerated expression, to build a ship around an old hawse-hole instead of being able to get an appropriation to build a new ship."[37]

And where would the Treasury find the money with which to rehabilitate the fleet, among the many other necessary functions of government? Why, it would levy taxes. And how might it collect those taxes? Here was a thornier matter. Honest and patriotic Americans would pay voluntarily. But a not insubstantial residue of opportunists would pay only if they thought somebody was checking up on them. To promote the belief that somebody was, indeed, checking, Reed supported a $75,000 appropriation for the commissioner of Internal Revenue to finance the honoraria of consultants whom Representative Charles E. Hooker, a Mississippi Democrat, characterized as "informers."

A graduate of the Harvard Law School, Hooker had fought the war in the First Regiment of Mississippi Light Artillery. In 1865 he was elected attorney general of Mississippi, but U.S. military authorities removed him from that post, as they did other former Confederate officers from theirs. Perhaps this experience reinforced an already developed distaste for intrusive government. In any case, Hooker delivered a heartfelt condemnation of federally financed tax spies. The Irish, especially, had no use for snitches, he added.

"I shall be unable to treat the House to such an uninterrupted flow of eloquence as has poured from the gentleman from Mississippi," Reed replied, before proceeding to best him. "I shall not be able to do it because I have not the power, and I shall not be able to do it because it is not necessary in a statement of facts." Stripped of its rhetorical plumage, Hooker's idea was to stop enforcing the revenue laws. "The gentleman from Mississippi proposes," Reed went on,

> under the guise of allusions to Irish history, to deprive the people of the money which belongs to them from the manufacture of whisky. Everybody knows that there is no such righteous tax in this world as the tax on whisky and tobacco. It is a tax which relieves the people every time it is imposed, and every dollar that escapes the Treasury has to be put upon the honest work and labor of the people.
>
> Now, for this Congress to cut down and limit the powers of the officers of the Government for the detection of crime is to limit the revenue, is to encourage illicit distilling, is to work an injury to the country. And if gentlemen want in this way to limit the powers of the officers of the Government, in the face of what they must know will be the effect of such a procedure, they have to cover it up with something like eloquence.[38]

More typically during the 46th Congress, Reed addressed the House on a question of parliamentary procedure. Here he directed a comment toward Speaker Randall concerning the still unresolved army appropriations bill. To the spectators in the galleries, it must have sounded like Greek: "I submit that the Committee of the Whole cannot give consent to a vote in the House and that it is not possible for the chairman of the committee or the gentleman in charge of the bill to give consent that an amendment which has been rejected by the Committee of the Whole shall come before the House for action." Randall's reply was as recondite as Reed's question: "The Chair has stated that the Committee of the Whole having failed to report the amendment, it could not come before the House unless it come in [a] manner as has not been done in this case, by unanimous consent in the Committee of the Whole or by allowance before the previous question was ordered upon the engrossment of the bill and the amendments. Then it would come in as an original proposition."[39]

Now and again, however, Reed raised a question of parliamentary law to political and rhetorical heights. Even in this, the first session of his second Congress, he had achieved that mastery of his emotions that so infuriated his adversaries when he later came to occupy the Speaker's chair. The more the Democrats raged at him, the more serene he seemed to become. His humor became sharper, his sarcasm more withering and his manner more imperturbable, the more he was provoked. On April 22, 1880, he rose to speak against some amendments that the Democrats were trying to attach to a routine appropriations bill.

Possibly, the Democrats were lulled by Reed's opening protestation. Straight-faced, he asked his Republican colleagues to sympathize with the unfortunates on the other side of the aisle. Put partisanship aside, the Republican partisan ironically counseled them. The Democrats had resolved to limit the time that they themselves had for discussion. You would too in their position, he continued. Suppose that you, like they, had forced a special session of Congress with the avowed purpose of cropping the powers of the executive branch, but that you had failed in that attempt and afterward gone "to the people and had by them been rebuked from all quarters of the compass . . . ?" Or, he asked them, "Suppose . . . you belonged to a party which was made out of odds and ends, a party that had no principle which ran through it, a party that could not command a score of votes upon any particular principle, would you expose them to discussion and to the utterance of their honest sentiments?" Or—or—he pressed, "[S]uppose you had men on your side who had contributed to that magnificent improvement of the African race which has been designated by radical malignity as the massacre and butchery at Fort Pillow; and suppose you knew that at any moment they were liable to get up and pronounce a discourse on the doctrine and duty of conciliation! How would you like to let loose such men as these?"[40]

But this was merely the preface to "the entirely non-partisan speech that I purpose to make here this afternoon," Reed ironically proceeded. Then, in earnest, he announced his intention to expose the iniquity of attempting to enact controversial legislation by attaching it to an appropriations bill. He was, he said, speaking in support of a principle, "the proposition that no House of Representatives or Senate has any right to put on appropriation bills legislation which is objectionable to another branch of the Government, for the purpose of coercing that branch of the Government to approve a bill which would not otherwise have its approval, by withholding appropriations for support of the Government unless such agreement was had."[41]

The particular amendment to which he objected would authorize the appointment of special deputy marshals to police federal elections. The marshals would be hired by the federal circuit courts and draw wages of $5 a day. The amendment directed the courts to strive for a fair representation of the various political parties in this projected Election Day corps of marshals, one from this party, another from that. Reed, however, would have none of it, least of all the supposed nonpartisanship of the design.

"[T]here is no such thing as a non-partisan republic," he insisted, "and the moment you get a non-partisan republic, that republic is tottering to its fall. Parties are created for some decent and respectable purpose; they grow out of the necessities and needs of mankind; and our system of Government is founded on the idea of ascertaining which party should be uppermost. That is the very basis upon which we go through elections. And by virtue of which we exist. It is not our object as my friend [Joseph R. Hawley] just now suggested to me, to produce twins. [Laughter.] . . . The best system is to have one party govern and the other party watch; and on general principles I think it would be better for us to govern and for the Democrats to watch. [Laughter.]"[42]

REED WAS ON hand when the Republicans convened in Chicago that June to nominate a presidential candidate. Among the star-studded collection of U.S. senators, power brokers and former Grant administration cabinet officials on display at the Exposition Building on Michigan Avenue the 6'2" congressman was rather lost in the shuffle.[43] Decently, Reed could support no other candidate than James G. Blaine, Maine's favorite son, but it's as certain as a surmise can be that he silently rooted for Garfield.

The Republican delegates were united in their platform but divided as to their candidate. They favored a protective tariff and restricted Chinese immigration. They supported the Constitution, the Union, the gold standard and public education. They excoriated the Democrats, mentioning and deploring by name the Garcelon fraud in Maine. Twenty years on, they still abominated slavery. Nor did they look kindly on "its twin barbarity, polygamy."

The incumbent, Hayes, was not in the running for a second term, but Grant was heavily promoted for a third. Nominating the onetime general of the Union armies, his name "the most illustrious borne by living man," Roscoe Conkling, senator from New York, brought down the house. "This convention," he declared in peroration, "is master of a supreme opportunity. It can name the next President. It can make sure of his election. It can make sure not only of his election, but of his certain and peaceful inauguration. More than all, it can break that power which dominates and mildews the South. It can overthrow an organization whose very existence is a standing protest against progress."[44]

The 15,000 Republican delegates and onlookers, screaming and stomping their feet for 15 minutes after Conkling sat down, were less unified than they sounded.[45] The Grant partisans—"Stalwarts," they called themselves—were up against a determined reform faction. "Half-breeds," the Stalwarts styled the earnest, progressive and improving good-government faction whose morbid honesty had caused President Grant to shake his head. Party, patronage and personal loyalty were the Stalwarts' credo. Reed was a full-blooded member of neither tribe, though Thomas Collier Platt, a thoroughgoing Stalwart from New York, would come to regard the man from Maine as one of theirs.[46] It was Platt, who, addressing a New York Republican convention, had famously claimed that there had not been one election in which he had not fought for "the ticket, the whole ticket and nothing but the straight Republican ticket." Reed might have said as much, though with a leavening dash of wit.[47]

The Stalwarts, who venerated Grant, believed that the party did too, and the first ballot seemed to bear them out. The tally was 304 votes for Grant, 284 for Blaine and 93 for Treasury Secretary Sherman, with a smattering for others; 379 took the prize. Twenty-eight ballots later, there was little movement, and the delegates retired to their hotels. Next day, June 8, the anti-Grant forces began tiptoeing away from Blaine toward Garfield. On the 34th vote, the Ohioan had 17 votes, on the 35th, 50. On the 36th came the break, and the dark horse was nominated. Conkling, ever the party man, moved to make the vote unanimous, to which the convention assented. As a sop to the Stalwarts, General Chester A. Arthur, a former collector of the Port of New York and a Conkling machine man, was nominated vice president.

The Exposition Building was vacant only for the time it took the Republicans to clear out and for the National Greenback-Labor party to move in. The Greenbackers, into whose spreading tent filed representatives of the Socialistic Labor Party, Hoyt-Pomeroy Union Greenback party, Social Workingmen, Working-Women, Kansas Workingmen and Eight Hour League, put forward General James B. Weaver of Iowa as their presidential candidate. The prohibitionists, whose views not even the open-minded Greenbackers could countenance, nominated General Neal Dow of Maine.[48]

Neither did the Democrats break with that postwar convention that only a former Union general was suitable presidential timber. General Winfield Scott ("the Superb") Hancock, went to the top of the Democratic ticket. The party platform condemned governmental overreaching, endorsed "honest money" (silver included) and "a tariff for revenue only." The previous presidential election, it decried as "the great fraud of 1876–77," and asserted that the party had yielded to this bald-faced theft only because a new civil war would have been worse. It had, it added, submitted to injustice in 1876 "in firm and patriotic faith that the people would punish this crime in 1880."

Economic recovery was the wind at the back of the Republican party, while vengeance filled the sails of the Democrats. Perhaps the Maine Democrats, post-Garcelon, had a weaker claim on righteous anger than did Democratic parties in the law-abiding states, but Reed noticed no diminution in the ferocity of his opposition. Not even his renomination by the First District Republicans was uncontested, though prevail he did, on August 10, in Saco. "We are going to bury these worse-than-Egyptian foes of ours in a sea of popular wrath," the incumbent vowed to the cheering crowd. "But we must expect no direct interposition from above. We must be the Red Sea ourselves."[49]

Reed campaigned hard, speaking once a day, often for as long as two hours, for Egypt—evidently—had united against him. Samuel J. Anderson, the peacetime militia general and railroad man, was again Reed's Democratic opponent, but this time there was no E. H. Gove to splinter the anti-Reed vote. The Greenbackers had thrown in their lot with the Democrats. In 1878, Reed had squeaked through a divided opposition. Now he faced a unified one.

Or so it seemed, as Reed shunted from one First District rally to another, reminding the voters that, as important as the presidential contest was, America was not governed by one man. "The great controlling influence in this country," he told a Portland audience at the start of the campaign, "is not presidents or holders of office, but the will of the party in power. There are those who are sorry this is so. I am not one of them. The wisdom of all is better than the wisdom of some." As for Garfield, Reed admitted that he did have one flaw, "but it is the only one: He does not dislike the Democratic party as much as he ought to."[50]

It turned out that this very flaw was pleasingly absent among ranking Maine Greenbackers. Solon Chase opted out of the Fusion project in July, decrying the Democrats' newfound devotion to hard money.[51] E. H. Gove himself—onetime chairman of the Greenback state committee and secretary of state under Garcelon—followed in August. His defection was complete. Once upon a time, the Greenback party stood for currency reform, Gove wrote in a letter of resignation to the Greenback higher-ups. Now it stood for beating the Republicans. To this exclusive end it had made common cause with the criminal enterprise known as the Democratic party. "A 'Solid South' is the boast of the northern Democrats," Gove observed. "It should be their shame and confusion. It is not a community of ideas, begotten of free discussion; it is the harmony of fear, the unity of terrorism cemented in blood. . . . I believe that the interests and the good of the country are best served by the defeat of the Democratic party. That I may contribute to that end in the most immediate and direct manner, I go to the Republican party."[52]

But Gove led no mass defection. The campaign was nip-and-tuck, easily the most closely run of Reed's long congressional career. Early election returns had Anderson ahead. The final tally put Reed over the top but by a meager 109 votes, 16,915 to Anderson's 16,806 (with a third-party contestant drawing just 250). Anderson protested, charging fraud and pursuing the matter both in the courts and in Congress. Reed spent $2,600 defending himself, not to mention the untold hours of brief-filing, evidence-gathering and, as one might suppose, sleeplessness. To the House Committee on Elections, he filed a reply to the Democrat's charge of voter intimidation. "If I could scare them as easily as the contestant seems to think and by means as inadequate as he has proved," Reed wrote, "I have certainly been recreant in a plain duty. I ought to have scared more of them." In 1882, a Republican Congress saw the matter exactly that way.

Chapter 10

For Want of a Quorum

THE REPUBLICAN CLEAN sweep of 1880 delivered political results well short of triumphant for the party of Abraham Lincoln. President Garfield was shot on July 2, 1881, as he waited for the train that would take him to his class reunion at Williams College. He had been in office for less than four months. "I am a Stalwart of the Stalwarts!" bellowed his assassin, Charles J. Guiteau, in an allusion to the rift in the Republican party that divided the good-government reformers from the U. S. Grant loyalists. Crazy Guiteau was a Grant man.

Blaine, Garfield's Secretary of State, was at the president's elbow when Guiteau pulled the trigger. In the new administration of Chester A. Arthur (Garfield died a long-lingering death on September 19), Blaine would remain in the State Department. Following this service he himself would surely ascend to the presidency; Blaine so expected, and Reed did too. However, Blaine's very proximity to that shocking event would forever damage the former Speaker of the House of Representatives, Reed came to believe. It was as if, Reed mused, "the hands which seemed to be the hands of Esau" were, in fact, Blaine's.[1] As for Garfield, his suffering moved Reed almost to tears.[2]

Still open was the question of who would become the Speaker in the Republican-controlled 47th Congress. Reed deprecated his own chances. "[T]oo badly situated," he advised George Gifford. Besides, "Maine is hardly big enough for Blaine alone."[3] Reed was right about his chances, though he did garner 11 votes out of the 285 cast. The Speakership went to 45-year-old J. Warren Keifer of Ohio, a former Union general and, in the early 1870s, commander of the politically powerful Ohio Department of the Grand Army of the Republic. Like Reed, Keifer was a third-term representative and a Republican partisan of the Stalwart type. There, however, the similarity ended. In Keifer, there was neither redeeming wit nor fundamental fair-dealing. Before long, the Speaker had a son and a pair of nephews on the House payroll. He fired a long-serving stenographer and replaced him with a family friend.[4] The House rolled its eyes at such indiscretions; Democrats justly condemned the Speaker's naked partisanship in doling out committee assignments.

These deficiencies were yet unrevealed when the Speaker-elect addressed the House on December 6, 1881. Keifer remarked on the fact that in neither branch of Congress did one party enjoy a commanding majority. Lucky it was, therefore, that at no time since the war had there been so few burning national issues. "While the universal tendency of the people is to sustain and continue to build up an unparalleled prosperity," he said, "it should be our highest aim to so legislate as to permanently promote and not cripple it. This Congress should be, and I profoundly hope will be, marked peculiarly as a business Congress."[5]

Keifer might have been the least surprised man in the House when the nonpartisan millennium did not immediately dawn. But it was a Republican, not a Democrat, who first rose up to challenge the Speaker's authority. Godlove S. Orth, 64, of Indiana, formerly the American ambassador to Austria-Hungary, had himself sought the Speakership. He was sorry to lose the prize, sorrier still when Keifer failed to salve that wound of disappointment with a suitable office. It was customary for the victorious Speaker to reward the runner-up in that contest with plum committee assignments. To protest this perceived slight, Orth resigned from the Rules Committee. To reiterate his displeasure, he introduced a resolution to strip the Speaker of sole discretion over committee assignments. This formidable power, Orth proposed, should rather be diffused among many members.

Reed shuddered at the thought. He himself had no quarrel with the Speaker. When Orth resigned from the Rules Committee, Keifer inserted Reed in his place. It was, therefore, Chairman Reed of the Judiciary Committee who introduced a resolution late in March to fix a date for the House to decide the long-unfinished business of the *Alabama* claims.

The *Alabama*, a steam-driven Confederate cruiser that wreaked havoc on northern shipping during the war, had long been a source of contention between the United States and Great Britain. Built in a British yard and launched over the protests of the American minister to the Court of St. James's, the Confederate raider was, by American lights, as much a British vessel as if she had flown the Union Jack. After the war, the United States entered a formal claim for compensation; $2 billion in cash or the cession of the Dominion of Canada would be suitable, Senator Charles Sumner proposed. The settlement secured in 1872 at Geneva by a five-man tribunal consisting of representatives from the United States, Great Britain, Switzerland, Italy and Brazil was slightly discounted from Sumner's number: There would be no Canada and only $15.5 million in cash. Obtaining the money turned out to be the easy part.

To whom to distribute it? Directly to the owners of the captured northern vessels and cargoes or to the insurers of those assets? Congress could not, or would not, decide. To not a few southern Democrats, there was no such thing as a deserving Yankee recipient of a war-related claim. Certainly, the southerners had received little enough satisfaction from northern Republicans concerning their war-related claims. And so the bulk of the $15.5 million remained on deposit at the U.S. Treasury over the length of six congresses. If the affair of the Geneva award were not so typical of the incapacity of Congress to function, it might have seemed more outrageous. Then again, each party had its own idea of proper functioning. To the Democrats, the fewer bills enacted, the less money spent, the less intrusive the federal authority on the powers of the states (especially, in the South, on the powers to restrict the franchise to white males), the better. It was, in general, the Republicans who pushed for activist legislation. It vexed them that the House produced so little besides speeches, motions and resolutions made in the service of obstruction.

Having paid his respects to the former Speaker during a 1902 presidential visit to Portland, Teddy Roosevelt doffs his hat to the crowd assembled outside Reed's residence.

Facing southwest, climbers to the top of the Portland Observatory commanded a view of Congress Street in the heart of the rising metropolis.

Sensitive to how little his birthplace resembled Lincoln's log cabin, Reed pointed to the new construction that had been put in place since his family left. "I was not born in all that house," he would say.

His parents, Mathilda and Thomas B. Reed, Sr. Everything he was he owed to his father, said Reed of the sailor and watchman.

Thomas B. Reed in the flush of his slender youth. "Oh, but what a student I was in those times," he recalled of his days at Bowdoin.

The gunboat USS *Sybil*, aboard which Acting Assistant Paymaster Reed served a mainly monotonous year patrolling southern waterways during the Civil War.

Mound City, Illinois, the desolate wartime naval station where the *Sybil* frequently called.

Reed, the mustachioed ornament of the Portland Bar. The future Speaker first served as a state legislator, Maine attorney general and Portland city solicitor.

Reed detested James G. Blaine, the powerful Maine Republican, though it's not entirely clear that the Plumed Knight hated Reed in return. Blaine fell short of the presidency but served three terms as Speaker of the House of Representatives.

Reed, lower left, and his congressional colleagues confronted a fiscal dilemma utterly unlike the one pressing so hard in 2011: The monstrous federal surplus refused to be shrunk.

The "Watchdog of the Treasury," William S. Holman, Democrat of Indiana, warned of the coming of the American superstate, with Washington, D.C., its imperial capital.

William M. Springer of Illinois was oil to Reed's water. "Bounding Springer," the Speaker styled the House Democrat who irked him more than any other.

President Grover Cleveland won Reed's admiration for his staunch devotion to principle. Washington tourists sometimes mistook the two amply proportioned men for each other.

Reed stands over the Speaker's chair during the fractious 51st Congress, his attention almost certainly directed to the Republican side of the House. The empty seats were the Democrats'.

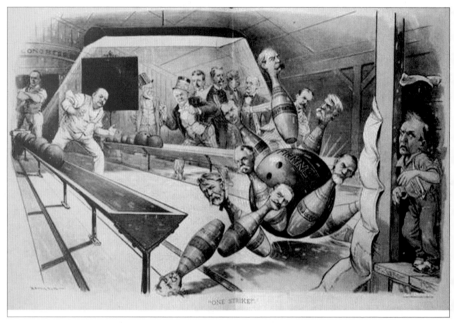

The new Speaker leaves not a political pin standing in the early days of the great quorum count of January–February 1890. The horror-struck pin-setter is John G. Carlisle, the Democratic Speaker of the prior three congresses.

An unfriendly cartoonist takes Reed to task for his alleged czarlike conduct during the quorum-counting tumult in 1890.

The Speaker—no clean-desk man—at the peak of his career and of his frustration.

Before their falling out over the war with Spain, Henry Cabot Lodge nominated Reed for president at the 1896 Republican convention in St. Louis.

ANOTHER EXPLOSION AT HAND.

Popular sentiment, here symbolized by William Jennings Bryan, made the peaceable William McKinley a war president. "He has no more backbone than a chocolate éclair," Reed is supposed to have said of his Republican rival.

Susan P. Reed, who married the Speaker-to-be in 1870. Herself a keen intellect and voracious reader, she is known to have opposed her husband's politics on only one issue: Mrs. Reed wanted no part of woman suffrage.

Katherine Reed Balentine, standing second from right, bears witness to Maine Governor Carl E. Milligan's signature on a resolution setting aside September 10, 1917, for a special vote on a constitutional amendment to enact female suffrage in the Pine Tree State (the men voted it down). Reed's daughter favored her father both in her looks and in her devotion to women's rights.

Reed; his wife, Susan; his daughter Katherine; and his books—the sum of which made the largest private library in Maine—shared the residence at 32 Deering Street, Portland.

"Well, I hope my enemies are satisfied," Reed reportedly quipped while laying eyes on his new portrait; the painter was John Singer Sargent

Reed was as vexed as the next Republican. The truth was that parliamentary obstruction, whether employed for high Jeffersonian reasons or low bigoted ones, made for long days and longer nights on Capitol Hill. Reed would go on to make a political revolution by sweeping aside the most tedious forms of obstruction. He did so for many avowed reasons, not one of which was to relieve the tedium of a filibuster-prone House. However, one may not unreasonably suspect that the sheer ennui of such proceedings as those of March 20, 1882, figured in some way in Reed's long-congealing plans for change.

It was late in the afternoon of that day when Reed got to his feet to move that the Geneva awards be brought before the full House. To do so required a motion to suspend the rules, which he made "under unanimous instructions" from the Committee of the Judiciary. The disposition of the tribunal's award had been pending since 1872, but that did not mean that the relevant bill had yet worked its way to the front of the legislative queue. On the contrary, many bills had the right of way. To hopscotch these measures, Reed needed the cooperation of the Democratic minority: "I hope opportunity will be given for a hearing, which is all the resolution asks," he said.

The minority was not disposed to give him one. Democrat William Springer of Illinois immediately moved to adjourn. He called for tellers to count the votes on his motion. He demanded the number of yeas and nays on that motion, and, finally, tellers to count the yeas and nays. The House voted not to adjourn, and other Democrats picked up where Springer had left off. There were motions for a roll call and learned discussions about whether there was or was not a quorum present. To decide the question, it was necessary to order a roll call, which Reed proceeded to do. One hundred and forty-one members didn't answer, even members who were present on the floor. "The Doorkeeper will now close the doors," Keifer intoned, "and the names of absentees will be called in order that excuses, if any, may be offered."

Then followed the ritual interrogation of the absentees, the clerk calling the names in alphabetical order. Plainly, if a member were truly absent, he could not explain himself. But the physically absent constituted only a small portion of the nonresponders. From the Record:

Mr. Aitken. No excuse offered.

Mr. Allen.

Mr. Valentine. Mr. Allen is very sick and unable to be here. I
move that he be excused.

The motion was agreed to.

Mr. Atherton. No excuse offered.

Mr. Barbour.

Mr. Cabell. Mr. Barbour has been sick for some days. I move that
he be excused.

Mr. Bayne. No excuse offered.

And so on, all the way down to the end of the alphabet; neither did
Mr. Young have any excuse. After which Reed moved "that the members for whom no sufficient excuse has been made and who are absent
without leave, be arrested by the Sergeant-at-Arms and brought in custody to the bar of the House."

Springer demanded that Reed make his resolution from the clerk's
desk, and not from the floor.

"It has not been reduced to writing," said Keifer.

"I ask that it be reduced to writing," said Springer.

"The gentleman from Maine will reduce it to writing," assented
Keifer.

So Reed wrote out his resolution and handed it to the clerk, who
read it aloud; the resolution was adopted.

Now followed a debate about whether a resolution was in order to
dispense with the further proceedings under the roll call. Keifer judged
that it was, others that it was not. Republican John Henry Camp was
quite sure it was not. "It is not in order," said Camp, "under clause 8,
Rule XVI, which provides that pending a motion to suspend the rules
the Chair may entertain one motion that the House adjourn, but after
the result thereon is announced he shall not entertain any other dilatory
motion till the vote is taken on suspension. This is a dilatory motion
under that clause of the rule which says that no dilatory motion shall be
entertained till the vote on suspension has been announced. I submit,
therefore, that the motion is not now in order."

Keifer, demurring, explained why he could not construe the motion in question as a dilatory motion to prevent the coming to a vote on Reed's original motion to suspend the rules.

Republican Roswell P. Flower was a rich New York banker who had been appointed to fill the congressional seat vacated by Levi P. Morton in 1881. The evening was wearing on, and Flower's stomach might have been growling. Certainly, the freshman congressman was impatient—parliamentary hair-splitting was not the way of Wall Street. "This seems to me to be a great waste of time," said Flower, "and therefore I move that all further proceedings under the call be dispensed with and we resolve ourselves into a Committee of the Whole to discuss the tariff-commission bill. I understand that there are some two hundred speeches to be delivered on that bill, and it seems to me that the quicker we get at it the better will the country be pleased."

Camp objected. Flower's motion was not in order. On the other hand, said Camp, "I move by unanimous consent that if the gentleman from New York has a speech to deliver he be permitted to do so. [Laughter.]"

So absentees began to appear at the bar of the House in the custody of the sergeant-at-arms. Keifer asked each for his excuse. Many had been at dinner. "Mr. Speaker," said Democrat Edward Bragg of Wisconsin, "I move that leave be given to all the members of the House who answered to their names to go to their dinners, and that those who have been to dinner be required to remain and hold down the fort until the others return."

This eminently sensible idea elicited an objection on a point of order, which Keifer sustained.

"I would like to know under what rule," Bragg parried.

"The Chair is not always bound to assign reasons," Keifer replied.

"It is sometimes easier to render judgments than to give reasons," Bragg said.

"The Chair recognizes that," allowed Keifer.

So the inquisition continued, its monotony broken once when a Pennsylvania-born Democrat, Robert Klotz, replied to Keifer in German. Many minutes later, John Hyatt Smith, a Brooklyn minister of independent party affiliation, replied in a comically deferential English.

"I would say, Mr. Speaker," began Smith, "that it is the first time in my Congressional experience I have been under arrest. [Laughter.] I say it in great deference to the authority of the House. I feel I am a prisoner in the hands of my friends. [Laughter.] I look upon it as an imprisonment of love. I look upon it as a token of regard of the House. [Laughter.] I apologize most humbly for the fact my absence has suspended the action of the Congress of the United States. [Laughter.] I promise hereafter I will be more faithful to my duty.

"But gravely, Mr. Speaker, the reason for my absence was sickness. I have nothing more to say and I submit myself to the courtesy and authority of the House."

Four congressmen spoke up in short succession:

"I move that my colleague be excused."

"I move that he be fined $20. [Laughter.]"

"I move to make it $10."

"I rise to debate the proposition."

It was Klotz, the Pennsylvania, who had moved to fine Smith $20. When challenged, he repeated his motion and promised to explain it. This he did in German until laughter drowned him out.

Reed, no closer to his objective than he was before hunger pangs began to winnow the ranks of his colleagues on the floor, now moved "that all further proceedings under the call be dispensed with." The motion agreed to, Reed demanded the regular order of business. It was an attempt to pick up where he had left off hours before.

However, neither the passage of time nor the onset of thirst and hunger made the Democrats more amenable to Reed's agenda. Joseph Blackburn, Democrat of Kentucky, moved to adjourn. Reed called the motion out of order. "Pending this motion to suspend the rules one motion to adjourn has been voted down," said Keifer, siding with Reed, "and that is all that is allowed." Blackburn protested, but Keifer insisted, rising on a point of order. At Blackburn's behest, the clerk read aloud the rule on which Keifer based his decision:

"Pending a motion to suspend the rules, the Speaker may entertain one question that the House adjourn, but after the result thereon is announced, he shall not entertain any other dilatory motion till the vote is taken on suspension."

Blackburn thought he saw a loophole. Yes, Reed had made his motion to suspend the rules in the service of fixing the date on which the House would consider this very old business of the $15.5 million. But in seeking to obtain a vote on that motion, the fact had come to light that there was no quorum. Whereupon followed the roll call and the Speaker's interrogation of the prisoners of the sergeant-at-arms. Reed himself had ended that phase of the evening's business with his motion to dispense with further proceedings under the call. So doing, in effect, he had wiped the House slate clean. No motion was now pending. "The gentleman from Maine," Blackburn wound up, "now takes the floor and makes a motion which, although couched in the same language as the former motion, is in reality a new motion, having abandoned the prosecution of the motion which was before the House when he moved to dispense with further proceedings under the call."

Reed refused to dignify Blackburn's argument with a reply, and he said so. Keifer did consider it, only to find it out of order. Now the Speaker called on the House to vote on Reed's motion. It was a voice vote, "a division by sound," and it sounded to Keifer as if Reed had won. But the Democrats insisted on a division by sight. The ocular vote was lopsided enough at a preliminary count, 99–1, but the Democrats weren't voting. Once again, there was no quorum. "Why do they not vote, Mr. Speaker?" William Andrew Jackson Sparks, the Illinois Democrat, addressed Keifer. "That is an inquiry which should be addressed to the gentlemen not voting," the Speaker replied.

The gentlemen not voting, or some of them, wanted to adjourn, but Keifer seemed unwilling to let them. "I rise to make a parliamentary inquiry," piped up Richard P. Bland, Democrat of Missouri. "It is claimed that no quorum has voted. I want to know if this House is to remain in session until next July before a motion can be made for adjournment, unless a quorum votes on this proposition?"

A freshman Republican from Tennessee, William R. Moore, was bewildered. "I wish to inquire," he said, "if there be no way by which the Representatives of the American people in Congress assembled can transact the business of the people for which we are sent here? I confess it seems to me we have been and are now enacting a very broad farce."

"The gentleman will state his point," said Keifer.

"I am trying to find out the point," returned Moore.

Moore wasn't the only one. Keifer had lost control of the House. The members were not voting but milling. The tellers stood by helplessly. "A quorum has not yet voted," the Speaker observed. "The Chair thinks a quorum is present, and requests members to vote on one side or the other."

"I rise to a point of order," said Sparks. "It is, that there is no order in the House." The point was well taken, Keifer allowed, and he called on members to return to their seats. Flower, by now feeling like an animal caught in a trap, moved that the poll be closed. Keifer ruled the motion out of order: "Gentlemen are requested to vote," he coaxed over the dull roar.

George Robeson, a New Jersey Republican, rising to a point of order, caused Rule 8 to be read aloud. It was the rule requiring members to "vote on each question put"; the Democrats themselves had instituted it in the 46th Congress. "I desire now, Mr. Speaker," said Robeson, "the attention of my friends on the other side of the House to the demand of the rule which they themselves made."

"And which," retorted Sparks, "gentlemen on the other side of the House in the last Congress invariably violated." He had Robeson there.

Now came another roll call. There were 106 yeas, 5 nays and 181 abstentions. There was a corporeal quorum, clearly, though not a parliamentary one. What could Congress do in the absence of a parliamentary quorum? Why, said William Springer, quoting from the Constitution, it could adjourn, and he so moved. Blackburn followed Springer in the same vein. He closed his speech with these words: "If a motion to adjourn is not in order now, a motion for a roll call of the House is not in order now; and I ask the Chair to tell me what motion beneath God's sun is in order when this House finds itself without a quorum, except it be one of these two motions?"

"Perpetual motion," a Republican called out.

"The gentleman's tongue represents the subject of his remark," the Kentucky Democrat parried.

Blackburn was one of the 181 members who had not answered the roll call. John Van Voorhis, an upstate New York Republican, had noticed the silence and called it to the attention of the House. "I rise to a point of order," said Van Voorhis. "It is that the gentleman from Kentucky is not in the House. The call of the roll which has just been had shows that he is not here."

The technically absent though physically present Blackburn flicked aside that point of order with the parliamentary truth that the Speaker may not entertain two points of order at once; Blackburn's had precedence.

"We all know perfectly well," Van Voorhis rejoined, "that there are one hundred and sixty members of this House present. The men who can complain that they want to adjourn are those who do not vote. Now, they have no right to violate their own rule, for this rule was made by a Democratic Congress. They violate their own rule which requires them to vote; they say they will not vote, and then they ask the Speaker to violate another rule and let them move to adjourn."

If the Democrats wanted to adjourn, said Robeson, piling on, let them vote on Reed's motion. "We seek to bind the conscience of no man," he said. "We do not ask them to vote for any proposition. We do not ask them to do anything they do not want to do. We ask them to put themselves on record against the thing, if they desire to put themselves on record against it. But they sit in their seats and refuse to vote, in violation of every proposition of reason or of logic, and then complain of the result of their own dereliction of duty."

It was clear how Blackburn saw his duty. It was to thwart the pretensions of an overbearing majority—specifically, in this case, Reed's attempt to jump the legislative queue with the Geneva award. The Kentuckian denied that any Geneva claimant deserved a red cent, and he vowed that there would be no quorum until Reed withdrew his motion.

Flower and Moore were not the only members who deeply yearned for a pillow, a drink or a bite of dinner. At length, a spirit of compromise began to enter into the tone of the debate. Abram S. Hewitt of New York moved that Reed's resolution be amended, such that the Geneva awards would come up for consideration in the House not on March 28 but April 11. To this, Reed was amenable. Others, too, expressed their approval. But there still was pending a motion to adjourn. Keifer considered the question at some length, concluding that no such motion was in order, "it having been disclosed by the last roll call of the House there was a much larger number present than a quorum. And the Chair will state it has no doubt there is within the bar of the House at this time much more than a quorum. That fact has been ascertained by a count of the House. The motion to adjourn is not in order."

Or was it? "Let me make a parliamentary inquiry," offered Bragg. "The roll-call having been made, if that vote is not completed on that roll-call does not it remain before the House as an unfinished roll-call? And when the rule provides that after a roll-call has been made and the call of the absentees or those not voting has been made, that the Chair shall not permit any member to vote thereafter, does it not leave this House in the condition under the ruling of the Chair with an incomplete roll-call which by the rules of the House never can be completed?"

To resolve this parliamentary complication another vote was ordered. The vote was not on the motion to adjourn. It was, rather, on a motion to table an appeal on the Speaker's refusal to entertain a motion to adjourn. The yeas were 79, the nays 42 and the number not voting 171. So the motion to lay on the table the appeal from the decision of the Chair was agreed to—or would have been, Springer quickly interjected, if a quorum were present, which, however, it was not. He raised this objection as a point of order.

Keifer replied that Springer had spoken too late, had missed the fast-closing parliamentary window to object that there was no quorum. Springer insisted that he had risen immediately to speak. Keifer bowed to Springer's insistence. But Dudley Haskell, a Kansas Republican (and one of the minority of nonlawyers in the House; he was a shoe merchant), wanted to hear Springer himself attest for the Record that he had, in fact, leapt to his feet and that he had done so before William Rice, a Massachusetts Republican, had been recognized and started to speak.

Keifer sided with Springer, but Haskell kept pushing. "I rise to a point of order," he said. "If we are to be bound by these rules, let us be bound by them. I submit that the gentleman from Illinois [Springer] has not yet said he made his point of order before the Chair recognized the gentleman from Massachusetts [Mr. Rice]. I ask under the rule that the gentleman from Illinois shall make that statement."

Bland of Missouri was outraged. Did Haskell mean to say that it was within the Speaker's power to refuse the minority the right to make a point of order by recognizing the first Republican who catches his eye? Keifer replied that he had no such intention. "The gentleman from Missouri is unnecessarily excited about this matter."

More minutes were devoted to the very same subject, Keifer all the while averring that there was nothing to quarrel about. Springer's point of order stood. It only remained to hold another roll call to determine if there was, indeed, a quorum. Reed so moved, and the clerk droned the roll. This time 161 failed to answer. "The clerk will now call the names of those who have not answered on this call," Keifer intoned. A member moved to suspend the ritual of seeking an excuse for their nonresponse from members who had previously been excused as sick. It was now after 11 PM, and the old and infirm were slipping out of the chamber. "I ask to have all the members excused," someone suggested; "they are all getting sick."

The laughter from this witticism had died away when Republican John Camp moved that the doors to the House be closed and that the sergeant-at-arms be directed to take into custody all members who were absent without an excuse. Reed proposed a compromise. Inasmuch, he said, as the Hewitt proposal to amend his initiative on the Geneva awards had seemed to find favor, might the House not adjourn with the understanding that there would be a vote on the Hewitt-amended measure after the reading of the Record tomorrow (or, rather, as it was now after midnight, later today)?

"Is there objection?" Keifer asked.

"I object," said Springer.

But the obstructionist starch had gone out of the minority party and even Springer was led to withdraw his objection. It was 12:38 in the morning when the yawning members filed out of the House and headed for home.[6]

THERE WAS NOTHING unique in this marathon of parliamentary posturing. In Britain only a year before, debate in the House of Commons over the so-called Coercion Bill had stretched for 41 continuous hours.[7] "Obstruction," decried the *Times* of London of the filibustering radical

Irish members of Parliament, "is no longer merely noxious in so far as it retards the enactment of important measures; it is inflicting deadly blows upon the credit of the House of Commons, and, indeed, of Parliamentary government."[8] Nor was the technique of the disappearing quorum an invention of the Springer-era Democratic party. In 1840 the patron saint of the Republican party had jumped out of a first-story window of the Illinois statehouse in order to prolong the meeting of the Illinois state legislature: Abraham Lincoln had leapt to deny the Democratic majority the quorum it needed to adjourn. The Democrats, in fact, were able to count a quorum, Lincoln's defenestration notwithstanding. The lanky future president was unhurt in his escape, as "his legs reached nearly from the window to the ground."[9] So the Washington press corps, inured to dilatory operations, treated the events of the evening of March 20 as little more than a reportorial footnote.

THAT DID NOT mean, however, that the majority was happy with the rules or that it did not push to revise them. The sultry Washington summer had long since devoured the sweet Washington spring when the case of a contested election tied up the House in knots. Under the Constitution, each house of Congress is the judge of the suitability of its own members; sitting, supposedly, as judges, the representatives and senators themselves, not the courts, resolve disputed elections. Reed himself was intimately familiar with the House machinery in such matters, as Samuel Anderson, his Democratic opponent in 1880, was waging a contested-election case against him, as noted earlier. (In response to Anderson's vaguely stated charges of voter intimidation and fraud, Reed entered specific accusations against Anderson, including one that he had procured the vote of L. S. Berry, "an insane man, and so disqualified."[10] Reed kept his seat.)

Late in May 1882, the case of Mackey vs. Dibble came before the House. A Republican, E. W. M. Mackey, charged that a Democrat, Samuel Dibble, had fraudulently taken his place as a representative from South Carolina in the 47th Congress. Dibble, in return, charged Mackey with forgery and evidence-tampering. In theory, the Committee on Elections, and the House as a body, weighed the merits of such cases

with judicial impartiality. In practice, the proceedings were unabash-
edly partisan, and the party in power invariably seated its member and
dislodged the pretender from the other side. Never far below the surface
in 1882 were recollections of the Hayes-Tilden contest, memories either
sweet or sour, according to party affiliation.

At full strength, the Republicans had the majority to force the vote
that would seat Mackey and dislodge Dibble. But they were not quite
at full strength. Lacking a quorum, they sat for a week of roll calls and
motions for adjournment and interrogations of members returned to
the House in the custody of the sergeant-at-arms. On the eighth day
of these proceedings, May 27, a Saturday, Reed secured the Speaker's
recognition to submit a privileged report from the Rules Committee.
His report was a new rule that would, if adopted, prohibit parliamentary
obstruction of an election case. The text was as follows:

> Pending a motion to suspend the rules, or on any question of
> consideration which may arise on a case involving the constitu-
> tional right to a seat, and pending the motion for the previous
> question, or after it shall have been ordered on any such case,
> the Speaker may entertain one motion to adjourn; but after the
> result thereon is announced he shall not entertain any other
> motion till the vote is taken on the pending question; and pend-
> ing the consideration of such case only a motion to adjourn or to
> take a recess (but not both in succession) shall be in order, and
> such motions shall not be repeated without further intervening
> consideration of the case for at least one hour.[11]

To the Republican side of the aisle, this serpentine sentence promised deliverance. If dilatory motions were out of order in election cases,
Mackey was as good as seated and the week-long torture by roll call was
as good as ended. But there could be no deliverance until Reed's new
rule was enacted. And there could be no such fruition until the Republicans could materialize their halt and lame on the floor of the House
to vote. That this triumph would not occur on Saturday was evident
as soon as the clerk finished reading Reed's proposed amendment. First
came the customary demand for recess (disallowed), followed by a point

of order (overruled), followed by an appeal of the Speaker's decision on that point of order (which the Speaker refused to entertain). At least the sides did agree to adjourn. They would resume the fight on Monday, May 29.[12]

Aficionados had the rest of the weekend to anticipate the best kind of Washington political theater. Reed was, to be sure, a skilled parliamentarian, with formidable intellect and fearsome wit. In reputation and experience, however, he seemed a very pale copy of Samuel Randall, his principal Democratic antagonist, 11 years Reed's senior and three-time Speaker of the House. In the Chair in March 1877, presiding over a Democratic majority, the Pennsylvanian had ordered the vote that turned the presidency over to Rutherford B. Hayes, the very man who, as Randall was convinced, had stolen it from Tilden. Better a peaceful and constitutional presidential succession than a chaotic, possibly bloody, one, Randall believed, and his conviction drove the House before it. Preceding this act of disinterested patriotism was a feat of endurance that won for Randall the worshipful wonder of every congressman of average stamina and ordinary bodily capacities. In the final session of the 43rd Congress, the Pennsylvania Democrat had remained on the floor or in the cloakrooms (in any case, within the sound of the voice of the clerk of the House) for 72 consecutive hours while leading the opposition against the Force Bill. And when his parliamentary triumph was complete, "after the most exciting and protracted parliamentary struggle ever known," Randall had led a procession of victorious Democrats down the main aisle of the House bearing the tin coffeepot to whose contents he modestly ascribed his staying power.[13]

So on the morning of Monday, May 29, eager political theatergoers jammed the House galleries. There was a capacity crowd too on the floor, a sign that the Republicans had rounded up stragglers to make their majority. After the prayer and the reading of the journal, Reed spoke up: "I now call up for consideration the proposition to amend the rules, reported from the Committee on Rules."

The parliamentary battle was joined. Knowing spectators perhaps opened a book or a newspaper to amuse themselves during the obstructionist preliminaries. There was a motion to adjourn, which was voted down. Reed moved that the House forgo reading of the names of that roll call. Blackburn objected, and so the roll was called. Randall moved that the House, when it did adjourn, should not reconvene until June 1. Reed rose to a point of order. "My point of order is that upon a proposition that the House change its rules, dilatory motions cannot be entertained by the Chair." Other points of order and additional procedural matters filled more minutes. But presently, the cognoscenti put down their reading material. The parliamentary track was clear for the gentleman from Maine. The crowd leaned forward to catch his Down East twang:

"The House of Representatives," Reed began, "acts under the Constitution of the United States. It has certain powers conferred upon it as a separate body, powers which it can exercise without either let or hindrance of any other body, powers which it cannot surrender if it would, under the Constitution, powers which it is obliged to retain, powers which it can never trade away. These powers are ever present with it, and it is bound to act in obedience and in furtherance of those powers."

The first of these powers was one conferred by the Founders; Reed read from Section 5 of the Constitution: "Each House shall be the judge of the election, returns and qualifications of its own members, and a majority of each shall constitute a quorum to do business."

Reed observed that the House had been busily not discharging this constitutional obligation for the past eight or 10 days. A quorum, certainly, had been present on the floor, but no business had been done. The Speaker might have overruled these obstructionist tactics, and Reed seemed to wish that Keifer had done so. But, he went on, "I have believed that the wisest way, the more orderly way to reach and remove the obstruction was to revise and amend the rules under color of which this transaction of the last eight or 10 days has taken place. It would seem, after we found our rules were not suitable in character and detail to enable us to discharge our constitutional duty, that it became the first duty of the House to change its rules under the other provision of the Constitution which I now read from the same Section 5: 'Each House may determine the rules of its proceedings.'"

It made no sense, Reed pointed out, that the House had enacted rules that served no other purpose than to stymie the House. It made still less sense to assert, as the Democrats did, that such rules could not be changed. He said he would waste no breath on the question of whether the Democrats' tactics were dilatory. "Every man with brains in his head knows that is the purpose of them," he proceeded, "knows that is the object and intention of them, and cannot be blinded by any suggestions. We have no right to go into questions of motives. . . . [T]o impute improper motives to members is unsuitable, but to proclaim their obvious purpose is the right of any man with organs of perception, and brains capable of recording the impressions made upon them—I shall take it for granted that this House comprehends what no schoolboy could fail to comprehend, that the series of motions made today were made for the express purpose of delay and preventing a change of the rules."

Reed now gave a preview of his own career in the Chair: "I maintain the proposition that wherever it is imposed upon Congress to accomplish a certain work, whether by the Constitution or by a law, it is the duty of the Speaker, who represents the House, and in his official capacity is the embodiment of the House, to carry out that rule of law or of the Constitution. It then becomes his duty to see that no factious opposition prevents the House from doing its duty. He must brush away all unlawful combinations to misuse the rules and must hold Congress strictly to its work. And I am fortified in my proposition in regard to law by a very distinguished authority acting upon a very distinguished scene, and occupying a position in which if he is wise he will be willing and glad to press into history."

Randall himself was, of course, that distinguished authority. Reed was pleased to remind the Democrats how their very own Speaker disallowed dilatory motions in the discharge of his constitutional duty in the electoral crisis of 1877. Now then, Reed continued, under the Constitution the House had the right to make its own rules. And it therefore had the right to change them. From which it followed, he said, that "No members, or set of members, have the right to use the rules which are to be changed to prevent the change which the House desires to make. . . . The very power which the House is exercising cannot be used to destroy that power. There is no such thing as suicide in any provision of the Constitution."

In a partisan flourish, Reed invoked a ruling by former Speaker Blaine to embellish the one by the Democrat Randall. So it is, he wound up his speech, that "Under the principles of law, under the principles of the Constitution and under the action of this House, the minority has no further right to delay public business."[14]

This was a potent speech, but it seemed to make few converts on the other side of the aisle. Reed's rule would leave the minority defenseless, the Democrats protested, Blackburn asserting that it would turn over control of the House, "without any limitation, without any restraint," to a partisan majority.[15] Debate was in its fourth hour when Reed rose to say that the House itself had made his case for him: "If argument on this side accompanied by argument on the other side has not been enough to satisfy the mind of the Speaker on the righteousness of the point of order I have made, I think no further argument could possibly have the effect of doing it."[16]

Speaker Keifer, at least, was convinced. Nor was he shaken in that belief when Springer, "his face white with rage" and shaking his fist over his head, cried out, "The Speaker ought to be deposed!" So the matter at last came to a vote, the Republican majority perfected with such heroes as Russell Emmett of Pennsylvania, who made his way unsteadily into the chamber on the arms of his friends, "his face and his head enveloped in bandages." The vote was 150 yeas, 1 nay (a Democrat, Augustus A. Hardenbergh of New Jersey, a banker and railroad man) and 140 sitting on their hands. "So," the Record said, "the House determined to consider the contested-election case."

It was, according to political taste, a victory of common sense over obstruction (the Republican construct) or of "MIGHT AGAINST RIGHT" (the editorial judgment of the Washington *Post*).[17] Either way, Reed had triumphed.

Chapter 11

Progress Stops in Washington

N EVER DID THOMAS B. Reed pine for the good old days. He no
more yearned for homemade anesthesia, outdoor privies and the
wooden plow than he did for the Puritan Sabbath. If Congress couldn't
hasten the pace of American progress, according to his political credo,
the least it could do was not to impede it.

One evening in 1882, the congressman found himself seated at a
small dinner with Alexander Graham Bell. The great inventor was
expounding on the "possibility of transmitting sight like sound and making us see in Washington what was going on in New York just as we can
now hear talk through the telephone." Reed thought it entirely plausi-
ble. And he was intrigued with Bell's observation that electricity might
harness remote sources of power. Capturing the power of the tides, or
of distant waterfalls, Reed mused in his diary, "we shall soon have to
work only for exercise. A dynamo machine under Niagara would feed
the world."

In the final decades of the 19th century, almost no technical, industrial or scientific feat seemed impossible. Between 1790 and 1860, the
U.S. Patent Office had granted fewer than 40,000 patents; between
1860 and 1890, it awarded 400,000.[1] Gray-haired people stared in wonder at the transformation of American life. Relentlessly did one new

machine displace another not-quite-so-new machine, along with not a few of the workers who had operated it. In 1879, a leading manufacturer employed 17 skilled men to produce 500 dozen brooms a week. By 1885, the same manufacturer, newly mechanized, paid 9 men to turn out 1,200 dozen brooms a week.[2]

Twice as much production with one-half the payroll was nothing out of the ordinary. The 1885 Report of the U.S. Commissioner of Labor recited chapter and verse on the revolution in American productivity. Shoes and boots? "Goodyear's sewing machine for turned shoes, with 1 man, will sew 250 pairs in 1 day. It would require 8 men working by hand to sew the same number. By the use of King's heel-shaver or trimmer 1 man will trim 300 pairs of shoes a day, where it formerly took 3 men to do the same. One man, with the McKay machine, can handle 300 pairs of shoes per day, while, without the machine, he could handle but 5 pairs in the same time."[3] Or breadboxes: "[W]hat was done in 1876 by 13 men and women working together, is now accomplished by 3 men."[4] And in oil production: No more were barrels hauled by horse-and-wagon from the wellhead to the railway. Pipelines carried the oil instead. The Commissioner of Labor ventured that 5,700 teams of horses and double the number of men were thereby rendered redundant.[5] Finance was itself a force for growth and up-tempo operations. Joint-stock companies were superseding partnerships and family proprietorships, just as King's heel-shaver had nudged aside human trimmers on the factory floor. Fitted out with more machinery and larger capitalizations than the firms of yesteryear, limited-liability corporations produced more things more cheaply than ever before.

The commissioner put pencil to paper. Out of a population of 55 million people, 11 million were grown men—one in five. Four million persons worked in the "mechanical industries" of the United States, which depended on steam power and water power equivalent to roughly 3.5 million horsepower. Now then, the muscle of six grown men was equivalent to that of one horse. So 21 million men (6 times 3.5) would be required to do the work of the present four million persons, in the absence of steam and hydro power. Twenty-one million able-bodied men working in the mechanical industries implied an overall population five times larger than the official tally, namely, 275 million.

And from the same census, the commissioner gleaned the fact that there were 28,600 locomotives in the United States. "To do the work of these locomotives upon the existing common roads of this country and the equivalent of that which has been done upon the railroads the past year would require, in round numbers, 54,000,000 horses and 13,500,000 men," he estimated. "The work is now done, as far as the men are concerned, by 250,000. . . . To do the work, then, now accomplished by power and power machinery in our mechanical industries and upon our railroads would require men representing a population of 172,500,000, in addition to the present population of the country of 55,000,000, or a total population, with hand processes and with horsepower, of 227,500,000, which population would be obliged to subsist on present means. In an economic view the cost to the country would be enormous."

However, that was not the commissioner's last word. Recovery from the depression of 1873–79 was only three years along when the world economy slumped again. The intervening boom had been sweet, albeit short. When a millionaire acquaintance of Reed's suggested that the congressman had better get out of politics, because "a bank account is better than fame," Reed paused to reflect. "If any were to come along and offer me what I am fairly worth in some other business," he confided to George Gifford, "this country would run great risk of losing a statesman."[6] It was just as well that Reed did not choose to seek his fortune in private business at that moment, as the boom, or boomlet, had ended. It was surely no accident, the commissioner speculated, that the blight of falling prices, falling interest rates and falling employment had occurred in the midst of a gale of innovation. New technology, deployed by immense new limited-liability corporations, was producing much more than consumers could afford to buy. The implication of the commissioner's analysis was that material progress was a decidedly mixed blessing.

Labor leaders, poets and social critics had long before reached the same conclusion. Alfred Lord Tennyson in 1842 published the antimodernist poem "Locksley Hall." Even the capitalists were not so sure about the newfangled media of communication. "The electric message is superseding the leisurely letter," one worn-out observer complained. "There is no quiet waiting for foreign correspondence. The cable announces a bargain struck on another continent, and the same day, before the goods have been shipped, the cargo is sold and the transaction ended." David Wells, one of the most thoughtful exponents of progress, joined in this lament: "If one trader keeps himself in instantaneous contact through the telegraph with markets and customers, all must do the same, or be left behind in the struggle for success. Thus dominated by new conditions, the merchant and financier of to-day has been rendered almost as much of a machine as the worker in the factories, whose every movement has been automatic, or subordinate to the physical forces acting through machinery."[7]

But to Wells, and to Reed too, these were quibbles. Hectic and fast-paced the modern life might be, but it was constantly getting better. People were living longer. They were healthier and better fed—they were, in fact, demonstrably bigger. Manufacturers of ready-made American clothing had bumped up the sizes of their trousers and coats in the 1880s to accommodate a taller, wider and better nourished customer.[8] Mark Twain could see the improvements as he traveled the country. He noted, unsentimentally, the displacement of his beloved steamboats by the railroads, and the displacement of harvest hands, who used to travel by steamboat, by automated reaping equipment.[9] "Lots of things have changed and all for the better," the author jotted in his notebook in 1884.

They have dry towels in the hotels now, instead of the pulpy-damp rag of former days, which shuddered you up like a cold poultice; and they have electrical buttons, now, instead of those crooked bell handles, which always tore your hand and made you break a lot of the commandments—all you could think of on a sudden call that way; and at table they feed you like a man and a brother, and don't bring you your dinner and spread it around your plate in a mass-meeting of soap-dishes; and you have the telephone instead of the petrified messenger boy. And then the new light. There was nothing like it when I was on the highway before. I was in Detroit last night and for the first time saw a city where the night was as beautiful as the day; saw for the first time the place of sallow twilight, bought at $3 a thousand feet, clusters of corruscating electric suns floating in the sky, without visible means of support and casting a mellow radiance upon the snow-covered spires and domes and roofs and far-stretching thorough-fares which gave to the spectacle the daintiness and delicacy of a picture and reminded one of airy unreal cities in the glimpses of a dream. Yes, the changes are great and marvelous and for number past enumeration.[10]

And then there was Congress. Reed was the sponsor of a bill to com-pensate a firm of Portland granite cutters for a loss it had borne on a gov-ernment job from years before. In the depression of the 1870s, Joseph Wescott & Son had aggressively bid on a federal contract to install a pair of staircases in the east wing of the new State, War and Navy Build-ing at Pennsylvania Avenue and 17th Street, in Washington (a wonder-ful old pile in the Second Empire style, known today as the Old Execu-tive Office Building). It was exacting work, as the design was spiral, and no one step was identical to another. In those hard times, the Wescott firm had bid just $15,000 to secure the work. It didn't hope to make a profit, Reed said, only to pay the help. And win it did, with plans, however, that significantly understated the scope of the project. Out of pocket by $10,000, the management of the company complained to the government supervisor, who promised an equitable sorting out of the claim when the work was done. But no compensation was forthcoming, though the government had paid $80,000 for work of similar scope on the same job. Wescott petitioned Reed, and Reed submitted a bill to reimburse the firm for a portion of the deficit, $3,468.[11]

This was four or five years before. The telephone, the transatlantic telegraph and the Bessemer steel rail had accelerated the pace of com-merce the world over, but the wit of man had done nothing to speed the passage of H.R. 3850. "Mr. Speaker," said Reed on February 10, 1883, in still another attempt to do right by his Portland constituents, "this bill was duly considered by the appropriations committee, was favorably reported, was considered and agreed to in the Committee of the Whole on the Private Calendar, and was passed there unanimously. All that I ask now is that it may have what may be termed its formal passage in the House. There was no objection to the bill; there can be none. It is not only equitable but it is legally correct. The only difficulty has been to get at it. I desire to have it passed now in order that it may reach the Senate in time to pass that body at this present session. It was before the last Congress, but was not reached, owing to the press of business. In the present Congress it was reached some two weeks ago, was carefully examined and fully explained, and no one found any objection to it." Not even William S. Holman, Democrat from Indiana, whose parsimony in the public's name earned him the sobriquet "Watchdog of the Treasury," was opposed. And so, at long last, there was justice, and a Treasury check, for Joseph Wescott & Son.[12]

Legislation to authorize construction of a new home for the overcrowded Library of Congress had a still longer period of gestation. The British had burned the first congressional reference library during the War of 1812. Thomas Jefferson had seeded a second with his personal collection of 6,487 volumes. By 1883, Jefferson's books had been augmented by more than 470,000 others, in addition to 150,000 pamphlets, the same number of musical works and a mass of photographs and engravings. The Library was literally bursting at the seams. Would Congress not spend the money to build a structure large enough to contain what was already on deposit and what would surely be deposited there in the decades and generations to come?

Congress would not. The people demanded lower taxes, not a literary cathedral. There could be no telling what the future would bring (or how many books the authors of tomorrow would write). "Let us," a Georgia Democrat, James H. Blount, urged, "take care of the present." Then too, there was lingering resentment among some of the members over the act of 1870 that required copyright applicants to send to the Library two copies of each work for which they sought protection. Not a few congressmen regretted that the taxpayers were committed to house this immense pile of material, half of which, estimated a representative from Maryland, was tripe.

But which half? Reed demanded of the members. "The half which the gentleman from Maryland does not like or the half which any other gentleman from the House does not like? Who is to determine?" Ordinarily, Reed would let his wit carry the argument, but his bibliophilic senses shocked him into uncharacteristic earnestness. "I say that in a great library no book is useless," he proceeded. "In a great library meant for a great nation every printed thing ought to be, and nothing pertaining to a library is out of place. What is trash in my library is not trash in the library of another man."[13]

Applause was the response to these high-toned remarks, but laughter was the more typical expression of the House's appreciation for Reed's forensic sallies. Three weeks after the Library of Congress debate, Reed was doing his best to promote a new federal subsidy for the shipping interests in which Maine happened to be so well endowed. Richard W. Townshend, an Illinois Democrat, had demolished the bill, and the premises on which it was written, arguing the matter from the perspective of free trade and free competition. "Mr. Speaker," said Reed, rising to rebut, "I do not purpose to take the present valuable time to answer the speech that has just been made. I could have answered that speech any time the last six years, and I apprehend I shall have the opportunity over the next two years. And making that speech I suppose must be of advantage, or else it would not be made. Only I can not quite understand why it should be made on this particular subject, to which it seems to have no special reference."[14] He was serenaded with laughter.

IN THE EARLY 1880s, the Democrats and Republicans clashed over what we today call globalization, but which they then called "the tariff." Did imported merchandise displace American products, jobs and profits? Should the United States be integrated into the world economy, or should it stand apart? In general, the Democratic party stood for unobstructed commerce with foreign nations, the Republicans for protective walls. "Free-trader" and "protectionist" were the epithets that the parties hurled at one another, each label utterly condemning in the eyes of the partisan who flung it. Reed, as partisan a Republican as any who sat in the House, loyally espoused protectionism, though he was too practical a politician to take that doctrine to its utmost illogical extreme.

The income tax, the all-too-familiar workhorse of 21st century federal finance, was an innovation of the Civil War; in antebellum times, the tariff was Washington's principal means of support. During economic expansions, imports into the United States provided a bounty of federal revenue, and the first seven years of the decade of the 1850s were just such a period of plenty. In 1850, the tariff brought in $39.7 million; in 1856, $64 million. In this period, there was a kind of national consensus: Duties should be set high enough to finance the government but not so high as to penalize foreign producers or to subsidize domestic ones. Congress, confident that the government was well provided for, voted a general reduction of duties in 1857. It fixed the maximum rate at 24 percent, while some kinds of imported goods—notably, raw materials—were admitted free. It was the closest the country would come to the ideal of free trade for the rest of the 19th century.[15]

It happened that the year of the passage of this enlightened legislation was a panic year. In the ensuing business depression, Americans imported fewer goods. Tariff receipts and the government's revenue accordingly fell. In 1857, tariff duties had brought in $64 million. But they yielded just $42 million in 1858 and $50 million in 1859. All at once, an apparent surplus of federal revenues gave way to a persistent shortfall. Justin S. Morrill, a Whig from Vermont, drew up legislation to solve not only that problem but also another. Higher customs duties, Morrill urged, would balance the federal books while furnishing needed protection for American industry.

Morrill, a so-called Conscience Whig, detested slavery but not that form of coercion that abridged the freedom of Americans to transact with foreigners. Vermont maple sugar and Vermont marble, for example, he regarded as products so innately precious as to deserve special federal protection. To that end, he held, the government, through the taxing power, should thwart the desire of any American who preferred Canadian syrup to Vermont syrup, or Italian marble to that produced in Morrill's own congressional district. Favored American products should be "nursed into perennial vigor by moderate and steady discrimination in their favor." So Morrill wrote a bill intended both to refill the Treasury and to nurture infant industries. No less an appraiser of fiscal legislation than John Sherman, the future Treasury Secretary, pronounced the bill a model of its kind—that is, as Morrill wrote it. "But," relates Ida Tarbell in her history of the tariff,

good as the bill may have been when it came from the committee, it was soon assaulted right and left by those who had something to protect or those who were affected by what it protected.
Much of the pressure, Mr. Morrill found, was impossible to resist.
What can you do when a Senator of the United States, one so
famous as Charles Sumner, "calls your attention" to letting cocoa
in free (though according to the principle on which you are
working it should pay a slight duty) because his friend, the head
of an "eminent house" . . . wants his cocoa free? What are you to
do when Pennsylvania iron men and Rhode Island manufacturers, who according to your theory of protection are established
and whose duties should gradually be lowered, come down on
you for higher rates, and your party colleagues tell you that if you
refuse their requests the election may be lost and the cause of
human freedom retarded?[16]

Morrill could not refuse, and his bill, heavily amended, passed the
House in May 1860. Next it was on to the Senate to face what seemed
certain burial. The Democratic party, which controlled the upper house,
flatly opposed protection. The southern wing of the party opposed it all
the more when it came with the imprimatur of the likes of the eman-
cipating Morrill. Though "Free trade and free men" would have made
a stirring campaign slogan, antebellum politics pitted one principle
against the other. If the federal government could protect one kind of
property, it could logically threaten another—slaves, for instance. One
of the earliest acts of the seceding states was to lay down a policy of
nonprotection: Tariffs, they declared in convention in Montgomery,
Alabama, in 1861, were for revenue only, not to enrich southern manufacturers (of which, in truth, there were but few).

It was Lincoln's election and the attack on Fort Sumter that
breathed new life into Morrill's pet legislation. As southern senators packed their bags to return to their seceding states, they gave the
Republicans a clear field in Washington. Unchecked, the new protectionist majority proceeded to festoon Morrill's bill with still more
amendments, including a 20 percent tariff on imported wooden screws.
The bestower of this gift, James F. Simmons of Rhode Island, happened
to represent the only state in the Union in which a wood-screw factory

was known to be situated—and in which the senator, thereafter known as "Wood-Screw Simmons," was "popularly supposed to be interested." America's trading partners protested, but President Buchanan, a Democrat elected on a free-trade platform, signed the bill that Morrill himself could hardly recognize.

The depression-induced deficits of 1858–60 were large enough to create the impetus for Morrill's new tariff schedules. The fiscal abyss of the Civil War set the stage for an entirely different order of things, indeed, for a preview of the modern American state. Before the war, the government taxed little and spent little. In the decades of the 1820s, 1830s and 1840s it spent no more than an average of $1.47 per year per capita. In the 1850s, it spent an average of $2.01 per year per capita. Then came the rebellion and its aftermath, and for 10 years, the government spent an average of $12.17 per year per capita.[17]

At first, the Lincoln administration was reluctant to impose taxes to fight a war that might be won in pleasantly short order. Bull Run and Shiloh forced a reconsideration of the timetable, and the government reached deep into the people's pockets. It instituted taxes on incomes (a maximum of 10 percent on incomes of $10,000 and up) and inheritances. It taxed legal documents, telegrams and safety matches, manufactured goods, luxuries and bare necessities. Tariff rates too went up, so as not to disadvantage the heavily taxed American producers. In 1864, the duties reached an average of 47 percent, a rate even higher than that imposed by the Tariff of Abominations of 1828, which so mightily contributed to making John Quincy Adams (like his father) a one-term president. It was a punitive rate but a temporary one, Congress and the administration insisted. It would come down with the peace.[18] "I regard all our present legislation as temporary or provisional in its character," said Massachusetts Senator Charles Sumner in response to a colleague's observation that American producers seemed to be getting awfully comfortable behind the wartime tariff wall.[19]

Came the peace, however, and the wall remained standing. There was no choice, the politicians now declared. The public debt, totaling almost $2.8 billion, must be honorably discharged. There were widows to pension, armies to disband and ships to decommission. There could be no immediate return to the antebellum bliss of low, or nonexistent, internal taxes and tariffs.[20]

In fact, excise taxes on domestic manufacturers were soon rolled back, in most cases eliminated. Not so the tariff—that is, the protective tariff. In 1872, Congress did see fit to eliminate the imposts on coffee and tea. And it reduced, in the same year, by a flat 10 percent, a host of protective duties. Both of these actions were properly counted victories for Republican principles. Coffee and tea, produced outside the United States, had yielded a handsome customs revenue to the government. Each dollar of tariff duty paid on those indispensable beverages had accrued to the Treasury. The duties on coffee and tea were of a different class than protective duties on items that Americans themselves produced. There was no domestic coffee- and tea-growing industry to protect.

There were, however, domestic manufacturers of books, cotton goods, linen, gloves, pottery, glass, steel, paper, et cetera, and they clamored for protection. Duties slapped on such items were, of course, paid to the Treasury. But the Treasury was not the only beneficiary of the tax. The American producers themselves were recipients of an indirect bounty. Encumbered by customs duties, imported merchandise cost more than it would have cost in the absence of the tariff. Observant American manufacturers did not fail to raise their prices higher to reflect the full tariff-inflated price of competing imports. And so the tariff was, in effect, paid twice: once by the importer, and a second time by the consumer. The importer paid his tribute to the government, the consumer to the protected American businessman.

Republican theorists retorted that this criticism failed to reckon with the lucky employees of the protected manufacturers. Americans earned good wages, the argument went, because sound Republican policy protected their livelihoods from the pauperized labor of such benighted lands as Canada.

One could imagine a nation that took the Republican gospel of protection to its limit, the free-traders replied, one that prohibited trade with every foreign people, relying, instead, on its own resources for all it consumed. Such a nation would resemble the farmer who made his own plow, the blacksmith who set his own broken arm or the lawyer who cut down the timber with which to manufacture his own paper. By setting aside the common-sense principle of buying from others what one could not easily make oneself, society would be busier, certainly—but also considerably poorer. No individual, family, town, county, state or region would choose to live this way, "like snails, each in [their] own shell." Nor would a right-thinking nation.

The champion expositor of these ideas was the Frenchman Frederic Bastiat (1801–1850). In logic, humor, clarity of expression and simplicity of argument, Bastiat was unsurpassed. The Democrats delighted in quoting him in congressional debate. The Republicans, having no ready answer for Bastiat's arguments, were reduced to pointing out that he was, indeed, French. Reed, who by the early 1880s was devoting his leisure hours to a serious program of French-language study, seemed to abjure that particular line of attack on Bastiat's ideas. Nor could he easily have refuted the Frenchman's logic.

It would be a pleasure to be able to relate that Reed's piercing intelligence led him to abandon his party on the protective tariff, as he subsequently left it on imperialism. That he did not was no fault of the persuasive economist. "A tariff, then," Bastiat observed in his free-trade masterpiece, *Economic Sophisms*, published in two installments in the late 1840s, "may be regarded in the same light as a marsh, a rut, an obstruction, a steep declivity—in a word, as an *obstacle*, the effect of which is to augment the difference between the price the producer of a commodity receives and the price the consumer pays for it. In the same way, it is undoubtedly true that marshes and quagmires are to be regarded in the same light as protective tariffs."[21]

Eliminating obstructions in time and space was the essential work of such inventors as Bell. Reed gloried in their achievements. And though the congressman was only too happy to participate in a Republican filibuster when the Democrats were in power, the political cause to which he largely devoted himself was the removal of parliamentary obstructions in the House of Representatives. When it came to trade between nations, however, Reed joined his colleagues in marsh-making, rut-digging and obstruction-building, though—let it be said on his behalf— others in his party made more obstacles than he did.

But not even the high-protection element could easily defend the patchwork of taxes and tariffs in place in the decade and a half before 1880. Americans had not forgotten that the duties of 1864 were imposed for the duration of an emergency that had ended in 1865. Nor had it slipped their minds that the Panic of 1873 had occurred in a time of high protection. Adherents of the protective doctrine had taught that such dislocations as that of 1857–59 (let alone those of 1873–79) were the consequences of low tariffs. Neither was it lost on students of the census that the decade of the 1850s, with its moderate tariffs, showed stronger growth—in employment, wages and capital employed, among other vital signs—than that of the 1870s, with its sky-high tariffs.[22]

As trade revived in 1879 and 1880, so did customs receipts. And as the government's coffers filled to overflowing, so did the demand for tariff relief. In response to the demand for lower and more equitable taxation, a Tariff Commission was empanelled in 1881. The free-traders held out no high hopes for the impartiality of this creation of a Republican (therefore protectionist) administration. Indeed, it was chaired by the protection-procuring lobbyist for the wool interests, and it called such witnesses as Joseph Wharton, the Philadelphia nickel-and-steel magnate and University of Pennsylvania philanthropist, whose very net worth was testament to the sweets that a tariff might inequitably bestow. There were, however, 603 other witnesses, some of whom, buyers of Wharton's protected nickel, wanted to know why the government was making him rich at their expense.

When, in December 1882, the commission submitted its report, lobbyists for the protected industries gasped. They had hung by the elbows of the commissioners. Over dinner and at the theater, they had patiently refuted the free-trade arguments put forth by such otherworldly theorists as William Graham Sumner. Yet the commissioners did not do what the lobbyists had been paid to assure that they would do. They did not recommend a mere token trimming in rates but rather a cut on the order of 20 percent to 25 percent. "[E]xcept for the establishment of new industries which more than equalize the conditions of labor and capital with those of foreign competitors," the report said in summary, "protective tariff rates were indefensible."[23]

As troubling for the high protectionists was the annual message of the president himself. "The present tariff system is in many ways unjust," wrote Chester A. Arthur, also in December 1882. "It makes unequal distributions both of its burdens and benefits." Arthur, a committed protectionist who had overseen customs operations at New York for seven years, "knew much from close contact of the ambiguities, the frauds, the injustice of the duties then in force," as Ida Tarbell puts it. Professor Sumner of Yale might be dismissed as a builder of intellectual air castles, but not the longtime collector of the Port of New York.[24]

If the House did not hear the president's foot impatiently tapping for remedial action, it could not have missed the electorate's. In the just-completed 1882 congressional canvass, the people had given the Democrats a clear majority in the House. Come December 1883, with the start of the first session of the 48th Congress, protection would therefore become the minority doctrine on the House floor. It behooved the Republicans to act while they had the votes.

It was February 3 when "Pig Iron" Kelley of Pennsylvania rose to lead the assault. Topic A was the duty on glassware, 50 percent on a simple tumbler.[25] Samuel Cox, a New York Democrat, pointed out that while human beings could enter the United States at will, inanimate objects were stopped at the doors of the custom house. Cox had wit and learning—he knew his Bastiat—and he was a dangerous opponent in debate.

Why, said the Democrat, waving some information supplied by an import house, a tariff of no less than 110 percent was collected on 1.3 million square feet of window glass. By taxing it, the government was effectively taxing sunshine. Did the House not know the Bastiat parable about the French candle-makers who petitioned the government to build a roof over France so to block out the free daylight? Many members groaned, but Cox spelled out the moral of the story: It was "almost a prohibition on Heaven's sunlight."

"Oh, no," countered a Michigan Republican, Roswell G. Horr.

"Oh, yes," retorted Cox.

"Who is this author?" asked Horr.

"He is a Frenchman," replied Cox.

"Do you go abroad for your authors as well as for your facts?" Horr demanded.

"I go wherever there is sunlight; wherever I can find a tallow dip or ray, in Michigan or anywhere. . . . If I could get my friend from Michigan [Mr. Horr] in some sort of a condition where I could put a wick into him I would illuminate this great country from Maine to the Gulf! [Great laughter and applause.]"

Interjected Reed: "If the gentleman from New York illuminates anything it will have to be by the aid of the gentleman from Michigan, as he seems incapable of doing it alone. [Laughter]"[26]

To Kelley, protection was a system of "exquisite harmony."[27] Reed omitted the beatific flourishes. In answer to cries from conservation-minded Democrats that the lumber tariff was denuding American forests, the man from the Pine Tree State answered, "Why, sir, the very purpose of forests in the economy of nature is to be cut down and have houses built out of them. . . . I tell you each generation can take care of itself; each generation is sufficient unto itself."[28]

As to the theory of the tariff, Reed espoused the straight Republican line. He argued, no more convincingly than others in his party, that big countries, unlike small ones, had nothing to gain by making the things they could make most cheaply, and buying from other nations the things they could not advantageously produce. "I tell you, gentlemen," Reed told the House, "the people of this country are in favor of giving to the whole people, the farmers, the manufacturers and every one else, the markets of this country. The great sophism of Bastiat is he always argues about what would be the effect if the city of Paris were cut off from the rest of the world. It would be as preposterous to ask Paris to supply all its own wants as to ask any single family; and that is always his argument. But when he and his imitators persist in reasoning by analogy from Paris to a great country like this with everything in it, he and they palm off worse sophisms than he ever pretended to expose."[29]

Though widely read in French authors, Reed seemed to draw the line at Bastiat. On equally distant terms with the French free-market theorist was the Arkansas Democrat Poindexter Dunn, with whom Reed locked horns 10 days later. Let the manufacturers of farm implements be compensated for the tariffs they pay on the raw materials they import, Dunn proposed; the Treasury should make it up to them. Somehow, Dunn insisted, this would help the poor farmer.

Reed wanted to know how.

The implement makers would be better off. Maybe they could reduce the price of their wares, Dunn replied.

"Then it does not go to the agriculturalist?" Reed persisted.

"I have no doubt it will reach him," Dunn unconvincingly replied.

It sounded to Reed as if the farmer would receive something less than a cheap plow in the bargain. Perhaps something more in the nature of a colored lithograph of a plow. The members laughed at Dunn's expense.

"The gentleman from Maine attempts to be facetious as he always does when he finds himself unable to oppose a just measure by fair argument—which he seldom attempts," Dunn shot back. "This is a question that has to be met and voted upon here, and the country will not be deceived by any exhibition of the gentleman's attempted wit, and if he attempts to get over it in that way he will find himself very much mistaken."

"The gentleman from Arkansas is very much mistaken if he imagines the country is paying any attention to this kind of performance," Reed replied.

Dunn drove ahead in the same vein. Reed, he said, was flippant because he could not be serious. "We all know his habit in that respect. He often essays the role of the funny man for that side of the House. . . . Let me advise him to abandon it. It does not become him. His efforts in that character do not comport with our ideas of the 'fitness of things.' His tonnage is too great for such a light character."

"The gentleman's time has expired," Reed reminded him, "and I have the floor; and I want to say it is an improvement to the floor."[30]

For all of Dunn's earnestness and all of Reed's wit, the House could not pass a tariff bill. It had, however, enacted a measure to reduce internal taxes—high time, all agreed, as the government was running a $100 million budget surplus. The case for tariff reform found a better reception in the Senate. Taking to heart the recommendations of the Tariff Commission, the upper house enacted wide-ranging reductions in import duties. This bill it sent to the House, where, in Reed's judgment, "a lingering death awaited it."

Everything was wrong with it. The 47th Congress was due to expire on March 3—the bill had arrived in late February. The Republican majority, though it knew the country expected lower tariffs, resisted enacting them. And, not least, the Senate had had the impertinence to write its own tariff bill. In the House was reposed the constitutional power to originate revenue bills, and this privilege the members jealously guarded. Anticipating protest from the lower chamber, the senators had presented their tariff bill as an amendment to the previously passed House measure to reduce internal, or domestic, taxes. The members were unplaced, however, and they delivered long addresses on the constitutional infringement of the tribunes of privilege and property on the representatives of the people. Reed admitted that he too had been tempted to gather up his learning and hold forth in this manner. However, he said on February 27,

> I intend but to make a simple statement. And that is, that I believe from the precedents and my study of the Constitution that the Senate has transcended its power in the bill it has sent to us. I had intended to go to some length to prove this from precedents, from the history of the formation of the Constitution, and from general principles in a manner which would be satisfactory to me at least if not to others. But I am about to perform a great act of generosity to the House and to the community. I am going to omit that speech; and the omission is the more singular favor because such an opportunity in the common course of events seldom happens to a man more than once in his lifetime. Anticipating the gratitude of both the House and of future generations, I call for the previous question. [Laughter.][31]

Reed was speaking in support of an ingenious new rule of the Rules Committee's devising. Under the existing rule, a two-thirds vote was required to bring the Senate bill before the House. Such a majority was not to be had. Under the rule Reed proposed, a simple majority could decide to consider the measure. But the rule was like nothing else the members had heard of. It said that a bare majority could take up a bill amended by the Senate but only for the purpose of disagreeing with its amendments. That is to say, the House would force disagreement.*

---

* The rule stated: "That during the remainder of this session it shall be in order at any time to move or suspend the rules, which motion shall be decided by a majority vote, to take from the Speaker's table House Bill No. 5538, with the Senate amendment thereto, entitled a bill to Reduce Internal Revenue Taxation, and to declare a disagreement with the Senate amendment to the same, and to ask for a committee of conference thereon, to be composed of five members on the part of the House. If such motion shall fail, the bill shall remain on the Speaker's table unaffected by the decision of the House on said motion."

Just barely, the rule passed, for the Democrats sat mum during the vote, forming themselves into a disappearing quorum. The Washington *Post* blamed Reed for this "Revolutionary Scheme," as its headline writer put it, which the Democrats, and a few bolting Republicans, had "Most Righteously Resisted." Though Reed did not himself write the rule, he did present it on the floor. The New York *Times*, so admiring of the parliamentary ingenuity that he had displayed in speeding disputed-election cases to a vote, had no use for this "preposterous and unprecedented" creation.[32]

What had Reed and his rules-writing colleagues wrought? They had sent the Senate tariff measure to a 10-man conference committee, of whom seven were high protectionists. The conferees thereupon set to work picking apart the work of the Tariff Commission. Thus, the experts had proposed a rate of 50 cents a ton on iron ore. The House and the Senate had agreed to it. The conferees, however, saw fit to raise that duty to 75 cents a ton.[33] Yet the five congressmen and five senators also saw fit to reduce certain wool duties, much to the distress of the representatives of the wool-gathering states. "I have voted with the protectionists of Pennsylvania and the protectionists of New England," cried Representative James S. Robinson, a Republican from Ohio, "with the assurance—the most positive assurance—that this great interest I represent should be taken care of . . . and you have stricken us down."[34]

The "mongrel tariff bill of 1883," its critics called it, and the name was supremely apt. There was no rhyme or reason to it, except as a testament to political influence in tariff legislation. In the Senate, where the original tariff measure passed by a 42–19 margin, the conference-mauled successor barely slipped through on a strict party vote, 32–31. John Sherman, the archprotectionist from Ohio, voted aye but sorely regretted it. Either every industry deserved to be protected or none did, he finally came to decide. President Arthur signed the bill only minutes before Congress adjourned on March 3, 1883.[35]

To Reed, the bill was "as brilliant a parliamentary maneuver as was ever made." It had "drawn the teeth of the Free Traders for years." It was, above all, a triumph of technique, though not—it is only fair to say—of statesmanship.[36]

Chapter 12

Votes for Women

DELEGATES TO THE annual convention of the National Woman Suffrage Association converged on Washington in the first week of March 1884 to present their petitions in support of a constitutional amendment to break the male voting monopoly. Gallant condescension was the attitude struck by the House and Senate committees that received them on these occasions. The suffragists had been at it for 15 years—this year marked the 16th—and for just that long had achieved no result more substantial than a pat on the head.[1]

As usual, the visiting ladies encountered chivalrous adversaries: President Arthur would receive them at the White House, and the Senate would convene a special committee to hear their petitions.[2] Perhaps, as in 1872 and 1876, the Republican party would consent to drop a few lines into the national platform expressing the hope that women might one day receive their due at the polling place. Nor was it out of the question that a committee of the House or Senate would draft a report urging constructive action on the proposed 16th amendment. Indeed, Ben Butler was the coauthor of just such a brief as long ago as 1871.[3] But the American male of 1884 was no readier to relinquish his control of the ballot than was his father or grandfather. For that matter, neither did most women seem any closer to demanding that men surrender their ancient prerogative.

Yet the suffrage movement drove on. Some of its members had fought for the abolition of slavery, and they knew something about brickbats and derision. It was, indeed, they believed, no exaggeration to liken the plight of women in 1884 to that of the slaves in 1861. The suffragists' moral certainty sustained them, but so too did the unmistakable, if incremental, signs of progress in the lot of the American woman. Long gone were the days when, as Julia B. Foraker reminisced, a woman's only two choices in a career were "the home and invalidism."[4]

In 1848, the year Elizabeth Cady Stanton helped to lead a few hundred like-minded radicals at Seneca Falls, New York, to bring to light the subjugation of women, the right to vote was far from the top of the feminist agenda. There were more basic injustices to redress. In marriage, a woman was a nullity, "civilly dead" under the law (as she was in France under the Napoleonic Code). She was barred from enrolling in college, let alone from teaching in one. She had no voice in church affairs (the Quakers were an exception on this point). If divorced—for reasons that men alone judged actionable—the courts might take her children away from her. Stanton had enumerated these grievances, and many others, in the manner of the Declaration of Independence, with American males *en masse* substituting for King George III. Stanton, after Jefferson, concluded her Declaration of Sentiments: "Now, in view of this entire disenfranchisement of one-half of the people of this country, their social and religious degradation—in view of the unjust laws above mentioned, and because women feel themselves aggrieved, oppressed and fraudulently deprived of their most sacred rights, we insist that they have immediate admission to all the rights and privileges which belong to them as citizens of the United States."[5]

Not immediately, but gradually, the disenfranchised were gaining a measure of satisfaction. It had taken five years of argument and an act of Congress besides, but Belva A. Lockwood had been admitted to practice before the Supreme Court, the first woman so elevated. "You ought to see Belva," a male newspaper correspondent wrote to his readers in Cleveland. ". . . Strong and healthy in spite of her years [she was in her mid-50s], she can make 10 miles an hour on the tricycle she rides daily to and from her office."[6] In Illinois, to pick only one state, women were holding jobs as school superintendents, cabinet makers, physicians, lawyers (a grand total of two of them were practicing in Chicago), real estate agents, journalists and preachers.[7]

It can't be said that the national government supplied the impetus for this remarkable change in mores; rather, women were making their way in the world almost despite the laws and the courts. The 14th Amendment to the Constitution, ratified in 1868, went so far as to write sexual discrimination into the federal canon by promising the protection of the law to "male" inhabitants, age 21 or older, at polling places for national elections. It didn't mention the other sex.

Women, however, were finding their own voice. Mrs. Virginia Minor, a citizen of Missouri, sued the registrar of voters who had refused to allow her to cast her ballot in the 1872 election. Did the 14th Amendment not prohibit a state from making or enforcing a law denying any person equal protection of the laws? It certainly read that way to her, and she took her case to the Supreme Court. There, however, the masculine American legal mind resoundingly held for the sexual status quo. In 1875, in *Minor v. Happersett*, the Court unanimously affirmed that it fell to the states to determine who might vote, that citizenship alone conferred no right to vote and that, therefore, "the constitutions and laws of the several states which commit that important trust to men alone are not necessarily void."[8]

This was just as it should be, most Americans seemed to agree. When, in 1884, Representative John H. Reagan, a Texas Democrat, attacked the measure to establish a special House committee to hear the plea of the suffragists to amend the Constitution, he spoke for a smug congressional majority. In the absence of that uncommissioned suffrage committee, the matter was handed off to the Judiciary Committee, on which sat Thomas B. Reed.[9]

On the tariff, Reed spoke the party line, but he was his own man on suffrage. Liberty was for all, he affirmed, not just for one sex. He had another reason to support the cause of women's emancipation: In no political context could he abide the pretensions of a would-be ruling class. It was not just the white man's violation of Indian treaties that he opposed in his freshman year in Congress, but also the theft of tribal lands dressed up in highfalutin language. "I am glad, at least," he said, "to see that there is grace enough left in this matter to sugar it over with pleasant phraseology. I am glad to see that no member of this House makes a proposition to take land away from people who own it unless he can convince his mind that the handsome phrase 'march of civilization' will cover the occasion as well as the country."[10]

By the same token, the Maine Republican heaped scorn on the attempts by certain southern Democrats to codify Jim Crow into the new interstate commerce legislation of the mid-1880s. "Nothing in this act contained shall be construed as to prevent any railroad company from providing separate accommodations for white and colored persons," was one offending amendment. To its author, Charles F. Crisp, a former teenage lieutenant in the Virginia infantry, the amendment was reason itself. It would in no way coerce the railroads into segregating the races. Rather, it would simply not require them to integrate the races. As it was, a black passenger holding a first-class ticket on a railroad journey originating in, say, Washington, and terminating in, say, Tallahassee, suffered a humiliating experience at the first station stop in Georgia. He or she was rousted out of his or her carriage and directed to a Jim Crow car for the duration of the ride through Georgia. The blacks-only car was typically the one hooked just behind the smoke-belching locomotive.[11]

Perhaps the Crisp amendment lacked delicacy. In its place, Clifton R. Breckinridge, an Arkansas Democrat, proposed that "nothing in this act shall be construed to deny to railroads the right to classify passengers as they may deem best for the public comfort and safety, or to relate to transportation between points wholly within the limits of one state." Breckinridge's indirection was, to Reed, a still greater provocation than Crisp's crudity. At least Crisp's bigotry had the courage of its convictions. After the man from Arkansas said his piece, Reed said his, expressing, first, his sarcastic approbation of the alternative amendment. A good thing it was that color and politics were out of the issue, which "has now become a question of assortment [laughter]; and now this House, which is determined to pursue these 'robber barons,' has before it the plain question whether it will not merely leave to them the privilege of assorting us, but whether it will absolutely confer upon them also the privilege of assortment by direct enactment on the part of Congress. [Renewed laughter.]

"Now," Reed went on,

I appeal to this House, engaged as it is in the pursuit of wicked monopolists, if it intends to confer upon them a privilege of assortment without rights by law? Why, surely we must have some Treasury regulations as to the method of assortment. [Laughter.] Are we to be assorted on the ground of size? [Great laughter.] Am I to be put in one car on account of my size and the gentleman from Arkansas into another because of his? [Renewed laughter and applause.] Is this to be done on account of our unfortunate difference of measurement? Or are we to be assorted on the mustache ground? Are we to be assorted on the question of complexion, or are we to be assorted on the beard basis?

If not any of these, what basis of assortment are we to have? For my part I object to having these 'robber barons' overlook and assort us on any whimsical basis they may undertake to set up. [Laughter.] Why, surely, Mr. Speaker, this House, engaged as it is in putting down discrimination against good men, can not tolerate itself an amendment of this character for an instant. [Applause.][12]

The Breckinridge amendment passed notwithstanding.

AS FOR DISCRIMINATION against women, the position of the Republican party was one of mollification, as the suffragists themselves did not need to be reminded. Stanton, some years earlier, had complained that her sisters and she had been sitting "on a limb of the Republican tree singing 'suffrage if you please,' like so many insignificant hummingbirds, long enough."[13] The male heirs of Abraham Lincoln were quite content to preen themselves on having "established universal suffrage" and "justice, perfect liberty and perfect equality for all," as if one-half of the adult American population did not somehow fall under the meaning of the word "universal."[14]

So the Judiciary Committee went through the motions of receiving the annual petitions of the revolutionaries in bonnets and petticoats.

Emma McRae of Indiana testified that women needed the vote to protect themselves and their families. Miss Jessie T. Waite of Illinois complained that, without the vote, women were powerless against the liquor interests. Mrs. Catherine A. Stebbins of Michigan speculated that, if they could vote, women could "bring a moral power to bear that shall make war needless."[15] As for the prevalent argument that women should not be exposed to the rough masculine edges of the polling place, Mrs. Elizabeth L. Saxon, of Louisiana, observed that, at home, when a cesspool backs up, it's the woman of the house who gets out the scrub brush and carbolic acid. "[A]nd, as they did this in private life, they would prove equally effective in scouring up the foul places in public life."[16]

Perhaps Mrs. Lillie Devereaux Blake of New York looked meaningfully at Reed when she recalled the attempted hijacking of the Maine gubernatorial election in 1879 by Alonzo Garcelon and his Democrats-and-Greenbacker alliance. It was surely a great wrong, she sympathized, that the people of Maine were denied the opportunity to express their will at the polls. If, then, the committeemen had nodded in agreement, Mrs. Blake would have had them where she wanted them. "Why, gentlemen," she pressed on, "I assert that a majority of the people of Maine have never been permitted to express their will at the polls. A majority of the people of Maine are women, and, from the foundation of the government to this day, have never been permitted to exercise any of the inalienable rights of citizens"[17] The famous Susan B. Anthony called the committeemen's attention to the sexual inequity in federal civil service work. Women, being voteless, were powerless against the males who could exchange their votes for jobs. "The tide is moving," she told them, "it cannot be swept back. I beg you, in the name of justice, humanity and mercy, that you will not keep woman coming back here for the next 30 years as she has been kept coming for the last 30 years."[18] (Perhaps, to her, it seemed like 30 years.)

It fell to one of the younger members of the Judiciary Committee, 35-year-old William C. Maybury, Democrat from Michigan, to remind the ladies of their place. A product of the University of Michigan Law School, Maybury brushed aside the constitutional arguments of the suffrage proponents as blithely as the Supreme Court had done in *Minor*. The amendments to the Constitution enacted after the Civil War to protect the emancipated slaves, he wrote, were necessary to protect the former slaves against their former masters. Surely, there was no meaningful analogy between free American women and benevolent American men. Chivalry and the generosity of spirit of the male were all the protection that women required, wrote Maybury on behalf of the committee's majority. Women in the same boat as the former slaves? "Woman is not the slave, but the companion, of man," he corrected the emancipationists.

> Her duties are as noble as his, though widely differing. Her true sphere is not restricted, but is boundless in resources and consequences. In it she may employ every energy of the mind and every affection of the heart, while within its limitless compass, under Providence, she exercises power and influence beyond all other agencies for good. She trains and guides the life that is, and forms it for the eternity and immortality that are to be. From the rude contact of life, man is her shield. He is her guardian from its conflicts. He is the defender of her rights in the home, and the avenger of her wrongs everywhere. In the shadow of this defense not only is she shielded and protected, but in it man himself is permitted to play his most exalted part in the social economy. The Christian system conserves the peace and harmony of their home and invests with sacred solemnity their relations of man and wife.

Then too, Maybury observed, it was by no means clear what kind of woman would avail herself of the vote if that privilege were accorded to her. His colleagues and he feared the worst: "[Y]our committee are of the opinion that while a few intelligent women, such as appeared before the committee in advocacy of the pending measure, would defy all obstacles in the way of casting the ballot, yet the great mass of the intelligent, refined and judicious, with the becoming modesty of their sex, would shrink from the rude contact of the crowd, and, with the exemptions mentioned, leaving the ignorant and vile the exclusive right to speak for the gentler sex in public affairs."

Reed was one of only four committeemen who recoiled at the majority's findings, and he took it upon himself to draft a dissenting brief.

One evening at home in Washington, he read this document aloud to his wife. Susan Reed, no suffragist, curled up on the sofa to listen "with every expression of scorn and disgust," as Reed interpreted her body language. He began reading, thus:

No one who listens to the reasons given by the superior class for the continuance of any system of subjugation can fail to be impressed by the noble disinterestedness of mankind. When the subjection of persons of African dissent was to be maintained, the good of those persons was always the main object. When it was the fashion to beat children, to regard them as little animals who had no rights, it was always for their good that they were treated with severity, and never on account of the bad temper of their parents. Hence, when it is proposed to give to the women of this country an opportunity to present their case to the various State legislatures to demand of the people of the country equality of political rights, it is not surprising to find that the reasons on which the continuance of the inferiority of women is urged, are drawn almost entirely from a tender consideration of their own good. The anxiety felt lest they should thereby deteriorate, would be an honor to human nature were it not for an historical fact that the same sweet solicitude has been put up as a barrier against every progress which women have made ever since civilization began. There is no doubt today that if in Turkey or Algiers, countries where women's sphere is most thoroughly confined to the home circle, it was proposed to admit them to social life, to remove the veil from their faces and permit them to converse in open day with the friends of their husbands and brothers, the conservative and judicious Turk or Algerine of the period, if he could be brought to even consider such a horrible proposition, would point out that the sphere of women was to make the home happy by those gentle insipidities which education would destroy; that by participation in conversations with men, they would learn coarseness, debase their natures and men would thereby lose that ameliorating influence which still leaves them unfit to associate with women. He would point out that "nature" had determined that women should be secluded; that their sphere was to raise and educate the man child and that any change would be a violation of the divine law which, in the opinion of all conservative men, always ordains the present but never the future.

So in civilized countries when it was proposed that women should own their own property, that they should have the earnings of their own labor, there were not wanting those who were sure that such a proposition could work only evil to women, and that continually. It would destroy the family, discordant interests would provoke dispute and the only real safety for woman was in the headship of man, not that man wanted superiority for any selfish reason, but to preserve intact the family relation for woman's good. Today a woman's property belongs to herself; her earnings are her own; she has been emancipated beyond the wildest hopes of any reformer of twenty-five years ago. Almost every vocation is open to her. She is proving her usefulness in spheres which the "nature" worshiped by the conservative of twenty-five years ago undoubtedly forbade her to enter. Notwithstanding all these changes the family circle remains unbroken, the man child gets as well educated as before and the ameliorating influence of woman has become only the more marked. Thirty years ago hardly any political assemblage of the people was graced by the presence of women. Had it needed a law to enable them to be present, what an argument could have been made against it! How easily it could have been shown that the coarseness, the dubious expressions, the general vulgarity of the scene, could have had no other effect than to break down that purity of word and thought which women have, and which conservative and radical, are alike sedulous to preserve. And yet the actual presence of women at political meetings has not debased them, but has raised the other sex. Coarseness has not become diffused through both sexes but has fled from both. To put the whole matter in a short phrase: The association of the sexes in the family circle, in society and in business, having proved improving to both, there is neither history, reason, nor sense to justify the assertion that association in politics will lower the one or demoralize the other.

Mrs. Reed might have seen this coming years ago. Her husband had revealed strong feminist leanings while prosecuting Edward Hoswell for the murder of Mrs. Hoswell's putative lover, John B. Laflin, in 1870. Back then, as Maine attorney general, Reed had scoffed at a long-encrusted body of precedent that treated the wife of the jealous husband as if she were an idiot, a child or a doll, and the husband as if he were God's own avenging angel. Curled up in her disapproving ball, Mrs. Reed fixed her eye on the author of the draft of the Judiciary Committee's minority report. "Hence," Reed continued,

we would do better to approach the question without trepidation. We can better leave the "sphere" of woman to the future than confine it in the chains of the past. Words change nothing. Prejudices are none the less prejudices because we vaguely call them "nature" and prate about what nature has forbidden when we only mean that the thing we are opposing has not been hitherto done. "Nature" forbade a steamship to cross the Atlantic the very moment it was, and yet it arrived just the same. What the majority call "nature" has stood in the way of every progress of the past and present, and will stand in the way of all future progress. It has also stood in the way of many unwise things. It is only another name for conservatism. With conservatism the minority have no quarrel. It is essential to the stability of mankind, or government and of social life. To every new proposal it rightfully calls a halt, demanding a countersign, whether it be friend or foe. The enfranchisement of women must pass the ordeal like everything else. It must give good reason for its demand to be or take its place among the half-forgotten fantasies which have challenged the support of mankind and have not stood the test of argument and discussion.

Is suffrage a right or a privilege? Reed went on to ask. That is, can one man govern another "except to the extent that the other man has

a right to govern him"? If the answer was no, the discussion was ended.
If suffrage was the right of one sex, it must be the right of the other. If
man needed the vote to protect his life, liberty and property, so, equally,
did woman. With this, Reed went off on a slightly different tack. It too
would have been familiar to Mrs. Reed:

> Our government is founded, not on the rule of the wisest and
> best, but upon the rule of all. The ignorant, the learned, the wise
> and the unwise, the judicious and the injudicious are all invited
> to assist in governing, upon the broad principle that the best
> government for mankind is not the government which the wis-
> est and best would select, but that which the average of mankind
> would select. Laws are daily enacted, not because they seem the
> wisest even to those legislators who enacted them, but because
> they represent what the whole people wish. And, in the long
> run, it may be just as bad to enact laws in advance of public senti-
> ment as to hold on to laws behind it.

Mrs. Reed was not persuaded, but her husband had not given up. The
next morning, she sailed into him for expressing his support of a certain
candidate for the presidency that year (enticingly, in Reed's account of
this exchange, the politician goes unnamed). Reed affected shock: "I
pointed out to *her* midly but firmly that there was an obvious impropriety in advice coming from a person disqualified by [her] sex from having
opinions on such subjects directed to one who was simply by reason of
his sex so entirely superior—that he alone was fit to participate in the
selection of a President. This evening she came to the conclusion that
she always thought there were some women who were fitted to decide
such questions etc. Such progress cheers one on the long road which
will finally lead to emancipation."[19]

But on that road, as Reed advised Anthony on subsequent occasions,
she could expect no overt political help from him.[20] When the time for
female suffrage finally arrived, the politicians would be fairly falling over
themselves to get behind it. They would not lead the movement—politicians never led any movement—but would rather follow the progress
in public opinion. Cynic though he often seemed to be, Reed believed

devoutly in the existence of that progress. Individuals might hold fast to bigotry and superstition, but society was irresistibly shaking loose from it.

He was vindicated soon in at least one particular. In February 1887, 153 Portland ladies signed a "remonstrance" against women suffrage on the ground that the ballot would "impair the integrity of their devotion to their domestic duties, and will deteriorate the character and consideration which give them the influence they now exert in society." Susan Reed's name was not among the petitioners.[21]

Chapter 13

"Monumental liar from the state of Maine"

R EED QUOTED WITH approval the witticism of Senator John James Ingalls, a Republican from Kansas, that "each party was trying to cheat the other and that both would be successful."[1] Perhaps the American people agreed—at no point during the first decade and a half of Reed's political career did the voters entrust both the executive and legislative branches of government to either the Republicans or the Democrats.[2] If the political history of the period lacks revolutionary drama, it's because neither party was in a position to effect a revolution.

That is, a political revolution. A revolution in industry, agriculture, commerce, science, technology and demography was hurtling on quite without reference to the legislative agenda in Washington. As a source of discontinuity and disruption to the familiar patterns of American life, nothing that Congress did could compare with the inventions of Thomas A. Edison, George Pullman or Alexander Graham Bell. Nor could mere politics compare in national consequence to the great human tide of the early 1880s. Between 1881 and 1886, almost three million immigrants made their way to America. In the 12 months through June 30, 1882, there were 788,992 new arrivals, a mass of humanity equivalent to the populations of Colorado, Delaware, Nevada, Oregon and Rhode Island.

The Founding Fathers might still have recognized the federal government of the mid-1880s as the modest enterprise they envisioned in 1787. Clerks were clattering away on typewriters, and the Patent Office was a museum of modern marvels, but the income tax, that indispensable prop of the superstate, had been kicked away in 1870. Law-abiding Americans had little to do with the federal apparatus, nor it with them. The government delivered the mails, maintained the federal courts, battled the Indians, examined the nationally chartered banks, fielded the army, floated the navy and coined the currency.

Reed arraigned the Democratic party as obstructionist and reactionary, so different from the party of progress, his own. A concomitant of national progress, he believed, was an energetic national government. It was a government, for example, that paid its diplomats a living wage, erected a public building worthy of the Library of Congress, subsidized the American merchant marine and protected domestic industry from the "pauper" wages prevailing in those benighted countries beyond the seas (and, indeed, in the dominion due north). In resisting such reasonable applications of federal power, he charged, the Democrats were stunting the nation's growth. The Democrats replied that the Republicans' objective was not so much the growth of the nation as that of the GOP. Under cover of a national emergency, the Lincoln administration had suspended habeas corpus and printed up hundreds of millions of paper dollars with not an ounce of gold or silver to back them. Now that same party, 20 years after Fort Sumter, was perverting federal powers to maintain an unnatural and corrupting regime of one-party rule. Was the Democracy the party of obstruction? The Democrats half conceded the point. Yes, they said, they were obstructing the government in Washington from trespassing on the powers that the Constitution had reserved for the states. Republicans replied with the observation that the Democratic solicitousness for the niceties of the Constitution was highly selective. Punctilious in their recognition of the reserved-powers clause, the Democrats cared not a fig for the 15th Amendment, which granted equal rights at the polling place to all male adults, black or white. If the Republicans legislated to prolong their hold on the

White House, the Democrats obstructed to tighten their grip on the electoral votes of what had by now become the "solid South." So flew the recriminations.

Builders of theories concerning the origins of the 21st century federal Leviathan can plausibly trace a pattern of governmental aggrandizement back to the Republican party of Lincoln's time, and, later, of Reed's. But big is a relative term. By the standards of any subsequent era of American politics, laissez-faire was the ruling doctrine of the mid-1880s. When, in 1884, the Democrats finally recaptured the White House for the first time since the war, they set out to rebuild a navy that the ostensibly free-spending and defense-minded Republicans had allowed to dwindle to decrepit obsolescence. "[W]e live in a world of sin and sorrow," Reed would say. "Otherwise there would be no Democratic party."[3] At times, what really seemed to distinguish the two major parties was not so much political philosophy as the war, as the victorious Republicans lost no opportunity to remind any and all.

Just because the two parties were so much alike in governing philosophy, however, did not mean that politics were dull, or that the life of a congressman was easy. The very precariousness of the party balance injected suspense and rancor into every national election and into many state and local contests. Never, in the 1880s, did Reed enter a campaign with the comfortable certainty of victory, although it would have set his mind at ease to know that between 1885 and 1901 no Maine congressional incumbent would lose an election; in no other state did inertia so favor the career politician. "I am getting to like the business," Reed confided to his soulmate George Gifford before the 1882 midterm elections, "but it is as insecure as living in a Powder Mill and very often as startling."[4]

On the national scene, it was a powder mill of the Republicans' own construction. After abolishing slavery and saving the Union, the party of Lincoln had seemingly put aside virtue for more remunerative pursuits. The Republican-controlled Post Office, for instance, had been caught paying grotesquely inflated fees to favored contractors to deliver the mails on routes in the thinly settled west. What was a fair rate of pay to carry not a great many letters between points in Montana or Dakota? Was it $2,350, the sum paid during one 12-month period? Or $70,000, the sum paid the subsequent 12-month period? Early in 1882, a Washington, D.C., grand jury handed up indictments against personages of the standing of Stephen W. Dorsey, U.S. senator from Arkansas and secretary of the National Republican Committee. All in all, in the estimation of the U.S. attorney general, the perpetrators of the Star Route frauds (so-called because the routes were marked by an asterisk in the postal guides) ranked as "the worst band of organized scoundrels that ever existed since the commencement of the government."[5]

Another source of self-inflicted trouble was party factionalism. The U. S. Grant loyalists, or "Stalwarts," were at pistols drawn with the reform element. To the basic Democratic critique of the Republican party's corruption, the reformers, or "Mugwumps," or, sometimes, "Half-Breeds," said "Amen." The Stalwarts counted Reed as one of theirs, and Reed, it is true, shared none of the reformers' uplifting zeal. Pure in his political conduct, he had no interest in instructing the impure. He had a practical politician's regard for that system in which the incumbent party was free to distribute offices to reward its friends. Not that he enjoyed the importuning of office-seekers or believed in the value of government work for its own sake. To a young man who had begged his help in securing a federal post, Reed advised a career in business instead. "I have thus written you as I should write to a son if I had one," he concluded his counsel, "and you will probably heed the advice just as he would—But it is good."[6]*

The Republicans were on the defensive as well, in the matter of the swollen U.S. Treasury, and this problem too was largely their own fault. Civil War–vintage tariffs delivered surpluses to the government in hard times and good, $100 million or more per annum in the early 1880s. Democrats urged that the tariffs that generated these redundant sums be reduced and that the surplus be returned to the people. Republicans resisted. Was not the protective system the very basis of the country's

---

* Office-seekers were every elected official's cross to bear, and Reed was no exception. To Gifford, he complained that he was assailed each day by supplicants who "refer to my greatness recent and future, say they hate to trouble me and then—'If you, situated as you are would only use your influence.'" All he had to do, they seemed to think, was to order the office desired "and have it smoking hot on a plate when [they] came around." See Reed to George Gifford, January 10, 1880. George Gifford Collection. Duke University.

prosperity? By the lights of 21st century economic orthodoxy, the years 1881 and 1882 would have been the very times for the government not to run a surplus. There was a business depression in the offing—March 1882 was the start, according to some modern recordkeeping—and no receding economy is the better for a swollen public treasury.[7] But there was no such thing, in those days, as countercyclical fiscal policy. Neither were there opinion polls. But hard times have never redounded to the benefit of the incumbent party, and Reed could sense that he was in for a hard fight.

For the first time (and the last time too), he would be running in a statewide race. The census of 1880 had stripped Maine of its fifth congressional district. Redistricting was underway but would not be completed in time for the 1882 election. So the Pine Tree State became, for this one election, one immense congressional district. To the top four vote-getters would go the available four House seats. Reed drew 72,925 votes, which placed him second, behind Nelson Dingley Jr., a one-term Republican who had none of Reed's national stature. And in the counties that made up his old district, Reed polled just 900 votes more than the rest of the local field.[8] He was beholden for even this relatively small margin to the breakdown of the Democratic-Fusionist alliance.

Not every Republican was so lucky in 1882. The voters expressed their unhappiness by transforming the 23-member Republican majority in the House of Representatives during the 47th Congress into a 79-member Democratic majority in the 48th. In New York State, the incorruptible mayor of Buffalo, Grover Cleveland, was elected governor of New York by the largest margin of victory in any American gubernatorial race up until that time.[9] All together in 1882, Democrats won 13 of the 16 contested statehouses.

"In politics nobody is ever safe," Reed had observed while the 1882 issue was still in doubt.[10] He might have added that in politics nothing is ever certain. Cleveland had come from out of the blue, a walrus-mustached lawyer who had never gone to college, had not served in the war (when conscripted, he had paid a substitute) and whose entire elective résumé, previous to the Buffalo mayoralty, had consisted of the office of sheriff of Erie County, New York. As sheriff, Cleveland had given fair notice of what the people could expect from him in higher office. Having discovered, by the use of his own tape measure, that the firewood contractor was shortchanging the county, he had forced restitution. For Erie County in the 1870s, this was an astounding display of public integrity. Then too, when the time came to hang a man whom Cleveland personally believed to be innocent, there was, for the sheriff, no delegating the task of working the scaffold to put the condemned man to death. Cleveland did the deed himself.[11]

Reed and Cleveland might have been mistaken for one another in profile, as each tipped the scale at more than 250 pounds. Cleveland, however, had a small store of learning, no sarcasm and not one recorded flash of wit. Hung over his bed in the sleeping room directly upstairs from his Buffalo law office was the illuminated motto, "As thy days are, so shall thy strength be" (Deuteronomy 33:25). Above the words were arrayed the allegorical figures of Life, Duty and Death. "If I have any coat of arms and emblem," Cleveland would say, "it is that." In the call of duty, he could be at his law books straight through the night and into the morning, stopping only for breakfast and a bath (cold water, of course) before resuming his labors, and seemingly none the worse for wear.[12]

Cleveland was a bachelor who loved to fish and loved his boon companions. Though raised in a strict Presbyterian household, he drank beer, played cards and had no compunction against traveling on Sunday. In no way was he morbid. But to the politicians who had grown comfortable in the grafting ways of western New York, he exhibited unmistakable signs of that grim and cheerless honesty that rankled President Grant.[13] Alarmingly, however, to the grafting politicians, Cleveland seemed not to care about money. He seemed indifferent even to popularity. He refused to compromise from his precious principles or to make the slightest concession to the rules by which his betters, the professional, or so-called machine, politicians, had gotten ahead. It was, to the bipartisan ring that ruled Buffalo, only mildly concerning that the reform element was pushing Cleveland for the 1881 mayoralty race. They were flabbergasted when the tyro had the temerity to accept the Democratic nomination on the condition that the boss of the Democratic convention and the incumbent city comptroller, John C. Sheehan, be dropped from the ticket. The delegates yielded, Sheehan retired and Cleveland won the election. "Public officials are the trustees of the people," was his not-so-memorable rallying cry.[14]

Mayor Cleveland rooted out fraud and waste in the Buffalo street department, built a water and sewer system the honest way and earned the sobriquet "Veto Mayor" for his tussles with a thoroughly debauched city council.[15]

He was not even two years into his term when his name was put forward as the Democratic candidate in the 1882 gubernatorial race. "A sound, plain, uncomplaining Democrat and an absolutely free man," was Cleveland's self-portrait, and it seemed exactly to correspond with the people's yearning for a better kind of politics.[16] For himself, Cleveland yearned for the office, and he cagily maneuvered for the nomination. The "unowned" candidate, he had nevertheless managed to enlist Tammany Hall and the Albany machine in his cause. Still, he had compromised not one of his principles. "I shall have no idea of reelection or any higher political preferment in my head," he wrote to his brother, the Reverend William N. Cleveland, on November 7, Election Day, "but be very thankful and happy if I can well serve one term as the people's Governor. Do you know that if mother were alive I should feel so much safer? I have always thought her prayers had much to do with my success."[17]

At the Albany statehouse, Cleveland carried on as before. He seemed barely to look up from his work. With 12 months on the job, he could take pride in reforms to the state's civil service, the creation of a bureau to "collect information and statistics touching the relations between labor and capital" (relations were destined to worsen) and no fewer than 44 executive vetoes.[18] By returning to the assembly legislation to roll back the fares on New York City's hated elevated railroads, the governor seemed to outdo himself. He could not have picked a more popular bill to veto, nor a more hated corporate entity to defend. Assemblyman Theodore Roosevelt spoke for many by referring to the management of the Manhattan Railway Company on the floor of the legislature as "infernal thieves and conscienceless swindlers." Cleveland did not necessarily disagree with that characterization, but he pointed out that the company had a contract. "The State," Cleveland's veto message said, "should be not only strictly just, but scrupulously fair, and in

its relation to the citizen every legal and moral obligation should be recognized. This can only be done with a firm determination to deal justly
and fairly with those from whom we exact obedience." As for Roosevelt,
who had voted for the bill, the veto message convinced him that he was
wrong and the governor was right. "It is not a question of doing justice
to them," the assemblyman declared, in announcing his change of heart.
"It is a question of doing justice to ourselves. It is a question of standing
by what we honestly believe is right. Even if in so doing we antagonize
the feelings of our constituents."[19]

Was the mushroom career of the good, the honest—above all, the
earnest—Grover Cleveland the herald of a new spirit in American politics? Was Senator Ingalls's quip, quoted above, a part of the spirit of a
now-receding past? Posterity may see that it was. Reed seemed not to
suspect it.

The burning issue of civil service reform was a light to the future. The
Republicans dearly loved the federal bureaucracy. As they controlled
the White House, so they ruled the executive departments of the government and did most of the hiring. The gratitude of those so employed
took the form of not-quite-voluntary contributions to the Republican
party. As a method of public administration, the spoils system had its
drawbacks, but there was never a mightier engine for the perpetuation
of one-party rule. Democrats condemned it, and Garfield's assassination
in 1881 by a crazed federal office-seeker softened some Republicans. So
Senator George H. Pendleton, Democrat of Ohio, found a receptive
Congress in January 1883 for his civil service reform legislation. His act
provided for the institution of a Civil Service Commission to assure that
merit, not political preferment, was the criterion for hiring and firing
senior federal employees. Reed joined Republicans and Democrats in
voting Pendleton's bill into law.[20]

But Reed voted with his tongue in his cheek. "We are just now having a spasm of Civil Service Reform, and statesmen are sprawling in
the mud in every street in their anxiety to prove their devotion for the
blessed principles which in their hearts they have always worshipped,"
he reported to Gifford late in December 1882. ". . . Think of the new
race of statesmen without henchmen or followers devoting themselves
from morning until the dewery [sic] eve to the perfection of those great

measures which statesmen always produce when not [hounded] by office seekers."[21]

Every congressman had a certain number of government plums to dangle before his political friends. Reed had his postmasterships and—a much greater prize—the collectorship of the Port of Portland. At least Reed assumed that President Arthur, with whom he was friendly, would let Reed choose the collector when that post became vacant in 1883. Alas, Senator Eugene Hale, a Maine Republican, had Arthur's ear, and the office went to Frederick N. Dow. Reed had had a run-in with Dow's father years before, and he was on none too cordial terms with the son. Reed counted the lost collectorship as one of his greatest political disappointments.[22]

Then, again, Reed well understood how badly things could go even for the politician who got his way. "The man who gets appointed knows that it is owing to his own virtues, and the man who don't, and his friends are sure to doubt about my being a statesman even if they acquit me of corrupt motives," so he wrote to a friend, Professor Henry L. Chapman of Bowdoin, early in 1884. "But then I suppose that even Professors have their troubles. In the shoes of all mankind there is sand and also unboiled peas."[23] Reed's shoes were presently filled to overflowing. In the 1884 election season, he removed the popular postmaster of Brunswick, Maine, and replaced him with someone instantly unpopular. The deposed employee had been through the war and had the wounds to prove it. By firing him, Reed ran afoul of the Maine veterans, including the most honored of the lot, Joshua Chamberlain. Before long, the old soldiers published a broadside announcing they would be voting for Reed's Democratic opponent, Judge Nathaniel Cleaves.[24]

A Bowdoin man too, Cleaves was no ordinary Democrat. His brother was Maine's Republican attorney general and he himself had won a probate judgeship in a predominantly Republican district.[25] The Washington Post proceeded to write the incumbent's obituary. "The cold, dark waters of affliction are gathering around the feet and slowly climbing up the shivering knees of Congressman Thomas B. Reed, of Maine," the paper said shortly before the election. "Reed has been a [condemner] of Civil Service Reform, and has held, in practice if not in words, to the old way of giving offices as rewards for political service. In accordance with that ancient method, Mr. Reed had the postmaster of Brunswick turned out and one of his own henchmen put in. . . . Slowly but surely— as sure as death and taxes—the Civil Service Reform is moving on. By and by the most thick-headed of the Stalwart Congressmen will have learned that he has no more business to interfere with the appointment of a postmaster than he would if, instead of going to Congress, he had remained at home to sell peanuts, dig the soil, carry bricks or do any other honest work."[26]

"Thick-headed" was not the Reed anyone knew, least of all the Democrats. Neither was he the kind of Republican who valued loyalty above truth. But, in common with such party regulars as James G. Blaine, the former Speaker of the House and ruling Republican of Maine, Reed valued partisanship above reform. He was a Republican who happened to support women's suffrage and the practical emancipation of African-Americans, rather than an idealist who happened to be a Republican.

Reed, however insecure he might have felt in his district, was one of the Republican party's rising stars and one of the House's foremost parliamentarians. Yet the congressman's wit and sarcasm might have seemed funnier in the boom times in which the decade of the 1880s began than they did in the hard times that had set in about 1882. Civil service reform was as earnest a cause as ever there had been, as serious and dull, indeed, as Grover Cleveland himself. An age of earnestness was dawning, and Reed was its greatest sardonic wit.

"THE LABOR QUESTION" was then thrusting itself into political prominence. A sign of things to come was the strike in 1883 by 12,000 telegraphers against the Western Union Company. Under the malign governance of Jay Gould, the strikers contended, they worked for as little as $39 a month, common laborer's wages, and seven days a week.[27] Capital, too, was disgruntled. The so-called robber barons, far from exploiting their customers, were devouring each other. In the bitterest battles of the railroad rate wars of 1881, humans, freight and cattle traveled for little more than free. The New York Central, according to Chauncey Depew, its president, was sometimes reduced to hauling cattle from Chicago to New York for a dollar a car and then rebating even that dollar.[28] In the half decade before 1885, the nation's railway mileage would grow to 125,000 miles from 86,500 miles, while railway-invested capital would more than triple, to $18 billion.[29] Here was capitalism irrepressible enough to scare even the capitalists.

In 1883, a Senate investigating committee set out to discover the source of the new rancor that was infecting the relations between capital and labor. The senators heard from dozens of witnesses from all walks of life, including, for instance, a New York sanitary engineer, Charles F. Wingate, who attributed the appallingly high death rate among the city's tenement-dwellers to the conditions in their four- and five-story dwelling places. One carried one's water into one's windowless, unventilated rooms, one waited to use the unspeakable privies—holes dug in the backyard—with dozens of other tenants, and one inhaled the mingled stench of unwashed bodies, wet cellars and human waste. "The filth (of the privies) oozes out all over the yard, and the stench is intolerable," was a representative complaint entered by a tenement-dweller to the New York Health Department.[30] In the wintertime, the people simply didn't bathe.

A 33-year-old Samuel Gompers took the witness stand to describe the conditions of American working people. Even in Massachusetts, where 10 hours, under the law, was the maximum length of the workday, employers found ways to extract their pound of flesh, he testified. Work would begin seven or eight minutes before the appointed time, lunch would start seven or eight minutes after the appointed time, and the end of the day's drudgery would come seven or eight minutes after everybody's watch except the boss's said it was time to go home. Thus did "minute thieves" grind down the mill operatives who earned each week as much as $6.30 and as little as $2.05. And if the employees complained? "There is no recourse here and no appeal," they would be told; "if you do not like it, get out."[31]

In Birmingham, Alabama, the senators questioned a lumber dealer and banker, Albert C. Danner, who said that blacks made better laborers than whites. They were uncomplaining and hardworking when you paid them promptly and treated them right. Danner said he paid his laborers $30 a month, of which, only the rarest nickel or dime went into the bank. "Since they were treated so badly by the Freedman's Bank," Danner testified, "they don't seem to have much use for banks. I consider that the failure of that bank was one of the worst calamities that ever happened to the people of the Southern country. . . . [T]hey deposited in that bank because they were ready to do anything that Washington wanted them to do; they understood that the bank was a Government institution, and that the Government in Washington wanted them to put their money into it, and so they did that as they would have done anything that the Government wanted them to do."[32] Reed, in March 1884, submitted a petition on behalf of some Maine residents to the House Banking and Currency Committee; the petitioners sought legislation to direct the government to assume the Freedman's deposit liabilities.

John Swinton, managing editor of the New York *Sun*, told the senators that he had seen such horrors in New York City in the "famine" winter of 1874 as he would never forget. Ever since, he said, he had tried to uphold the cause of the working people. Restore the income tax, he urged the panel. In 1870, at a rate of just 2½ percent, it had yielded $27 million, collected from a mere 75,000 people who clearly didn't need the money. "This tax, collected from these few," he said, "must have relieved over ten million of our people from one-half of their taxes; relieved them without a burden being felt by those who paid the tax." And he implored the senators to bring the power of the national government to the work of improving the wretched New York tenements. Ten thousand New Yorkers died every year of what deserved to be called by its plain and shocking name: starvation. Why were there no reliable facts and figures on this outrage? "[U]nless some national power takes hold of the local imbeciles the results which are seen in the death-tables are likely to continue, and grow worse."[33]

Jay Gould himself, the "best-hated man in America," was called to testify in November 1883.[34] Prompted by the senators, he told his life story. The topic seemed to embarrass him, and he spoke so softly that they asked him to raise his voice—the reporters were straining to hear. At one point in his narrative, Gould remarked that he had passed the point of caring about money. "Railroads had then got to be a sort of hobby with me."[35] Still, they were a lucrative one. He told how he had transformed the Missouri-Pacific from a 287-mile stretch of track between St. Louis and Kansas City with gross weekly earnings of

$70,000 to a 10,000-mile-long complex grossing more than $1 million a week. As the railroad grew, Gould went on, so did the territory through which it passed. "[W]e have made [it] rich."[36]

Under questioning, Gould said he would sell his interest in Western Union to the government at a fair price, if that is what the government determined to do. But rather than nationalize Western Union, he said, Congress would be better advised to privatize the Post Office. "It is a nice, genteel occupation—telegraphing," Gould mused when asked about the Western Union strike. He insisted that the company bent over backward to treat its employees fairly. As for the labor agitators, "Your best men don't care how many hours they work, or anything of that kind; they are looking to go higher up; either to own a business of their own and control it, or to get higher up in the ranks."[37]

"For some reason," a senator observed, "labor is restless, uneasy and to some extent unemployed."

"Well," Gould answered, "there is a little [surplus] of labor. In the first place, we have been importing an enormous amount of new material in the way of immigration; all those people had to be placed. Then we were building railroads too rapidly, and now we have stopped. That leaves a surplus of labor."[38]

A six-foot-tall truckman had appeared before the committee. He was out of work, hungry, at wits' end. His family was hungry. What should he do? Gould replied that he knew that there were many such cases in the big cities. "It is a very difficult thing to say exactly how you are going to ameliorate everybody's condition. I have noticed, though, that generally if men are temperate and industrious they are pretty sure of success. In cases such as the one you describe I could almost always go back behind the scenes and find a cause for such a person's 'misfortunes.'"

"This is a free country," said Gould in concluding his remarks, "and I think we had better give every man his free choice."[39]

The May 1884 failure of the criminally mismanaged brokerage house of Grant & Ward bore a peculiarly Republican stamp. The Grant on the door of the firm was U. S. Grant Jr., but it was the father who gleaned the shame for the bankruptcy. It was, after all, the ex-president who imbued the enterprise with prestige, a patriotic luster not unlike the kind that attached to the Freedman's Bank.

A financial panic precipitated by the loss of confidence occasioned by the failure of a crooked Wall Street firm bearing the surname of the era's most illustrious public figure—was such a fact not fodder for the political platform of the party to which the illustrious figure happened *not* to belong? It was not in the presidential election season of 1884. The Democratic party platform, which indicted the Republicans for offenses ranging from theft (an allusion to the 1876 election) to "Mongolian" wage slavery (a reference to its supposed encouragement of Chinese immigration), made no explicit reference to the financial crisis or the depression that was beginning its third year.

Then again, the Democrats had a ready-made campaign issue in the person of the Republican nominee, James G. Blaine. Short of the presidency, Blaine had done almost everything in politics that there was to do. He was an orator and parliamentarian, published author, Maine state legislator, three times Speaker of the U.S. House of Representatives, U.S. senator, Secretary of State under Presidents Garfield and Arthur and now—at last—Republican nominee for president. In his days in the House, the voters of Kennebec never failed to reelect him by lopsided margins.[40] At the close of the 43rd Congress, as he brought down the gavel on the close of his third term as Speaker, the Democrats contended with the Republicans as to which side of the House could do him the noisiest and most emotional honor.[41] It was said that when Blaine shook your hand, he held it as if he intended to keep it. He looked into your eyes and asked about your family, not just asking but actually seeming to listen to the answer. A great many Republicans revered the white-bearded, gentle-featured "Plumed Knight" from Maine, and so, off and on, did a great many Democrats. "Now there's Blaine, damn him! But I do love him!" one southern congressman was overheard to say to another as they caught sight of the then-Speaker walking down the Capitol steps following an especially contentious debate.[42]

But the devotion Blaine inspired in the North came at a cost to his acceptance in the South and with independents and progressive Republicans in every section. In January 1876, he introduced an amendment to a bill designed to extend amnesty to former officers of the Confederacy on condition of their taking an oath of allegiance to the Constitution of the United States. From such amnesty, Blaine's amendment would exempt Jefferson Davis, but not because he alone had led the rebellion (for many had helped to march the South over that cliff). Rather, said Blaine, what made Davis unfit for amnesty was the fact that "he was the author, knowingly, deliberately, guiltily and willfully, of the gigantic murders and crimes at Andersonville." It did not escape the attention of the Democrats that 1876 was a presidential election year, that Blaine was running hard for the Republican nomination and that a good stout wave of the bloody shirt would do him no electoral harm with the northern veterans. Cox of New York abused him for "raking up again the embers of dead hate," while Robert G. Ingersoll, the Republican orator from Illinois, extolled him for having "snatched the mask of Democracy from the hideous face of Rebellion."[43]

No longer did those who would damn Blaine also love him. Enemies of the former Speaker and 1876 presidential aspirant now wished to do him harm. And to the consummation of that project, Blaine himself unexpectedly lent a hand. His own correspondence, then coming to light, showed that the former Speaker had been willing to barter his office for the sake of his personal dealings with the Little Rock and Fort Smith Railroad. He incriminated himself in a series of letters he wrote, while Speaker, to a promoter of that property. Before these documents could be entered into the record of the congressional committee that was investigating him, however, Blaine snatched them out of the hand of the man who was to have turned them over to the investigators. James Mulligan was that man, and the letters were henceforth, inevitably, known as the "Mulligan letters." A lesser, or less audacious, politician than Blaine might have burned the evidence. Blaine dramatically read it aloud on the floor of the House—taking care, however, to read the letters in such a jumbled order as to deny to the packed galleries any real understanding of what he had meant when he wrote them. Still, no context was necessary to catch the drift of such passages as this one, which then-Speaker Blaine had addressed to his would-be business partner in 1869: "I do not feel that I shall prove a deadhead in the enterprise if I once embark on it. I see various channels in which I can be useful."[44]

If Blaine's devotees smelt only the roses of exoneration in this dramatic production, others recoiled at the stink of venality, and it was Hayes, not Blaine, who wound up heading the 1876 Republican ticket.

In his defense, Blaine had pointed out that his dealings with the Little Rock and Fort Smith were ultimately unprofitable. But even if that fact could expunge the impropriety of dangling the power of his office in front of (among others) the financier Jay Cooke, it does not explain how this public servant and father of six managed to live like the partner of a prosperous Wall Street banking house. Blaine maintained a house in Augusta that required a staff of six, and he built and furnished a $100,000 Washington mansion at Dupont Circle. The source of that dollar figure is Thomas B. Reed, whom the proud statesman led on a tour of the place: "the noble monument to his economy and financial genius," as the visitor sarcastically put it. Writing to Gifford, Reed observed that Blaine meant to "rule Maine. . . . Well, why not? Is virtue not virtue because out of office? Is not truth as stainless out of the Congress as in? Is not honesty the best policy and do not the lives of our prosperous men show it?"[45]

Without imputing to Reed a purity of character beyond the capacity of mortal man to uphold, one may observe that Blaine and he occupied opposite ends of the spectrum of political rectitude. Reed was, from time to time, a supporter of the railroads in Congress. In 1883, he presented a report opposing the Democratic demand that the Northern Pacific forfeit the public lands that Congress had granted it. For this disinterested recommendation the Democrats abused him as a tool of the robber barons.[46] The next year, Reed and Richard W. Townshend, Democrat of Illinois, locked horns over a postal appropriation bill. Townshend lost his temper and took a rhetorical roundhouse swing at Reed, calling him an unfailing defender both of "extravagant appropriations" and of misappropriation. "If ever the interest of a railroad corporation was at stake in this House, I have found the gentleman from Maine its champion and defender."

Reed's friend Frank Hiscock demanded that Townshend's words be struck from the Record. Reed declined the courtesy. He didn't want to invest his antagonist's attack with any such significance. "But," Reed added of Townshend, "when he talks of extravagant appropriations and of peculators, if he looks at the record in the star-route cases he will find that I voted with the committee in condemnation and that he was not here. [Applause on the Republican side.]"

Still, Townshend persisted: "I have never heard peculation assailed on the floor of this House but that gentleman from Maine has sprung to his feet and defended it."

"Name one single instance," said Reed.

"I remember an instance that the gentleman from Kentucky brought up," said Townshend; "charges that were made in the last session of Congress. I do not now remember the name of the party, but the incident all will remember."

"Name one," Reed repeated.

"I decline to yield," said Townshend.

"Just give us the name," said Reed.

"Mr. Speaker," Townshend returned weakly, "I have not time, and decline to be interrupted. [Derisive laughter on the Republican side.]"

At length, Townshend resumed the assault: The man from Maine was a "defender of every railroad scheme that has been brought in here, and . . . an obstructer of every character of legislation that has been attempted to put a restraint upon the railroad corporations and compel them to comply with their obligations and to meet their duties to the Government."

"I desire to say only a word," Reed concluded. "Fortunately the observation from the gentleman from Illinois—the Shawneetown district of that State—has had the kindness to make [his accusation] in the presence of this House, that knows both of us. Now I say to this House that my record is open to the world upon any and all topics. And there are only two sets of people for whose opinion I care a great deal. The one is my constituency, which knows me, and the other is this House, which knows him. [Applause on the Republican side.] And it is hardly necessary to say that I shall stand vindicated before them both. . . .

"I desire to say another thing," Reed concluded: "that if I have at any time been found upon the side of a railroad corporation, which is a term of reproach upon his part, it has been because I was defending the cause of justice upon the floor of the House; and while I stand here as a member of this House there is no man on the face of the earth so poor nor any corporation so rich that I will prostitute myself to injustice for the sake of that temporary advantage which comes of maintaining a false position because some dishonest men are clamoring against me. [Applause.]"[47]

Ten days later—this was in March 1884—Reed was in correspondence with a representative of the Northern Pacific who had made him the offer of some free or discounted train tickets. "I need not say to you, who have so much experience in public affairs, that I don't expect by acting in this fashion thus strictly to escape public slander," the congressman told his would-be benefactor. "I only expect not to deserve it."[48]

Reed had none of Blaine's knack for living a plutocrat's life on a public servant's salary. He, like Blaine, bought and sold stocks and real estate. But, unlike Blaine, he could never coax enough out of his investments to build a Washington house of any scale of grandeur (rather, he put up at hotels while Congress was in session: the Hamilton House during the 48th, 49th and 50th Congresses and the Shoreham Hotel thereafter). How Blaine accumulated his money is evidently past knowing: "We hear much of outgo, but almost nothing of income," his biographer, David Saville Muzzey, relates.[49]

So Blaine, not Reed, was the grandee of Washington. Reed dearly loved the kind of dinner parties that the Blaines seemed so effortlessly to stage—"the best theater in the world," he attested. But to be a guest at such entertainments, one reciprocally had to host them, and this expense Reed could ill afford. "And so a man not rich has to decline too often."[50]

THE WEALTH OF reputation, however, Reed was fast accumulating. He was once again working to make Congress more productive—or, at least, less sclerotic. Never confuse the U.S. House of Representatives with the Maine legislature, he advised one of his constituents in 1884. In a given session, the Maine assembly might complete 100 percent of its business; the U.S. Congress, less than 10 percent. "You and the community little realize how hard it is to pass a bill under the rules of our house," Reed consoled Andrew Hawes, whose pet legislation Reed had been unsuccessfully sponsoring. "I have tried my very best to have them changed."[51]

Reed's latest efforts in that direction came in the shape of his proposed amendments to the rules governing the sequencing of legislation for consideration by the House. Under the system in place, bills were considered in the order in which they were minuted on the calendar.

And because committees typically reported the least complex, least controversial and least significant bills first, it was these issues, not the weightier ones, that were likely to thread their way to the floor in time for the members' consideration. Thwarted, the sponsors of neglected legislation jockeyed to have it passed by "unanimous consent," without debate and without consideration. It was a poor system. But at the end of a long and typically unproductive session, the evils attending unanimous consent seemed preferable to those of complete inaction. "At least one half of the public building bills of the last session were passed in this way," Reed noted in an appeal to his colleagues in February 1884; "and it is a most vicious and pernicious system of legislation."[52]

To break the legislative dam, Reed proposed a series of steps by which the committees of the House could more easily direct their bills to the floor. A "morning hour" would be set aside for the purpose; and the way would be cleared for the House to take up business now buried on the Speaker's table. The object, said Reed in pleading his case, was not more legislation, "but a better class of legislation." His proposals got nowhere, and the debate continued. "Here we are," observed Reed two months later, "with the business of three Congresses piled upon this House and with the prospect that the business of four Congresses will be piled upon the next." One thousand two hundred committee reports rose in a huge stack, while the House does "no business, because under our rules we deliberately sacrifice our time in such a way that it is impossible to do business."[53] And a good thing too, replied the Democrats. If there was one thing the country didn't need more of, it was federal laws. Reed surely had a point—"We undertake to run Niagara through a quill," he said—but then so did the Democrats. Reed pronounced himself scandalized in 1884 when the House hurriedly took up a sundry civil appropriation bill of 86 pages in length and representing an outlay of $22.3 million. Behold the spectacle, Reed exclaimed—the sight of such an immense document being passed "without examination, without reading and without knowledge?"[54]

"CIVIL SERVICE REFORM," "honesty in government" and "tariff for revenue only" are political slogans never to be confused with "No taxation without representation" or "Liberty and Union, now and forever." But the presidential campaign of 1884 was emotionally charged from the very beginning. "Chet" Arthur, as the incumbent was known to his former friends in the New York Republican machine, might have deserved to be renominated—the 1884 platform praised his "wise, conservative and patriotic policy"—but his friends had left him. By championing a little bit of reform, the former collector of the Port of New York had neither mollified the progressives nor rallied the conservatives. He made enemies on both sides. "All in the world that we want of him," remarked Whitelaw Reid, publisher of the New York *Tribune*, a few months before the convention, "is to die with reasonable decency when the necessity of his political death at last dawns on his vision."[55]

That moment arrived when Blaine's name was read into nomination at the Chicago Exposition Building: "Whole delegations mounted their chairs and led the cheering," the New York *Tribune* reported, "which instantly spread to the stage and deepened into a roar fully as deafening as the voice of Niagara. The scene was indescribable. The air quivered, the gas lights trembled and the walls fairly shook."[56] A little later in the proceedings, one of the delegates-at-large, former Ohio governor Joseph B. Foraker, made a speech nominating John Sherman for the presidency. In passing, Foraker happened to mention his "admiration for that brilliant genius from Maine." A quarter-hour of frenzied cheering ensued before Foraker could return to the business of extolling the merits of the dull former Treasury Secretary.[57]

Democrats moved into the Exposition hall a month after the Republicans departed. Scenes of joy greeted the nomination of the Democratic standard-bearer too, but it wasn't the nominating speech that brought down the house. In seconding the nomination of Grover Cleveland, General Edward S. Bragg struck the theme of the campaign to come. "We love him for the enemies he has made!" said Bragg of the nominee, the general's eyes ummistakably clamped on the delegation from Tammany Hall.[58] "It was a remarkable victory," a historian of the Democratic party rightly observes of Cleveland's nomination for the presidency—"for a man without money, without organization, without effort, without even expressing his views on national questions, without an issue or an asset save his own rugged and powerful personality."[59]

Blaine too had his enemies, though, unlike Cleveland—or, for that matter, Reed—he did not seem to go out of his way to make them. Among the most implacable of these accidental foes was Roscoe Conkling, the Republican boss of New York State. In 1866, Blaine and Conkling, both congressmen, had traded insults on the floor of the House during debate over an army appropriations bill, Blaine remarking on Conkling's "majestic, supereminent, turkey-gobbler strut."[60] Blaine intended no malice—the words had just come to him in the heat of the moment, as Conkling's words, no less cutting, had come to the New Yorker. But, as Reed could readily testify, the scars left by cruel wit can be slow to heal. Conkling's wounds never did, and he diligently worked to sabotage Blaine in New York.

Carl Schurz's opposition to Blaine, on the other hand, was more of the cerebral type. The German-born lawyer, newspaper editor, Union army veteran and reformer insisted that the man from Maine was morally unfit to lead the nation. What was the overriding issue of 1884? Schurz posed to a Brooklyn audience in August. Neither the tariff nor the currency. "At other times," Schurz allowed, "they might absorb our attention. But this time the Republican National Convention has, with brutal directness, so that we must face it whether we will or not, forced upon the country another issue, which is infinitely more important, because it touches the vitality of our institutions. It is the question of honesty in government." Compared to the honor of the American people, demanded Schurz, a nominal Republican, of what conceivable significance was party loyalty?[61]

So Schurz and Conkling, each for his own reasons, lined up with the former mayor of Buffalo, who had no known views on any national issue except honesty, which he favored. He was, indeed, brutally forthcoming shortly after the Democratic National Convention disbanded on a subject that Schurz had never dreamt would even come up. The topic was the out-of-wedlock son of Maria Halpin, an attractive, thirty-something Buffalo widow. Cleveland, a bachelor, allowed that he could have been the father. He wouldn't swear to it—there were other candidates—but as he was the only one who happened to be single, he resignedly acknowledged responsibility. Because Cleveland was blameless in public life but flawed in his private dealings, whereas Blaine was corrupt in his public conduct but beyond reproach as a husband and father, some quipped that the obvious course was to keep Cleveland in government and send Blaine back to private life. Long faces in the good-government contingent smiled wanly at the joke.

Before the Halpin revelations, it had been so clear, the Mugwumps lamented. In Blaine, there was black, in Cleveland white. Now, to the distracted average voter, it would all appear rather gray. Before Cleveland's "woman scrape," as the candidate delicately put it, the Democrats had the edge in mocking verse:

> Blaine, Blaine, James G. Blaine,
> Continental liar from the state of Maine.
> Burn this letter!

But now they heard an echo:

> Ma, Ma, where's my paw?
> Gone to the White House
> Haw, haw, haw![62]

The fact was that, in policy matters, one party sounded much like the other. Each stood for the gold standard, for reduced taxation and for sensible reductions in the tariff. The Democrats, it is true, were by conviction the low-tariff party and the Republicans the party of protection, but the Democratic platform pledged that the party would pull the rug out from under no protected industry by precipitously slashing the tariff that kept foreign competition at bay. The Republicans, for their part, committed themselves to correcting "the inequalities of the tariff," whatever they might be. Blaine, in writing and on the stump, tried to bring the tariff issue front and center. The Democrats would dismantle the very system of protection that had sustained 20 years of American industrial prosperity, he contended. Nor did he neglect to wave the bloody shirt. "I do not believe," Blaine harangued a crowd in Fort Wayne, Indiana, "that the men who added luster and renown to your State through four years of bloody war can be used to call to the administration of the Government the men who organized the great Rebellion

('No! No! Never')."[63] Blaine was the first Republican presidential candidate of the postwar era not to have served in the Union army (the rest had been generals). But because Cleveland too had avoided service, the Democrats had no ready response to Blaine's postdated bellicosity.

Cleveland, indeed, hardly said a political word. He had asked for no votes in the Buffalo mayoralty race. For the presidency, he chose, for the most part, a lofty silence, as most candidates for the nation's highest office had customarily done. Blaine decided to take his case to the people. Even if he had wanted to, he could have hardly ignored Carl Schurz haranguing midwestern audiences in both English and German on his supposed moral turpitude. Besides, Blaine's charisma was his greatest political asset; it would be wasted on his front porch in Augusta. So on September 17, Blaine and his traveling party embarked on a whistle-stop campaign tour into the Midwest and back East again.

Reed joined the rail caravan for a portion of the journey. One can imagine his sense of happy relief, for he had nosed out Judge Cleaves in the September 9 congressional balloting. His plurality of 915 votes was one of the weaker showings in a strong canvass by Maine Republicans that year. But he had won, confounding the Washington *Post* and Joshua Chamberlain alike. And he had received a stirring testament to his congressional service from none other than Abram S. Hewitt, the Democrat from New York. "I am glad you have been re-elected," Hewitt congratulated him, "for although you are a pronounced enemy to the Democratic party, your great abilities, and your sleepless vigilance, have been of great service in the cause of sound legislation. I have always admired your capacity and fearlessness; and if my political adversaries are to be found in the House at all, I know of no one whose presence is more acceptable than yours. You always give and take the blows which are incident to free political life with courage and calmness. But you never allow political differences to interfere with your personal friendships; hence I am proud to class you among my friends."[64] Politics indeed makes strange bedfellows, Reed might have reflected as he rode along, however briefly, with the presidential candidate he so little resembled or, indeed, supported.

Blaine was six weeks on the stump when he received a summons to New York. Cleveland was showing all too well, the Republican scouts reported. Besides, the prohibition candidate, former Kansas governor John P. St. John, was drawing 80 percent of his support from the Republican party.[65] Did Blaine have enough energy for a final push in New York? Answering in the affirmative, the candidate checked into the Fifth Avenue Hotel on October 28.

Next morning, Blaine received the benediction of a gathering of Protestant clergy, one of whom, the Reverend Samuel D. Burchard, pledged that, as Republicans, his brethren and he "don't propose to leave our party and identify ourselves with the party whose antecedents have been rum, Romanism and rebellion."

Blaine was perhaps too tired, bored or distracted to listen. In any case, he did not think to repudiate this alliterative insult to the Catholic vote. Nor did it seem to cross his mind that Delmonico's was not the best place to be seen to dine that evening, where he did, in fact, remind 200 of the city's moguls how much they owed to the Republican protective tariff. "The Boodle Banquet," the next day's headlines read.[66]

Not that the money power was all Blaine's. On the Saturday before Election Day, an army of Cleveland supporters marched up Broadway from lower Manhattan to catch a glimpse of their hero in a reviewing stand at Madison Square. A lawyer, marching with other members of the bar, recalled that "Veteran Democrats marched side by side with gray-bearded men who had participated in the formation of the Republican party. . . . As we marched up Broadway and Fifth Avenue reaching from curb to curb and with inspiring strains of martial music, we could see ahead of us, with their banners waving, and we could hear constantly repeated the war-cries of 'Blaine, Blaine, James G. Blaine, The monumental liar from the State of Maine.' . . ."[67]

The hosts of cheering Democrats, however, foretold no landslide. Just as he was expected to do, Cleveland carried the so-called Solid South, as well as Connecticut, New Jersey, Indiana and Delaware, a total of 183 electoral votes out of the necessary 201. New York was the prize, the state that Cleveland had carried by so pleasing a margin in 1882. But this time, the race went neck-and-neck. It was, indeed, a photo finish, without—for days on end—a clarifying photograph. Hotheads on the Democratic side, having long before braced themselves for another stolen election, threatened to install their man in the White

House by force. Cleveland himself seemed to entertain that possibility. "I believe I have been elected President," the Democrat wired a friend on the Thursday after Election Day, November 4, "and nothing but the grossest fraud can keep me out of it, and that we will not permit." Blaine feared another civil war. But trigger fingers unflexed on Thursday when the president of Western Union tendered his congratulations to the Democrat: "All concede that your administration as governor has been wise and conservative, and in the larger field as president I feel that you will do still better, and that the vast business interests of the country will be entirely safe in your hands." So wired Jay Gould.[68] Cleveland did, after all, squeak to victory in New York, but by a margin of less than 1,200 votes out 1,167,169 cast. In the national popular vote, Cleveland edged Blaine by a bit more than than 25,000.[69]

Contemplating Cleveland's victory, Reed commented thus: "The Democratic party now has thrust upon it the business of doing something."[70]

Chapter 14

Champion of Protection

F OR BREAKFAST, REED favored fish balls, beans and potatoes. "I have retained the simple tastes of my ancestors who were nearly all fishermen," he noted in a diary entry dated October 4, 1885. "I love fish balls dearly. But as they make me fat I ought to give them up."[1] He wrote these words in French.

A part of Reed fit the stereotype of the American provincial who supported high protective tariffs because he had no use for foreigners. Playfully, he could cast himself in the role of a Yankee rustic, for instance, on the occasion of his hearing the sound of Latin being spoken on a summer evening in 1886. "It is a remarkable thing," the former Latin instructor recorded, "at least as it appears to a citizen of Maine. I've never seen anything like it."[2]

In truth, the congressman was a man of refined taste and wide-ranging interests. Especially did he love the French language. He engaged a French tutor, read French novels (he loved Octave Feuillet for the purity of his prose), attended French-language theatrical productions, took long vacations in Europe, corresponded with Gifford in French and kept a French-language diary. Except for its wage structure and exports, he seemed to love the old continent.

"I have studied French very hard," he wrote in April 1885, the month after Cleveland's inauguration. "I get up at half past seven every

day, have breakfast at eight o'clock and I am at my office at nine, astonishing my friends."[3] He did not astonish them for long, however. A
night owl, Reed often slept badly and usually slept late.

Overeating was only one source of the congressman's insomnia. "The
cigars were strong," he related of the dinner party on March 20, 1886, at
the home of his independently wealthy Republican colleague Representative Ira Davenport of New York. Other guests included the civil service
reformer Dorman B. Eaton, Chief Justice Morrison R. Waite and Republican Senator William M. Evarts of New York. Reed returned to his hotel
abuzz with the talk and the nicotine. He tossed and turned for two and
a half hours, got up and ate some caviar and drank some mineral water.
"I spent a frightful night," he wrote the next day. "I couldn't sleep until
5 am, and I could only fall asleep after having taken a sleeping powder.
I have to eat less." Desperate for sleep, he sometimes employed desperate measures. "Last night," he jotted in November 1887, "I found sleep
an impossible thing. I got up at midnight and had two glasses of whiskey and put around my neck a cord to which I attached an onion." The
patient slept till 11:30 in the morning, a result that perhaps owed more
to the whiskey than the onion, Reed speculated (the mayor of Scranton,
Pennsylvania, had suggested this home remedy to him).[4] At times he felt
depressed—in Washington in January 1888, for example. "I had the black
sickness all day today," he wrote to himself. It was, indeed, not possible to
be happy in Washington, he mused. And, in homage to the great German
philosophical pessimist, he jotted, "Long live Schopenhauer!"[5]

What topics crowded into Reed's mind in the wee hours of the first
term of Grover Cleveland? Money, for one. Reed wanted more of it—a
fortune, if possible. "I desire to be greatly rich myself," he wrote after
an evening spent in the company of rich men.[6] He seemed not to want
for income. What he craved was capital. Yet he lacked that unerring
instinct for getting paid that no aspiring accumulator of great wealth
can afford to be without. One may observe a curious inattention to the
main chance in the record of five profitless months he spent as counsel
to a couple of Texas land speculators in London in 1883.

Reed met one of these men on a trans-Atlantic steamship. The congressman was on vacation, his first in many years, a meandering, unstruc-
tured tour without Susan or Kitty. But he was not so bent on sightseeing

that he refused to listen to a business proposition presented by a new shipboard acquaintance. Would Reed lend his time and talent in London to raising money for just about the biggest real estate project in creation? "Very well!" said Reed to the proposition, without, however, stopping to spell out the terms on which he would be paid, let alone how much.

John V. Farwell was that acquaintance. He and his brother, Charles, with whom Reed served in the 47th Congress, had entered into a contract with the state of Texas. They would build a new state capital in Austin, a building taller, even, than the Capitol in Washington, D.C. At 566.6 feet long and 388 feet wide, it would be the seventh largest building in the world. In exchange, the brothers would receive three million acres of land in the Texas panhandle. This spread, they would call the XIT Ranch, as in "Ten counties in Texas." It would take 781.25 miles of barbed wire just to fence it all in. What the Farwells needed was a good lawyer.

Throwing himself into this project, Reed holed up at the British Museum to study the relevant law. He attended meetings with prospective buyers and led the partners around London in the capacity of a tour guide. Weeks slipped by, then months. By and by he sent for his wife, who joined him in London just as "the bottom had nearly dropped out of the whole situation." Now it was time to settle accounts. But when Reed broached the subject of his fee, his erstwhile clients became vague. Was he not to be paid a contingency fee, a certain percentage of the profits in case of success, little or nothing in the event of failure? they inquired. Not at all, Reed replied. He had "inferred" that the Farwells would pay him "as lawyers are usually paid." It was they, not their lawyer, who would bear the risks and keep the profits (if any). Reed, spinning out his sad story to the lawyer he engaged to try to salvage his fee—$7,175, as he calculated it—did not neglect to blame himself. John Farwell had acted "just as I ought to have known he would."[7] Reed's lawyer finally threw in the towel. Without the prodding of a lawsuit, Reed's clients would pay no more than $3,000. "They are not simply ugly," the congressman's attorney signed off, "they are vicious."[8]*

---

* The Farwells did, in fact, build the capital and developed the ranch. John Farwell died in 1909, leaving an estate of $1,775,000. He remembered the Moody Bible Institute in his will.

A little more than two years later, in February 1886, we find Reed gnashing his teeth over his stockbroker, Stanley Pullen. The congressman had been carrying 100 shares of Delaware, Lackawanna and Western Railroad. The share price had lately climbed, but as Reed was about to order a sale, he received news, through the mails, that Pullen had previously sold him out, thereby nullifying an anticipated $600 profit and turning it into a $750 loss. "It makes me sick," Reed recorded, in French. ". . . I am completely upset and thoroughly frustrated. I am furious at everything this morning. The wealth that I desire to give me the leisure for my career always escapes me. But I will succeed nevertheless."[9] There would be worse. Eleven months later, Pullen would cost him "another $4,000." This loss, however, the diarist bore without comment.

Reed was not so intent on success, either in his speculations or on the floor of the House, that he failed to make time for the finer things in life. He doted on Kitty, as she entered adolescence. "It is the birthday of my little girl," he recorded as she turned 13. "She has become very charming and becomes more so each day."[10] In Portland, he found time to visit the Cumberland Club, where he played cards (though not on Sunday, the bylaws prohibiting that breach of the Sabbath) and billiards ("as well as a cow," he judged).[11] He bought books until he had amassed a library of more than 5,000 volumes, including 500 in French and 35 bound volumes of *Punch*.[12]

In Washington, Reed and his French tutor, M. Larroque, would converse for two or three hours at a time, often parting company at 11 PM or midnight. Sometimes the two would converse while walking, the professor attracting curious glances for his stove-pipe hat. "After the walk," Reed wrote of one such excursion in an entry dated March 14, 1886, "we went back to my place, where he spoke to me about Father Lacordere, his eloquence, his story, and about Lammennais and other wonderful preachers of the Church. Afterwards, we played a game of *ecarte* in order to learn gaming vocabulary."[13]

Reed read heavily and happily in French. "I finished the first volume of Mérimée's *Lettres à une inconnue*. The day before yesterday I bought six volumes of Montesquieu's *Oeuvres*, two volumes of Pascal's *Pensées* and his *Lettres Provinciales*, and the *Théâtre de Clara Gazul*, etc. by Mérimée. Two evenings ago I glanced through *Pepita Jiménez*, translated from the Spanish."[14]

Then there was the attractive Mrs. Hillyer, who, on consecutive evenings in mid-March 1886, happened to be seated in front of Reed at the theater. It pleased Reed that this charming woman spoke French during the intermission on the first evening. Her French was capable and her figure was arresting. On the second night, Mrs. Hillyer was seated beside her husband. "But he seems to me an inferior man," Reed noted. "She has a waist so tiny as to excite a strong feeling of curiosity. I would like to see for myself how she is made."

The reader may share the biographer's strong feeling of curiosity about Reed's conduct. Was, or was not, this exponent of woman's suffrage faithful to Susan, whose name rarely figures in his diary? The congressman's descendants excised such passages as they deemed unsuitable for posterity, though in so doing they may have merely succeeded in whetting our salacious curiosity. Thus, for instance, on April 19, 1886, after attending a dinner party with a portion of Washington's political "A" list, Reed took a walk with another dinner guest, his colleague Frank Hiscock. And to Hiscock, noted Reed, "I recounted my affair with Miss [indecipherable]." Presently, the family editors allowed another line of text to surface, but without context: "to begin a lawsuit against them in Albany and employ Mr. Hamilton Harris."[15]

Whether Reed was, with respect to his marriage vows, a strict or liberal constructionist, he liked women as fellow human beings, not merely for the favors they might or might not choose to bestow on members of the male sex. His hat was off, for instance, to Mary Logan, wife of Blaine's 1884 running mate, General John "Black Jack" Logan. Reed saw in Mrs. Logan not merely a beautiful being but also a consummate diplomat. To see her at the height of her powers, he reminisced after the general's death late in 1886, "you have to see her in the middle of a room crowded with society people. . . . I saw her in Portland surrounded by a crowd of strangers, and I have never seen such a perfect show. She walked from one side to the other, waving, shaking hands. She answers all of her questioners. Never a word amiss, never an awkward answer."[16]

We learn in these French-language jottings that Reed liked Cleveland—liked him "a lot"—though so hard did the president push himself that Reed feared for his life. Did Reed himself have designs on the presidency? "Being President, my friend, what does that mean?" he wrote in French to Gifford in April 1886. "Here is a man who can do nothing according to his wishes, who is always loaded with sycophantic behavior, to whom no one tells the truth, who is forced to receive overwhelming numbers of men. And when all is over, what does he become? A man, who resembles the President in the way that a shipwreck resembles a ship at full sail."[17]

We may take it with a grain of salt that Reed did not aspire to the presidency. He pretended not to want the Speakership, either. When the 49th Congress assembled for its December session in 1885, the Republicans caucused to nominate their floor leader. To his chagrin, Reed discovered that Hiscock had been campaigning hard for the honor. Reed, characteristically, had lined up not one vote. "[T]here was nothing left for me to do but pretend I didn't care," as he related to Gifford. However, when the votes were cast, Reed had 63 to Hiscock's 42. The victor was jubilant: For some time the de facto Republican floor leader, he was now that man in name as well. "But now," he added to Gifford, "I am like a young bear, all my difficulties are ahead of me."[18]

Minority leader or not, however, Reed feared for his seat, and organized labor was one of the sources of his insecurity. A prosperous lawyer and friend of the railroads (or, at least, a defender of the railroads' valid contractual rights), Reed was exactly the kind of politician whom the Knights of Labor wished to return to private life. "I took a walk tonight with a Knight of Labor, who gave me his opinions on several subjects," he recorded in April 1886. "I wasted a lot of Science on him."[19] However, Reed chose not to antagonize his trade-union adversaries but rather to try to mollify them. For his trouble he was castigated on the editorial page of the New York *Times*. It happened this way.

On April 12, Representative Frank Lawler, Democrat of Illinois, resolved that a House committee conduct a study, at a cost of $5,000 or less, into the rapidly escalating conflict between labor and capital. Lawler was that rare bird of plumage in Congress, a nonlawyer. He had been a news agent on a railroad, a brakeman, the president of the Ship

Carpenters and Calkers' Association and—for nine years—a letter carrier in the Chicago post office. He had been in Congress just one year.

On his feet to object was John H. Reagan, a Texas Democrat. No mere letter carrier, Reagan had served as postmaster general of the Confederacy. He was, besides, a student of the Constitution, as he proceeded to remind the House. The root principle of the Founders of the United States was their assumption "of the capacity of people for self-government," Reagan reminded the members. "The Constitution assumed to distribute and partition the powers of the Government on the idea of the capacity of the people for self-government. It delegated certain powers to the Federal Government. It reserved other powers and all the powers relating to local legislation to the State governments. These questions which relate to the employment of laborers and local contracts belong to the State authority; and when Congress passes this resolution, as I suppose it will do, or anything else that violates the Constitution [laughter], it assumes the incapacity of the people for self-government."[20]

Another former Confederate, James B. Morgan, Democrat of Mississippi, seconded Reagan: The House had a duty to disabuse the Knights of the delusion that Congress could, or should, solve their problems. "[W]hy not speak to these men and tell them that this is like the case of every other contract known to the laws of the land, that they are at liberty to say to the railroad companies, 'We will work for you,' or 'We will not work for you,' and that the railroad companies are at liberty to say to them, 'We will employ you,' or 'We will not employ you,'" and that is the end of the transaction."[21]

"This matter is a very simple one," Reed replied. "The Congress of the United States, like every legislative body, sits for the hearing and for the redress of grievances. Even if it be true . . . that we have nothing to say to these men after the investigation is over, we certainly are bound to give them the investigation. We are bound to hear what the facts are, and, if we can, to act upon them. . . . If it turns out that the facts are such that they can not be acted upon within the purview of the Constitution, then there will be time for the gentleman from Texas [Mr. Reagan] to repeat his constitutional discourse. But, for my part, I beg leave here and now—and there can be no better opportunity than in a time of trouble like this, when there seems to be great disturbances in the land—to protest this everlasting putting up of the Constitution of the United States against every proposition which is presented in this House. I say that the total effect of such action will be to make a mockery of the Constitution and to give point to that jest which was made here long years ago, that the Constitution of the United States, in the mind of a strict constructionist, was in favor of every bill that he wanted and against every bill he opposed."[22]

In an election year, the petitions of 700,000 working men were unlikely to be ignored in Washington, Constitution or not. Nor were they in 1886. Hiscock spoke up in support of the proposed congressional investigation, as did Democrat Sam Randall of Pennsylvania. Of all people, William M. Springer, the Illinois Democrat—"I cannot restrain myself when I see that man," Reed told his diary[23]—threw his weight behind the investigation too.

"Mr. Speaker," Springer began, "I regret that the gentleman from Texas [Mr. Reagan] should have placed his opposition to this resolution upon constitutional grounds."

Reagan interrupted him: "I want to ask the pardon of this House for having given offense to Democrats, including the gentleman from Illinois [Mr. Springer], as well as to the gentleman from Maine [Mr. Reed], by referring to the Constitution."[24] The *Times* reproached the two strange bedfellows, Reed and Springer, for dangling out to America's workers the false hope that legislation could be the constitutionally lawful solution to their troubles.

Having fallen afoul of temporal authority in April, Reed managed to offend a Portland minister in July. In delivering the city's Centennial Oration, the congressman had paused to recall the death, at the Second Battle of Bull Run, in 1862, of his college friend Samuel Fessenden. "Can it be that I shall never look into those cheerful eyes again?" Reed had said. "Can it be that neither the quaint jest of the happier hours, nor the solemn confidence of the heart . . . will ever again fall upon the ear of friendship or of love? It can be no otherwise. He can only live in my memory—the dead, however sweetly embalmed, are but the dead."[25]

The Reverend H. C. Dunham disapprovingly quoted those words to his congregation from the pulpit of the New Jerusalem Church. Did Christianity not hold out the promise of life everlasting? "Interpret this language as we may," Dunham told the congregation, "it is not the sweet, beautiful teaching of Christianity, but of bitter and unlovely infidelity."

Dunham was of a mind to turn the text of his sermon over to the Portland newspapers, but a friend and neighbor of Reed's protested that the congressman had meant no such thing. Actually, Dunham wrote to Reed, Stephen Berry was the only friend of Reed's who had so protested. The rest had seen the matter exactly as Dunham did. Would not Reed consider issuing a public disclaimer?

Reed would not. He had meant to take no stand on the question of the Christian afterlife. Nor had he done so, he insisted. To his diary alone he later confided that "I sometimes have a great desire to be a religious man, but I know from experience that there is no peace in that."[26] To Dunham, on this occasion, he replied that "it has been the custom of my life to submit in silence to any criticism which seems suitable to the one who makes it." And that was that.

Ahead loomed the fall election. For the Maine Republicans that year, the campaign season began on August 24 with a picnic on chilly Lake Sebago. Politics, however, was not the foremost attraction for most of the 3,000 spectators who arrived on foot, in carriages or by rail. Farm families came for a day of eating and socializing, the women wearing "the inharmonious and blazing colors common among the country people of this State," according to an out-of-town reporter. Reed and Blaine, sharing the same special train, alighted together at 1:30. "Isn't he handsome!" cried a woman in the crowd, and nobody could doubt that the politician to whom she referred was the Plumed Knight, natty in gray suit and white hat.[27]

Blaine, not enamored of open-air speaking, read from his text. The crowd listened distractedly as he ran through his familiar election-year repertory. They could, he told them, thank the Republican party for protecting them against pauper wages, including the wages paid to poor southern blacks. (How, exactly, Republican policies shielded the white workingman against this alleged source of economic peril was not spelled out in news reports.) Reed, in his turn, "commended" Blaine's "eloquence and conservatism," and unfavorably compared the promises of the Democratic party in 1884 with the Cleveland administration's first-year achievements.[28]

It was a mark of Reed's growing prominence that the Knights of Labor chose to target him for defeat. A week after the picnic came a report that an agent of the union's national office was on the ground in Portland spreading the word among the estimated 6,000 Knights in Reed's district. Of such overriding importance was Reed's defeat that the Knights had determined to abandon their own candidate, a certain Mr. Moulton, in the First Congressional District and throw all their support to Reed's Democratic opponent, William Henry Clifford. Not that the Knights particularly liked Clifford, either: He was a lawyer, not a proper son of toil. But the president of the national order liked attorney Reed even less.

News of the Knights' offensive elicited nothing short of glee from the New York *Times*. Had the editorial page of that newspaper not rebuked Reed in the April debate over the Lawler resolution? By demagogically disparaging the constitutional objections to federal intrusion into local labor matters, the Maine Republican had tried to insinuate himself into the Knights' good graces. See, now, how labor returned the favor! Not that Reed's defeat at the polls would be such a bad thing even for Reed, the *Times*'s editors insisted. "He would probably be returned to Congress two years later a more courageous and self-respecting man."[29] But Reed again confounded his detractors, polling 15,625 votes to Clifford's 14,299.[30]

The winner was amazed: "It's too bad that I have no chance in my district," he had glumly mused in his diary in March.[31] Reflecting on this, his sixth consecutive victory, Reed doubted there would be a seventh. "I am not a skillful liar," he confessed to Gifford. Nor could he hide his anger or his feelings, as a successful politician must. "Ruin will swallow me up soon," he predicted, before knowingly adding, "But I have always thought like that."[32]

WITH ONE EXCEPTION, the conscientious Cleveland refused to put his name on a document of a public policy nature that he himself didn't write. That exception, in 1885, was a preinauguration letter to members of the 48th Congress, warning against an attempt to weaken the gold standard. Samuel J. Tilden, the grand old man of the Democratic party, had pushed Cleveland to make the statement—and not without cause, as foreign dollar holders, in the wake of the 1884 panic, were having their doubts about the integrity of the currency.[33] However, the president-elect, though he subscribed to the message, chafed at Tilden's meddling. Neither, one imagined, could he have been happy with the purple prose of Tilden's draftsman, the ex-newspaperman and Democratic factotum Manton Marble.[34]

Certainly nobody but Cleveland contributed to the drafting of the president's second State of the Union speech. It was the custom in these annual messages to deliver a comprehensive national status report. Cleveland, in a radical departure from form, devoted his entire discourse to the-then third rail of American politics, the tariff laws.

Cleveland wrote urgently, fearful that the country was on the verge of another financial panic. The autumn was ordinarily a time of stringency in American banking. Farmers needed credit to haul their crops to market; to accommodate that demand, farm banks withdrew the funds they had placed on deposit with their big-city correspondents. So dollars left Wall Street for employment in farm towns throughout the interior. It happened every year.

In 1887, however, a business depression exacerbated the ordinary seasonal pressures, while an indigestible surplus in the federal Treasury compounded the usual cyclical strains. According to modern dating methods, the downturn had begun in March.[35] And though Cleveland, for better or worse, had no econometric experts on whom to call, he could see for himself that the times were hard.

The prevalent fiscal problem in the 1880s was too much cash in the public till, not too little. In Cleveland's administration (as in Arthur's before him), the Treasury took in much more than it spent. What to do with the surplus taxed the finest minds in public life.[36] Should Congress spend the money on river and harbor improvements and national defense, as Senator John Sherman urged? Or should it return the money to the people, as assorted Democrats demanded? The parties could at least agree that removing dollar bills from circulation and imprisoning them in the Treasury's vaults was no way to fight a depression.

Treasury officials knew as well as anyone how much the dollars yearned to be set free, and they did what they lawfully could to liberate them. What avenues of economic stimulus were open to the constitutionally correct politicians of the 1880s? They could—and did—purchase the government's own outstanding bonds, evidences of the long-lingering financial cost of the Civil War. And they could deposit a modest sum of this money in private banks, thereby returning it to circulation. But the number of outstanding bonds was finite, as was the number of banks authorized to accept federal deposits. Do what it might to mitigate the damage inflicted by its own overflowing exchequer, the government was finally forced to concede that it was simply overfed. Or, rather, President Cleveland, in the name of the government, finally chose to make that acknowledgment.

The politically attuned portion of the nation was electrified by Cleveland's message. Posterity too may stop and stare, especially at the principles on which the president based his prescriptions. Taxes being "exactions," the government was bound to hold them to the bare minimum; it had no moral, political or constitutional claim on the people's income. The "theory of our institutions," declared Cleveland, "guarantees to every citizen the full enjoyment of all the fruits of his industry and enterprise, with only such deduction as may be his share toward the careful and economical maintenance of the Government which protects him." By taking more than the bare minimum, the government was guilty of "indefensible extortion." The Treasury thereby became "a hoarding place for money needlessly withdrawn from trade and the people's use, thus crippling our national energies, suspending our country's development, preventing investment in productive enterprise, threatening financial disturbance and inviting schemes of public plunder."

In fiscal year 2009, the federal government ran a deficit of $1.4 trillion, or 10 percent of the national output. A deficit meaningfully smaller would have deprived the struggling economy of the "stimulus" necessary to restore prosperity, so the ruling theory had it. At the time that Cleveland wrote, the national output (likewise impaired by a business slump) was on the order of $12.5 billion. The federal surplus, in the sum of $100 million, was about 0.8 percent of that grand total.[37] In the so-called Great Recession of 2007–08, the Treasury, Congress and the Federal Reserve together pulled out more countercyclical rabbits from more hats than a benumbed citizen could easily count. In the hard times of 1887, there was really only one hat, the Treasury; and one rabbit, the purchaser of the 3 percent bonds (redeemable at the option of the government). But, as Cleveland explained, these bonds had finally been retired, "and there are no bonds outstanding the payment of which we have a right to insist upon." Alexander Hamilton's sinking fund, the pot of money earmarked for retiring the public debt, was still in operation. And the Cleveland administration had paid into this fund the maximum permissible for the current fiscal year. What then? How might the government meet the financial emergency that, to Cleveland, seemed all too near at hand?

Well, the Secretary of the Treasury could buy government securities in the open market, paying what the sellers demanded. But the authority for such purchases stemmed from an appropriations bill passed many years before. To Cleveland, it seemed an awfully tenuous legal basis for such an important fiscal initiative. To other Democrats, including the House Speaker, John Carlisle, the notion of paying prices well above 100 cents on the dollar for the Treasury's obligations seemed inherently inequitable; the creditor class had done nothing to deserve such a windfall.[38] Then too the president bridled at the idea of conferring on the Secretary of the Treasury such immense and arbitrary powers over the financial part of the American economy.

Indeed, Cleveland wanted no part of any contemplated intrusion by the Treasury into the nation's business. And that went for the proposed deposit of most or all of the government's overflowing balances in the commercial banking system. "Exceedingly objectionable in principle," the president judged it, "as establishing too close a relationship between the operations of the Government Treasury and the business of the country and too extensive a commingling of their money, thus fostering an unnatural reliance in private business upon public funds." If it were to be done at all, he went on, let it be done as an emergency measure. "Legislative and executive effort should generally be in the opposite direction, and should have a tendency to divorce, as much and as fast as can be safely done, the Treasury Department from private enterprise."[39]

Having nailed his principles to the door, Cleveland raised the hammer against the tariff laws themselves, "the vicious, inequitable and illogical source of unnecessary taxation."[40] Customs receipts levied on some 4,000 items furnished the largest share, by far, of the federal revenue: in 1887, $217.3 million out of $371.4 million, an amount more than twice the size as that year's $103.5 million surplus.[41] Not that the overstuffed Treasury was the only adverse consequence of the tariff laws. They raised prices to domestic consumers as well and—another baleful effect—contributed to the formation and prosperity of monopolies, i.e., the "trusts."

Republicans had long asserted that the high customs duties protected against low foreign wages. They were the armor and shield of the American workingman, Reed and likeminded protectionists never tired of asserting. Certainly, something positive was at work in the labor market. Prices, as noted, were falling throughout the final quarter of the 19th century, as advances in technology pushed down the cost of production. But in the decade of the 1880s, wages zoomed higher. Thus, from 1879 to 1889, an index of consumer prices fell by 4.2 percent, while indices of farm and urban wage rates rose. "No decade before or since produced such a sustainable rise in real wages," a historian of the period relates.[42]

Midway through the decade, Cleveland had no such data at hand. He did, however, make some penetrating observations. Out of a work force numbering 17.4 million, 7.7 million worked on the farm—the tariff protected them not at all. And of the 3.8 million employed in "manufacturing and mining," 1.2 million really had nothing to do with the fabrication of marketable goods (such workers included carpenters and joiners, blacksmiths, tailors et cetera). Which left 2.6 million conceivable direct beneficiaries of the so-called protective system. Yet, observed Cleveland, even these employees were also consumers. Granted that the tariff inflated their wages, it also inflated the prices of the things that those wages bought.[43]

What, then, was to be done? A "radical reduction" in duties on raw materials, Cleveland proposed, would lower the cost of life's necessities while enabling American manufacturers to compete more effectively in foreign markets. Both major political parties were agreed that the groaning federal surplus was an evil to be corrected. So, then, the president beseeched, let us have no partisan bickering over "free trade," the Republicans' favorite bugbear. It is, he said, "a condition which confronts us—not a theory." And, in ringing conclusion: "The simple and plain duty which we owe the people is to reduce taxation to the necessary expenses of an economical operation of the Government and to restore to the business of the country the money which we hold in the Treasury through the perversion of governmental powers. These things can and should be done with safety to all our industries, without danger to the opportunity for remunerative labor which our workingmen need, and with benefit to them and all our people by cheapening their means of subsistence and increasing the measure of their comforts."[44]

Far from depoliticizing the tariff debate, Cleveland's message put a new partisan charge into it. From Europe, Blaine cabled his condemnation. From the Mugwump ranks came extravagant praise: There had been no such magnificent utterance since the Emancipation Proclamation, they cried. From the protectionist Democrats—notably Sam Randall from the iron-manufacturing state of Pennsylvania—rose cries of lamentation.[45]

Professional politicians of whatever stripe needed no reminder that 1888 was a presidential election year, or that, by broaching no topic but the tariff in his State of the Union address, President Cleveland had drawn the electoral battle lines around that single, emotional issue. The 50th Congress convened on December 5, 1887, the opening ceremonies enlivened by the ejection from the public galleries of a man who bade the House join him in the singing of the Doxology: "Praise God from whom all blessings flow . . ." His neighbors scattered when they saw the singer reach under his seat and produce a bundle that—in view of recent violent collisions between capital and labor—might have been a bomb. Happily, it was not; the singer was escorted from the premises and the ordinary opening-day business resumed. The Democrats, of whom there were 168 on hand, voted John G. Carlisle of Kentucky the Speaker; the Republicans, of whom there were 152, nominated Reed. Little Samuel S. Cox of New York and the massive Reed walked Carlisle down the aisle to a waiting Judge Kelley, the 73-year-old patriarch of the House, who administered the oath of office to the third-term Speaker.[46]

Carlisle's views on the protective tariff—and on the urgent need for legislation to whittle it down to size—exactly matched Cleveland's, but the 50th Congress was slow off the mark. The Speaker's own electoral troubles were one source of delay. The Knights of Labor had run their own man against Carlisle in Kentucky's Sixth District. Nobody expected the upstart to make a showing—certainly, Carlisle did not—but George H. Thobe gave the national statesman a run for his money. Nor did he accept that Carlisle had, as the results seemed to show, won by the skin of his teeth. In keeping with the rules of the House, the disputed contest was thrown to the House Elections Committee for adjudication.[47]

Did it not therefore make sense to adjourn for the holidays, reconvening on January 5? William H. Hatch, Democrat of Missouri, so moved in mid-December. No, Reed protested, it did not. Both sides of the House were agreed on the need to shrink the fiscal surplus. And both sides were agreed that a reduction in the federal tax on tobacco would be a place to start (Blaine had proposed as much, venturing that 95 percent of American workingmen chewed while on the job). Or, Reed needled the Democrats, were they frozen in fear by their own president's radical State of the Union address?

"If the other side of the House find it somewhat difficult to range themselves alongside of the recent message which has been sent them we can all well understand it," said Reed in his best incendiary manner, "and we can all give them the assurance of our respectful sympathy [Laughter on the Republican side.], because it was a summons from, I hope to some of the Democracy, a very great way off, and it requires that they traverse a very great distance before they can get alongside of their pioneer brother at the other end of the avenue. [Laughter.] If time is wanted for that purpose, I hope the gentleman from Missouri will frankly say so. If there is a proposition—if gentlemen on the other side of the House have grave doubts how they shall comply with the suggestions of the message; if after they have made up their minds, in the interest of moderation and reform, that the more advanced of them will be contented with the destruction of a few of our industries, and they need time to select which they see fit to destroy, that would be ground, of course, for his motion; and I hope the gentleman from Missouri, with the frankness which always characterizes him, will tell us if that is the reason underlying his resolution."

Hatch, a former assistant adjutant general in the Confederate army, listened to Reed with mounting annoyance. "Mr. Speaker," he replied to his tormentor, "I had hoped that it would be possible to introduce a resolution of adjournment in this House and yield to the gentleman from Maine without his improving the opportunity—"

Mr. Reed (interrupting). "I think I have improved it."

Mr. Hatch. "To make a political harangue. I do not think he has improved it. It is the same old speech that we have been listening to for the past ten years."

Mr. Reed. "And the same old enemy. [Laughter.]

Mr. Hatch. "If the gentleman from Maine had not had the opportunity time and again during both sessions of the Forty-ninth Congress to vote for the consideration of a tariff bill, and always voted against it, there might be some strength and sincerity in the position he is occupying today. [Applause on the Democratic side.]"[48]

The newspapers were as amused as was Reed himself at this small tumult on the floor. In his diary, the perpetrator jokingly protested his innocence: "But after all, I only threw a stone through the window to see if the family was home."[49]

ROGER Q. MILLS, chairman of the House Ways and Means Committee, brought a ready-made tariff bill with him to Washington from his home in Texas.[50] He knew what he wanted. As liberty was his credo, so free trade was his policy. A thrice-wounded ex-Confederate infantry officer, Mills had had long service on Ways and Means. He had sat through all too many hearings into the relationship between the tariff and American manufacturing, and he laid down the law for 1888: There would be no more such investigations—the facts and the theory were abundantly clear.

"Mr. Mills," relates Ida Tarbell in her history of the tariff, "was an out-and-out free-trader. After Mr. Carlisle, he was the ablest and best-informed man in Congress on the tariff."[51] Ideologically pure and perfectly briefed though he might have been, however, Mills failed to persuade his less determined colleagues to root out the protective system root and branch. The southern Democrats on Mill's committee represented districts heavily involved in sugar and iron. In the way of politics, each received special consideration in the details of the tariff-drafting.[52]

Not until April, the month following the famous blizzard of 1888, was the watered-down Mills bill presented to the House.[53]

It was quite pure enough to enflame the Republicans—a threat, as they saw it, to the very foundation of American prosperity. Debate raged for over a month, encompassing 151 speeches, including a stem-winder by the ordinarily terse Thomas B. Reed. The Democrats' position was simplicity itself. The tariff was a tax, they observed. It did not fall on the manufacturer, who could charge higher prices, and earn a higher profit, than he could do in the absence of government protection. The burden, rather, was borne mainly by the workingman, who paid tariff-inflated prices but enjoyed no share of his employer's tariff-inflated profit. The moguls didn't pay their hired help a share of their earnings but rather the market wage. Jay Gould, if the spirit came over him, could pay his bootblack $500 a day. But the spirit never did seem to descend. No, Mills observed, the millionaire tossed him a nickel, the same as anyone else.[54]

"Suppose," Mills added by way of illustration, "that a laborer who is earning a dollar a day by his work finds a suit of woolen clothes he can buy for $10 without the tariff. Then the suit can be procured for 10 days' work, but the manufacturer goes to Congress and says, 'I must be protected against the man buying this cheap suit of clothes.' And Congress protects him by putting on a duty of 100 per cent, or $10. Now it will require the laborer to work 20 days to get this suit of clothes. Now tell me if 10 days of his labor have not been annihilated?"[55]

On the floor of the House, Reed was one for brevity. Repartee and the parliamentary thrust were his stock in trade. Fluent as he was in the five-minute speech, however, the great debate over the tariff now demanded more from him. President Cleveland and Representative Mills had dropped the Democratic gauntlet on the floor of the House, and it fell to the minority leader to pick it up. This Reed proceeded to do.

Reed was, it is true, no deep student of international trade. He read Henry M. Hoyt's *Protection vs. Free Trade* (1886) and sampled the writings of that progenitor of the American School of Economics, Henry C. Carey. "After dinner I read the work of Mr. H.C. Carey," Reed recorded on December 15, 1887, "where I found many ideas I had already thought of myself."[56] Among these ideas was the doctrine that, under a properly administered system of protective tariffs, labor and capital, far from fighting with one another, thrive together harmoniously. However, for the new House minority leader, economic questions never held the charm that the French language did. "Last night I studied Protection," he reported on May 4, 1888. "There is a Sahara."[57]

Dry the tariff might be, but it was the issue of the year for 1888. The fiercest of the Republican protectionists, old Pig Iron Kelley, struck a rhetorical tone on the floor of the House fully in keeping with the size of the political stakes. "The enactment of this bill would instantly paralyze the industry and enterprise of the people," he thundered. Not forgetting the bloody shirt, Kelley continued: "Mr. Chairman, having devoted the years of my vigorous manhood to the overthrow of the political influences of the slave oligarchy, I intend to devote my remaining years to the emancipation of its political affairs from the fatal embrace of the most fruitful source of poverty, ignorance, vice, crime, disease, insanity and ignominious death known to the civilization of the nineteenth century, and whose subtle and insidious power is arrayed alike against the mining and manufacturing interests of the country and the diversification of its agriculture." Kelley was referring to the Democratic party.[58]

Kelley's, however, was a voice from the Republican past. Reed and William McKinley, of Ohio, were the party's principal standard-bearers in the great tariff debate. Carlisle (who successfully repelled the challenge to his election by his Knight of Labor opponent), Mills and William L. Wilson of West Virginia were the champions of the Democratic side. McKinley and Wilson and Mills could dazzle the galleries with the facts of the case and Carlisle with the logic, but Reed was unsurpassed at combining facts and argumentation with wit. He closed the Republican side of the debate on May 19.

True to his partisan temper, Reed attacked the Democrats more than their legislation. If, as they insisted, protection was federally sanctioned theft, why did the Mills bill not seek to eliminate the evil rather than only to mitigate it? If the consumer bore 100 percent of the cost of the tariff, as President Cleveland himself asserted, the cost had been horrific—$6.6 billion since 1880, Reed calculated. By the Democrats' own admission, the American robber barons had exacted the greatest tribute

in history. Yet the Mills bill contemplated merely a marginal reduction
in tariff rates:

"If it be a tribute," Reed jabbed at the Democrats, "be bold and
sweep it away. Why do you hesitate? Is it because you dare not be caught
lowering the wages of the laboring men who have the votes? Have the
courage of your leader's convictions—for has not the gentleman from
Texas, godfather of this bill, who has promised to bring it up in the nurture and admonition of the Lord, loudly proclaimed to the open day that
tariffs have nothing to do with wages? Is it out of mercy to the capitalist
that you falter? [Laughter.]"

As for protection, the system the Democrats would destroy, Reed
said he felt no need to defend it. The mighty growth of the United States
since the Civil War was defense enough. "It has survived the assaults of
all the professors of the 'dismal science' called political economy. . . . It
is the instinct of humanity against the assumptions of the book men. It
is the wisdom of the race against the wisdom of the few."

American producers deserved America's markets, and it was the
duty of government to keep the foreigners from trespassing in them.
Reed took it as given that, under free trade, "the richest country gives
the most; in fact, it levels itself down and levels the other countries
up." Now then, he demanded, which is richer, Europe or America?
America, of course. Nobody doubted it. The Democrats, conceding the
point, nonetheless proposed to demolish the very reason for American
prosperity. As for the Republicans, said Reed to the sound of enthusiastic protectionist applause, "We mean to keep the wealth here. We
mean to do it even if we build a 'Chinese' wall of tariff taxes around
this country."

Reed brushed aside the Democrats' complaint about the bloated
profits of the protected domestic manufacturers. Perhaps the critics merely wished that they too were rich. "Whenever I walk through
the streets of that Democratic importing city of New York and look at
the brownstone fronts my gorge always rises," said Reed, who himself
yearned for the wealth he didn't have. "I can never understand why the
virtue which I know is on the sidewalk is not thus rewarded. I do not feel
kindly to the people inside. But when I feel that way I know what the
feeling is. It is good, honest, high-minded envy. When some other gen-

tlemen have the same feeling, they think it's political economy! [Great laughter.]"

The president's party condemned the tariff-empowered monopolists. There were no such creatures, Reed asserted; no imagined trust could long withstand the competition that always sprang up to skim off extraordinary profits. "That is one of the laws of God working for his children," he said. "Compared with one of your laws of Congress, it is a leviathan to a clam."

Reed had, the previous summer, toured the West in the company of some wealthy friends. He had seen the land from the vantage point of a private railcar, "in good company as rich people do," as he remarked to Gifford, from Chicago to Minneapolis and thence to the Pacific northwest and into Alaska, then home again, via Salt Lake City and Denver.* At Pike's Peak, the New England intellectual had, for the first time, ridden a horse. At Greeley, Colorado, he had marveled at the potato fields, "unequalled in Aroostook itself."[59] For years, he had heard western congressmen complain that the tariff had picked clean the pockets of their constituents. Reed, however, now knew better.

"In the fullness of time," he related, "I traveled West myself. You may well imagine my astonishment, who had never seen 10 acres together in corn, to behold fields of that great staple stretching way out to the horizon's edge, to see tracts of land which seemed to have no boundaries but the visible sky; land so rich that if we had an acre of it in Maine we would have sold it by the bushel [Laughter.], while on every side were the great brick houses, such as only the squire lived in in our villages. After some days of this I became sulky. I said, gentlemen, of course we have robbed you; your Congressman would not lie about trifles like that. But what disgusts me is that we did not do it more thoroughly. The gleaning looks bigger than the harvest. These crumbs are bigger than the food we put on our tables. Then they confided to me that the Western Congressmen were great orators and did this for practice. [Laughter.]"

---

* "I must confess," Reed added, "the world is very sweet for men who have enough money. They say it was possible by means of faith to send an abyss to hide a very tall mountain. Do you believe all that? It's quite possible today by means of money. Faith in times past, money today." See Reed to George Gifford, August 29, 1887. Thomas Reed Collection. Bowdoin College.

Reed had spoken for almost two hours. Many had doubted that he had the stamina or the intellectual discipline to mount such a sustained effort. But the speech was a triumph. Half a million copies were printed and distributed by the nation's business interests. "In truth," he allowed himself to reflect, "I have arrived at the summit of the climb."[60]

Chapter 15

Great Plains Land Bubble

R EED WAS WORRYING about the 1888 elections even before he was officially in them. News that the hometown Republicans had selected him as their candidate for the seventh consecutive season reached him in Washington in the first week of May. The nominee picked the item out of a newspaper. "[N]o one sent me a single telegram!" he marveled, then mused: "It is always like that. The District and I don't bother each other."[1]

Reed, along with much of the rest of America, had Blaine on his mind. Would the Plumed Knight make another run for the presidency? The nomination was his for the asking, such authorities as former president Rutherford B. Hayes and former senator Benjamin Harrison agreed.[2] None of the other aspirants—neither John Sherman, the "Ohio Icicle," nor Chauncey Depew, the railroad president and Fourth of July orator, for instance—commanded anything like Blaine's worshipful following. "In the spring of 1887," relates a modern historian, H. Wayne Morgan, of the 1884 Republican standard-bearer, "his head-cold rated front page discussion. Reporters trailed him in Europe like spies in a Balkan war, donning servants' costumes, bribing grooms and butlers for gossip from the coach and table."[3]

"Blaine can be nominated by acclamation . . ." acidly remarked

Roscoe Conkling, his blood enemy, "and be defeated in the same manner."[4] Neither had Blaine ever worked his charms on Reed, though few seemed to know it. Most assumed that the younger man was the elder's protégé. En route to Alaska the summer before, Reed was constantly presented with the rumor that he was traveling as Blaine's political agent.[5] On the contrary, Reed believed—however implausibly—that Blaine had opposed him from the time he ran for attorney general of Maine. "[H]e is a capable man, a man of genius," Reed confided to his diary of his supposed mentor in October 1887, "but he is a liar, an egoist, without moral principles. It is true, undoubtedly, that all great men have had in their makeup a bit of the charlatan, and that it is not possible, even though it might seem so, to govern men at a level of moral perception of the greatest men, but Mr. B. is surrounded by a crowd of corrupt and corrupting men." Reed went on to describe an investment Blaine had made in a Hocking Valley, Ohio, coal venture. To attract other investors, the statesman had allowed the company to say that he, Blaine, was a stockholder. But when the venture failed, Blaine turned out to occupy a more senior, and therefore a safer, position in the capital structure. To the surprise and dismay of those who thought they had invested alongside him, the Plumed Knight was revealed to be a creditor, a status sealed in a secret agreement that he had negotiated with management. "But without doubt, that doesn't mean much," Reed ironically wound up the story. "Great men are above morality."[6]

Whatever Blaine did in 1888, it looked to Reed like trouble. If he ran and won, he could damage Reed from the White House. If he didn't run, it would be because he doubted his party's chances of winning—and Reed would miss the helpful presence of Blaine's name at the top of the national ticket. There was a worrying element of truth in the boast of Reed's 1884 congressional opponent, Judge Cleaves, that only the presence of Blaine on the ballot had tipped a close race to the Republican incumbent.[7] Such were Reed's downcast notes to himself, in French, a year before the polls opened.

If Reed was uneasy, so were many others in the company town of Washington, D.C. Which way would Blaine jump? He was positively unavailable, Blaine himself insisted in early 1888 in a series of communiqués from Europe, where he was vacationing. By March, the non-candidate was privately pushing Benjamin Harrison, the lawyer he had retained in Indiana to silence ugly, Democratic-fomented rumors about his marriage during the 1884 campaign.[8] Blaine's legions would not be easily dissuaded. In time, they could understand the word "No," but only if it were issued, repeatedly, from the lips of their hero himself. On June 19, the Republican National Convention got underway in Chicago. Listening to temporary chairman John M. Thurston sing the noncandidate's praises, the delegates might have supposed that Blaine was out of the running on account of a martyr's death: "[T]he gallant leader, that chevalier of American politics, the glory of Republicanism, the nightmare of Democracy, our Henry of Navarre . . ." and so forth, Thurston proclaimed.[9] But Blaine had no stomach for another campaign, and he cabled his emphatic decision to the Maine delegation. So it was to be Sherman—or Harrison or, perhaps, William McKinley. The latter loyally declined all consideration; he, like every other faithful son of Ohio, was pledged to Sherman. "Sherman won't do; he is too cold," an unnamed skeptic remarked to an Ohioan. "Why," replied the Sherman loyalist, "he is a red hot stove compared to Harrison."[10] At last, on the eighth ballot, the Blaine-less and McKinley-less delegates pushed Harrison over the top.

Late in July, the Mills bill too went over the top, in a party-line vote. It passed under the gaze of the president's stylish wife, Frances Folsom Cleveland, who was seated in the House galleries, and over the mocking insistence of the Republican minority that the Democrats had achieved nothing but a slightly smaller rate of plunder. For all the president's principled sound and fury, noted Reed and the others, the Democrats had brought forth a bill that reduced the average duty to 40 percent from 47 percent. Why had the Democrats retreated so far from the principles their own president had so recently and ardently enunciated? Reed had the answer: "It is because they recognize the fact that the people of the United States are in favor of the American doctrine of protection [Applause on the Republican side]; that they are in favor of having the articles which the people of America use made by American workingmen; and from now until election time their greatest effort on the other side will be to explain away the declarations which they so bravely made, and to say that even Mr. Cleveland himself is a genuine protectionist and never meant anything else. [Applause on the Republican side.]"[11]

Waylaid in the Senate, the Mills bill never became more than a bone of partisan contention, but it was the bone of bones in 1888. The Republican platform denounced it by name without so much as a word of acknowledgment for the need of reform through other means. "We are uncompromisingly in favor of the American system of protection," the party thundered; "we protest against destruction as proposed by the President and his party. . . ."

For the Democrats, "taxes" were the all-encompassing evil, and the tariff was a tax, that and no more. Republican policies, the Democrats alleged, left American enterprise "fettered and bound to home markets," but the party made no other direct attack on Republican trade doctrine. It rather concentrated its fire on the consequences of that doctrine, notably the redundant $125 million Treasury cash balance: "Debauched by this immense temptation," the Democrats charged, "the remedy of the Republican party is to meet and exhaust by extravagant appropriations and expenses, whether constitutional or not, the accumulation of extravagant taxation."

To a resident of such western boomtowns as Wichita, Kansas, Lincoln, Nebraska, or Los Angeles, California, the jousting platforms were of little more consequence than the weather report for the nation's capital. A higher or lower tariff might have meant a few dollars to the family budget. But those dollars shrank to insignificance when the very dirt under the family's feet was turning to gold. As the train bearing Reed and his party sped west from Chicago in the summer of 1887, a spectacular property boom was burning itself out in southern California and the Great Plains. In Los Angeles, the average price of a business lot had jumped to $5,000 from $500 in only 12 months. In Wichita, according to the historian John D. Hicks, "A clerk who put his $200 into a lot sold it two months later for $2,000. A barber who dabbled in real estate made $7,000. Real estate agents, many of whom made much larger fortunes, swarmed over the place by the hundreds; they were so numerous that the city derived a considerable revenue from the license fees they had to pay."[12]

Mortgage debt was on the rise throughout the United States. From 1880 to 1889, the value of cumulative mortgage transactions reached $9.5 billion, up 156 percent from the previous 10 years. In comparison, population grew by a quarter and wealth by a half. In other words, observed a senior official of the Census Bureau, "real estate mortgage debt increased proportionately about three times more than wealth and about six times more than population."[13] "Subprime mortgage" was a phrase for the future, but the lenders and borrowers of Reed's day anticipated the excesses of a later time even without their descendants' specialized vocabulary or their evolved financial and regulatory systems. Reed himself, an investor in land in Holt County, Nebraska, was a loser in the speculative collapse of the early 1890s.

For a proper bubble, the prerequisites are a compelling story and a ready source of finance, and these the western land markets had in spades. The story seemed to write itself: The frontier was vanishing, and land, long cheap, would soon become dear. Advertisements promised would-be emigrants to the Plains and Dakotas rich soil, easy mortgage lending terms, big crops and—of all things—salubrious weather. The weather was indeed a pleasant surprise in Kansas and Nebraska. Eighteen to twenty inches of rainfall was necessary to make a good crop, and this quota was annually met in the early and mid-1880s, even in the normally arid western portions of the states. Old-timers scratched their heads: What could explain the anomalous succession of wet seasons? Human activity, some authorities reasoned: By breaking sod, irrigating crops and planting trees, the settlers had effected a kind of benign climate change. A professor at the University of Nebraska lent his authority to this pleasing hypothesis.[14]

Mortgage money was available on terms that a 21st century borrower might find hauntingly familiar. Thus, for instance, the Union Pacific lent up to 90 percent of the value of the property at 7 percent over an 11-year term, with no principal amortization until the fourth year; for the first three years, the borrower paid interest only. Loans were available for the asking, though it was not always strictly necessary to make a formal application. The loan companies would come knocking at the farmhouse door.

American savers (and some foreign capitalists) were in the throes of a great yield hunger. Interest rates had peaked with the war-induced inflation of the 1860s. By the mid-1880s, New Englanders were earning just 4 percent at the bank and slightly less on high-grade railroad bonds. Inasmuch as the cost of living was actually falling (down by an average of 0.50 percent a year in the 1880s), a modern-day economist would judge that inflation-adjusted, or "real," interest rates were generous. But western mortgages, yielding 6 to 8 percent, were still more generous. Loans secured by livestock, farm implements and rolling stock—so-called chattel mortgages—fetched 10 percent and up. To the objection that nothing is actually free in investing and that pioneer agriculture is inherently risky, the promoters smilingly pointed to the good crops and high prices of recent seasons. Why should they not persist? And again to quote Hicks, "The mortgage notes themselves, 'gorgeous with gold and green ink,' looked the part of stability, and the idea spread throughout the East that savings placed in this class of investments were as safe as they were remunerative. Small wonder that money descended like a flood upon those who made it their business to place loans in the West!"[15]

Back east, bank regulators urged the smitten depositors to go slow. "Eastern states found it necessary to pass laws for the examining and licensing of western investment companies in order to protect individuals who were being induced to withdraw their deposits from savings banks and invest them in western securities," relates the historian Hallie Farmer. A lot of good it did: "Competition existed not between borrowers but between lenders. 'I found drafts, money orders and currency heaped on my desk every morning,' said the secretary of a western loan company. 'I could not loan the money as fast as it came in.' The manager of another company stated that 'during many months of 1886 and 1887 we were unable to get enough mortgages for the people of the East who wished to invest in that kind of security. My desk was piled high every morning with hundreds of letters each enclosing a draft and asking me to send a farm mortgage from Kansas or Nebraska.'"[16]

Presently, the demand for lendable funds rose to meet the generous supply. No self-respecting town wanted to be without its streetcar line, jail, school or—especially—railroad junction. "Confidence was high," recounts Farmer, "money was easy to obtain and the West entered upon such an orgy of railroad building as the world had never seen before. Old companies extended their lines. New companies were organized. Within six weeks in the spring of 1887, the *Northwestern Railroader* recorded the incorporation of 16 new railroad companies and the letting of contracts for work on 13 new branches of old roads. Kansas more than doubled her railroad mileage between 1880 and 1887. That of Nebraska was quadrupled and Dakota had 11 times the mileage in 1890 which she had in 1880."[17] And when, as sometimes happened at around this time, the railroad magnates fell to cutthroat competition, the traveling public was the winner. At the peak of the price wars of 1886, the fare between Kansas City and Los Angeles on the Santa Fe Railroad cost exactly $1.[18]

Frontier standards of due diligence in the 1880s proved little better than the big-city kind 120 years later. "Securities which could not have been sold in ordinary times found a ready market," according to Farmer. "Bonds of Capitola Township, Spink County, Dakota, were sold in this period and changed hands many times in eastern markets before it was discovered that no such township existed."[19]

None could doubt the existence of Los Angeles. Settlers by the thousands saw the place for themselves, and they watched the levitation of its real estate values. By 1885, Isaias Hellman, president of the Farmers and Merchants Bank and leader of the boomtown's banking community, had decided that a good thing had gone far enough. Against the ever-present temptation to run with the herd (especially if the herd seemed to be running in the direction of money), Hellman ordered his bank to restrict its lending. And in the fall of 1887, he announced that the Farmers and Merchants would have nothing more to do with the speculative bubble. Hellman's example was evidently a powerful one, for at that critical juncture less than half the assets of the Los Angeles banking community were out on loan. Within six months, only a quarter were. It was thanks to the restraining influence of the bankers, notably Hellman, that the southern California economy did not burst along with the local property bubble.[20] But rare, then as now, is the financier of detached and sober judgment. More common in 1887 was the attitude of the editor of the Nebraska *State Journal*, who protested that there was nothing like a bubble in property prices in Nebraska or Kansas. "It is simply," he asserted, "the effect of the exhaustion of the public lands and the prosperity of the trans-Missouri region."[21]

That prosperity was then receding. The alleged new era of man-made moisture ended in 1887 and a persistent drought began. Grain prices peaked; by 1890, the price of a bushel of corn was 28 cents; it had been 63 cents in 1881. Lending dried up with the moisture. In the years 1884 to 1887, 6,000 farm mortgages, in the sum of $5.5 million, were written in Nebraska, Farmer relates. "In the next three years, only 500 such mortgages were placed with a total value of $633,889. . . . Eastern investors refused to place more money in the West and much of the money already invested was withdrawn as the lenders became frightened over the agitation of the debtors for relief in the form of stay laws."[22]

The available data suggest, if anything, that the citizens of Kansas borrowed not recklessly but in moderation. Mortgage debt was just 26.8 percent of the value of Kansas real estate, according to estimates compiled by the 1890 census-takers. Per capita private debt, counting only adults, amounted to $347. However, those statistics paint a misleadingly conservative picture. Per capita indebtedness in Kansas, for instance, was four times the national average. And though just 60 percent of the taxed acres in the state were encumbered by mortgage debt, that was the highest such proportion in the union.[23] Then too, any debt is oppressive in the absence of income with which to service it, and such was the plight of the drought-stricken Jayhawk farmers. By 1892, half the population of western Kansas had trekked back east. On some of the wagons that bore what remained of the settlers' possessions, there was emblazoned the motto "In God we trusted, in Kansas we busted."[24] To this portion of the American electorate, the tariff battle seemed rather an abstraction.

THE STIFF-NECKED BENJAMIN Harrison proved to be a potent campaigner, at least when he kept beyond handshake range from the voters. He refused to travel far from the front porch of his home on North Delaware Street in Indianapolis, but no matter. The people came to him. They tromped over his lawn, made off with sections of his picket fence and listened to the words exactly suited to the crowd of the moment.

"My father," Julia Foraker related in her memoir, "who was in the thick of the campaign and heard hundreds of the speeches, said that Harrison *never once* repeated himself."[25] But there was a repetitive theme, and that was the Democratic threat to the American system of protection. Though the Mills bill would hardly institute free trade, the Republican candidate admitted, it was a clear step in the wrong direction. Give the Democrats four more years, and they would import the English system of radical laissez-faire in its entirety. Blaine, returning from Europe to stump for the ticket, did his all for Harrison, and the Republican campaign machinery hummed.

The Democrats' machinery wheezed and sputtered. In Cleveland, they had a noncampaigner: Going Harrison one better, he not only refused to tour but also to make a speech. He would sit behind his desk and do his duty, as he always did. And his running mate? Former senator Allen G. Thurman was known to break down in front of campaign crowds. "God knows," he once pitifully remarked to a visiting delegation of Indiana Democrats, "that I would rather be at home with my dear wife than in any office in the world."[26]

In 1884, the Democrats loved Grover Cleveland for the enemies he had made in Buffalo and Albany. In 1888, they should have loved him more for the ones he had made in Washington. Like poor Chet Arthur, Cleveland had made a good-faith effort at civil service reform but had done just enough to alienate the office-hungry Democrats without winning over the purest of the Mugwumps. Unlike any previous postwar president, he had dared to veto some of the most transparently fraudulent special pension bills that the House and Senate annually pushed through to reward their ex-soldier constituents. And if that were not politically inexpedient enough, Cleveland—who had sat out the war in Buffalo—had stirred up the mighty veterans' bloc with a maladroit attempt at sectional reconciliation.

With Lee's surrender, the captured battle flags of the Confederate armies were rounded up and sent to the War Department for storage, along with the flags of the North, and there they remained for 20 years. Why not return these dusty relics to the states from which they had come, even to the states of the former Confederacy? Secretary of War William C. Endicott proposed the idea to Cleveland just before Decoration Day 1887. Certainly, Cleveland replied; anything to advance the good work of sectional healing. On the national day of commemoration itself—the Day of the Dead Soldiers, as Reed irreverently called it— Cleveland went fishing.

The president's attitude toward the keeping of Memorial Day, however, was that of a distinct and mostly silent minority. To the principal organization of the veterans' lobby, the Grand Army of the Republic, Cleveland's fishing trip was a studied insult to the veterans of the Union army. The battle flag order, which came to light two weeks later, was an unforgivable act of treachery. Words could not express the rage of some of the ex-soldiers, though Lucius Fairchild of Wisconsin, national commander of the G.A.R., did make the attempt. The commander of a regiment of the Iron Brigade at Gettysburg, Fairchild addressed his fellow veterans at a meeting in Harlem: "May God palsy the hand that wrote that order. May God palsy the brain that conceived it, and may God palsy the tongue that dictated it." "Fairchild of the three palsies," the old hero was playfully known in the press thereafter, though it would have taken more than that jest to lighten the mood at the White House.[27]

If Cleveland brought on the battle flags imbroglio himself, he was the innocent victim of a political trick that cast his administration as a feeble tool of Queen Victoria. To the British minister to the United States, Sir Lionel Sackville-West, a Republican citrus-grower from Pomona, California, had artfully addressed a letter asking which candidate in the upcoming election might better support British interests. Sackville-West seemed to understand little about the potency of the Irish-American vote. He was, however, if nothing else, attentive to his correspondence. Taking the bait, he responded by virtually endorsing Cleveland's bid for a second term. "Murchison," as the Republican trickster signed himself, turned over this epistolary dynamite to his lawyer, who slipped it to the publisher of the Los Angeles *Times*. The story broke in late October, days before most of the country went to the polls. The administration's anguished disavowals—and demands on the British Foreign Ministry to recall its dim diplomat—repaired only so much of the damage.[28]

*   *   *

REED AND BLAINE made an odd and unaffectionate couple, but they campaigned together in Maine. Never before had Reed spoken to such large and enthusiastic crowds. The candidate pushed hard, singing the praises of the protective tariff, for he was no shoo-in. Indeed, political observers considered his seat, alone among the four contested House seats in Maine, to be up for grabs. On September 6, two weeks before the voting—Maine, as usual, got off to an early start—a visiting Chicago newspaperman reckoned that the incumbent might pull out a victory, if only on account of his Democratic opponent: William Emery, a moneylender from York County, was "rich but unpopular."[29] Reed did, in fact, handily prevail, with 18,288 votes to Emery's 15,855 (805 went to the prohibition candidate).[30] The victorious incumbent caught his breath and then a train for Massachusetts, where he campaigned for (among others) Representative Henry Cabot Lodge, who was seeking reelection to the House. "Today, or rather yesterday," Reed noted on September 29, "I went to Springfield and gave that night a speech to the citizens of that town. It [was] said that that was the largest meeting that had ever been seen there."[31]

It was a glorious autumn for the Republican party. Though Cleveland outpolled Harrison in the popular vote by almost 1 percent, the Republican captured 233 electoral votes, including New York's, to the incumbent's 168. Many Democrats shook their heads. The tariff was their undoing. "I don't regret it," said Cleveland. "It is better to be defeated battling for an honest principle than to win by a cowardly subterfuge."[32] Mrs. Cleveland was unbowed. On her way out the door, she issued instructions to the White House staff to take care of things in her temporary absence. "We are coming back just four years from today."[33]

Reed, like President Cleveland, was preoccupied with a principle. For Reed, it was a kind of idée fixe. He believed in majority rule. It seemed a reasonable enough principle on which to conduct a political career in America. Yet Congress, especially the 50th Congress (1887–1889), was a model of nonrule. In its conduct and organization, it might as well have been dedicated to the proposition that the minority was in charge.

The 50th Congress, though immortalized as the "Do Nothing Congress," did not literally do nothing. Among its slim legislative achievements it could count a reduction in the fee for obtaining a passport to $1 from $5, the creation of the Department of Labor and the fixing of the standard workday of a Post Office letter carrier at eight hours. However, in Reed's judgment, the things it did paled next to the things it failed to do—or, rather, under its own rules, refused to do. For days in tedious succession, the members answered roll calls, listened to filibustering speeches, voted on motions to adjourn or—to prevent the formation of a quorum—refused to vote at all. In one six-week span, they enacted just four bills. To all who continued to believe that that government is best which governs least, four was more than enough. The Washington *Post* editorially scolded "this unwieldy and self-shackled body," but the paper did not thereby shame it into action, or into a change in the rules that gave a minority free reign to obstruct.[34]

On the contrary, a generally popular measure to rebate a Civil War–era tax to the states—or, at least, to some states—was presently subjected to the full gamut of parliamentary obstruction. The states to which the rebate was due were those that had paid it. To the states that had not paid it—i.e., the states of the former Confederacy—nothing was due. Not surprising, then, a representative from Alabama, William C. Oates, a Democrat, led resistance to the measure. On April 4, 1888, he and others began a filibuster that stretched until April 12, a 192–hour epic of roll calls, interrogations of absentees, motions for adjournment, inquiries into the existence of a quorum, calls for a division, calls for the yeas and nays, the reading aloud of the names of the members who had voted, the calling of the names of those who had not, et cetera.[35] Long after midnight on the first day of this ordeal, a member objected to a motion to recess "until tomorrow." "But tomorrow will not come," Reed interjected. "It will be today under this arrangement. The gentleman is laboring under a misapprehension."[36] Reed and his forces, and Oates and his forces, ultimately reached agreement to allow the bill to come to a vote in the next session of the 50th Congress. It did, and passed in both the House and Senate, only to die on President Cleveland's desk.[37]

Reed gave full vent to his frustrations in an essay he wrote for the *North American Review* and which that egghead journal published in October 1889 under the headline "Obstruction in the National House." In it, Reed did not deny that dilatory motions could serve a noble purpose by curbing a tyrannical majority. Having himself employed such devices in democratically controlled congresses, he could hardly have argued otherwise. But in recent times, especially in the 50th Congress, obstruction had become the instrument of a tyrannical minority. And, indeed, not so much of a defined minority but of a changing cast of willful individuals. Representative Albert Raney Anderson, an independent Republican of Iowa, for instance, had personally blocked the House from voting on a bill to settle accounts with the Union Pacific Railroad, then the government's biggest debtor. And how had Anderson managed this feat of obstruction? By introducing a measure to codify the laws of the District of Columbia, a bill then already before the House, and demanding that it be read aloud—which it was, to groans and slumping shoulders, until the House adjourned for the day. Reed observed that the plan for settling with the Union Pacific, encased in the pending legislation, had been blessed by a commission appointed by President Cleveland. Whether the bill would have met with the approval of a majority of the House after a full discussion, Reed said, he did not know. "[B]ut it does seem as if, under a republican form of government, two-thirds of the House of Representatives ought not to have been deprived of the power to say whether the subject should be discussed or not."[38]

Reed wrote with a purpose, as he was then maneuvering to win the Speakership of the 51st Congress, which would convene in December 1889. "The next House," he noted, "will contain no large and successful majority tempted by its largeness and success to ride over the minority." It seemed that the Republicans would have a majority of only three, which would "hardly cover the percentage of loss from sickness and disability." Four new states had just entered the union—North and South Dakota, Montana and Washington—and they would send five new congressmen to Washington, as soon as they could hold elections. But even if the Republicans should capture each of those five seats, they would hold just three above a quorum, "which is hardly enough for business, let alone tyranny."

Reed closed with a preview of what the Democrats might expect when Congress reconvened. There would be some effort "to change the rules so that business can be done and the scandals of the last Congress avoided." But no, he immediately corrected himself, that was not right. "Change the rules" conveyed the wrong idea. "No rules have to be changed, for the new House will have no rules. What should have been written is that there will be an effort to establish rules which will facilitate the public business—rules unlike those of the present House, which only delay and frustrate action."[39]

Roger Q. Mills, the Texas Democrat of tariff fame, replied to Reed in the December issue of the same journal as the House convened. It was obvious to Mills that, in constructing his elaborate arguments against the tyranny of the minority, Reed and the Republicans were bent on mischief, "some desperate enterprise . . . that their prophetic souls tell them is beyond the boundary of rightful jurisdiction." While they would not go so far as to repeal the Bill of Rights, it would not be above them to cheat some honestly elected Democrats out of their seats in contested election cases or re-create the unscrupulous returning boards to which Hayes owed his presidency. "It is to prepare the way for the advent of this higher civilization that the rules have been indicted and arraigned before the bar of public opinion."[40]

Mills, like Reed, deprecated the chances of the Republicans accomplishing very much in the House of Representatives with a majority of only three votes. Unlike Reed, Mills insisted that the new majority party would find some sinister way to get what it wanted. Seventeen challenges to duly elected Democrats were already in the queue. The new Republican Speaker could defeat a dilatory motion by refusing to recognize the Democrat who was making it. However, the Texan continued, there was no such easy way around the arithmetic of the constitutional quorum.

To work their will in the 51st Congress, the Republicans would need the votes of 166 members. If every Republican were at his post, they would muster 169 votes. But, as Reed had noted, sickness and absences would almost certainly deny them that minimum number. How, then, might the new Speaker conjure a quorum if the Democrats withheld their votes? Many parliamentarians had puzzled over this very riddle. On February 24, 1875, at the tail end of the 43rd Congress, the Republicans were in the majority but, on that particular day, fielded no quorum. To a proposal from the floor that the chair command a quorum by compelling members of the minority to vote, Speaker Blaine made his famous reply. "The chair knows of no way of making a horse drink, although you may lead him to water." Others persisted. The Speaker could see with his own eyes who was in the hall. Why not mark down as present those who were actually present, whether or not they chose to vote? To which Blaine replied, "The moment you clothe your Speaker with power to go behind your roll-call and assume that there is a quorum in the hall, why, gentlemen, you stand on the very brink of a volcano."

Four years later, in 1879, the partisan roles were reversed, with the minority Republicans sitting mum while the majority Democrats scratched around for a quorum. Mills related how John Randolph Tucker, a Democrat from Virginia, tried to cut short the Republicans' filibustering with an amendment to allow Speaker Randall to count a quorum. But the minority sent up such a howl of protest that Tucker withdrew his amendment. Among the indignant Republicans was, of course, Thomas B. Reed. "All of them concurred with Speaker Blaine," Mills wrote, "that the majority party must make the quorum to do business; and that the majority of members present, when less than a quorum, can only compel the attendance of absentees, but cannot compel the vote of a member."

There was not a shadow of a doubt, Mills asserted, that the Republicans would revert to their cheating ways, reviving the methods of 1876 to steal the votes they couldn't fairly win. He did not actually assert that the next Speaker of the House would count a quorum, but he let the suggestion hang in the air. "The measure they propose is bold and revolutionary," he wound up, "and it remains to be seen whether they will succeed in passing it, and, if it is passed, what the popular verdict will be when it comes to be enforced."[41]

Chapter 16

To Count a Quorum

IT WAS IRKSOME to Reed that four Republicans chose to challenge his rightful claim for the nomination for the Speakership in the 51st Congress. He, not they, had led the party in opposition during the previous two Democratic-controlled congresses. To be passed over now that the Republicans were back in the majority would be a slap in the face, as Reed made note—"which rebuff I hope has not been deserved by any failure to do what was entrusted to me."[1] He addressed these sentiments, in November 1888, to his young admirer Theodore Roosevelt, the ambitious New York Republican who had hitched his star to the victorious presidential campaign of Benjamin Harrison. Roosevelt was behind Reed four-square.

The late autumn of 1888 was a season for Republican job-hunting. For four long years, Republican aspirants to federal offices had wandered in the Democratic wilderness. With Harrison—already, hopeful prospective jobholders were calling him "Benjy"—came the hope of deliverance. Ascribing his narrow victory over Cleveland to providence, the president-elect seemed rather above the employment scrum. Reed had no such luxury, where, in Portland, Republican office-seekers were making his life a misery. One of these supplicants was a figure from the congressman's youth. Reed had never liked him when the two were boys, but they had played together because they had a common friend to whom Reed was devoted. Then one day, out of the blue, the two boys, the one he liked and the one he didn't, stopped talking to Reed, stopped playing with him. Why had they done it? No reason, just a whim, the favored one later told him. Now, 38 years on, the unfavored one wrote Reed with a small request. Would he please get him appointed postmaster of Portland?[2]

Blaine too, the former U.S. senator, House Speaker and presidential candidate, was looking for work. His heart's desire was to return to the State Department, where he had briefly served as Secretary under Garfield and Arthur. In pursuit of this ambition, the Plumed Knight visited Washington in January 1889, a guest of William W. Phelps, a rich Republican congressman from New Jersey. Well did Reed know the Phelps household. Marian, Phelps's 20-year-old daughter, often drew him there. He had been seated next to her in February 1887 at a glittering dinner party that Representative Phelps had hosted in honor of Reed's old House colleague Frank Hiscock, now a senator-elect from New York. "I spent a very pleasant evening seated next that charming young lady, who pleased me extremely," Reed noted in his diary.[3] The teenager continued to delight him. He was captivated by her charm, her figure and her astuteness. (Nor was he the only one; Mark Twain later dedicated a book to her.) Now that she was 20, she seemed to have his number, as he confided to his diary that January: She had "growled at me, in a thundering manner. Oh well, it serves me right. It is hard to be reprimanded by one so young, but the worst part is that she was justified. She said that I am a slave to my conditions, of my wit which I always give the whole world, my emotions and my hates, which I am going to lose by my lack of patience the work of a lifetime. Oh, but how she scolded me without mercy. I know her well, that young lady, but it was astounding to be so thoroughly known."[4]

A couple of weeks later, Reed was again at the Phelps home, talking with Marian, when in walked her father accompanied by the wife of Robert R. Hitt, a Republican representative from Illinois. Presently, the talk turned to the Blaines. Reed couldn't stand it, and he stalked out of the house. Not long afterward, Phelps, Marian and Mrs. Hitt went for a walk, and whom should they encounter but Reed? He fell in step with

Marian. After enough distance had opened between them and the other couple, Marian asked him why he had left so suddenly. "After a promise not to betray me," Reed recorded, "I told her that the interminable conversations about the Blaines and their affairs seemed banal enough to give me goosepimples. She scolded me because of my impatience but didn't protest at all."[5]

And where, one may wonder, was Mrs. Reed while the congressman was keeping company with the likes of Miss Phelps? "This evening," Reed recorded in his diary in early 1889, "I intended to see two of my female friends, but my wife had her migraine, her terrible headache, and I stayed home reading some more in the Count of Monte Cristo."[6]

Reed yearned for the Speakership. But it was not just his four congressional rivals who stood in his way. Blaine too, for some reason, had decided to oppose him. Reed had come by this intelligence from his French tutor, who had gotten it from a Virginia judge, who had heard it from Blaine himself, in a chance meeting on the street. Actually, said the judge, it was "Blaine's friends" who were against Reed, "not Mr. B. himself" according to this succession of informants. Not that it surprised him, the diarist reflected. Blaine "is my nemesis. He is a man without principle. If he becomes a cabinet minister, my head will be in a basket, believe me."[7]

Blaine got his wish, becoming Harrison's Secretary of State, but Reed's head remained joined to his neck. Blaine's intrigue, such as it was, presented a less immediate threat to Reed's ambition than William K. McKinley. Putting her finger on Reed's vulnerability, Marian Phelps had also identified McKinley's strength. In Mack, there was no wit, mild or astringent. He was good-looking, well-spoken and polite. He listened well and sympathetically, even to the Democrats. "What a priest he might have made!" a monsignor had said of him.[8] He was married to an invalid, and he stayed by her side, needy and mentally unbalanced though she was. And for this too, he gained friends and sympathy. McKinley had none of Reed's intellectual curiosity or doubt, and not one drop of cynicism. A Mason and a churchgoing Methodist, he raised the Republican gospel of protection to a kind of secular faith.

McKinley liked to be addressed as "Major," his wartime army rank. The son of an Ohio ironmaster, he enlisted as a private in the commis-

sary section of the 23rd Regiment, Ohio Volunteer Infantry. His commanding officer, Rutherford B. Hayes, was not present when the then-
sergeant delivered hot coffee and rations to his comrades under heavy
fire at the Battle of Antietam in 1862. But he heard reports of McKinley's utter disregard for his own safety. Presently, the sergeant became a
lieutenant, then captain and finally—for his "gallant and meritorious
services" at Opequhan, Fisher's Hill and Cedar Creek—brevet major.[9]
Nobody had addressed Reed as "Assistant Paymaster" since 1865, which
was exactly what the former reluctant sailor preferred. As for the Major,
Reed privately called him "Napoleon."[10] Still, the cynic had reason to
fear the cheerful believer. "My opponents in Congress go at me tooth
and nail," Reed said, "but they always apologize to William when they
are going to call him names."[11]

At the recent Republican National Convention, McKinley had been
talked about for the presidency. In House debate over the Mills bill, he
had spoken long and ably, and he had a moneyed backer in the Ohio
industrialist Mark Hanna. Furthermore, McKinley had campaigned for
Harrison, while Reed had not lifted a finger.[12] On this last score, at least,
Reed had no regrets. Friends of Reed's—Hiscock, for instance—were
buzzing around the White House seeking some kind of preferment from
Harrison or the party in exchange for their good work in the campaign.
"I am very comfortable due to the fact that I had not helped the candidate in any way," Reed reflected to himself. "Happy are those who
expect nothing!"[13]

Alone with his diary, Reed appraised McKinley. A "sly" one was the
Major, but "he is a man of little scope, believe me. He will be in the near
future exposed to critics, and the result will be that one will find that he
is at present above his own level. He was wrong in presenting himself as
a candidate for the Speakership."[14] Filling out the field of Reed's rivals
were Joseph G. Cannon of Illinois, Julius C. Burrows of Michigan and
David B. Henderson of Iowa.

Reed's 1888 letter to young Theodore Roosevelt expressing his
apprehension about the Speakership contest in the Republican caucus
was dated almost a year to the day before the issue was decided. He won
on the second ballot on November 30, 1889, with 85 votes out of 166.
McKinley was next, with 38, followed by Cannon with 19, Henderson

with 14 and Burrows with 10. Watching these proceedings, Reed's old Democratic sparring partner, William Springer of Illinois, listened to a railroad lobbyist predict that Reed would walk away with the prize. In that case, Springer retorted, the House was destined to become "a body corporate, not politic."[15]

The victor had just turned 50, though, as a newspaperman noted, you could hardly tell it, so smooth was the brow on his massive head. Blaine had been 39 when he first occupied the chair. Henry Clay was only 34. Then too, Blaine had been in Congress only six years before he was elected Speaker, and Clay served his first term in the chair (though Clay had previously served in the Senate despite being under the legal age for that distinction). Reed had been waiting his turn for 12 years.

What human material did the Speakership require, and what portion of these requisite qualities did Reed possess? Henry Clay, by general consent, was the 19th century's greatest Speaker. If, however, his was the model personality for the job, Reed must have wondered what he was getting himself into. "In public," Carl Schurz, the Mugwump newspaper editor and former U.S. senator, wrote in his biography of Clay, "he was of magnificent bearing, possessing the true oratorical temperament, the nervous exaltation that makes the orator feel and appear a superior being, transfusing his thought, passion and will into the mind and heart of the listener; but his imagination frequently ran away with his understanding, while his imperious temper and ardent combativeness hurried him and his party into disadvantageous positions."

In his drawling, sardonic imperturbability, Reed bore not one speck of likeness to Schurz's Clay. In bearing, the Speaker-elect was certainly impressive, but it was his sheer fleshy mass that commanded attention, rather than his magnetism. Nor did he achieve, or even strive for, rhetorical exaltation. He spoke well and fluently but, whenever possible, briefly. Reed was not without imagination, nor was he averse to a fight—far from it. It was his formidable self-control that conquered the urges that, according to Schurz, sometimes betrayed Clay. Reed could storm out of a drawing room at the mention of Blaine's name but could also sit unflinching on the floor of the House as his enemies pelted him with abuse.

Reed had not craved the Speakership for the glory alone. Seated at its head, he would bring the House into the age of electric lights and telephones. Professor William Graham Sumner of Yale contended that obstruction was, on balance, a positive force in congressional politics; though it thwarted passage of some useful legislation, it blocked the passage of much more unnecessary legislation. Reed rejected the thought. Under his leadership, the majority would legislate and be held to account for its works. Reed was, of course, well aware that the Speaker got a raise: The job paid $7,500, or $2,500 more than the ordinary congressman earned—no small sum to a husband and father who had just bought a spacious $12,000 house in Portland and who wrote magazine articles at not unimaginably high space rates.* The diarist never mentioned the money, but he had long been contemplating the power and responsibility.

The Speaker did not, in fact, speak—or speak much; to that extent, Reed's title was a misnomer. What he did do was control the political destiny of every member of the House. He distributed committee assignments, named the chairmen, settled parliamentary disputes, directed the legislative agenda and chose to recognize (or not to recognize) a member who wanted the floor. "Mr. Speaker!" that member would have to respectfully petition the chair, keeping a civil tongue in his head as he did so. No verbal fencing was permitted with the leader of the House. When, during one of the many heated moments of the 51st Congress, Colonel Mills addressed remarks to the Speaker that were beyond the pale of parliamentary decorum, Reed responded thus: "The chair does not wish to have any personal controversy with the gentleman from Texas and thinks that if the gentleman from Texas will reflect he will see the impropriety."[17]

THE 51ST CONGRESS convened at high noon on December 2, 1889. Political spectators thronged the galleries as the members went through the formality of validating the choices their respective caucuses had made for Speaker.[18] Reed polled 165 votes; John G. Carlisle, of Ken-

---

* Reed had a professional author's facility. On deadline, he could write 1,000 words an hour. In January 1889, writing for the *Century* magazine, he wrote a 3,000-word piece for $5, the equivalent, in those days, of not quite one-quarter of an ounce of gold. For the same rate of pay in terms of gold, he would have earned $300 in 2010.

tucky, the Democratic runner-up and Reed's immediate predecessor,
154. The closeness of the margin was testament to the slimness of the
Republican majority; at maximum strength, the party might seat 168
members, only three more than necessary to make a quorum. The
vote completed, the swearing-in proceeded. Judge Kelley, father of the
House, waited at the rostrum for Reed and his escort to make their way
from the north entrance of the chamber down the main aisle to the
Speaker's chair. It was McKinley on one side and Carlisle on the other,
with Reed's "man-mountain shape," to quote the historian H. Wayne
Morgan, "dwarfing the escort and much of the furniture."[19]

Taking the gavel, Speaker Reed did, in fact, speak:

> I thank you for the high office which your voices have bestowed
> upon me. It would be impossible not to be moved by its dignity
> and honor. Yet you may well imagine that I am this moment
> more impressed by its responsibilities and duties.
>
> Under our system of government as it has been developed,
> these responsibilities and duties are both political and parliamen-
> tary. So far as the duties are political, I sincerely hope they may
> be performed with a proper sense of what is due to the people of
> this whole country. So far as they are parliamentary, I hope, with
> equal sincerity, that they may be performed with a proper sense
> of what is due to both sides of this Chamber. [Great applause.]
>
> To the end that I may satisfactorily carry out your will, I
> invoke the considerate judgment and the cordial aid of all the
> members of the House. [Applause.]

That bipartisanship would not be the outstanding feature of the new
Congress was evident when a parliamentary struggle developed over the
election of the House chaplain. Each party had its candidate, and each
party expected its members to vote the straight party ticket. The Democrats' cleric, however, being blind, laid claim to bipartisan sympathy.
The Reverend W. H. Milburn, who had served in the 50th Congress
(and who, according to the bolting Republicans, had no means of support outside the House), prevailed over the candidate put forward by the
Republican leadership.[20]

There were other sources of partisan contention. The evergreen tariff issue was one. The plight of African-American voters at southern
polling places was another. The nature of the dollar was a third. Finally,
there was the perennial embarrassment of the Treasury surplus.

There are proverbially no easy answers for many public issues, but
the Republicans had a simple enough solution for the surplus: They
would spend it. Of course, as President Harrison insisted in his State of
the Union message, his administration stood for economy in government and lower taxes. But equally, it favored stronger coastal defenses,
harbor and river improvements, a bigger navy, more and better army
artillery, a proper merchant marine and, not least, decent pensions for
Union veterans of the Civil War. "I am not unaware that the pension
roll already involves a very large annual expenditure," Harrison told
Congress; "neither am I deterred by that fact from recommending that
Congress grant a pension to such honorably discharged soldiers and sailors of the Civil War as, having rendered substantial service during the
war, are now dependent on their own labor for a maintenance and by
disease or casualty are incapacitated from earning it."[21]

Reed took a lighter view of the pension situation, complaining
ironically that he had been so coddled in the navy—with free board, a
pair of servants, free clothing and a more than adequate salary—that
he had run himself into debt as a civilian to try to re-create the luxuri-
ous life he had regrettably left behind. Did not he too deserve a pension? Harrison, not sharing Reed's wry outlook on life, named James
"Corporal" Tanner, a well-known lobbyist for the Grand Army of the
Republic, his commissioner of pensions. Tanner, who had suffered the
amputation of both legs below the knee at the Second Battle of Bull
Run, had unbounded sympathies for the veteran and not one ounce of
concern for the creditors of the United States. "God help the surplus,"
he said.[22]

But the Harrison administration's legislative program was only as
solid as the frail Republican majority in the House. Not for Reed the
luxury of his party brethren in the Senate, where the Republicans had
a majority of 51 to 37. In the House, to make and keep a quorum, every
Republican vote was critical. A Speaker began a new session by making
committee assignments and simultaneously, by long custom, discharg-

ing the political debts he had incurred in being elected. Reed had made no promises, but it was the decent thing to show respect for one's vanquished rivals. Thus to McKinley went the chairmanship of the Ways and Means Committee; to Cannon and Henderson went places on the Appropriations Committee; and to Burrow went the chairmanship of the Committee on Manufactures. As for the all-important Committee on Rules, on which Reed had formerly shone, it consisted of Reed himself—the Speaker was ex-officio chairman—McKinley, Cannon, Carlisle and Randall.[23]

However, the Rules Committee did not meet. At least, it did not meet to draft a set of rules for the conduct of business in the 51st Congress. Reed rather chose to carry on the proceedings under "general parliamentary law," a somewhat amorphous body of precedent derived from common practice in American and British legislative assemblies. That the general parliamentary law was an unwritten canon suited Reed to a "T," enlarging, as it did, his scope for interpretation and narrowing the opportunity for obstruction. Democrats opposed it for the very same reasons. Much better, they argued, the rules adopted by the 46th and later congresses that made the minority every bit the parliamentary equal of the majority. These were just the rules, Reed complained, that had held the House hostage to anyone who would move to adjourn, to fix the date of adjournment or to take a recess. For the convenience of the forces of obstruction, such motions were in order at all times.[24]

The new Speaker may have assumed "an office no less consequential than the Presidency of the United States," as the Washington *Post* put it, but that did not mean that its occupant was relieved of the usual cares of an elected politician.[25] A power play at the Deering Centre, Maine, post office required the Speaker's immediate attention—indeed, on the very day he appointed McKinley to the chairmanship of Ways and Means. The postmaster was quarreling with a Mr. Hoegg, in whose store the post office was situated, "and while Mr. Hoegg was willing that the Post Office should remain in his building," the Speaker said, "he was apparently not willing that the Postmaster should."[26] Such were the early claims on the time and attention of the man who was preparing to turn the Capitol on its ear.

It was an open secret in Washington that Reed had a trick up his sleeve. The Republicans' small majority and the Speaker's iron will were reasons enough to doubt that the Democrats would be allowed to talk the 51st Congress to death. A month after the chaplain squabble, there arose a seemingly innocuous procedural debate over an appropriations bill for the District of Columbia. The chairman of the committee that oversaw the District brought the measure before the House and moved that the members resolve themselves into a Committee of the Whole to consider it.

The white-haired William C. P. Breckinridge, Democrat of Kentucky, was on his feet to object. Breckinridge was an orator born and bred, descended from John Breckinridge, an attorney general in the administration of Thomas Jefferson, on his father's side, and from Patrick Henry on his mother's. The scion of this illustrious clan was born in 1837, in Danville, Kentucky, then the "Athens of the West." In the Civil War, he was a cavalry officer of sufficient pedigree, dash and bearing to be selected to serve on the bodyguard of Jefferson Davis.[27]

"I now raise the question of consideration," declared Breckinridge, meaning the question of whether the House wished to attend to that item of business at all. Any member had the right to raise the question of consideration, but it had to apply to the "main question"—i.e., the business in front of the House.

"The question of consideration cannot be raised on a motion," Reed ruled.

"But, Mr. Speaker," Breckinridge pressed, "this is more than a motion. It is not a simple motion to go into Committee of the Whole, but a motion to go into Committee of the Whole upon certain conditions and with certain limitations contained in the resolution, which constitute virtually the adoption of the rule or rules for the guidance of the House. It is not, therefore, a simple motion, but it is a motion separate and divisible."

"It is a motion to instruct the committee, which is created by the motion itself," said Reed.[28]

This was on January 7. On the 21st, Reed again raised the Democrats' ire by refusing to order tellers to count the yeas and nays on a motion to adjourn. He evidently thought it was a waste of time. Richard P. Bland, Democrat of Missouri, had so moved, and Colonel Mills had rallied to Bland's defense. "The vote by tellers," said Mills, "is a part of parliamentary law, and has been used, within the memory of every gentleman sitting on this floor, from the oldest down to the youngest, as much as a motion to adjourn. It is the only way by which we can correct the decision of the Speaker. When the Speaker decides the question, whether he decides it right or wrong, if there is no verification of his decision by a vote, he becomes a mere Czar in the seat now occupied by the Presiding Officer of the House."[29]

Not far beneath the thicket of these parliamentary technicalities was Reed's vision of a return to the principle of majority rule. The Democrats, jealous of the rights of the minority, protested that there were no rules, but only that thing called general parliamentary law, which meant the Speaker could rule by caprice. Former Speaker Carlisle, an acknowledged master parliamentarian, supported Breckinridge, who now quoted Jefferson, the Democrats' patron saint, warning against the "caprice or passion" of a presiding officer—the Speaker of the House, for example.

"When there are rules," Breckinridge went on record as saying, "each of us will have knowledge of what he must be bound by in carrying out his duty to his constituents upon this floor. But, sir, if we have no rules, and nothing but the will of the Speaker, based upon some vague parliamentary law, casting aside all the experience of the past, we will find ourselves constantly involved, as we are today, in apparent confusion."[30]

The House voted to sustain Reed's ruling by a vote of 134 to 125, with 71 members sitting mum. The Democrats could take consolation in the margin, if not in the result. Unless the Republicans could materialize 166 votes on the floor, there would be no quorum, hence no legislation. Barring a parliamentary coup, the Harrison administration was in the Democracy's power.

The finances of the District of Columbia were not an inherently emotional subject, but every disputed election brought out the fight in the minority party. Under the Constitution, the House was the supreme judge of the qualifications and elections of its members. There was, however, in these contested-election cases, none of the ordinary suspense of a judicial proceeding. As Reed observed, "The decision of election cases invariably increases the majority of the party which organizes the House, and which therefore appoints the majority of the Committee on Elections. Probably, there is not a single instance on record where the minority was increased by the decision of contested cases."[31] So it had gone for Reed in 1881 when his Republican brethren rebuffed a challenge by Reed's defeated Democratic rival, Samuel Anderson.

So close was the margin between Republican and Democratic forces in the 51st Congress that every contested seat might have tipped the legislative balance. The Democrats, it is true, could expect to win no disputed election on the merits. But they looked forward to filibustering the Republicans into a state of reasonableness if not of submission. They had their chance in the matter of Smith vs. Jackson, an election case from the Fourth Congressional District of West Virginia. It was the first of the new session, with Smith, the Republican, being the favored contestant. John Dalzell, a second-term Republican from Pennsylvania, and a Yale man to boot, moved that the case be taken up. Crisp, Democrat of Georgia, objected, raising the question of consideration. Reed put that question to the House "The ayes seem to have it," he announced.

Crisp called for a division, or vote, then the yeas and nays. The yeas prevailed, 162–3, with 163 not voting. Therefore, Crisp observed, there was no quorum—or was there?

Now Reed proceeded to make history. "The Chair directs the clerk to record the following names of members present and refusing to vote," the Speaker said, eliciting applause on the Republican side.

"I appeal," cried Crisp. "[Applause on the Democratic side.] I appeal from the decision of the Chair."

Reed was now calling out the names of the Democrats by whose refusal to vote the House had fallen short of quorum: "Mr. Blanchard, Mr. Bland, Mr. Blount, Mr. Breckinridge of Arkansas, Mr. Breckinridge of Kentucky."

"I deny the power of the Speaker and denounce it as revolutionary," roared the last-named Breckinridge. "[Applause on the Democratic side, which was renewed several times.]"

Bland called for Reed's attention. "Mr. Speaker— [Applause on the Democratic side.]"

"The House will be in order," Reed interjected.

"Mr. Speaker," Bland continued, "I am responsible to my constituents for the way I vote, and not to the Speaker of this House. [Applause.]"

Reed kept calling out the names of the nonvoting Democrats: "Mr. Brookshire, Mr. Bullock, Mr. Bynum, Mr. Carlisle, Mr. Chipman, Mr. Clements, Mr. Clunie, Mr. Compton."

"I protest against the conduct of the Chair in calling my name," Compton called out.

Seeming not to hear, Reed continued: "Mr. Covert, Mr. Crisp, Mr. Culberson of Texas [Hisses on the Democratic side.], Mr. Cummins, Mr. Edwards, Mr. Enloe, Mr. Fithian, Mr. Goodnight, Mr. Hare, Mr. Hatch, Mr. Hayes."

Hayes protested, but Reed proceeded: "Mr. Holman, Mr. Lawlee, Mr. Lee, Mr. McAdoo, Mr. McCreary."

"I deny your right, Mr. Speaker," said McCreary, "to count me as present, and I desire to read from parliamentary law on that subject."

"The Chair is making a statement of fact that the gentleman from Kentucky is present," replied Reed. "Does he deny it? [Laughter and applause on the Republican side.]"

Over cries of "Order!" and bursts of applause, McCreary read from Mays's *Parliamentary Practice*, a copy of which the Speaker of the House customarily kept close by. To wit: "A call is of little avail in taking the sense of the House, as there is no compulsory process by which members can be obliged to vote."

More applause, more cries of "Order!"

"The gentlemen will be in order," said Reed, to the mirth of the Republican side. "The Chair is proceeding in an orderly manner," again raising laughter from the same side of the aisle.

The naming of names resumed: "Mr. Montgomery, Mr. Moore of Texas, Mr. Morgan."

Down through the alphabet Reed continued, deadpan. He might as well have been back calling the roll in his old Portland schoolroom: "Mr. Owens of Ohio, Mr. O'Ferrall. . . ."

"It is disorderly," cried Breckinridge, jumping into the aisle dividing the Republican and Democratic sides of the House. ". . . It is a disorderly proceeding on the part of the Speaker. [Applause on the Democratic side.]"

Reed continued: "Mr. Stewart of Texas, Mr. Tillman—"

"Will the Chair answer the parliamentary inquiry?" demanded Cooper of Indiana.

"Mr. Turner of Georgia—"

Again Cooper interrupted: "I demand an answer to the parliamentary inquiry. By what rule of parliamentary law, and by what right, does the Chair undertake to direct that men shall be recorded as present and voting?"

"The Chair will answer the gentleman, if he will be in order, in due time," Reed responded.

But Cooper would not pipe down.

"The gentleman must not be disorderly," Reed chided him.

Joe Wheeler of Alabama, an ex-Confederate general, took no notice of that small rebuke: "Must the Representatives of the people remain silent in their seats and see the Speaker of this House inaugurate revolution?"

Presently, Cooper cried out again: "Mr. Speaker, I insist upon my appeal."

Returned Reed: "The gentleman must not mistake his situation. He is not to compel the Chair to do certain things. The Chair must proceed in regular order, and the gentleman, as a member of this body, will undoubtedly permit the Chair to proceed."

The Democratic side of the House, in fact, wanted nothing less. Many were up on their feet. "The Chair will proceed if gentlemen will take their seats," Reed admonished them. As the hubbub subsided, Reed began to explain to the members what he had done, and what he meant to do.

The question before the House was, of course, whether a constitutional quorum was present, and upon this question the Speaker would rule, "from which an appeal can be taken if any gentleman is dissatisfied therewith," Reed added.

Crisp piped up: "In advance, I enter an appeal. [Laughter and applause on the Democratic side.]"

Reed continued:

There has been for considerable time a question of this nature raised in very many parliamentary assemblies. There has been a great deal of doubt, especially in this body, on the subject, and the present occupant of the Chair well recollects a proposition or suggestion made ten years ago by a member from Virginia, Mr. John Randolph Tucker, an able constitutional lawyer as well as an able member of this House. The matter was somewhat discussed, and a proposition was made with regard to putting it into the rules. The general opinion which seemed to prevail at that time was that it was inexpedient to do so, and some men had grave doubts whether it was proper to make such an amendment to the rules as would count the members present and not voting as part of the quorum as well as those present and voting. The evils which resulted from the other course were then not as apparent, and no such careful study had been given to the subject as has been given to it since.

That took place in the year 1880. Since then there have been various arguments and various decisions by various eminent gentlemen upon the subject, and these decisions have very much cleared up the question, which renders it much more apparent what the rule is.

It so happened that the-then Democratic governor of New York, David B. Hill, had counted a quorum in the New York State Assembly when he was the lieutenant governor and presiding officer of the Senate in 1883; and a Democratic governor of Tennessee had similarly counted a quorum in the Tennessee General Assembly in 1885. Those precedents, for Reed, "covered the ground." However, for good measure, he observed that it was not uncommon for the House of Representatives itself to disregard the absence of a quorum when there was pressing work to do. Besides, he reasoned, the Constitution gave the House the power to compel the members' attendance. But if the members, so seated, were then at liberty to sit silent, was the Constitution not defeated? Reed proceeded to a reading of the lengthy decision of the New York State quorum decision.

Then there was bedlam. However, in the tumultuous sea of political humanity, there was one island of serenity. Reed remained seated at the Speaker's desk, "his face pale and determined and his right hand firmly clinched around the butt end of his gavel." Then again, Reed had a naturally pale complexion—before very long, he would be twitted as the "Great White Czar"—and he rarely betrayed emotion. On a stifling Saturday in April 1888, Breckinridge and he had been skirmishing on the floor of the House over the expenses of the Secretary of the Navy. Breckinridge's temper flared, and he blurted out something well outside the bounds of parliamentary courtesy. Reed, keeping his temper, made a barbed, but proper, response.[32] "I kept my hate sweetly and responded in a very parliamentary manner," he recorded in his diary.[33]

Nobody could tell what emotions were playing out behind Reed's hazel eyes, though Crisp, now face-to-face with the Speaker, was looking deep into them at very short range. He had clamored down to the Speaker's desk to appeal Reed's decision. And he appealed too against a Republican attempt to quash debate.

"Mr. Speaker, I appeal to your fairness as a man; gentlemen [Addressing the Republican side of the House.], I appeal to your fairness as men, to give us simply an opportunity to reply to the argument which the Speaker has seen proper to make. Are you afraid to hear the rulings that have been made in this House for over a hundred years?"

As men, the Republicans assented, and Crisp was off and running. In support of the proposition that Reed was a czar, tyrant, revolutionary and usurper, the Georgian invoked the authority of the "most eminent of living Republicans," James G. Blaine. But, of course, as Reed well knew, there was another eminent living Republican whose authority Crisp would not overlook. A quorum "'is not the visible presence of members, but their judgment and their votes that the Constitution calls for,'" Crisp went on, quoting Reed's own arguments against the quorum-counting rule put forward by Tucker of Virginia in 1880.[34]

"The applause on the Democratic side was deafening," the Washington *Post* reported, "and there was hand-clapping in the galleries. When it had subsided, Mr. Crisp exclaimed dramatically, 'I appeal, Mr. Speaker, from Philip drunk to Philip sober,'" an allusion to the sometimes tipsy king of ancient Macedonia. There was another outburst of applause, which the Speaker met in his blandest manner: "The House will have the kindness to be in order."[35]

Joseph Cannon, in support of Reed, spoke after Crisp; and Carlisle, in opposition, followed Cannon. McKinley would resume the debate the next day. At long last, the House adjourned. Returning home to the Shoreham Hotel that evening, Reed would ask his wife about her day, for she too had been through the wringer. It was Wednesday, the day in Washington reserved for receptions in the homes of Cabinet officers and other ranking officials. In what the *Post* diplomatically described as the "dainty drawing-room of the Shoreham," she had hosted an "unusually brilliant reception." A vision of black silk net, Mrs. Reed, in the *Post*'s opinion, "makes a delightful hostess, as pleasant to converse with as she is pretty to look at." Reading this notice the next morning, the Speaker could reflect that his wife's reviews were better than his.[36]

Day 2 of the Reed revolution was no less impassioned than Day 1, but the revolutionary language was losing its shock value. The inflammable Bland, denied recognition from the chair, torched Reed with words that, only two days before, few could ever have imagined hearing in the House. "I denounce you," said he, "as the worst tyrant that ever presided over a deliberative body."[37] The remarks drew jaded applause. Springer and McKinley, each seeking the floor, simultaneously addressed the chair, talking over one another for long and noisy minutes before Reed ruled on behalf of the Major. Besides McKinley, Benjamin Butterworth, Republican of Ohio, spoke up for Reed, while Henry G. Turner of Georgia denounced him. The running debate was a model of decorum, but pandemonium returned with McKinley's motion to lay the appeal on the table—that is, the Democratic appeal against the Speaker's decision to count the quorum. Into the melee sprang Springer with a motion to adjourn. The motion failed. A Democrat's call for the yeas and nays produced a roll call, but the Democratic side of the aisle sat silent through it. And once more Reed said, "The Chair will direct the Clerk to enter the following names of members upon the Journal who were present and declined to vote." So he called the roll of the reluctant again. By and by, the motion to lay the appeal on the table was carried. "Shame!" the Democrats cried, as Reed pushed himself away from his desk and made his way home and to bed. There—according to his family's later telling—he lay "prostrated with a nervous chill."[38] It would have astonished the Democrats to know it.

The third and final day of the first phase of the Reed revolution began with a prayer by the Reverend Milburn that the House might have an orderly session. It was not to be. Springer moved to adjourn; the motion was defeated. Bynum moved to adjourn, and so did Bland, but neither were these motions carried. The roll was called on the approval of the previous day's journal, but the Democrats withheld their votes. Reed thereupon directed the clerk to record the names of members present but not voting. William Bynum's name was among those called.

"I appeal from the decision of the Chair in announcing those not voting," the Indiana Democrat cried.

"That is a statement of fact which can not be appealed from," Reed returned. Pausing to let the Republican laughter subside, Reed announced, "On this vote the yeas are 161 and the nays are none."

"No quorum," Bynum stated, and indeed, in prerevolution days there would not have been.

"And accordingly the Journal is approved," Reed declared.

"No quorum has voted," Bynum repeated. "I rise, Mr. Speaker, to a question of personal privilege."

Reed allowed him to proceed.

"Before the vote was taken on this question, I rose and addressed the Chair and made a motion to adjourn, which was a proper and parliamentary motion," said Bynum. "The Chair, in defiance of parliamentary law, in defiance of right and justice, in defiance—"

"The gentleman from Indiana will be in order," Reed interjected.

"The gentleman from Indiana is in order. [Applause on the Democratic side.] I propose, Mr. Speaker, to stand here in behalf of the rights of the constituency I represent on this floor [Applause on the Democratic side.], a constituency equal in intelligence, equal in patriotism—"

Someone called out, to Republican mirth, "But they are not here."

"Ah, sir," Bynum continued, "they are now present, and I am standing here as their representative to sustain their rights against the arbitrary, the outrageous and the damnable rulings of the Chair. [Applause on the Democratic side.] And so far as I am responsible the people I represent shall not be silenced or gagged on this floor. [Applause on the Democratic side.]

"You, sir," he went on, pointing at Reed, "have violated more than any man on this floor parliamentary rules, parliamentary practice. You may consummate what you have undertaken to do. You have the power, backed up by a mob. [Applause and cheering on the Democratic side.]"

"Gentlemen will refrain from expressions of opinion," Reed replied.

"They may as well refrain, Mr. Speaker," Bynum continued. "The people of this country are witnessing this proceeding. They have spoken through the press of this country, and they have spoken in condemnation of these proceedings which will bury you beyond resurrection. [Applause on the Democratic side.] You may consummate these proceedings as you did similar ones before, when at the hour of midnight a Federal judge made a ruling to perpetuate the Republican party in power, and his name has dropped out of history. [Applause on the Democratic side.] And, more than that, it is but in keeping with the practices of your party when you stole the Presidency and counted in a man who was not elected. [Applause on the Democratic side.]

"It is in keeping with the practice of your party in the State of Montana, where you have attempted to steal two Senators. It is in keeping with the acts of the Federal judiciary today, which has violated the law, which has trampled on laws to screen from punishment the greatest political criminal and greatest political outlaw of this country. [Applause on the Democratic side.] And you look and laugh at this scene."

Reed's colleague from Maine, Charles A. Boutelle, spoke up: "As this member has denounced every department of the Government, executive, legislative and judicial, he had better sit down now or secede. [Laughter and applause on the Republican side.]"

"You had better put me down," retorted Bynum.[39]

This too was met with laughter and applause. But there was also an undercurrent of violence. Many members of the 51st Congress had done their share of killing in the Civil War. William H. "Howdy" Martin, Democrat of Texas, had raised a company for the Confederate army in 1861. Mustered into the Fourth Texas Regiment, he had fought under Robert E. Lee straight through to Appomattox. At one of the hottest moments during these three days of violent talk, Martin felt the wolf in his throat. He got up out of his seat and cried out for the leader who would give him the order to remove Reed bodily from the Speaker's chair. It was clear to Charles Tracey, Democrat from upstate New York, that Martin meant what he said, and he so apprised Reed. The Speaker didn't flinch.[40]

The Republican side of the aisle was as one behind the Speaker—had it been otherwise, Reed later said, he would have resigned the Speakership and gone to New York to practice law with the eminent corporate attorney Elihu Root. Long after the quorum battle, Reed was reminiscing with Henry St. George Tucker, son of John Randolph Tucker. The son himself was a Democratic congressman, a member of the 51st Congress and present for the three-day melee. "Right in the midst of that tumult, when you fellows were behaving in that outrageous way," Reed said, "old Anderson from Kansas (you remember that godly man, don't you?), rushed up to the Speaker's desk, his face flushed with excitement, his fist clenched, and shaking it at me, he said, 'Mr. Speaker, you have sent the party to hell, but I am going with you.' Tucker, I knew then that the victory was won."[41]

Bynum did, finally, sit down, though not for long. Returning again and again to the fray, he was finally censured for crossing a line that, during the three days of Reed's revolution, seemed to be drawn somewhere around bloodshed. Springer next took the baton of Democratic resistance, which he passed along to Crisp. It was the Georgian who finally bowed to overwhelming Republican might. "I do not know what effect it will have," he said late in the afternoon, "but I appeal to my friends to hear the gentleman from Pennsylvania"—i.e., Dalzell, who was trying to begin the arguments over the disputed West Virginia election case.[42] Crisp did, indeed, calm the waters, and Dalzell was allowed to proceed. Decorum returned, and with it a new era in the life of the House—and of Thomas B. Reed.

Chapter 17

"I hope my enemies are satisfied"

NEVER WAS AN ambition more transparent than Reed's bid to streamline the rules of congressional procedure. The House over which the Speaker presided, "the most unwieldy parliamentary body in the world," in Reed's estimation, needed more than patchwork repairs.[1] The time had come for a gut renovation.

That there must be rules, Democrats did not dispute. They had been grumbling since the start of the session about the lack of progress in that direction. The Rules Committee, consisting of Joseph Cannon (chairman), McKinley and Reed for the majority, and Carlisle and Randall for minority, had been studiously indolent. Every Congress drew up its own rules and procedures, borrowing as much as it chose from the usages of its predecessor. Yet eight weeks into the session, the 51st Congress was operating under what the Speaker was pleased to call "general parliamentary law." It was, cried the opposition, the contrivance for one-man rule.

So saying, the Democrats were under no illusion that the Rules Committee's handiwork, when completed, would restore their treasured minority rights or retain the desired amount of gum in the legislative gears. But they might not have anticipated how thoroughly the rules unveiled on February 6 would consolidate the Speaker's power and undermine what was left of theirs. Of the 47 rules in place during the preceding Congress, Cannon, McKinley and Reed left just 29 untouched. As for the rest, the minority contended, they might as well be called what they were, a revolutionary manifesto.[2]

There was, to begin with, the quorum. One proposed rule formally empowered the Speaker to count it. Another, in a mere nine words, promised changes almost as far-reaching. "No dilatory motion shall be entertained by the Speaker," said Subsection 10 of Rule 16.[3] So it would fall to Reed to decide if a motion from the floor was intended to obstruct the business of the House. Might obstruction, if serving the right cause, serve the public interest? The new Speaker seemed to deny the possibility. For him, obstruction was inherently undesirable. A third innovation concerned the Committee of the Whole, formally known as the Committee of the Whole for the State of the Union. It was a miniature House into which the members could resolve themselves to discuss legislation and broker amendments outside the structure of a formal session. Under the Reed rules, only 100 members would make a quorum in that useful body. The order of business was the object of a fourth kind of innovation. Here the cumulative frustrations of Reed's long service in the House found expression. For instance, no more would Mondays be given over to the call on the states and the territories for the introduction of bills, memorials and resolutions, a ceremony that devoured minutes and hours to no good end. Henceforth the Speaker, in silence, would direct such items to the appropriate committees. The Speaker's table, on which unfinished business had been wont to pile up, would henceforth be swept clean of messages from the president, bills and departmental reports, among other documents. Expeditious new processes would be put in place to deliver committee reports to the clerk, rather than to consign them to oblivion, as had so often been the case before. And so forth: It was as if the Committee on Rules had been captured by a time-and-motion man.

It took no prophetic power to anticipate the argument that the Reed rules would institute one-man rule in the people's chamber. "If the suggestion should be made that great power is here conferred, the answer is that as the approval of the House is the very breath in the nostrils of the Speaker," the Republican triumvirate on the Rules Committee wrote (the style was plainly Reed's) in their committee report to repel that line of attack, "and as no body on earth is so jealous of its liberties and so impatient of control, we may be quite sure that no arbitrary interruption will take place, and indeed, no interruption at all, until not only such misuse of proper motions is made clearly evident to the world, but also such action has taken place as will assure the Speaker of the support of the body whose wishes are his law."[4]

Cannon defended the new rules as the triumph of common sense over encrusted tradition. And as to the alleged dictatorship of Tom Reed, had the minority forgotten that their own Speaker Carlisle had personally blocked the Blair education bill from coming to a vote in the House for the six consecutive years in which he held the gavel, although that legislation had passed the Senate in each successive congress?[5] And surely the members recalled how James B. Weaver of Iowa had talked for three days straight to force consideration of a bill to confer territorial status on Oklahoma. Sixty million Americans demanded to know why their well-paid representatives could not organize themselves in such a way as to complete more than 5 percent of the business in front of them.[6]

Cannon's appeal for legislative efficiency fell flat on the Jeffersonian side of the aisle. A faster gait of lawmaking was exactly what the Democrats didn't want and the country didn't need, argued Roger Q. Mills of Texas. "We believe with our fathers," he said, "that we do not want many laws and we do not want them rapidly made. One of the greatest authors that ever wrote in the English language, second only, in my judgment, to Shakespeare, I mean Henry Thomas Buckle, who wrote the *History of English Civilization*, was so disgusted with the constant interference of government with the rights of the citizens that he laid it down as a rule that there is but one wise act that any legislative assembly can pass, and that is an act to repeal a former law. . . . We want to have as little law as possible, as little intermeddling as possible with the affairs of the people."[7]

"Mr. Speaker," protested James Blount of Georgia, "you have specified in these rules every proceeding you could think of that had been used, as you thought, to delay business. And when you had done that, when you had cut off all inventions you could conceive of for delay, you feared there might be something still left, and so you put in a clause that covers everything allowing the Speaker to declare that he will entertain no proposition that in his judgment he considers dilatory." Throw in the other innovations in rules and procedures, and what you have is a spectacle unique and heretofore unimagined, "without precedent in this country and without precedent in any country where liberty is recognized. Ay, and in doing this you have ridiculed the suggestion that the precedents you contravene are hoary with age and venerable with the wisdom of many generations of statesmen. You have discovered that you are wiser than your fathers."[8]

At 67 years of age, William S. Holman, Democrat of Indiana was one of the House graybeards. He was first elected to the 38th Congress, in 1858, and had, for that reason, a different view of partisanship than most of his younger colleagues. Not a few members kept pistols at their desks in those tempestuous days. Once a careless politician, fishing around for a piece of paper, accidentally discharged his weapon, sending a ball blasting into the desk in front of him, narrowly missing human flesh. "In an instant," as Holman told the story, "there were fully 30 or 40 pistols in the air, and the scene looked more like a Texas bar-room than the Congress of the United States."

No one could accuse Holman, a war Democrat, of hiding Confederate bigotry behind lofty Jeffersonian language. He meant it when he quoted Jefferson—he had made a close study of the third president's life and works. And he meant it when he called the Reed rules an open call on the Treasury. Perhaps no one in Congress was more conscientious than he in the cause of governmental economy—or more annoying to his fellow members in his grim pursuit of it. Some years earlier, the Subcommittee on Indian Affairs, of which Holman was chairman, had conducted an inspection tour of the western Indian reservations. All but the chairman elected to travel from Washington in a Pullman car, Holman declining that comfort to preserve the Treasury from the exorbitant extra expense. The Republicans loved to bait him for his parsimony, but it was a fellow Democrat, Alexander M. Dockery, of Missouri, who caught Holman out in the rarest of extravagances. The "Watchdog of the Treasury" had, seemingly inexplicably, lent his support to an appropriations measure. When it came to light that the funds would be spent in the capital city of Holman's own home state, Dockery rose to quote Lord Byron:

> 'Tis sweet to hear the honest watch-dog's bark
> Bay deep-mouthed welcome as we draw near home.[9]

Holman's bill was lost in laughter. For the sponsor, it was an uncharacteristic lapse. Tearing into the Reed rules, Holman was his old self, observing, first, that taxing and spending were the essence of legislation. "These schemes of plunder," Holman declared in reference to lawfully enacted federal taxation, "which are often successful even under rules most favorable to the minority, have, during the last 25 years, aided to create the enormous private fortunes which now threaten our free institutions, for the possessors of these overgrown estates, distrustful of the people, are plotting for a stronger government, which enlarged navies and armies well express. Let us see whether at this time greater facilities for reaching the money of the people in the Treasury than now exist demand these new rules."[10]

The 36th Congress was Holman's first, and it was the last before the war; it enacted 384 laws and appropriated $61 million. The 44th Congress, which convened 10 years after the war, enacted 579 laws and appropriated $299.1 million. And only six years later, the 47th Congress, 1881–83, managed to spend $529.3 million, an increase of $230 million in just six years over the outlays of the 44th. "Surely," Holman went on, "this enormous increase does not indicate the necessity of amending the rules to enable the Speaker and chairmen of committees more readily to reach the people's money! Coming down to the last Congress, the fiftieth (1889 and 1890), Democratic, 1,824 laws were enacted, appropriating for both sessions $543,632,004.95."

No doubt, Holman allowed, there had been cases of unwarranted obstruction of congressional business in the past. "[B]ut shall such instances, which did no harm, justify rules that ignore the minority and leave the majority without any restraint whatever? It is only the lobby that could demand such a state of the rules.

"Only a word in addition," Holman prefaced his peroration, but the Democrats wanted more. "Go on! Go on!" they called out to him, and he obliged: "There never has been a time in my experience in Congress . . . when a greater number of schemes of plunder were seeking access to your Treasury than now. Three hundred and fifty million dollars, not for the present moment, but to be fixed and settled for early expenditure for ships of war and fortifications, and that, too, in time of profound peace; millions for subsidies, millions for irrigation, by which a few men are made to be rich at the expense of the laboring masses of our people, and cart-loads of old Southern war claims that have been examined and rejected by the proper Departments of Government—these measures are all crowding upon us. The public bills alone now pending involve in the aggregate a sum exceeding the public debt. Go into your corridors. Have you ever seen so many syndicates and organized lobbies here before? Have you ever seen such manifest preparations for an onslaught on your public Treasury as now? Have you ever known of as many schemes and projects to draw money from the Treasury as are to be found among the bills already introduced?

"No man can misunderstand—" said Holman, now coming into the homestretch, "I think no gentleman does misunderstand—exactly what this change of rules means. It means that the Speaker, instead of being, as for the past 100 years, the servant of the House, shall be its master; that the Speaker and the chairmen of committees shall be a petty oligarchy, with absolute control of the business of the House. It means the striking down of the manhood and proper influence and control, in legislation, of every other member of the House on your side, gentlemen, as well as ours. It means more than all that; it means a great navy, an enlarged army, a great zoological park and other embellishments in this city, and all else that creates a splendid government and gives a sense of security to the owners of overgrown and imperial estates who have no faith in the people and long for a stronger government."

In sum, said Holman, the Reed rules pointed to a "splendid government and an impoverished people," and—begging another minute from the chair—he ventured a prediction. The next Congress would roll back the Reed rules "with the same spirit that animated our fathers when they struck the alien and sedition laws from the statute books of the United States. [Great applause.]"[11]

The Republicans did not wholly dispute Holman's argument.

Indeed, in substituting "action for inaction" and "legislation for obstruction," the proposed overhaul was "revolutionary," Byron M. Cutcheon, of Michigan, chairman of the House Military Affairs Committee, conceded. Then again, this was a new age, and a break from past practices was overdue. The Founding Fathers no more foresaw the railroads and steamboats than they did the Department of Agriculture—now a Cabinet-level agency of government, if you please, Cutcheon noted. Holman had mentioned the 44th Congress. In its two years of life, 4,708 bills had passed before its eyes. The 50th Congress had seen 12,664. And in the first two months of the 51st Congress, no fewer than 6,776 bills had been introduced and referred. The sheer volume of business before the House compelled reform.[12]

Libertarian critics—they were the Democrats—had harkened back to the simplicity and economy of government before the Civil War, the days before a national debt, a national banking system, the Interstate Commerce Commission, the U.S. Life-Saving Service (later a part of the Coast Guard), the enormous war-related federal pension obligations, et cetera. There was no going back, Cutcheon argued. "The school of Jefferson, for the time being, has been retired by the people, and the school of Hamilton and of Washington has been placed in control. The party of strict construction has been ordered to go to the rear, and the party of broad and liberal construction and of national constitutional powers has been entrusted with the helm of the ship of state, and changes in the mode of procedure and of policy must inevitably follow this change of political control."[13]

The Democrats argued not in the hope of changing the outcome—the inevitable vote produced the foregone decision on February 14—but to speak for the record and to posterity. It only remained to be seen what the Republicans would do with their newly minted powers. The tariff was, of course, a GOP evergreen, and it ranked high on the agenda of the Harrison administration. Election reform was another priority: The Grand Old Party stood for a free and fair ballot in the old Confederacy and the vigorous enforcement of the 15th Amendment of the Constitution (which guaranteed the vote to African-American men), if it stood for anything. In 1888, Harrison had campaigned hard on that very proposition. Then too, the party was committed to reducing the nettlesome federal surplus. The new pensions commissioner, James R. Tanner, was as good as his word: "I will drive a six-mule team through the Treasury," he said.[14]

This was, however, the agenda of the established Republican party of New England and the East. Admission of a half-dozen new western states since 1889 had added a new wing to the old party. To a man, the new senators and representatives—12 of the former, seven of the latter—were Republican. But they were a different kind of Republican. The farmers, miners, ranchers and storekeepers who sent them to Washington had no particular interest in black voting rights or in the doctrine of the protective tariff. What they wanted was inflation and its imagined happy consequences: higher commodity prices and a lighter burden of debt.

Reed, an investor in a Nebraska land-development business as well as in some undeveloped lots in Las Vegas, in New Mexico Territory, was presently to learn firsthand about the condition of affairs west of the Mississippi. In 1890, however, he gave no sign of understanding the difficulties of the people who were signing up to join the Farmers Alliance. The prices of agricultural products were falling. So too was the price of silver. But creditors did not, for that reason, humanely reduce the size of the balances that the struggling farmers, ranchers and miners owed. It took more and more corn, beef or silver to earn the dollars with which to stay solvent. In Kansas, farmers were burning corn for fuel.

So the 12 new senators and seven new congressmen arrived in Washington with monetary ideas not conforming to New England's.[15] For Reed, sound money was gold. If the party of Lincoln had taken the country off the gold standard in 1861 to fight the Civil War, it had restored that system with the peace (albeit with a 14-year delay, in 1879). A dollar in 1890 was worth slightly less than 1/20th of an ounce of gold, just as it had been in 1860. It was what Alexander Hamilton had stipulated and what, in the 1870s and 1880s, the leading commercial and financial nations of the world had come to rally around.

The westerners, though not so steeped in tradition as their eastern brethren, did point out—over and over—that the Founders had instituted a bimetallic monetary standard, silver and gold. Hamilton's dollar was exchangeable into gold or silver, at a fixed ratio of value. That ratio, under the 1792 Coinage Act, was one ounce of gold for 15 ounces of silver. The dastardly act of 1873 undid Hamilton's great work by making silver nonmoney—that is, by "demonetizing" it. No wonder the price of silver had collapsed, the bimetallists cried. On average in 1890, an ounce of the white metal was quoted at $1.04633, representing a ratio of silver value to gold value not of 15:1, as the first Secretary of the Treasury had intended, but of 19.76:1.[16]

To right this great wrong, the Silver Republicans, as they soon came to be known, determined to restore the metal they loved to its proper place in the American change purse. Their hearts' desire was "free and unlimited coinage," meaning that the Treasury would purchase, with IOUs, all the silver that the miners could deliver, turn that metal into silver dollars and set them into circulation, in this way consummating a general rise in prices. Failing free coinage, the Silver Republicans would consider a compromise whereby the Treasury would buy enough silver to put some starch back into its price. Whereas the Harrison administration had many items on its legislative plate, the Silver Republicans had just this one.

To hear the silverites tell the tale, the rich were conspiring to bankrupt the masses by making money ever scarcer. As recently as 1870, only Australia, Canada, England and Portugal were on the pure gold standard. The rest of the world used gold and silver, or silver alone. Then began a movement to push aside the people's money and raise up the plutocrats'. By consent of international bankers and foreign governments, the gold standard wormed its way into Europe, starting with the International Monetary Conference in Paris in 1867. Germany abandoned silver for gold in 1872. Sweden, Denmark and Norway followed in 1873, that infamous year in which the United States Congress demonetized the white metal as casually as it might have built a post office. France, Belgium and Switzerland exchanged bimetallism for gold alone in 1878. John Sherman, Hayes's Treasury Secretary, returned the United States to the gold standard in 1879.[17]

A fair-minded reader of the monetary record would likely have found no conspiracy but rather a worldwide expression of preference. Gold, being 15 or 16 times more valuable than silver, was handier to use and carry. Its value was more stable than silver's. A real-life demonstration of that particular monetary virtue took place between 1850 and 1875. The midcentury gold strikes in Australia and California had brought forth more gold production in 25 years than the world had known "in the 357 years preceding 1850," yet the value of the metal was not thereby depressed, observed the Harvard economist J. Laurence Laughlin. "This is a striking fact in monetary history: increase the production of gold enormously, and it is eagerly absorbed."[18] Not so with silver. Miners were producing more of it too, while European bankers and merchants were demanding less of it. Some compensating demand arose in India and China, both of which clung to the silver standard, but not enough to offset the roaring growth in supply. The price of silver weakened in the 1870s and crumpled in the 1880s. The Silver Republicans, and a growing number of Democrats besides, demanded inflationary redress.

WITH REED IN the Speaker's chair and his rules in the books, the 51st Congress got down to business. As McKinley chaired the Ways and Means Committee, the tariff bill was his to manage. The high priest of protection at last was free to devise a plan of his own to enlarge and extend the prosperity of the United States by the imposition of taxes on merchandise. The GOP leadership, brooking no obstruction, allotted just four days of debate on this centerpiece legislation. "The people have spoken," said McKinley, as he reported his bill on April 16, "and want their will registered and their decrees embodied in public legislation."[19] The people's will took the form of a very long act—"to reduce the revenue and equalize duties on imports, and for other purposes"—which the people finally despised.

The McKinley Act was not, as some historians contend, the victim of bad press and uninformed prejudice; its deficiencies were its own. As advertised, it did lay an ax into the federal surplus by repealing the duty on raw sugar, one of the Treasury's top money-makers. But it raised a host of other duties on the kind of consumer goods that registered voters seemed to buy: tin pans, blank books, pocket knives, table cutlery, clocks, Cuban cigars, kid gloves, a variety of groceries, crockery, carpets, buttons, shotguns, stockings, towels, linens and men's and women's clothing.[20]

As a sop to American sugar-beet growers, the bill delivered a bounty of two cents a pound on domestically produced sugar. Democrats sputtered in disbelief and even some Republicans chafed. Lightening one set of pockets in order to line another for the sake of stimulating production of a politically favored commodity seemed not at all what the Founders had had in mind.[21] No less singular were the duties on tin plate, a commodity produced in the United States in only trace amounts. Democrats balked at the argument that the tariff would, by itself, conjure a tin-plate industry. They had railed against protection lavished on infant industries, on stripling industries and on mature industries, but now they had seen everything. McKinley proposed to protect a nonexistent industry. And never before had a tariff measure levied duties on food products, as did the McKinley bill: Foreign eggs, heretofore untaxed, now bore a duty of a nickel a dozen. Imported bacon was taxed at five cents a pound and potatoes at 25 cents a bushel. Consumers might chafe, the Republicans seemed to reason, but the farmers deserved to partake of the blessings of the protective system no less than the industrialists. Perhaps the farmers would remember their benefactors in the autumn elections.[22]

Though there was no more zealous a protectionist on the party rolls than McKinley, his tariff was not a purely protectionist measure. Secretary of State Blaine had conceived a vision of a pan-American commercial union, and he prevailed on a reluctant House (including its reluctant Speaker) to incorporate a clause to empower the president to conclude commercial treaties with countries that opened their markets to American goods. If the GOP had, by this principal of reciprocity, hedged its bet on protection, it seemed to do so again on the issue of corporate giantism. Antitariff critics like former president Cleveland contended that the protective system promoted domestic monopoly just as it stifled international trade. McKinley and Reed might deny that indictment, but Senator Sherman implicitly seemed to concur, and his bill to declare illegal every "contract, combination in the form of trust or otherwise, or conspiracy, in restraint of trade or commerce" was signed into law on July 2, 1890.

McKinley's tariff bill enjoyed no such quick journey to President Harrison's desk, and neither did the Federal Elections Bill. Southern Democrats loathed the "force bill," as they styled Lodge's bid to revitalize the 15th Amendment, and prophesied horrid scenes of a new Reconstruction if it were enacted. The bill, in fact, provided legal, not military, remedies for election fraud, and its scope was national, not sectional. Not a few northern and western politicians feared too-close scrutiny of local polling practices, and Reed struck a somewhat less than idealistic tone in a speech in Pittsburgh in April. The Republican party, he asserted, had a right to the Republican vote in the South, whatever the educational attainments of the voter. "If ignorant, we need it to off-set the Democratic ignorance which votes in New York and other large cities. Why should they poll their ignorance and we not poll ours?"[23]

Obviously, came the southern retort, because federally supervised elections would bring "Negro rule." It was the risk of this abomination that justified ballot-box stuffing, as not a few prominent southerners had no compunction against publicly stating. To Reed, the race question was also a power question. For purposes of representation, slaves had counted as three-fifths of a person. Emancipated, they now counted as fully human, but were no more welcome at the ballot box for that. "If it be a race question," the Speaker proposed to the readers of the *North American Review*, "is there any reason why the white man in the South should have two votes to my one? Is he alone of mortals to eat his cake and have it too? Is he to suppress his negro and have him also? Among all his remedies, he has never proposed to surrender the representation which he owes to the very negro whose vote he refuses. The negro is human enough to be represented, but not human enough to have his vote counted."[24]*

To Republicans who had grown up in the party of Lincoln, the Elections Bill was a call to party colors. "A Republican can believe in tariff reduction or even free trade and yet properly adhere to the party," William E. Chandler, now a senator from New Hampshire, wrote to Reed. "But he cannot fail to advocate the Fifteenth Amendment and all proper laws to supplement it and to enforce it and yet be a Republi-

---

* As the rich man and the poor man each deserved his vote, Reed believed, so did the black man. A clever partisan in most matters, Reed was unmistakably earnest in his defense of the principle of majority rule. For a statistical analysis of Reed's highly liberal voting record on racial issues, see Richard M. Valelly, "The Reed Rules and Republican Party Building: A New Look," *Studies in American Political Development*, 23 (October 2009), 115–42.

can. His only proper place is with the Negro-baiting, Republican-killing Democracy."[25]

In this allusion to murder, Chandler's meaning was literal, not rhetorical. Republican deaths at the hands of Democrats featured in a pair of disputed-election cases involving sitting House members from Arkansas. In all, the 51st Congress heard 17 election cases, of which three concerned black Republican candidates who had lost by reason of white Democratic fraud. And in at least 10 of the 17 cases, the Democratic winner owed his seat to the black voters who, by reason of fraud or intimidation, had never been allowed to cast their ballots. The Reed rules would have been inflammatory enough to the Democrats even if race had played no part in the balance of political power in the House. As it was, the Republican majority's ability to settle such cases expeditiously (and, it need not be said, with the virtually inevitable partisan outcome) was the very factor that delivered to the GOP enough votes to make its precarious initial majority unassailable. Early in the session, Reed and Jonathan H. Rowell, a fourth-term Republican from Illinois and the chairman of the House Elections Committee, pushed through in quick succession a pair of election cases, each of which resulted in the seating of a black Republican and the unseating of a white Democrat. "A Democratic newspaper man in the press gallery," related the journalist Arthur W. Dunn, "looking across a gallery which was filled with negroes, said: 'Reed has just sent up there to see if there is another likely looking nigger in the gallery; and if they find one he's to be brought down and sworn in as a member of the House.'"[26]

Such was the racial temper of the House in late June 1890, when Lodge brought his Elections Bill, more than 70 pages worth, to the floor. Democrats were outraged, though not surprised, to hear the Speaker rule that debate would be limited to six days and that no speech could last for more than 40 minutes (later, he capped the length at five minutes). Anyway, the outcome, as all knew, was preordained. Republicans had the votes and the rules. All that remained to the Democrats was an appeal to public opinion and, perhaps, to the conservative instincts of the Senate.

To judge by the subsequent political difficulties of the Republicans who were chiefly identified with the Elections Bill, the Democrats did not misread the country's mood. The Civil War and Reconstruction were over and done with; let the southern blacks make their own way. Not a few northerners listened sympathetically to James C. Hemphill, of South Carolina, the Democrats' floor leader on the Lodge bill, as he appealed to their sympathy and common sense. "A good deal has been said in this country of late about the New South," Hemphill said.

> What this country really needs is a new North. It needs a North that will take a view of all the facts and not be guided by their own preconceived prejudices. It needs a North which will not waste all of its time and energy in reforming other people's abuses. It needs a North that will sometimes look at its own shortcomings and not always on those of people a thousand miles away; and it needs a North which will believe that when a man in the South of the Anglo-Saxon race happens by any untoward circumstance to come into serious collision with another man of the African race that it is not always because the other man is black.[27]

The Elections Bill provoked opposition on the Republican side of the aisle too. If the GOP was sincerely interested in helping African-Americans, said Hamilton Coleman, a freshman from Louisiana, let the Republican Congress do something tangible. Of the 9,000 votes he had garnered in the 1888 election, Coleman told the House, 7,500 were cast by blacks, who cared not that he had fought in the Confederate army but only that he was the regular Republican nominee. What these constituents of his needed least, Coleman went on, was friction and trouble, which the Elections Bill would surely bring them (and when there was trouble, blacks bore the brunt of it). Meanwhile, Coleman observed, bills to establish and support common schools and to reimburse the depositors of the failed Freedman's Bank awaited action. "Both of these bills quietly sleeping," he marveled, " 'under the new rules,' notwithstanding the fact that this Administration with its Republican majorities in the House and Senate and Republican President could have enacted both bills into law several months ago. Gentlemen, why do you not show your sympathy for the colored people in a practical manner when you have such a favorable opportunity?"[28]

Anathema though the Elections Bill was to a substantial minority of representatives, it sailed through the House on the wings of the Reed rules. The vote, when it came on July 2, was 155 for, 149 against and 24 members absent and not paired (meaning one absentee Democrat was not offset with one absentee Republican) for the tally.[29] Here was the people's chamber reconstituted: Make a caucus measure, let the Rules Committee stipulate the time and date for its consideration, along with a time certain for a vote—and let the opposition howl.

But there were no Reed rules in the Senate. There the minority could talk itself hoarse, as it proceeded to do in a 56-day debate over the Election Bill. Not that the senators, in all that time, never changed the subject. The silver senators were especially keen to move on. William M. Stewart, Republican of Nevada, said he opposed the Elections Bill on its merits.[30] Edward O. Wolcott, Republican from Colorado, was similarly opposed, and would have been, he added, even if there were not other, more pressing items on the legislative agenda. There were, however, "many things more important and vital to the welfare of this nation than that the colored citizens of the South shall vote." Financial legislation, for one, proposed Henry M. Teller, senior senator from Colorado and himself a Republican. "[T]he best minds in this country assert to-day that we are on the very verge of a financial panic."[31]

If Chandler was right about the essential body of belief of a Republican, the silver senators had no place in the GOP. It wasn't the almighty dollar they worshiped, rather the underdog, silver dollar, but for this idol they would gladly sacrifice someone else's civil rights. And it was in their hands that the Lodge bill died in January 1891. "The Confederacy and the western mining camps are in legislative supremacy," mourned Senator John C. Spooner of Wisconsin, a Republican of the original type.[32]

In the House of Tom Reed, the Confederacy and the western mining camps held no controlling influence. Indeed, according to the New York *Times*, Reed himself *was* the House, assisted from time to time by his loyal minions McKinley and Cannon, and some others. The Speaker reminded the editors of no historical figure so much as Robespierre, and if Reed had not yet chopped off his enemies' heads, they could thank their lucky stars that he had no guillotine. "But," said an editorial dated

July 8, 1890, "he will crush them politically; he will silence their voices in the House of Representatives; he will strip them of the power to exercise their rights; he will use every means, right or wrong, to prevent any change in the system he builds up." Yet this too shall pass, the editorial concluded: "The Reign of Terror was not more certainly the precursor of the downfall of the Revolution as Robespierre understood it than Mr. Reed's unbridled despotism is sure to be followed by the overthrow of the party for the benefit of which he is exercising it."[33]

By this time, the Speaker had confounded his enemies again by blocking one silver bill and ensuring the passage of another. The bill he helped to speed on its way to the desk of the president turned out to be the catalyst for a decade of American monetary upheaval. However, as Reed correctly observed, the bill he thwarted was worse.

For "free coinage" a modern reader may mentally substitute "inflation," as inflation was the object of the silver forces. In the Senate, they prevailed. A measure to direct the Treasury to purchase and mint into dollars all the silver offered for sale was passed into law on June 17, by a vote of 42–25.[34] Now it went to the House, where the tall and wide form of the Speaker blocked its path. Though he favored majority rule, Reed was prepared to make an exception now and then. The disposition of the monetary question was about to turn on a parliamentary trick.

For three days in June, beginning on the 19th, Reed presided over a House seething to express its will. The substantive question was whether the Senate free-coinage bill would be allowed to come up for a vote. Reed decided it would not. In these political calculations, Benjamin Harrison was a cipher. The president had gone on record against free and unlimited coinage of silver. But he had likewise gone on record supporting "the use of silver in our currency. We are large producers of that metal and should not discredit it. . . . The evil anticipations which have accompanied the coinage and use of the silver dollar have not been realized."[35] If Congress passed a free-coinage bill, would the president sign it? Sherman thought yes, some of the silver senators, no. Reed didn't care to bet.

Counting noses on June 19, the Speaker saw that the free-coinage proponents commanded a slight majority. As usual, attendance was well short of 100 percent. Some members were indisposed, others indifferent, others ministering to sick relatives. The Speaker needed time to rally the sound-money side to full strength. Now the nation's leading proponent of congressional efficiency worked for delay.

On the first day, the issue was joined over the House journal. Did the record of the previous day accurately record the Speaker's referral of the bill to the House Committee on Coinage, Weights and Measures? It was a question as important as it was obscure. In that committee, chaired by the friendly Edwin H. Conger, Republican of Iowa, the bill would disappear from view. In the Committee of the Whole, on the other hand, the bill might very well pass, so closely balanced were the contending forces. Reed's foil, the Democrat Springer, lashed out at the Speaker's strategy to sidetrack free coinage. "You can ignore the rights of representatives of the people," said the annoying man from Illinois, "but the people will pull you down, sir, at the polls next November, and your party with you."[36] Reed was imperturbable, as usual, though the silver forces very nearly scored a victory.

Neither did the pro-silver camp push their measure over the top and onto the agenda on June 20. Only later was the issue clarified: For the free-coinage side, it was to be that day or never. On the 21st, the halt, lame and reluctant representatives of sound money, responding to their party's summons, at last answered the roll call. And it showed that they, not the silverites, were in the majority. Drolly conceding that parliamentary law "was not an exact science [Laughter and applause on the Democratic side]," Reed said he had every intention to allow the House full latitude to decide the technical question.[37]

Now then, Reed posed, did or did not the Senate free-coinage amendment come within the purview of a certain rule, Rule 20? He considered the question from one aspect and then from another, and finally he judged that the bill should, in fact, be referred to the Committee on Coinage, after which (as he did not have to add) it would never be seen again. Democrats protested in vain, Crisp exclaiming that Reed's rules, in this instance, empowered not the majority but a gold-standard clique. "REED'S WAITING GAME" cried the first deck of the *Post*'s headline the next morning: "He Rallied the Republican Members and Emerges from Defeat." And, finally: "After Two Days of Fighting the Silver Bill

Remains with the Coinage Committee to Which It Was Originally Referred—The Silver Men Meet with Defeat." The Speaker had saved sound money—and at some political risk to himself. When, six months later, ex-President Cleveland committed to writing his opposition to "the dangerous and reckless experiment of free, unlimited and independent silver coinage," his handlers despaired of his ever winning another election.[38] To Reed's and Cleveland's lions in this opening round of the monetary bout of the 1890s, Harrison played the lamb.

In June 1890, however, few foresaw just how much fight remained. Foreign holders of American railroad bonds breathed a sigh of relief over Reed's sidetracking of the full-strength silver bill. The low interest rates then prevailing were not the kind to compensate a creditor for the risk that the money in which he expected to be repaid would be inferior to the kind he lent. Now that danger seemed to pass.[39] Besides, the Treasury was, in those days, an actual repository of treasure. There was $300 million of gold in the government's coffers, a pile that had grown steadily since the resumption of gold convertibility in 1879. Holders of paper claims on gold hadn't felt the need to present them at the Treasury for the lawful equivalent in coin or bars. Confidence in the capacity of the Treasury to meet its obligations in gold was unquestioned.[40]

It would not remain so for long, however, as the silver proponents did not walk away empty-handed. The Bland-Allison Act of 1878 had directed the Treasury to buy between $2 million and $4 million of silver a month. In practice, the Treasury bought less rather than more, between $27 million and $35 million a year. The Sherman Silver Purchase Act, passed in July 1890, upped the ante, committing the Treasury to buy 4.5 million ounces of silver a month, essentially the entire American mine output. And how would the government pay for these purchases?[41] Why, with new paper dollars—officially, the Treasury notes of 1890—which might be exchanged for gold at the option of the holder. They were full-fledged legal tender. The intention of the promoters of the Sherman Act was, of course, to make dollars more plentiful. That the realized consequence would be to send dollars into hiding was not widely anticipated. Perhaps Senator Henry W. Blair of New Hampshire spoke for the average legislator when he explained why he, a Republican, was prepared to vote for the bill:

I think nothing so adds to the happiness of the surroundings as for a sick man to take his medicine cheerfully; and as I intend to vote for this bill, after listening to one Senator from Oregon who finds in it the gold standard, that it is a gold measure, and the other Senator from Oregon who finds in it unlimited or free coinage in substance, and the Senator from Kansas who is satisfied that it is a free-coinage bill, and the Senator from Colorado who is not satisfied precisely what it is, but is very well satisfied with it, I thought I would vote for the bill, but I would give notice to the Senate that under no circumstances whatever, here or elsewhere, would I ever give a single reason for so doing.[42]

"During the whole session," Crisp of Georgia taunted Ben Butterworth, Republican of Ohio, "the gentleman and his party, if I may be permitted to borrow a simile, have seemed to bow before the Speaker with much the same feeling with which the Hindu bows before the hideous image of his god. 'He knows he is ugly, but he feels that he is great.'"

"Well," Butterworth good-naturedly replied, "I do not dissent from the good looks of the Speaker, and I agree that he is great."[43]

On the point of political greatness, Republicans saw it as Butterworth did. The Democrats would filibuster and obstruct. Under Reed, Congress would legislate. It was always the way, the Speaker told partisan audiences: "Hanging on to the old traditions is the business of the Democratic party, and it does that business well; we can never rival it."[44]

They loved the Speaker on the stump, and they loved him in the First District of Maine. In September balloting, Reed was reelected by 4,826 votes, the biggest plurality of his career. The victor was jubilant, the friendly Maine Republican press amazed. Reed had prevailed in this fashion over not only the Democrats but also his enemies in the state Republican party, the Blaine faction not least.[45] As for Blaine himself, speculated the Boston *Globe*, "He now has a more formidable rival than ever before for the office of 'uncrowned king' of the Republican party."[46]

What, exactly, had put Reed so far over the top? According to charges leveled by the New York *Times* and the minister of the Congregational Church of the seaside village of Wells, Maine, among others, the answer was corruption. Ten dollars apiece was the going rate for Reed ballots in Wells, the *Times* reported. According to the Reverend Mr. Gleason, at least, there was no "alleged" about it. A former state senator, the Honorable Barak Maxwell, was buying ballots as openly and casually as he might have been buying tomatos. The pastor denounced this electoral commerce from the pulpit on the Sunday after the election. Nor was Wells unique or even unusual: Reed's "boodlers" were buying votes all over the district, the *Times* charged. The Speaker seemed to have made no public denial of these allegations, which conflicted with virtually every other known facet of his public character. Reed had plenty of enemies, the *Times* among them. The Reverend Mr. Gleason was characterized as a Republican, although there were certain Republicans who were no friendlier to Reed than most Democrats. What to make of these disturbingly specific charges? Was Reed complicit in electoral fraud? To know Reed was to doubt it, though to know the politics of Reed's era was to wonder. In indignant retort to President Harrison's claim that providence had put him in the White House, Matthew Stanley Quay, the Republican boss of Pennsylvania, famously remarked that Harrison would "never know how close a number of men were compelled to approach the gates of the penitentiary to make him president." Notable is the fact that Reed's election went uncontested in the overwhelmingly Democratic House, a sign that the charges were even less credible than the ones that Anderson had hurled at him a decade before.

In any case, the sheer scope of Reed's victory seemed a happy omen for the Republican party in the upcoming off-year elections. Reed got on the train to do his bit for the party. He addressed audiences, some of them immense, a few of them adulatory, in New Haven, Connecticut; Champaign, Illinois; Burlington, Iowa; and Chicago. He made whistle stops in upstate New York: Utica, Rochester, Buffalo, Little Falls.[47] At Cedar Rapids, Iowa, the farmers looked so prosperous that the visitor from Maine quipped that he couldn't figure out what they did for a living. Where, he wondered, were "the sad-eyed, poorly clad men covered all over with mortgages and Democratic pity"?[48]

But Portland proved no bellwether of the national mood. A more accurate indicator was the zeal infusing the Wisconsin Democratic convention that met in Milwaukee in late August. Of the nine congressional districts in the Badger State, Republicans occupied eight. To the end of righting that manifest wrong, Colonel William F. Vilas, chairman of the committee on resolutions, rose before the delegates to read the party platform. It was, he stated, a document to "challenge the judgment of the voters of this state in the coming election."

The Democrats of Wisconsin, Vilas began, "declare our continued opposition to all forms of paternalism and centralization." He denounced the McKinley tariff, the force bill (by which the GOP was allegedly attempting to perpetuate itself in power through the familiar agency of election fraud), extravagant federal spending and—at the state level—a Republican-enacted education bill that required English to be the primary language taught in every Wisconsin schoolhouse. Here was a characteristic bit of GOP paternalism, Vilas protested. The state was populated by immigrants; let them learn English at their own pace and for their own reasons. And he had this to say about the Republican party's devotion to Tom Reed: "By its slavish support of the Speaker of the present House of Representatives in his arbitrary assumption of authority, it attempts to disenfranchise its political opponents."[49]

The "shouts and yells" that greeted the reading of the manifesto lingered long enough in the frosty autumn air to send seven of the eight Wisconsin Republican congressional incumbents packing, Nils Haugen being the sole GOP survivor. As Wisconsin went, so, approximately, went the nation. Out of 332 congressional seats, Republicans won just 86, while the Democrats took 238; Populists carried eight. It was a measure of the GOP disaster that, at the Capitol, there were not enough seats on the Democratic side of the aisle to accommodate the new majority; 75 had to find a desk with the humbled Republicans. As much as the people had lost patience with the "self-shackled" 50th Congress, they seemed no happier with the activist 51st.

Alleged Republican extravagance was a gift to Democratic office-seekers. "It's a billion-dollar country," someone—not, originally, Reed—replied in lighthearted defense of the appropriations record of the 51st Congress, but the voters didn't smile. As for the McKinley tariff bill, its timing was as bad as its economics. Enacted on October 1, it was the catalyst for a wave of election-eve price increases. "Every woman who went to a store and tried to buy went home to complain, and a wild unrest filled the public mind," Reed grumbled. "The wonder is that we got any votes at all."[50]

When the last of the appropriations measures of the 51st Congress were tallied, the New York *Sun* strove to grasp the enormity of the number. "Over a billion dollars in two years!" the Democratic editors marveled. "Such is the record of unchecked Republican rule during the existence of the body which President Harrison correctly describes as 'a most remarkable Congress.'

"The acknowledgment of the billion in the semi-official statement of the person lately Chairman of the House Committee on Appropriations closes the incident and makes the issue. Contemplate it:

"$1,000,000,000.

"In these ten figures there is a Democratic President for 1893."[51]

THAT SUMMER, THE summer of 1891, was an off-year for congressional elections, and Reed sailed to Europe on vacation. He visited Italy, where he conscientiously refused to read the newspapers but gloried in the paintings, churches, monuments and landscapes. "I couldn't have enjoyed them more at age 20," he reported. Then it was on to Paris, where he took a ground-floor, one-bedroom apartment and lived as a Parisian.* "I can speak French like a native," he boasted—"of the United States." In truth, he was a more than competent French speaker. Conversing with a reporter from *Le Figaro*, he almost felt as if he were home.[52] Though he was without his wife, he was anything but lonely, "for half of Washington is here and all New York," as he advised his friend Henry Cabot Lodge. Besides, there were books to be bought, statesmen to meet (including the 49-year-old Georges Clemenceau) and a portrait to sit for.

John Singer Sargent, a Paris-dwelling American expatriate, was the

---

* Though he did not always eat like one. One day, while shopping in Paris, Reed came across some canned New England codfish balls. He bought them and took them back to his room, where he had a small gas stove. "I went out and bought a bar of butter," as Reed told the story, "put some of the codfish with it on a bake pan, then ate the whole thing with a pint of claret. The best meal I had in France." See Asher Hinds Diary, January 28, 1897. Asher Hinds Collection. Library of Congress.

portraitist. He knew many subjects better than he did American civics. But Lodge, who himself had sat for Sargent and who helped to arrange the sitting for Reed (with the understanding that the picture would hang in a place of honor in the Capitol), had told him about the fuss in Washington and how Reed had met the storm with superhuman serenity. Reed's imperturbability was, to Sargent, instantly and troublingly evident.

Subject and painter sat closeted together in a borrowed Parisian studio, the massive Reed, looming beyond the painter's brush. Sargent found him charming in all respects except his exterior, which he could not seem to capture on canvas. He threw away his first attempt. "His exterior does not somehow correspond with his spirit," the artist wrote to another progenitor of the project, "and what is a painter to do? I am afraid you and your friends will be disappointed and . . . I could have made a better picture with a less remarkable man. He has been delightful." And to the American sculptor Augustus Saint-Gaudens, he added, "I didn't find much character where his face ought to be. Perhaps a full-length nude would have been the thing to do. What I have done is insignificant, and I beg all your pardons."

It was Sargent himself who quipped, "A portrait is a picture in which there is something wrong with the mouth." And he was right about Reed's friends. They did hate the painting. As for the subject himself, he judged that the likeness, though not so handsome as the original, was a notable work of art. Still, he did not forget to amuse his friends at the unveiling. Pretending to share the general sense of disappointment at the object upon which all eyes were fixed, its subject spoke up. "Well," said Czar Reed, "I hope my enemies are satisfied."

Chapter 18

For the Gold Standard

Opening day of the lame-duck session of the 52nd Congress—it was December 6, 1892—began with a reading of the State of the Union address of the recently defeated Republican president. The House was lightly attended and the members gave less than their full attention to the reading clerk. It was a topic of gossip in the galleries that the desk of the ex-Speaker was unadorned with the customary opening-day bouquet of flowers. "Oh," Reed quipped, "it is because I am nobody's darling." But he remained his party's leader, no small thing in that time of defeat.

"There has never been a time in our history when work was so abundant or when wages were as high, whether measured by the currency in which they are paid or by their power to supply the necessaries and comforts of life," spoke the clerk on behalf of the absent Benjamin Harrison. ". . . If any are discontented with their state here, if any believe that wages or prices, the returns for honest toil, are inadequate, they should not fail to remember that there is no other country in the world where the conditions that seem to them hard would not be accepted as highly prosperous."

Reed detested Harrison. In 1890 the president had not only failed to consult Reed on whom to present the plum of the collectorship of Portland. He had done worse: He had conferred that lucrative office on one of Reed's political enemies (just as Arthur had done). For this and for his regal aloofness and personal frigidity, the ex-Speaker would have nothing to do with the president. At the Republican National Convention in Minneapolis the previous June, Reed had gone so far as to throw his support to Blaine rather than contribute his mite to Harrison's renomination. (Newspaper reporters stared wide-eyed at the sight of Tom Reed cheering the name of his nemesis, but in Harrison, Reed had at last met a politician he disliked even more than the Plumed Knight.) His own election handily won in September, Reed had ridden the rails to campaign for Republican candidates in the national elections in November. However, he uttered the name of the president no more than was absolutely necessary. He would not, he said, "ride in the ice wagon." Election results made Mrs. Grover Cleveland a prophet. On her way out the White House door in 1889, she had predicted that her husband and she would be back. Now they were packing for the move.

No more than the other members milling around the floor of the House on that December 5 did Reed pay overly close attention to Harrison's evaluation of the state of things in the United States. If, however—while shaking hands and making funny remarks by the Speaker's desk—he had happened to catch the passage of the address just quoted, he might have winced. More than most easterners, Reed was beginning to develop some firsthand idea of just how unprosperous were some of the farmers, storekeepers, school teachers, railroad men and ranchers in the west and Great Plains. An investor in Nebraska farmland, he had, in 1889, subscribed $1,000 for 10 shares in the Pacific Town Site Company, a real-estate development corporation under the direction of a onetime Nebraska congressman, George W. E. Dorsey. Town Site's strategy was to enhance the value of the acres it owned by building a railroad close by, for which purpose it would borrow funds to supplement its investors'. The boom had ended even before Reed invested his money. In 1890, the eminent London banking house of Baring Brothers nearly came a cropper over its investments in Argentina. All at once, capital was in retreat. Kansas, Nebraska and the Dakotas were far from the pampas of the Argentine, but to frightened and overextended British financiers, they suddenly all looked the same. In the United States, financial pan-

ics customarily originated in New York and radiated west. In the early
1890s, the trouble started in the West and crept east. Though he couldn't
have known it, Reed was in on the ground floor of the Panic of 1893.

"In reference to business," Dorsey had apprised Reed in August 1891,
"the fact is this country is practically dead. It is impossible to get money
from the sources that have heretofore been open, and consequently there
is no speculation in anything. People are buying absolutely nothing
except what is necessary to support life, and this is the condition notwithstanding the fact that Nebraska never had such magnificent crops." Rain
was ample, even to the normally parched western portions of the state.
All would have been well, wrote Dorsey, if the company had not gone
into debt. "I went into Holt County some time since," he added, "and
made a personal examination of our lands. I have advertised the property,
endeavored to trade it for horses or cattle and have done everything I possibly could to dispose of this and get out, but so far without success."

Some things change in investment markets from generation to generation, but the human heart remains the same. Bear markets begin
with hope (really, things must get better). Then comes resignation (this
too shall pass), despair (no, it won't) and revulsion (if I ever buy another
share of stock, acre of land or what have you, just have me committed).
In 1891, Dorsey was still hoping, as were the Holt County farmers. They
would consider selling at between $15 and $20 an acre, "but at the same
time you can buy adjoining farms held by non-residents who purchased
equities as we did, for from $5 to $7 an acre," as Dorsey apprised Reed.

The market was frozen. The locals had no money, and emigration
had stopped. There was no confidence. For the lack of trust, Dorsey
blamed "our idiotic friends" in the Farmers Alliance. Only a year before,
mortgages endorsed by sound Nebraska banks had found a ready market
back east. "Today you could not sell a note of $5,000 signed by ten of
the best men in the state."

Dorsey, at least, was confident: The Town Site Company would succeed, although he did add that his brother-in-law, with whom he had
entrusted management of the Holt County lands, had left town after
losing everything he had in speculation on the Chicago Board of Trade.
"[A]nd I," wrote Dorsey, "have been trying to unravel the ragged ends
that he dropped. Have had a very difficult task and am not through yet.

If we could pay up what is due in Holt County, and hold the same for two or three years, there is no question but that money could be made by so doing. This depression cannot last."[1]

But the depression did last. There was drought too, and a "political cyclone" in the shape of the rise of the Populist party, successor to the Farmers Alliance. Dorsey and Reed lost everything they invested, Dorsey as much as $25,000, in part on account of a swindling business associate. Never, however, Dorsey implored, should Reed doubt Dorsey's honor and good intentions.[2]

Harrison proved no better an economic diagnostician than he had a second-term presidential candidate. Quite clearly, all was not well in America. One could have inferred as much from the showing of the Populist presidential candidate in November. James B. Weaver, drawing more than one million popular votes, became the first third-party candidate to win any Electoral College votes since before the Civil War (he gleaned 22). In Reed's financially adopted state of Nebraska, Weaver won 41 percent of the vote. Populists, furthermore, had won the gubernatorial races in Kansas, North Dakota and Colorado, as well as eight seats in the U.S. House of Representatives.[3]

There were other evil omens. The lethal, pitched battle between strikers and Pinkerton guards outside Pittsburgh at Carnegie's Homestead iron and steel works in the summer of 1892 was not the work of contented people. "I will never recognize the union, never, never, never!" cried Henry Clay Frick, general manager of the Carnegie property, who had imposed a wage cut on 8.5 percent of the hands, a decision seemingly at odds with the then-ruling industrial prosperity. Frick made his declaration while recovering from wounds he had sustained in an attack in his office by Alexander Berkman, an anarchist. Shot and stabbed on July 23, the executive had had his wounds bandaged at his desk, where he remained until his usual leave-taking time. Though Berkman was not a union man, his attack did nothing to soften Frick's obstinacy. Was not the protective tariff, of which the Carnegie Steel Company was such a large beneficiary, supposed to guarantee high wages for the American workingman? Some voters stopped to reconsider the theory and practice of the GOP's tariff. Carnegie won the strike and Harrison lost the presidency.[4]

FOR THE GOLD STANDARD

As organized labor was angry, so gold was restive. More of it was leaving the country than was coming in. Proverbially, money goes where it is wanted and well cared for. In the 1880s, gold was money, and its destination was the United States. In 1879, the year that Treasury Secretary John Sherman reinstituted the gold standard, the Treasury held a gold reserve of $120 million. In 1890, the year Senator Sherman reluctantly allowed his name to be affixed to the Silver Purchase Act, the reserve stood at $190 million. It was the operation of that law that set the monetary exodus in motion. Now the Treasury was commanded to buy 4.5 million ounces of silver every month with paper currency. The dollars thereby printed were, however, a charge on the gold reserve—one could present them at a Treasury office for the statutory equivalent of gold coin. The clock was thus set ticking on the gold standard. The more paper the Treasury issued to buy silver, the greater the number of pieces of paper—the Treasury notes of 1890—that might be lawfully presented for gold.

At $1.2929 to the ounce, at which silver was 1/16th as valuable as gold, the two metals would have been aligned to the perfect satisfaction of the silver interests. At that value for silver, and at the settled, $20.67-per-ounce value for gold, the Treasury could indifferently pay out either metal in exchange for such paper as might be presented to it. The Sherman act, in fact, wrote that equivalence into the statute books. It is "the established policy of the United States," the law stated, "to maintain the two metals on a parity with each other upon the present legal ratio."[5] In other words, a silver dollar could be exchanged for a gold dollar. Or, at the nation's custom houses, an importer could hand over silver dollars, rather than gold ones, to the customs agent. No matter that the value of the silver in that silver dollar was at a deep and deepening discount to the value of gold in the gold dollar. Congress had ordered the Treasury to treat them as if they were identical.

Opportunists the world over reveled in this artificial equality. Anyone could see that there was everything to gain and nothing to lose by exchanging silver at a discount for gold at full value. For nothing like the old $1.2929 value for silver was prevailing in the early 1890s. Shortly after enactment of the Sherman bill, an ounce was quoted at $1.21. Hopeful speculators had pushed up the price in expectation that federal buying would restore the 16:1 ratio. But not even the Treasury's monthly bid for 4.5 million ounces at market prices could stay the resumption of the silver bear market. By 1893, the value of an ounce of the white metal had fallen to 78 cents. Here was a powerful demonstration of the impracticability of a bimetallic standard in one country, but the silver interests only shouted louder. Mere federal stockpiling was not the answer (nor had they ever believed it was). Nothing would do, they insisted, but free and unlimited coinage. The decline in the value of silver, expressed in gold, was part and parcel of generally falling prices, the argument went. It was proof of the shortage of money—that is, of the scarcity of gold. That the very agitation of the free-silver enthusiasts had driven gold into hiding made no difference to the inflationists. As silver was abundant and dollars were scarce, the answer to the crisis was obvious: Let there be more silver dollars.

Such pleas from across the Mississippi did not fall on deaf ears in Washington. William McKinley, whose ear was forever to the ground, laid into the gold-standard Democrats in a speech in Toledo in February 1891. The now lame-duck congressman took no great interest in the monetary question. He was for gold, and for silver too: Practical bimetallism was the way forward, he vaguely believed.[6] But listening to the Major, a spokesman for the party that had restored the gold standard in 1879, an investor in New York, London or Paris might well have wondered what the dollar was coming to. Grover Cleveland, charged McKinley, "was determined to contract the circulating medium and demonetize one of the coins of commerce, limit the volume of money among the people, make money scarce, and therefore dear. He would have increased the value of money and diminished the value of everything else—money the master, everything else, the servant."[7]

Was the dollar really as good as gold? The answer would have to await the resolution of an epic political struggle. So money went into hiding. "New enterprises were abandoned, present business was curtailed and the more timid proceeded to hide their talent in a napkin," a contemporary historian wrote of the mood in 1891. That year, Europe drew heavily on American gold, with net exports in the 12 months to June 1891 totaling $68 million. In the succeeding 12 months, sales of big American crops reduced the net outflow to a trickle. But the huge net exports resumed in June 1892. In the next seven months, more paper dollars were exchanged for gold than in all the preceding 13 years combined.[8]

Thomas B. Reed Sr. had died in 1887 at the age of 83—"Capt. Reed," said the funeral notice in the *Eastern Argus*, out of respect for the deceased's long-ago command of a merchant vessel.[9] "I loved him with all my heart," his grieving son attested in his diary. Reed's mother, Mathilda Mitchell Reed, died three years later, at 80. Blaine, another fixture in Reed's life, was taken ill in May 1892 during a Cabinet meeting and was rushed to his home in Lafayette Square. Not knowing if he would live or die, the Secretary of State entrusted a message to a colleague to deliver to Harrison: Let the president know that he supported his renomination for a second term. In June, on the eve of the GOP National Convention, Blaine was still not well, but he was well enough to have reconsidered his options. He had, in fact, changed his mind. No longer was he explicitly a noncandidate. And while he was not, avowedly, a candidate, he could hardly support Harrison's renomination. Resigning from the State Department, he traveled to Boston to await the outcome of the balloting in Minneapolis. "It will be Blaine on the first ballot," "Boss" Matthew Quay, who had no more use for Harrison than Reed did, had emotionally predicted. And when Blaine's name was put into nomination on June 10, the delegates and the galleries went into a 27-minute rapture. "Blaine, Blaine, James G. Blaine," they stamped their feet as they chanted. The journalist William Allen White had the correct interpretation of that jubilant demonstration. It was "at once a salutation and a requiem," he wrote.[10]

Adore Blaine though they might, the Republicans nominated Harrison, on the first ballot and with 100 votes to spare. Before the motion to make the vote unanimous, the tally showed Harrison with 535⅙ votes out of 904⅓ cast; Blaine was next with 182⅙, then McKinley with 182 and Robert Lincoln of Illinois with 1. Reed received four votes, though he had not campaigned. His presidential strategy consisted of a pleasant thought. If, he had mused, Harrison and Blaine fought to a stalemate, and if the party needed a compromise candidate, perhaps he could be that dark horse. This was, however, "only the remotest possibility—too remote even to be considered by a provident man," Reed reflected.[11]

So the delegates dispersed to pull the ice wagon on which Reed refused to ride. Blaine, having no job to hold or work to do, except to fend off importuning publishers who sensed a final fleeting chance to cash in on his celebrity, rattled around his palatial Washington home. He died on January 27, 1893, three days before his 63rd birthday.[12]

It was to Stanley A. Pullen, of Portland, that Reed conveyed his feelings on Blaine's death. The former owner of the Portland *Press*, Pullen, in 1886, had bought a seat on the New York Stock Exchange. Reed was a client of the firm of Pullen, Crocker & Company and he had given Pullen wide discretion in managing his money. The two of them maintained a joint account in which, using borrowed money, they speculated in stocks and commodities.

Reed told Pullen that Blaine's wife had asked him to be a pall bearer at the funeral. She said that Blaine had intended to call on Reed after the opening of the new Congress but that his health by then had failed him. And she added her thanks to Reed for his help at the Minneapolis convention in steering the Maine delegation to Blaine. This had persuaded her that there was no basis in some of the stories that she had heard about him.

"Mrs. Blaine's measure to me was very gratifying," Reed wrote to Pullen. "I am feeling bitter and resentful and Mr. Blaine has tried me fiercely hard, but I tell you as I sit in the church with his aspect before me and the old solemn words put together in the old uncouth fashion of the Congregational Church so filled with associations for me, all my quarrels with Blaine seemed so trivial that only the wholesome fear of seeming in the eyes of an unloving world an awful hypocrite prevented a burst of tears—can you credit it? It was so."[13]

ALMOST TWO YEARS earlier, at the close of the 51st Congress in March 1891, Democrats had refused to make the customary resolution of thanks to Speaker Reed. Now, on the final day of the 52nd Congress, March 3, 1893, Reed rose to perform the office that they had shunned.

Speaker Crisp and the Democrats wondered what form this gratitude might take. They had wasted no time repealing "Reedism," especially its quorum-counting feature, when it was their turn to make the rules for the 52nd Congress. Nor had they thought to reconsider when, in February 1892, the Supreme Court upheld the validity of the quorum count in *United States v. Ballin*. They had defeated the Republicans and uprooted nearly every vestige of their parliamentary revolution. Unbowed, Reed had excoriated the Democratic Congress for having wasted a 3:1 majority. "In history," he had written, "it will present all the dead level of a Dutch landscape with all its windmills but without a trace of its beauty and fertility." The Democrats had failed to revise the tariff, to reach agreement on an international copyright law, to subsidize the merchant marine. The Democratic House was the "Citadel of Do Nothing." It had "shirked its duties and led a gelatinous life, to the scorn of all vertebrate animals." And now the author of those pungent phrases was going to express his heartfelt thanks to Speaker Charles F. Crisp, Democrat of Georgia.

"Mr. Speaker," Reed began:

> The Speaker of this House holds an office of dignity and honor, of vast power and influence. The extent of that power and influence cannot be described even by one who has been honored by its possession. All this dignity, honor and influence were created not to adorn or glorify any individual, but to uphold, support and maintain the well-being of the people of the United States.
>
> That that officer should be respected and esteemed concerns every member of this House not only as a member, but as a citizen of the United States. . . .
>
> While, therefore, my associates and I have not forgotten the past, I am sure that I speak the sentiment of them all when I say that the Republican party, without regard to what any other party may do, or what any other party has done, will buttress, by the respectful behavior of each and every one of its members, this high office. [Applause on the Republican side.]
>
> Therefore, placing patriotism above partisanship, placing duty above even a just resentment, notwithstanding we do not

approve of the parliamentary law of the Speaker and his asso-
ciates, and deem that the system re-established is undemocratic
and unwise, nevertheless, by offering the customary resolution,
we tender to the Speaker of this House the expression of our
belief that he, like all his predecessors, has performed the trying
duties of his office with upright intention and honorable purpose.
[Applause.][14]

THE INCOMING PRESIDENT and his Treasury Secretary seemed polls
apart on the question of the hour. There was no sturdier advocate of the
gold standard than Grover Cleveland. John G. Carlisle, on the other
hand, had a soft spot for inflation. He had opposed the resumption of
the gold standard in 1875. He had denounced the contraction of the
greenbacks, and he had supported the Bland-Allison Act of 1878 (under
which, as we have seen, the Treasury was directed to buy between $2
million and $4 million of silver each month). "The idea that there was
a conspiracy of the moneyed classes of the whole world to subjugate the
poor man was apparently fixed in Carlisle's mind," Carlisle's biographer
relates of the Treasury Secretary before he became the agent of Cleveland's monetary orthodoxy.[15]

Cleveland, however, was willing to forgive the Kentuckian his check-
ered past. He had taken a shine to Carlisle during his first administration.
At a low-stakes poker game among Cleveland intimates, Carlisle, then
the Democratic Speaker of the House, exhibited a miraculous strain of
good luck. The game was five-card draw. At the end of a spirited round of
raising and bluffing and back-raising, Cleveland stood pat. Senator James
Cameron of Pennsylvania drew one card. The newspaper editor Henry
Watterson stood pat. Then it was Carlisle's turn. He announced that he
would draw four cards, which he held awkwardly, as if he were new to the
game. Astoundingly, each card he drew was a king. "Take the money,
Carlisle; take the money!" Cleveland roared. "If ever I am president again,
you shall be the Secretary of the Treasury. But don't make that four-card
draw too often."[16] Later, away from the poker table, the president-elect
praised Carlisle's knowledge and experience. "[H]e knows all I ought to
know," said Cleveland, "and I can bear all we have to bear."[17]

Cleveland's burdens were waiting for him on the day of his inauguration, March 4, 1893. The Treasury was in nothing like the condition he had left it four years earlier. To the Harrison administration, including Pensions Commissioner Tanner, he had bequeathed a cash balance of $281 million and a gold reserve of $197 million. From the Harrison administration, he had inherited a cash balance of $24 million and a gold reserve not much more than $100 million. Against this gold had been issued $809 million of paper dollars, including $346 million of greenbacks, or legal tender notes; $328.2 million of legal tender notes issued under the Bland-Allison Act; and $135.5 million of the Treasury notes of 1890, paid out in conjunction with the Sherman Silver Purchase Act.[18] The Treasury's policy was to exchange any and all of this currency for gold at the statutory rate, whether or not it had been printed in order to buy silver. Not since Resumption had the Treasury's gold balance sunk below $100 million. By common consent, it was the prudent minimum.

Now doubt displaced confidence. It was confusing enough for Americans to try to parse the words and comprehend the deeds of the contending political parties on the great monetary question. It was no easier for foreign investors. There were Republican bimetallists and Democratic gold-standard adherents. There were also, however, confusingly, Republican silverites and Democratic bimetallists. Formerly, America's political fault line ran east to west, whereas now it seemed to travel north to south. "We denounce the Republican legislation known as the Sherman Act of 1890 as a cowardly makeshift, fraught with possibilities of danger in the future," the 1892 Democratic party platform stated in admirably clear language, "which should make all of its supporters, as well as its author, anxious for its speedy repeal." But neither did the Populist party mince words when it demanded "free and unlimited coinage of silver and gold at the present legal ratio of 16:1." What and whom was the British investor in American railroad debentures to believe?

In 1890, Reed had insisted that the choice before Congress was between bad and worse: the Sherman act or free silver. By 1892, however, there seemed precious little to choose between those monetary alternatives. Free silver meant the immediate end to the gold standard, the Sherman act the certain end but at some unknown date. It was silver now or silver later.

Unless, that is, the leading commercial nations could be brought together to agree on a plan to embrace both metals at a satisfactory ratio. Unilateral inflation would be commercial poison to the nation attempting it. Collective inflation might do no one nation any harm and all nations some good (or so the theory went). Thus Harrison, himself a keen bimetallist, called an international silver conference. Delegates from 20 nations gathered in Brussels in November 1892. The American delegation, which consisted of a couple of western senators, a former comptroller of the currency and a Brown University professor, among others, got its marching orders. It was to win international consent to plan for ushering silver back into the monetary mainstream. Failing an agreement on worldwide bimetallism, it was to secure some means of propping up the tumbling silver price. But two months of talking availed little except for the month in which the delegates would next convene—May, they decided. The Europeans liked the gold standard, had pledged themselves to it. Besides, they wondered, which was the authentic American monetary voice, the well-modulated sound of the Brussels delegation or the Babel of the representatives and senators in Washington, D.C.?

Cleveland's return to the White House set the nerves of American business on edge. The president and his party were pledged to reduce the iniquitous tariff. Anticipating foreign competition, the protected wing of the industrial economy waited to see how much, if at all, its profit margins would shrink. The Democratic platform demanded sound money and the repeal of the Sherman act. A laudable expression of intent, orthodox financiers agreed. But how and when would the administration redeem that pledge? Half of the Democratic party opposed it, including a second-term congressman from Nebraska named William J. Bryan.

Property owners lay awake at night wondering how much they would be worth if, by some congressional act of omission or commission, their gold dollars were reduced to silver ones. "People are in a state to be thrown into a panic at any minute," the Boston banker and philanthropist Henry Lee Higginson advised Attorney General Richard Olney on April 19, "and, if it comes, and gold is withdrawn, it will be a panic that will wake the dead. . . . I believe it to be a very great mistake, if the gold reserve is allowed to fall below $100,000,000, for that point has been held sacred and had better be kept so. Do not forget how much imagination has to do with all business operations. People as old as we are [neither Higginson nor Olney had reached 60] dread panics very much, because there is no reason left and because there are terrible sacrifices for most excellent people."[19]

Rumors were then flying that the Treasury would cease redeeming its silver notes in gold. There was an element of plausibility to the tale. Obviously, the financial bleeding had to stop. Then too, the pro-silver sympathies of the man who would presumably have to take action were all too well known. In an attempt to allay the rising panic, Secretary of the Treasury Carlisle issued a press release on April 21 pledging to continue to pay gold value for the silver notes. It would have been better if the statement had stopped right there. Instead, the sentence continued, "so long as he has gold lawfully available for that purpose." Now monied Americans had something else to worry about in the middle of the night. Which gold was "lawfully available"? Was it lawful to pay out gold from a reserve that had fallen below $100 million?[20]

Suddenly, it was no hypothetical question. On April 22, the reserve did slide below $100 million. What now? The Treasury might borrow gold, preferably from Europe, at an interest rate of perhaps 3 percent. Cleveland and Carlisle took it under consideration but with heavy hearts. They would be making unwanted history, as never before had the United States issued bonded debt in peacetime. The administration was weighing its options when, on May 4, National Cordage Company, one of the high-flying new industrial consolidations, went broke. Bankruptcies had been common enough in that time of financial trouble. The Philadelphia & Reading Railroad had failed in February. But National Cordage had seemingly gone bankrupt out of a clear blue sky. It had, indeed, just declared a cash dividend at the annual rate of 12 percent. It was as if a July 4 picnic was canceled on account of a blizzard.

Now the bottom fell out: of Wall Street, farm prices and of the economy itself. Industrial companies like National Cordage (quoted at $75 a share in February, at $18.75 on May 4) bore the brunt of the stock-market decline. "It has been a very bad day," a Washington broker friend of Reed's advised the former Speaker, "one of the worst I ever saw, and while there may be a God in Israel, we want him in Wall Street now. Notwithstanding the turmoil I have thought forty times of you and your affairs today, and I hope you saw enough in New York on your way home to drive you out of the game."[21]

New York, in fact, was not the best vantage point for watching the 1893 panic unfold. For once, bank runs were concentrated outside the American financial capital, notably in Denver; Kansas City, Missouri; Kansas City, Kansas; Louisville, Kentucky; Milwaukee, Wisconsin; and Portland, Oregon. Financial historians are not entirely sure what the depositors were afraid of: the quality of the institutions at which they banked or the quality of the dollars in those institutions' vaults. In any case, the people ran, and their gait picked up in June and July. Dollars were everywhere except where they had been or were supposed to be. The political movement to make money abundant had instead made it scarce.

If it were up to the Populist party, the government would place in circulation $50 for every man, woman and child in America.[22] In 1893, half of that per capita sum was issued and outstanding, though it was definitely not circulating. Hoarding of cash had placed a premium on dollar bills.[23] There was, in that day, no Federal Reserve to print up money on demand. If one's bank had closed, or if, still open, were rationing withdrawals, one had to make do. Cash could be had at a price. Brokers brought together those who had never trusted banks—whose money was under the mattress or between the sock and the sole of a shoe—and those who wished they had never trusted banks but who, in any case, needed money. The haves lent to the have-nots for a premium of as much as four percent, the brokers routinely finding it necessary to fumigate the haves' hoarded bills.[24] The Chicago World's Fair had opened in May. Unless one were prepared to cancel one's long-planned trip merely on account of a shortage of $10 bills, one improvised. Scrip proliferated. Perhaps $100 million of clearing-house certificates (used to settle interbank debts), cashier's checks, certificates of deposit, due bills from manufacturers and other such monetary inventions passed from hand to hand in lieu of legal tender that panicky summer. "It is worthy of note," recorded former comptroller of the currency A. Barton Hepburn, "that no loss resulted from this makeshift currency."[25]

But this successful experiment in privately issued money ignited no alternative political movement; it remained the government's business to put monetary matters right. The Democratic party was pledged to repeal the Sherman act: When would it act?

Cleveland had resisted ever-more-insistent demands that he call Congress into special session, but, in a June 4 interview with United Press, he seemed to relent. An August session was, indeed, now in the cards.

Cleveland presently wondered if he would live to see it. On June 18, the president's doctor discovered a tumor the size of a 25-cent piece on the roof of Cleveland's mouth. It would have to come out immediately, but no one must know, lest the panic rage harder. The operation was scheduled for June 19 aboard a yacht, the *Oneida*, on which Cleveland had often been seen in the past. Dr. W. W. Keen, the lead surgeon, left this picture of the patient on the eve of his ordeal: "On arriving on the yacht, the President lighted a cigar, and we sat on deck chatting and smoking until near midnight. Once he burst out with, 'Oh, Dr. Keen, those office seekers! Those office seekers! They haunt me in my dreams.'"[26]

Two weeks later, Olney visited his recuperating chief at Gray Gables, the Clevelands' summer cottage on Cape Cod. The president had lost a lot of weight, and his mouth was stuffed with cotton. A sizable piece of his left jaw had been cut out. "My God, Olney," Cleveland exclaimed through the antiseptic wads, "they nearly killed me." But the still-living president, with Olney's help, found the strength to compose his message to Congress urging repeal of the Sherman act. "[O]ur government," one resounding passage said, "cannot make its fiat equivalent to intrinsic value, nor keep inferior money on a parity with superior money by its own independent efforts." It was dated August 8, 24 hours after the scheduled start of the first, special session of the 53rd Congress.

Reed did not look his best in the summer. Whether on account of his girth or the climate in which he was born and raised, he thrived in the cold and snow. August in Washington was an ordeal he was generally spared by the legislative calendar, but 1893 was the rare, imperative exception. "This matter rises above party politics," Cleveland had asserted in his silver message, and Reed emphatically agreed. On the monetary issue, he was for the public interest, and for that reason with the president.

"He was observed by all observers," related the Washington *Post* of Reed at the opening of that sweltering special session, "an object of awe to the far Western member who saw him for the first time and has been used to regard him as a modern ogre, and was kept busy shaking hands with new acquaintances and old."[27] He was again elected minority leader, Republican strength having increased to 128 from 88 since the 52nd Congress. Exactly none of his celebrity did the ex-Speaker seem to owe to the flash of his appearance. He could be seen that summer, according to the *Post*, in a coat that "hung about him in folds innumerable, and to every fold there were a thousand creases; the vest crawled up to his chin and left exposed a not always immaculate shirt; the trousers fit him as stockings would a rooster. He was a sight to make the heathen rage and kind hearted women weep."[28]

Preliminaries out of the way, the emergency session of the 53rd Congress fell to debating the Sherman act, the issue that had called them to Washington. No member could doubt what the fuss was about. Unemployment was climbing and businesses were closing. As the congressmen gathered, the Treasury's gold reserve was $4 million below the $100 million mark. Prime commercial paper was quoted at 15 percent, though the quoting of any rate flattered the state of the money market. On the authority of the railroad titan James J. Hill, wiring the president from St. Paul, Minnesota, "No grain or farm produce can move for want of money."[29] On the other hand, the more radical of the silver partisans were prepared to suffer much worse than commercial paralysis in the name of their cause. "It is better, infinitely better, that blood should flow to the horses' bridles rather than our national liberties should be destroyed." So spoke Colorado Governor Davis H. Waite—subsequently known as "Bloody Bridles Waite"—at a silver convention held in Denver in July.[30]

The debate in the House was a curious show, as a Democratic speaker was almost as likely to condemn his own party's platform, and his own president's monetary agenda, as he was to support it. The Republicans, heavily for repeal, listened bemusedly as the majority party faced off against itself, the eastern gold faction versus the western inflationists. No Republican, not even Reed, put the case for repeal better or more eloquently than the eastern Democrats, notably Bourke Cockran of New York, who begged to remind his wild-haired colleague Bryan that the gold value of wages, according to data from "a Democratic Bureau of Statistics," had never been higher in the whole course of civilization than it was at that moment.[31]

Cockran had spoken for 90 minutes. Bryan would go for three hours. "The Democratic Party stands today between two conflicting forces," said the radical from Nebraska. "On the one side stand the corporate interests of the United States, the moneyed interests, [aggregated] wealth and capital, imperious, arrogant, compassionless. . . . On the other side stand an unnumbered throng, those who gave to the Democratic party a name and for whom it has assumed to speak. Work-worn and dust-begrimed, they make their mute appeal, and too often find their cry for help beat in vain against the outer walls, while others, less deserving, gain access to legislative halls."

Reed chose himself as the orator to deliver the last word for the Republican side of the debate. He did, for him, the unusual thing of preparing a set-piece speech, 60 minutes in running time. It was shortly before 10 in the morning on Saturday, August 26, when he rose to speak. Vice President Adlai E. Stevenson, a silver man, had come to listen, as had Secretary of the Treasury Carlisle. Reed had covered his imposing form with a loose-fitting suit. He wiped the perspiration from his brow, the air being hot and oppressive even by Washington summertime standards. The show of shirtsleeves being a breach of decorum, he did not, of course, doff his jacket. At the gallery entrances, men stood on chairs to get a better glimpse of the Republican giant, though they had no trouble hearing him. His voice, "less nasal than usual," the Washington *Post*'s reporter judged, "carried to the remotest ends of the hall."[32] On his desk, there were a couple of books but no notes or manuscript pages. He had committed his talk to memory.

Reed began humbly, as not a few of the members had done, by admitting how little he knew. Yet, though he had serious doubts about the wisdom of any individual, including himself, "and no doubt whatsoever of the difficulty of the task," he took comfort in falling back on "the wisdom of all," even when that collective wisdom was embodied in the decisions of the U.S. Congress.

As for the crisis at hand, it fit an age-old pattern. Boom and bust—cycles of confidence and distrust—followed one after the other. "The general progress has always been onward, but there have been many times when the movement has seemed to be to the rear." What was new was the "obliteration" of time and distance by the railroad and telegraph and ocean steamer. Magellan was three years in circumnavigating the earth; now it took two months. So it was a world economy, as the reverberating consequences of the Barings crisis attested. As it never needed it before, America had need of the world's capital, not only its own.

Now then, Reed continued, he would point no finger of blame at the passage of the Sherman act. A "variety of circumstances," which he would not enumerate, "conspired to make the passage of that act an absolute necessity." In consequence of that alleged necessity, foreign investors in American business had called for their gold and domestic depositors in American banks had run for their deposits.

Repeal of the Sherman act was, therefore, imperative, though repeal alone was unlikely to restore prosperity. The Democrats' intention to roll back the tariff was an equal weight on American enterprise. Which topic naturally led Reed to the enemy across the aisle. For the first time in 30 years, they held the White House along with a majority in both houses of Congress. "The time will come," said Reed, "when the Democratic members of Congress, instead of disputing with each other what the Democratic platform means [Laughter.], will be disputing with each other what the necessities of the country demand."

He paused to reflect how little was new under the sun. As a new member of Congress, he had listened to the inflationists assail the resumption of the gold standard. It would deliver the United States into the hands of the British and would prostrate the debtor, they said. "[A]nd yet, I lived to see every one of those prophecies forgotten, and every man connected with them forgotten, too. [Laughter.]" Out of the misplaced fears of the 1870s had sprung the boom of the 1880s.

Though the silver debate split the House by section more than by party, Reed closed on a note of pure, uninhibited partisanship. The president had had to appeal to the patriotism of the Republican party to push the repeal legislation by the obstacle of his own party. Nor had he appealed in vain. "What we were in our days of victory the same are we in our days of defeat—champions of true and solid finance. [Applause.] And when the time comes, as it will surely come, for us to lead this land back to those paths of prosperity and fame which were trodden under Republican rule for so many years, we shall take back with us our ancient glory undimmed by adversity; our ancient honor, unsullied by defeat."[33]

The vote came the next day, and it was better than two-to-one for repeal, with Republicans lining up four-to-one behind their triumphant minority leader. "Free Coinage Gets its Deathblow," boomed the fifth bank of a towering New York *Times* headline over the report of a "Grand Victory for Honest Money in the House." It was a grand victory in a skirmish. The Senate was yet to vote (not until October 30 would it follow the House), and far greater struggles lay in the future. Not only were the monetary infidels undefeated but neither were the battle lines permanently drawn. The radical silverites and the gold monometallists had no doubts. Bryan was for inflation, Cleveland for gold. Cockran too was for gold. But many disputants weren't sure what they believed. The monetary questions were complex, and each side laid vehement claim to the higher morality. It wasn't only McKinley who could wind up sounding like Cleveland one day and like Bryan another. Gold-standard Democrats of Cleveland's day had been free-silver men in Harrison's.

The truth is that Tom Reed himself wavered. In his speech to repeal the Sherman act he had sagely remarked that "the foundation of all disputes is difference in definition." One senses, reading him, that he was not quite sure what the gold standard was all about. It was clear to all that, under a gold standard, currency was exchangeable at a fixed rate for a certain measure of gold. Gold ballasted and collateralized paper claims. But, as Reed was not heard to say, the gold standard was an international system that maintained an equilibrium of prices and costs among the participating nations. Free trade, or something close to free trade, characterized the system. Impediments to trade were equally impediments to the synchronizing ebb and flow of gold between and among the concert of gold-standard nations.

So rock-ribbed gold men shuddered when Reed spelled out his monetary views next spring in an interview with the English journal *Fortnightly Review*. The editors presented the ex-Speaker as a likely Republican candidate for president in 1896. They quoted him floating an idea that, to the eyes and ears of the City of London, must have sounded only a little different than pure Bryanism. What Reed proposed was a consortium of countries joined in a policy of managed currency depreciation. This protective union would, somehow, raise up the price of silver in terms of gold. It would exclude from its commercial clique the products of those countries, like Britain, that insisted on remaining on a pure gold standard, without a silver filigree. The United States would lead this imagined bimetallic enterprise.

You see, Reed explained, the underlying trouble lay with the silver-standard countries of the East, notably India. Their cheaper money made their wares more salable in the world's export markets. Let us therefore emulate them, he urged, by promoting an international agreement to turn silver into money, alongside gold. To which a reader of the *Review* presently rebutted, Why not go all out? If inflation were the road to prosperity, why not be done with it and just print the money, omitting gold and silver altogether? In which case, this correspondent, Lord Farrer, a former Lord Chancellor, ironically observed, the United States would be just as prosperous as Argentina. "The policy goes still further," His Lordship wrote. "It says in effect to England not merely 'Take our silver,' but 'There are debts we have promised to pay you in gold; take them in silver, or, in other words, at a fraction of their gold value, or we will deal with you no longer.' Of such a policy the epithet 'disastrous' would be a very inadequate description."[34]

If Reed was at sea, in the monetary way, so were many Republicans. Henry Cabot Lodge, by now a U.S. senator, was pushing a kind of international bimetallism similar to Reed's ("anarchical," judged the *Nation*). State Republican parties in Kansas, Maine and Vermont endorsed some species of bimetallism. The Republican party of the Golden State of California GOP threw in its lot with free silver.[35] This was in 1894, the year of the march on Washington by a few hundred ragged unemployed men—"Coxey's Army," it was styled—to demand federal action to cut short the depression. It was the year of the violent strike against the Pullman railcar company, of a failed corn crop, of hunger and plunging investment values.[36] In 1892, American manufacturers had produced 2,011 locomotives. In 1894, they were on their way to making just 695.[37] Reed, returned that year by another comfortable margin to what would prove to be a strong Republican Congress, was one of the lucky ones. He had remunerative work for as long as the voters of the First District of Maine continued to reelect him.

He knew perfectly well, however, how hard was the lot of the less fortunate, and he would presently learn much more. His friend and broker, Stanley Pullen, was caught in the autumn of 1894 with a long position in the plunging grain markets. His difficulties were compounded by the fact that he was speculating with borrowed money. Perhaps Reed was caught with him, since Pullen, when presented with a demand to post more collateral, enlisted his lender's sympathies by saying that he was trying to carry his clients too. The lender held out the hope of leniency.[38]

Come January 1895, Pullen was evidently in deeper trouble, and he let Reed know it. "Your letter very naturally startled me," Reed replied on the 12th, "since the stocks etc. with you bear a very large proportion to my whole assets and hence I should like to know precisely how I am situated." What was the condition of his joint account with Pullen? Of his personal account? Could Reed, by remitting the necessary funds, buy his way out of the joint account? "I do not know that I can borrow the funds needed but think so," he advised Pullen.

Reed had no Washington bank, and he was low on cash. He was anxiously awaiting a check from Pullen. Altogether, Reed was in the dark about his affairs. He had made plans for 1896 (the nature of which he did not specify). Now, he advised Pullen on January 30, he might have to change them.

Shortly thereafter came the devastating news that Pullen, Crocker & Company had failed. It was no ordinary bankruptcy but one tainted by malfeasance. Reed's funds had been improperly commingled with the firm's. Reed was heartsick and impoverished to a degree he could not even know. Pullen, through his attorney, had asked his famous client to assume a posture of forbearance toward his claims on the bankrupt estate. On February 9, Reed replied that he would not do so. "I am entirely willing to have your property distributed among your creditors and take my share but I do not intend to go any farther," he advised Pullen. "I had protected myself against any disaster by an ample margin which would have enabled me to wait until my property should reach its full value. I was even in train to pay off all margins and take up the securities. I had taken every precaution except the precaution that you should not use my property as if it were your own."

Reed bemoaned the forced sale of his stocks that, he was sure, would have eventually recovered. "Nor will I undertake to say how badly off you have left me," he went on, "since your suggestion that Mr. Millikin lend me money shows that you know you have taken from me almost all I have. I will not say what reasons arising from our past relations gave me not only confidence but certainty that you would not and could not leave me in such a plight. Reference to them however may remind you why I think you should not be discharged from any indebtedness which the law retains. If you should ever repay what the law gives it would still leave me injured irreparably."

A shakier hand held the pen that wrote the final paragraph. "What the loss means to me and my family is useless to dwell on for you must have known all that. I have deferred writing this letter in order to think the matter over calmly after the first shock of the news had passed."

Pullen felt sorely used by the tone of Reed's letter (from the draft of which Reed had excised another paragraph announcing to Pullen that he would have nothing more to do with him outside business channels). His error was one of judgment, Pullen insisted. He had been borrowing money to keep the firm afloat, and he could have kept borrowing, hoping that values would recover (and that, as he did not add, he would not be found out misappropriating client funds). "I have grievously erred and have been grievously punished," wrote Pullen, "but I do not deserve treatment at your hands which implies more than I have been guilty of." He wanted to talk things over.

Reed wanted no reconciliation: "I have read your letter with much care," he replied on April 27.

I do not desire to do you any harm. I have avoided the expression of my opinion to any one except yourself. I do not sit in any judgment of you. On the contrary I wish it were in my power to take the same view as you do. You think your action was only an error in judgment. It does not seem so to me. My property was not yours to risk without my consent. That you have hurt me very much you know. How much you do not know, nor do I care to talk about it. It is done and cannot be helped. Whether I shall recover from this I do not know. I intend to. But it obliged me to ask favors which it has not been my custom to ask and to deny things to those I love what they ought to have, to myself expenditures which I ought to make. Time may wear all this away. I hope it will.

So unbearable was the whole matter to me that only the necessity of living within my income would have brought me to Portland. You cannot regret my state of feeling more than I do.

Nor was Reed any more inclined to forgive George Dorsey for his failed management of their shared Nebraska land investment. Dorsey, flat broke, had expressed to Reed the wan hope that, if he ever got back on his feet, he would "see that you are protected from loss." Yes, Reed coldly replied in April, that "is just what you ought to do."

As Reed came to terms with the destruction of his life's savings, he led Republican debate over contending plans to resolve the raging crisis of the dollar. If his thinking on this great financial question was not so crisp as it might have been, the wonder is, perhaps, that he was able to think about money at all.

The Treasury had become a gold sieve. No sooner did the administration raise the funds with which to replenish its reserve than suspicious dollar holders showed up to exchange their paper for the newly obtained bullion. In 1894, the Treasury had purchased $103 million in gold, but paid out $172 million worth. Nor was there any end in sight. It was a quirk of the law that the Treasury was required to send back out into circulation every unit of paper currency that it received. So in came the paper and out went the gold—and in came more paper and out went more gold. It was an "endless chain." Some $500 million of the government's paper dollars were outstanding, and more than $300 million had been exchanged for gold—and thereupon sent back out into the world and, very likely, into the hands of the very people who would exchange them for more gold. These people—the bears and the doubters—were in an enviable position. They could bet against the dollar without fear of loss. The dollar's gold value was not going to be raised. The only alternative to a return to monetary stability (which, in January 1895, seemed remote) was debasement.

On January 28, 1895, Cleveland, in a special message to Congress, asked for authorization to float a 50-year, 3 percent bond made explicitly payable in gold. Under prevailing law, which was the 1875 Resumption Act, bonds of the United States were payable in "coin." Now Cleveland wanted no one to doubt that "coin" meant "gold." But since the market did doubt, Cleveland sought to assuage it. He asked Congress to bless the bonds by stamping them "gold" (it would mean a substantial savings to the taxpayer in interest expense) and to allow the government to retire the boomerang paper dollars, thereby breaking the endless chain. "We should be relieved from the humiliating process of issuing bonds to procure gold to be immediately and repeatedly drawn out on these obligations for purposes not related to the benefit of our Government or our people."[39]

In the absence of prompt congressional action, Cleveland, on February 8, invoked executive powers to issue enough bonds to finance the purchase of $65.1 million in gold. To the fury of the silver faction, he outsourced the sale to a Wall Street syndicate led by J. P. Morgan and August Belmont. Nor was the rage of this faction stilled when it came to light that the bankers had collected an underwriting profit of between $6 million and $7 million for their not very laborious work.

It had fallen to William Springer, Reed's old sparring partner, now chairman of the House Banking and Currency Committee, to sponsor a bill to comport with Cleveland's January 28 message. Reed produced an alternative bill. Under the Reed plan, the Treasury would be split in two, the banking or monetary function divorced from the operating function. And in place of the long-dated gold bonds in the Springer measure, Reed proposed the issuance of two-year, 3 percent "certificates of indebtedness." The certificates would be payable in "coin," not, explicitly, gold.

To Reed, the absence of the word "gold" was a timely stroke of statesmanship. In the ideological hothouse of the 53rd Congress, "coin" was a soothing compromise. But the House was not to be soothed. On February 7, a succession of monetary bills came up for a vote. Reed's and Springer's among them. All went down to defeat. Reed himself had suffered a moment's embarrassment when a Populist member, Jerry Simpson of Kansas, ripped into his use of the word "coin." To which metal did the gentleman from Maine refer? Why, Simpson allowed, if Reed would only promise that silver is what he meant, the Populists would nominate him for president in 1896. And with that, the papers reported, Reed "broke for cover," hastily retiring to the corridor.

By the lights of the monetarily conservative East, nothing about Reed's conduct during the great debate over the gold bonds was exactly discreditable. But it lacked clarity, or, one might even say, courage. Cleveland had one unshakable conviction, and it was gold. Reed had many convictions, only one of which—no free silver—was strictly non-negotiable. In New York City, Theodore Roosevelt, the newly installed president of the Board of Police Commissioners, was discovering how deep ran support for the gold dollar among faithful Republicans. To them, a bimetallist was almost as objectionable a creature as a silverite. They were, he reported to Reed in June 1895, "exceedingly distrustful of anything which they regard as ambiguous on the question. . . . I have had long talks with them about you, and in case after case was met at the outset with a resolute misunderstanding of your position." Roosevelt reassured his friend that he had straightened out every Republican with whom he spoke, "but there are countless individuals to whom I didn't talk."[40]

The fact is that Reed had missed his moment. "I regret more and more all the time," Roosevelt confided to Lodge on July 30, "that Tom Reed did not make a strong anti-free coinage speech. . . . Had he done so, and come out in a ringing speech as a champion of sound money, there would not now be the slightest opposition to him in New York."[41]

So it was that, in the 1896 presidential election season, the banners hung on the exterior of 23 Wall Street, Morgan headquarters, said, "McKinley."[42]

Chapter 19

"God Almighty hates a quitter"

Reed savored his victories—his Portland constituents handed him one every two years—but he often shone brightest in defeat. As the minority leader of a defeated party in the 53rd Congress, 1893–95, he had the indescribable pleasure of watching a Democratic Speaker count a quorum. He creditably upheld the losing side in a bruising tariff battle and contemplated a run for the presidency. Outgeneraled for the Republican nomination by, of all people, William McKinley, he spared no effort to put his rival in the White House.

It was to repeal the Sherman Silver Purchase Act that President Cleveland called the 53rd Congress into special session in August 1893. But even as the struggle over the monetary standard raged, a parallel debate took shape over the rules by which the House would govern itself. As it was a Democratic House, they would be Democratic rules. It was a source of gratification to Reed, however, that—despite themselves—the majority party chose not to renounce every feature of the code of the 51st Congress. Retained, for instance, was the 100-member quorum for the Committee of the Whole as well as a watered-down check on dilatory motions.[1] Still, as Reed lost no opportunity to observe, the Democrats had stopped well short of the Republican ideal of majority rule.

If the parliamentary dispute masked a partisan cleavage over the nature of government, it could hardly obscure a clash of personalities. No love was lost between the current Speaker, Democrat Charles F. Crisp of Georgia, and his Republican predecessor. On March 4, 1890, during one of the heated contested election cases that marked the 51st Congress, then-Speaker Reed had called on the members to stop talking and be seated. Crisp, choosing to take this call to order as a personal reproach, informed Reed that he resented being singled out. Reed replied that he had done nothing to single him out. "The Chair looked directly at me," Crisp returned. "I was not saying a word but was about to resume my seat."[2] And so it went, back and forth, for some unedifying minutes.

Crisp was the son of Shakespearian actors. Born in Sheffield, England, he was taken to America by his mother in the year of his birth, 1845. Mother and father and children, reunited, eventually settled in Georgia, where Crisp, age 16, answered the call to the Confederate colors in 1861. For three years, he served in a Virginia infantry regiment. Captured at the Battle of Spotsylvania, he spent the final 12 months of the war in Union captivity, much of that time at Fort Delaware, a prison only slightly more hospitable to its inmates than such Confederate deathtraps as Andersonville. Come the peace, Crisp completed his legal studies (he had begun them in prison) and was appointed a Georgia superior court judge.[3] Elected to the U.S. House of Representatives in 1882, and every two years thereafter, he became a free silver-coinage man. On that account, he gave his gold-standard president fits.[4]

On August 29, Reed rose to critique the rules that Crisp and the Democratic majority were about to enact. It was encouraging, he allowed, that the majority had followed the lead of the 51st Congress to the extent of denying absolute and unchecked power of the individual member to filibuster. It was a start. But Reed wondered why the Democrats, having seen that much of the truth, did not accept it all. The House had the right to listen to any man, or to none. It depended on the man and the circumstances. Let the rules give true sway to majority rule, he went on, and the quality of debate would measurably improve. You would, in fact, he said, arrive at that rarefied level of discourse in which "a man knows enough about the subject to tell it without writing it down." The members laughed appreciatively.[5]

Still, inexplicably, the Democratic rule-makers had refused to stamp out dilatory motions. "What is the use of going on in this way?" the former Speaker demanded.

> Why not adopt a system of rules which will give the majority of the House control and which will take away from the filibuster his right to stop business. Why, sir, we deliberately incorporate into the rules a proposition that a motion to adjourn, a motion to take a recess, and a motion to fix the time to which the House shall adjourn shall always be in order; and two of these motions are amenable ad libitum; and upon each there may be a roll call, consuming three-quarters of an hour. We deliberately establish the principle of filibustering.[6]

Concluding, Reed said that, if permitted, he would introduce a motion to substitute the rules of the 51st Congress for those proposed by the Democratic majority of the 53rd. If successful, his motion would grant the House all the power it needed to control its deliberations and "to do its work."[7]

As the Republicans applauded their leader, Crisp was seen to turn over his gavel to James D. Richardson, a Tennessee Democrat, and step down to the floor. Acknowledged by Richardson, Crisp did a most unusual thing. He proceeded to make a speech condemning Reed's rules and Reed himself. Speakers did not often descend from the heights of their office to contend in the scrum below. Lacking Reed's storied imperturbability, Crisp was determined to strike back.

Yes, he began, some portion of the rules of the 51st Congress had merit, and this portion he and the Rules Committee would not for a moment exclude from the proposed new rules merely on partisan grounds. However, another portion of the Reed rules the country had "absolutely condemned," and this segment Reed had conveniently failed to mention. "The gentleman from Maine—and this is a hobby with him—when he stands up before the country and speaks of the rules of the 51st Congress nearly always omits, or fails to refer to, the practices in the 51st Congress which were so odious to its members and which were so odious to the country."

Reed had a great deal to say about majority rule, Crisp continued. But under the Reed rules it was the Speaker who decided which motions were, or were not, dilatory. Under the system proposed by the Rules Committee of the 53rd Congress, the majority of the House made that determination.

In partisan feeling, Crisp was fully Reed's match, though he had none of Reed's lightness of touch. So it was with a battering ram that the Speaker launched his assault. The Democracy, Crisp declared, believed in government by the people, not a tyrant. The people seemed to prefer it that way. It was a fact that, over the past 20 years, the Republican party never controlled the House for more than two years running. The voters removed them at the earliest opportunity. Crisp was beginning his second consecutive term as Speaker; Reed, in keeping with this happy custom, was out after just one.

"Mr. Speaker," Crisp ended,

> this is all I wanted to say. Perhaps I should not have said so much; and yet, for a good while, in certain quarters the methods and practices of the 51st Congress have been applauded on the floor of this House, and I have had no opportunity to say anything in reply. What I have said now has been provoked by the arrogant assertion that the 51st Congress, in its rules and in its methods, was an example which should be followed by all Congresses which should come after. Against that proposition I desire to enter a protest and say, so far as I am concerned, taking the methods and practices and rules as a whole, I feel exactly as felt the people after the first election after its organization, that it was destructive of the rights of the people and ought to be repudiated and condemned.[8]

Reed closed out the exchange with a prediction. The time will come, he said, when the Democrats adopt the Republican rules: "[I]t is as sure as anything on earth that the House of Representatives which meets to do business will follow upon the lines of the 51st Congress. [Applause on the Republican side.]"

Democrats scoffed. They had the Republicans outnumbered, 218 to

124. Though their majority was not so overwhelming as the 238 to 86 they had commanded in the 52nd Congress, it was lopsided enough to assure 179 votes, which—approximately, for there was some art in the definition—constituted a quorum. There could be no conceivable need to stoop to quorum-counting, the most odious (to use Speaker Crisp's term) of the Reed rules.

Reed, however, was in a position to make himself a prophet, and he began on November 2. The House had voted to adjourn on the next day at 3 PM, and large numbers of Democrats had made an early beeline home. In their flight from Washington, however, they had played into the parliamentary hands of Tom Reed. The House could not properly adjourn without passing a resolution empowering the Ways and Means Committee to sit during the recess to write a new tariff bill. It had not yet done so. Reed counted votes. Finding that the Democrats could field no quorum, he objected to the draftsmanship of the Ways and Means resolution. He filibustered on other subjects and only stopped filibustering when he decided he had taught the remaining Democrats a lesson. "The suggestion might be made," he concluded, "that we are quite ready to have the Chair count us."[9]

If the Democrats were still complacent about the adequacy of their numbers in the House, they had reckoned without Reed. No longer a mere practicioner of the parliamentary arts, the ex-Speaker was a published author on the subject. *Reed's Parliamentary Rules*, released in February 1894, was a pocket-sized primer on general parliamentary law. The book was apolitical, its author pointed out, nothing to do with quorum-counting or score-settling. Still, Reed's enemies affected amazement. "A work by the Czar of Russia on 'Constitutional safeguards' would not be more incongruous," the editors of the New York *Times* remarked.[10]

Neither had the Democrats reckoned with the centrifugal force of the monetary question. On February 7, Richard "Silver Dick" Bland, Democrat of Missouri, introduced a bill to conjure $55 million out of the Treasury's silver horde. This wealth he proposed to materialize by harvesting the difference between the intrinsic value of the monetary silver and the value the government conferred on it. By early 1894, the market price of silver was considerably less than its legally defined value. The difference was called "seignorage," and it was this value that Bland sought to pluck out of the government's mint. The country was deep in depression. Here, Bland urged, was a cheap and sensible way to give the people the money they needed.

It did not seem so cheap and sensible to Cleveland, who was desperately trying to persuade America's creditors that the dollar was as good as the metal that Bland would, if he could, drive out of circulation. Nor did the Bland seignorage bill meet with the approval of most Republicans or with the few dozen gold-standard Democrats. Reed now raised the point of order about which he had warned the Speaker in August: There was no quorum, he would say over and over, as the Democrats insisted on defining a quorum.

There were members enough in the hall, but the human forms sometimes lost either the will or capacity to speak, especially during roll calls. The roll would be called, the yeas and nays taken, motions to adjourn made, absent members sent for, the absentees retrieved by the sergeant-at-arms and hauled back to the floor, this and that procedural question taken. The result was a state of parliamentary suspension. Days and weeks dragged by, as the obstructionists, led by Reed, devoted themselves to parliamentary navel-gazing. It was very like the old days. Frequently, Reed's name would turn up on the long list of members (just enough to impede the progress of Bland's seignorage bill) marked "not voting."

"I am sorry, Mr. Speaker," said Reed to Crisp on February 24, "to notice the absence of a quorum."[11] This followed a vote on Reed's motion to adjourn that had tallied only 135 votes, 8 ayes and 127 nays. It would be so much simpler, as Reed would now and then remind his victims, if they would hark to reason, the Supreme Court, the Constitution and the example of the 51st Congress. How he hoped, Reed addressed the Speaker, that the House "will take warning from what has happened and will proceed to the right way," namely the way of the Reed rules. Naturally, the ex-Speaker archly added, such a course of action would be "more or less unpleasant for individuals who have been very vociferous at times upon this subject."[12] If Crisp once more felt Reed's eyes focused tightly on him, he did not say so.

On March 1, Bland's bill finally came up for a vote. It passed, 168–129, with 49 Democrats siding with their president but against their Missouri colleague. The legislation then motored through the Senate, only to land on the desk of the immovable Cleveland. "[S]ound finance," the president's March 29 veto message said, "does not commend a further infusion of silver into our currency at this time unaccompanied by further adequate provision for the maintenance in our Treasury of a safe gold reserve."[13]

Reed, meanwhile, continued to filibuster and Crisp to preside over a House held hostage to that obstruction. Millions were unemployed, business activity had collapsed (modern-day record keepers would designate June 1894 as the month the economy stopped contracting) and the once-sound dollar was an object of international speculation. Activist government was but a dream of the radicals and Populists. Still, even a mainstream Democrat might have expected more of the House of Representatives than the chaplain's morning prayer though on some days, those soothing words were the only constructive ones spoken. For the rest, they centered on roll calls and other such foot-dragging motions that Speaker Reed had summarily refused to entertain because, he alone judged, they were dilatory. Crisp knew full well that Reed's objective was to obstruct the business of the House, but he gave no sign of any willingness to adopt the worst part of Reedism. No doubt the Speaker genuinely held to the Jeffersonian tenets of minority rights that infused the Democratic party of this era. But his detestation of Reed would have sustained him in his resistance to copying the code of the 51st Congress, even if Thomas Jefferson had never been born.

On March 29, Crisp gave vent to his accumulated frustrations by paying Reed one of the handsomest compliments the ex-Speaker had ever received. It was, to be sure, a backhanded compliment, but not even a reformulation of the sentiments in the forehand style would have added much to the pleasure it gave its recipient. "[G]entlemen on that side," meaning the Republican side, said Crisp, who had again handed off the gavel to say his piece on the floor, "blindly follow him, no matter how their own convictions may differ from his. He is the great leader of that side. You will hear them privately saying, 'Reed ought not to do that,' or 'This is wrong,' but when Reed says 'Do it,' they all step up and do it. [Laughter and applause on the Democratic side.]"[14]

The Georgian was losing his battle, his surrender coming by degrees as he adopted one Reedism after another. On March 30, he refused the Republicans' tactical motions to adjourn. He announced that he would be under no obligation to explain the reasons behind his decisions and that he would entertain no appeals from those decisions. "This is very much like tyranny," drawled Reed. Late that afternoon, Reed was standing near the clerk's desk to supervise the counting of votes. All day long, roll calls had surfaced a quorum on the button, 179 votes, or, once, 180. In one of these nose counts, a second-term Pennsylvania Democrat, William A. Sipe, had been counted as voting though he was nowhere near the District of Columbia. Reed was keeping a watchful eye.

Seeing Reed standing over the clerk, Crisp announced that the House would be in order and directed every member to return to his seat. Reed quietly appealed—"I would like to be permitted to see the roll call"—but in vain. As Reed slowly walked away, he protested the Speaker's decision, thereby drawing a sharper direct order: "The gentleman will take his seat."

"The man from Maine," reported the Washington *Post*, "bowed and smiled in mock humility as he backed further down one of the aisles to the extreme right. 'I am going to do it,' he said."

Now Crisp called over the sergeant-at-arms and directed him to enforce the order. Reed had been "ambling down the aisle, his back to the Speaker," the *Post*'s account continued:

> He staggered and turned as if he had been shot. His face flushed and he looked scornfully at a black-haired deputy, who, in response to the Speaker's command, now stood in front of his burly form. Mr. Reed surveyed the deputy and then glared defiantly at the Speaker. "That is strictly unnecessary," he said, uttering each word with a deliberation that sent it hurtling like a catapult through the air.
>
> Mr. Crisp retorted quickly. "It is not," he exclaimed. "Instead of taking your seat"—the Speaker forgot parliamentary propriety and used the personal pronoun—"you respond to the Chair every time."

"Certainly I do," said Mr. Reed, heated but unabashed, "because the Chair attacks me."

Without paying attention to this remark, the Speaker uttered his ultimatum, "The gentleman must take his seat," was his emphatic command. Mr. Reed hesitated just a moment and then, amid a deathlike silence in the House, he moved across the floor from the Democratic to the Republican side. He walked like a man following a corpse. His head was bowed and his feet, weighted with unwillingness, dragged heavily.[15]

In a stage whisper, a Democrat broke the silence: "See Jumbo go back to his stake."[16]

The perpetual exchange of greenbacks and Treasury notes for the government's shiny gold coins was known as the "endless chain." The unending succession of dilatory motions in the House of Speaker Crisp was called the "merry-go-round." In happier times—say, in the 51st Congress under Speaker Reed—the obligatory approval of the previous day's journal was the work of a minute. In the 53rd Congress under the Republican siege guns, it could fill much of a fruitless day. One-fifth of the members on hand could order a roll call, the Constitution stipulated. And under the rules of the House no business could be conducted until the prior day's journal was approved. Reed, therefore, marshaled his disciplined troops to demand the yeas and nays as soon as the journal was read. Next came the roll call, the Republicans sitting mum as their names were called. Democrats lacking the numbers to create their own quorum, the Republican silence condemned the House to inaction. "Two days of actual work have not been accomplished in a month," Springer of Illinois moaned in April.[17]

And when they could stand it no longer, the Democrats gave up. They would, they said, count a quorum after all, but it wouldn't be the Speaker who, tyrant-fashion, did the tallying. Rather, one teller from each side of the House would report to the Speaker the names of those who were present but not silent on roll calls. This information in hand, the Speaker would declare the existence of a quorum. The business of the House would proceed—as, indeed, it did after the rule was adopted by the House on April 17. "Mr. Speaker," Reed addressed his antagonist in his moment of victory, "I do not desire to address the House again on the general subject. This scene here today is a more effective address than any I could make."[18]

The House met at noon the next day. Reed was late getting to the Capitol, and as he entered the House chamber he stopped and stared at the flowers heaped on his desk. It seemed as if the hothouses of Washington had been emptied in his honor. To this floral display, the Republican side of the House added a great cheer. No sergeant-at-arms accompanied the conquering hero. It happened that John Randolph Tucker was visiting his son, Henry St. George Tucker, the Virginia Democrat, and both were seated at the younger Tucker's desk. It was the father who, in 1880, while himself a Virginia Democrat, had proposed the quorum-counting rule that Reed had famously opposed. So Reed, spotting the senior Tucker, now 70 years old, seated next to his son, made his way over to the Democratic side of the House to greet his long-ago parliamentary adversary. He draped his big arm over the older man's shoulder. "Old gentleman," said Reed, "I am ready to divide the flowers with you."[19]*

IT WAS A new tariff bill that provided the opportunity for Reed to lay one of his first parliamentary traps in the 53rd Congress. In order to draft a proper Democratic alternative to the hated McKinley bill, the Ways and Means Committee proposed to remain behind in Washington during the 1893 autumn recess. For this it needed a resolution from the House—which Reed magnanimously allowed to pass after catching the Democratic majority napping without a quorum.

---

* Reed divided more than flowers. When the Republican-controlled 54th Congress adopted a rule affirming the essential quorum-counting reforms of the 51st Congress, Reed—once more Speaker—was content to allow that it take the form of the old Tucker amendment, under which the clerk of the House, and not, unilaterally, the Speaker, did the counting. Evidently, it was more important to Reed to advance the bipartisan acceptance of his reform than to affix his name to it.

The end of filibustering meant not only a more efficient House but also a more thoughtful one, Reed believed. "He thinks," Asher Hinds, Reed's clerk, recorded, "the pendulum has of necessity swung rather far in the direction of shutting off debate, because of the old and vicious system of using debate to kill and not to consider. With the power of killing by debate taken away, there may be fuller consideration without trouble." See Asher Hinds Diary, December 7, 1895. Asher Hinds Collection. Library of Congress.

If Reed had quorum-on-the-brain, the Democratic party was obsessed with the tariff. For a generation, it had dreamt of rolling back the iniquitous subsidies that the Civil War–era schedules conferred on favored American industries. And not for a generation had the Democrats had the opportunity that now lay within their easy grasp. With a 100-vote majority in the House, with a majority of one in the Senate and with Grover Cleveland in the White House, they could at last give life to the president's words. "A tariff for any other purpose than public revenue," said he, "is public robbery."[20] The reformers—tariffs for revenue only, they cried—fairly hugged themselves.

To William L. "Billy" Wilson of West Virginia, chairman of the Ways and Means Committee, fell the happy responsibility of turning slogans into law. A lawyer and former college professor, Wilson sometimes elicited smiles for his academic approach to life's problems. But the bill he produced was so far from being utopian that it sparked complaints from free-trade idealists. A mere "Sabbath Day's journey on the way to reform," complained Roger Q. Mills of Texas, now a U.S. senator.[21]

Wilson's measure removed the tax from imported coal, wool, flax, iron ore and hemp. For the sake of the poor farmer, it eliminated duties from agricultural equipment, binding twine and salt. Tax was reduced, though not eliminated, on foreign-manufactured cottons, woolens and linens. Sugar, both raw and refined, was added to the free, or untaxed, list. Rates were lowered on tin plate, a product that was never manufactured in the United States until the McKinley tariff literally called the tin-plate industry into existence.[22]

Thus, the Wilson bill: The author himself regarded it as a compromise measure, his free-trade critics as pusillanimous. But, the majority party could agree, Wilson's handiwork represented a profound improvement over the McKinley outrage, "the culminating atrocity of class legislation."[23] Besides, the government needed the revenue. As a revenue measure, McKinley's tariff yielded much less than advertised.

Beyond its generally moderate reductions in the tariff, the Wilson measure added the novel feature of a 2 percent tax on incomes of $4,000 and up.[24] It wasn't Wilson's idea of enlightened tax policy. Neither was it Cleveland's. Not since 1872 had the government had recourse to an income tax (at a rate of as much as 10 percent on incomes of as little as $5,000).[25] That tax was a wartime expedient, but leveling elements both inside and outside the Democratic party—Greenbackers, Populists, the Farmers Alliance—regarded it as a fiscal beacon for modern times. The Treasury needed fattening, they argued, and the bloated bondholders needed thinning. Benton McMillin, Democrat from Tennessee, heard their cry, and he took it up with his colleagues on the Ways and Means Committee.

Most of his fellow Democrats, of whom there were 12, opposed the idea, and they would walk out of the committee room when McMillin began to expound. If the committee were at full strength, the members left seated on these occasions would have been McMillin and 7 Republicans, led by Reed—just a quorum. The ex-Speaker had no doubt but that an income-tax amendment would haunt the party that enacted it. Happy to assist the Democrats in their pending blunder, he agreed to hold the Republicans in place when the other Democrats walked off.[26] If tax-paying posterity can find it in its heart to forgive McMillin for his infernal brainchild, perhaps it can also see its way to forgiving Reed. In any case, Wilson presented his bill to the House a week before Christmas.

In the 12-page brief that accompanied the legislation, Wilson acknowledged that, despite the favorable political auguries, there was a hard fight ahead. "So many private enterprises have been taken into partnership with the Government," he noted; "so many private interests now share in the rich prerogative of taxing 70 millions of people, that any attempt to dissolve this illegal union is necessarily encountered by an opposition that rallies behind it the intolerance of monopoly, the power of concentrated wealth, the inertia of fixed habits and the honest errors of a generation of false teaching." It was a fair preview of the obstacles ahead.[27]

Wilson traced the history of the tariff, noting the initial opposition of the early New England manufacturers. "They argued," he wrote, "that by laying a protective tariff their business would be thrown out of its natural channels and subjected to fluctuation and uncertainty. But, as usual, the clamor of selfish and less far-sighted men, and the ambition of lawmakers to usurp the place of Providence prevailed. The country entered on a protective policy with the unfailing result that Government help begot a violent demand for more Government help."[28]

Never had the country's growth been so fast or harmonious as in the low-tariff era, 1843–61, preceding the Civil War. The high wartime tariff schedules left more or less intact, the protected industries came to regard themselves almost as independent branches of the House Ways and Means Committee. Literally, they wrote their own tariff schedules, which obedient congresses copied directly into the statue books.[29] Based on the 1892 level of imports, Wilson calculated, the proposed new duties would lighten the burden of tax by one-third, but that was only the beginning of the benefits he anticipated. "Such a reform of the tariff must quicken every industry, must open a larger field for employment of labor, must secure to it more working days at steadier wages, a larger return in the comforts and goods of life for its labor."[30]

Reed, answering for the Republicans, expertly struck at the majority's point of vulnerability. The Democratic party had run for office against the alleged "public robbery" of the Republican tariff. And it had, indeed, won. Yet, now that it was in power, it proposed not to abolish this fiscal crime but only to tinker with it, and in a manner calculated to shatter what little commercial confidence remained. The Democratic stand against the supposed inequity of protection, wrote Reed, "is comprehensible and sturdy. The new movement on behalf of mitigated and sporadic robbery is contrary alike to good morals and public faith. All false pretenses are unwise, contrary to sound policy and sound statesmanship. Hence many of us, sure that the Democratic platform is utterly untrue, admitted to its straightforwardness and directness. This bill, framed by those who represent the platform, can not receive that kind of praise. It pretends to be a revenue tariff, and does not raise revenue. It pretends to give protection, but destroys it in every indirect way."[31]

Whatever the ultimate ambitions of the Democratic draftsmen, they did not so much as lay a glove on the underlying protective doctrine. Indeed, as the New York *Journal of Commerce* pointed out, there was nothing in the conservative Wilson revisions of the tariff to change the status of the American economy as the world's most highly protected.[32]

Debate over the Wilson bill would occupy seven months, most of them in the Senate, including a 12-day filibuster by the high-tariff

Republican Matthew Quay of Pennsylvania.[33] In the House, the out-come was never in doubt. Not for Democrats the almost martial party discipline of the Reed GOP, but even these free spirits consented to toe the mark for the sacred cause of tariff reform. In opposition, Reed prepared one of his very few great orations, writing out a draft equiva-lent to 60 double-spaced typed pages, then committing the text to mem-ory. When he rose to speak on February 1, 1894, a colleague sat near with cue cards, but the once and future czar, 54 years of age, had lost none of his formidable memory. Ordinarily, at his request, Susan stayed away from the House when he spoke, but here she was, alone with their daughter, Kitty, now 19, to hear him close out the debate on the Wilson bill for the Republicans. It seemed as if the rest of Washington were in the House chamber too. So tightly packed were the galleries, and so intense was the feeling, that the sergeant-at-arms took precautions against a possible riot by calling in a squad of city police to reinforce his own constabulary.

Anticipating a memorable speech, the people in the galleries applauded Reed before he even opened his mouth. When he did speak, he expressed his sympathy for them. "[F]or if anything seems to have been discussed until human nature can bear it no more," he said, "it is the tariff." Yet, as it was quite plain, the last word had not been said. Indeed, the subject was yet misunderstood. Economists were no help. They couldn't even agree with themselves. "I do not mean," Reed allowed, "that studious men have not discovered great truths and had glimpses of still greater, but in the main . . . they have forgotten that the whole race is wiser than any man. [Applause.]"[34]

The British political economists may preach laissez-faire, Reed con-tinued, but their more perceptive countrymen stare in wonder at the prosperity of the protected markets of the United States. Americans too should look about them (not so much, one could infer, at current busi-ness and labor-market conditions but at the trends long in place): "With wages rising, prices of manufactured goods falling, with lessening hours of labor, what more do you want except more of the same?"

Reed drew a comparison between low-wage Chinese labor, which Congress had voted to exclude from the United States, and imported merchandise produced with low-wage labor. Higher forms of civilization could not compete fairly, and win, against lower forms. Such eloquent free-traders as Bourke Cockran, Democrat of New York, never tired of singing the praises of the American system. It could meet any competition, they insisted. Reed demurred. "Compare the strong bull of Bashan* with a salt-water smelt. Who doubts the superiority of the bull? Yet if you drop them both into the Atlantic Ocean, I will take my chances with the smelt. [Laughter.]"

As Reed finished, Crisp handed off his gavel. Once more the Speaker descended to the floor to confront his parliamentary tormenter. He did so to the sound of long-sustained cheers for the departing Reed. Surveying his audience, Crisp acknowledged that there was no wittier defender of an unsound doctrine than the gentleman from Maine (on whose empty desk now stood a large congratulatory floral piece). But the House should not mistake repartee with logic or brilliance with substance.

"When we ask the gentleman from Maine to give us a reason why a high-protective tariff increases the rate of wages he fails to give it," Crisp continued, "but points to the glory, the prosperity and honor of our country." It was, indeed, true. Reed had asserted such a connection but had not proved it. "The gentleman," the Speaker charged,

> belongs to that class who believe that by a system of taxation we can make the country rich. He believes that it is possible by tax laws to advance the prosperity of all the industries and all the people in the United States. Either, Mr. Speaker, that statement is an absurdity on its face, or it implies that in some way we have the power to make some persons not resident of the United States pay the taxes that we impose. I insist that you do not increase the taxable wealth of the United States when you tax a gentleman in Illinois and give the benefit of that tax to a gentleman in Maine. Such a course presents the natural and honest distribution of wealth, but it does not create or augment it.[35]

Wilson, frail and stooped, closed out the argument for the Democrats. Moving and fluent, he was a worthy opponent even of Reed,

---

* A beast alluded to in Psalm 22.

spectators judged. The West Virginian's eloquent appeal for party unity inspired his colleagues, Bryan among others, to hoist him up on their shoulders and carry him out of the chamber. It was the high point of his legislation.[36]

Easily passing the House by a vote of 204–140, with only 18 defecting Democrats, the bill went next to the Senate. By head count alone, the Democrats should have had a clean and speedy victory. They mustered 44 votes, a majority of one, but a majority nonetheless. The truth, however, is that there was no one party of senatorial Democrats but a number of different Democratic factions. Some were true to the low-tariff faith of their president, others to the more conventional doctrine of getting a little something for themselves and their constituents. Democrat David B. Hill of New York announced that he would never consent to an income tax, whereas his New York colleague, Democrat Edward Murphy Jr., demanded protection for the manufacturers of collars, cuffs and shirts in his hometown of Troy.[37] Millions of dollars hung in the balance on each detail of the legislation.

In the end, the senators insulted Wilson's bill with 634 amendments, each an affront to the Democratic dogma on which Grover Cleveland, for one, had supposed that he had been elected.[38] After all, there would be no clean break from the McKinley doctrine, rather an embarrassing relapse into Republican heresy. To Wilson, Cleveland poured out his frustration, coining a phrase—"party perfidy and party dishonor"—on which the GOP joyfully seized for its propaganda value in the upcoming 1894 congressional elections.[39] The Democracy had indicted itself.

Wilson was as downcast as his chief, for Senate negotiators yielded nothing in negotiations with their counterparts in the House. All that was left to him and his party was the not-altogether-persuasive pledge to do better next time. But greater humiliations awaited the author of the Wilson tariff than the lower chamber's surrender to the demands of the upper one, or even of the enactment of his mutilated measure without the political cover of the president's signature. Wilson's greater ordeal was the merciless Reed. "So far as the gentleman from West Virginia is concerned and his compatriots," said the minority leader on August 13, "there is not the slightest necessity of my commenting on the difference between this scene of sorrow and the triumphal procession which carried him out of this House. [Laughter and applause on the Republican side.]"

Would Reed take pity on his vanquished rivals? The thought had not seemed to occur to him. He rather professed astonishment at the Democrats' determination to bring yet another tariff bill forward. "Not content with what you have done," he mocked them,

> you have threatened the people of this country with yourselves again. [Laughter on the Republican side.] We shall not write your epitaph. That has been done by a nearer and dearer. That has been done by the man whose name must be affixed to this bill before it can discredit the statute book. His name must be on it. He tells you that this bill is an instance of perfidy, injustice and dishonor. We have got nothing to do in the next campaign except to read the testimony of your Chief Magistrate, under whose protecting wing the Committee on Ways and Means of the House of Representatives have lived, so that we did not know at any moment whether they were a committee of the House or of the Executive. [Applause on the Republican side.] Out of your own household has come your condemnation. Nay, out of your own mouths has your own condemnation come.[40]

Reed's personal triumph in the 1894 election—17,086 votes to his Democratic opponent's 8,091—was the herald of the Republican landslide in November. Wilson could take some consolation in his defeat in West Virginia. At least he wouldn't have to listen to Reed anymore. Neither would Springer of Illinois nor Bynum of Indiana, two of the czar's other defeated Democratic enemies. The electorate had wiped away the Democrats' majority as ruthlessly as it had erased the Republicans' four years before. Crisp had won his race, though his victory condemned him to a return to the Capitol to face the music of the Speakership election. In that contest, the Georgian polled 95 votes to Reed's 240. Reed was thereby returned in glory to the chair from which the Democrats had ejected him after a single tumultuous term. "It will not be unbecoming in me, I hope," said Reed, addressing the House on December 2, 1895, upon taking the oath of office again, "if I acknowledge to this assembly that it is very agreeable to me to stand once more in the place which I left four years ago. Of the past, however, I shall not speak, for the past speaks for itself"—at which point the House burst out in applause. If it was any consolation to the Democrats, the sheer size of the Republican majority took some of the sting out of Reed's reascension. The 145-member GOP majority rendered quorum-counting unnecessary; the Republicans had the run of the hall.[41]

By the looks of things, they would almost certainly have the run of the White House too at the next opportunity. If possible, the Democratic party was in worse condition than the American economy. The only question was which Republican would have the honor of displacing Mr. and Mrs. Grover Cleveland from 1600 Pennsylvania Avenue.

Reed not unreasonably thought it could be him. McKinley's was the name on the famous tariff, but his was the one in the newspapers. He had led his minority Republicans to a famous victory in the House, had, indeed, revolutionized that institution through sheer force of will and intellect. His epigrams were on the nation's lips. It could not have helped but turn his head to hear that the North Carolina Republicans, convened on August 30, had voted to support him in 1896. "If the same course is pursued throughout the Southern States," Representative Thomas Settle, a two-term North Carolina Republican, advised the candidate-in-theory, "you will receive a flattering vote in our next National Convention from this section."[42]

McKinley would be competing for the same vote. Defeated for reelection to the House in 1890, the Major had won the 1891 Ohio gubernatorial race. At the national GOP convention in Minneapolis in 1892, the crowd applauded him whenever he showed his face.[43]

It was McKinley's very personableness that was almost his undoing. Robert Walker, an old friend of his, needed a guarantor's signature on a small promissory note. Would McKinley do him that favor? The Major obliged Walker by signing repeatedly—it was only to renew the one loan, Walker assured him. In fact, McKinley had guaranteed not one loan but many. And when, in February 1893, the friend's business failed, McKinley was on the hook for his debts.

The fair-haired politician's life and career were suddenly in ruins.

All McKinley knew about the size of his obligation—obtained through fraud but no less binding for that—was that it was more than he could pay. Evidently broke and certainly bamboozled, he seethed. What would he not say to Walker when he finally had the chance to confront him! But the sight of his suffering friend brought out the Major's abiding empathy. "Have courage, Robert, have courage!" he comforted the scoundrel. "Everything will come out all right."[44]

Poor McKinley! Worse than a bankrupt, he was a dupe, an aspiring chief magistrate of the United States who could not manage even his own not very grand affairs. And to top it off, Walker was in the tin can business, a branch of domestic manufacturing that did not even exist until McKinley's own tariff made it economically feasible (or had seemed to). McKinley's deep-set eyes seemed to recede ever farther into his tormented head.

McKinley now threw himself on the mercy of the people, disclosing all, or as much as he himself knew; the size of the debt was yet a mystery. He had, he told himself, worked so hard, had come so far, only to become the ridiculous victim of his own gullibility. But, to his joy and disbelief, his ordeal struck a popular chord. The public turned out to be as forgiving of him as he had been of Walker. Rich friends seeded a bailout fund, and contributions came pouring in. Wartime comrades returned small sums that the Major had kindly lent them 30 years before. Five thousand donors warmed to a politician who was as hard up as they were. The storied McKinley luck had not, after all, deserted him. The trustees of the McKinley fund bought his way out of $130,000 of his co-signed notes, and no Walker-related claim was ever filed against the McKinley estate. There was redemption too at the polls. In the 1893 gubernatorial election, the Major was returned to office in a landslide.[45]

THE GREATEST OF McKinley's inner circle—greatest, probably, in wealth, certainly in sagacity—was the Cleveland industrialist Marcus Hanna. Reed had been Hanna's house guest in 1891 when he traveled to Ohio to help in McKinley's first gubernatorial campaign. The Speaker made a favorable impression on his host, and Hanna sent his employees to mingle in the crowds that Reed addressed to discover how the voters felt. The verdict, as far as Hanna sized it up, was negative. In the words of Hanna's biographer, Reed was "an Eastern product."[46]

Harrison had taken from his Presbyterian faith the conviction that he was preordained to be president.[47] McKinley entertained a Methodist's variation on the same presentiment.[48] If so, Hanna was the essential part of the divine plan. The industrialist—coal and steel, shipbuilding and real estate—believed in McKinley as ardently as McKinley did in himself, or in the protective tariff. Early in 1895, Hanna dropped his business interests to devote himself to putting McKinley in the White House.[49] He took that decision at about the time that Reed discovered that Stanley Pullen had dissipated his life's savings. There was, however, no public disclosure of Reed's difficulties, no Reed fund and no outpouring of sympathy for an honest politician brought low by the wrongdoing of a friend. By choice, Reed suffered alone. People admired the Speaker for his head, but they loved McKinley for his heart.

Licking his financial wounds while occupying the Speaker's chair, Reed did not see, let alone understand and appreciate, the unfolding of the Hanna/McKinley plan. The grand design was to apply the business methods of efficiency to American electoral politics. So it was that Hanna and his candidate systematically began to capture the southern Republican delegations. As to technique, Hanna was open-minded. What worked was what suited him. Even so calloused a practitioner as "Fire Engine" Joe Foraker, the career Ohio politician, blanched at the crassness with which Hanna had bought up the votes of African-American delegates to the 1888 Republican National Convention. Hanna just shrugged.[50]

Reed was still basking in the flattering news from North Carolina when Joseph Manley, chairman of the Maine Republican party, discovered that McKinley was building an organization in Massachusetts, right under the nose of Henry Cabot Lodge. It was easy for Reed to dismiss this intelligence after the GOP clean sweep of November 1894. "The victory is overwhelming," Joseph Pettigrew, Republican senator from South Dakota, advised Reed. "You will be Speaker of the next House and I shall be much rejoiced if you are also the next President of the United States. . . . McKinley has many followers among our people, but I know he is not a true or sincere man, and I don't propose to have him nominated if I can help it."[51] Pettigrew could certainly not help it. Against the energy and organization of Hanna, neither could anyone else.

"Now, Major," Hanna announced to his candidate upon returning from a series of meetings with eastern Republican bosses early in 1895, "Quay wants the patronage of Pennsylvania; Aldrich, of New England; Manley, of Maine. Platt wants New York, but he wants it in writing; you remember he was fooled on Harrison."[52] In response to this declaration of certain victory, McKinley is supposed to have replied that if that were the price of the White House, he didn't want it. He would, he declared, go beyond refusing the help of the party bosses. He would flatly run against them. At length, the candidate turned to his strategist and asked, "How would this do for a slogan: 'The Bosses Against the People'? How would that sound?" Hanna liked it fine. But better still, the war council presently agreed, would be "The People Against the Bosses."[53] And so it stood.

Men of the world would credit only so much of that slogan, of course. Hanna, at the age of 57, was not about to undergo a personality change, even under McKinley's wholesome influence. So the McKinley-for-president organization went forth into the country in search of delegates and funds. It dunned manufacturers especially hard. Did they not owe their prosperity to the candidate's tariff? "McKinley's commercial travelers," critics of Hanna's methods privately sneered at the Majors's fund-raising emissaries. Not satisfied with sotto voce witticisms, Senator William E. Chandler publicly accused the campaign (though not the candidate himself) of seeking to raise no less than $250,000, a sum far beyond any needed for honest political methods.* The campaign, however, motored on.[54]

Reed had no Hanna and, therefore, no organization to call an organization. But he did have Police Commissioner Theodore Roosevelt working behind the scenes in New York and Henry Cabot Lodge openly

---

* Chandler knew a little something about the uses of cash in politics, as we have seen. In the wildly corrupt 1876 presidential election grab, he personally carried $10,000 to Florida.

campaigning in Massachusetts.* The Hanna steamroller could not, in fact, make headway in the Bay State, in which 1,851 Republicans convened in Boston on March 27, 1896, to pledge themselves and their delegates to Reed at the National Convention in St. Louis in June. There were hopeful indications from Alabama and Maryland as well. "The sentiment in Maryland is for him without the shadow of a doubt," declared the editorial page of the Baltimore *American* in endorsing Reed for president on March 28, "and when the time comes the South will rise spontaneously to his name."[55]

The editors failed to notice that Hanna and McKinley were winning the race before the other candidates had even heard the crack of the starting pistol. The men from Ohio conceded nothing, not even Reed's stomping ground, New England.† The first McKinley club in the nation was raised in Hartford, Connecticut, in 1895.[56] Addressing his fans that spring, McKinley was gratified and, possibly, inspired. It had begun to look as if Reed were a sectional candidate without a reliable section.

Though he had made a career of asking his constituents for their votes, Reed refused to beg for anything else. He would not seek financial support, for himself or for his campaign, and he would not, personally, ask Republican delegates for their votes in St. Louis. Especially would he not pay cash for those votes, even if the funds were available (as much as the pastor of the Congregational Church of Wells, Maine, might have doubted it).

---

* Reed had ceded some advantage to McKinley in the West by announcing that no new territories would be admitted to the Union during the 54th Congress. The Speaker's policy, complained an Albuquerque lawyer, Frank W. Clancy, to Senator Chandler, "is a great disappointment to us in this part of the country and has caused a feeling of hostility towards [Reed] which cannot be overestimated." Whatever the political advisability of Reed's decision on the territories, it was not his alone. New Mexico did not become a state until 1912. See Frank W. Clancy to Chandler, March 16, 1896. William E. Chandler papers. Library of Congress.

† In February 1896, New England's own *Atlantic Monthly* had published an essay questioning Reed's fitness for the presidency. A "party hero," the Speaker lacked the moral and administrative capacity to lead the government and the nation, the anonymous author contended. He was master of no subject, exponent of no great cause: "He has never set a moral force in motion." Reed, according to this critic, had put partisanship before the nation's solvency by refusing to support the Cleveland administration's plan to issue gold-backed bonds. The essayist was a better observer than prophet. As president, he predicted, Reed "might encourage the worst Jingoes—of his own party." Time would show very much the opposite. See the *Atlantic Monthly*, February 1896.

"They were for me, until the buying started," he said of the general run of southern delegates.[57] The Speaker did not poll much better in those northern reaches of the country where electoral commerce was conducted by subtler means. On March 19, the New Hampshire Republicans resolved to endorse not Reed alone, as most had expected (for indeed, the Reed delegates outnumbered the McKinley men by at least two-to-one), but either Reed or McKinley; Chandler was complicit in this compromise with the McKinley forces, which he himself subsequently denounced as "cowardly." On April 29, an Associated Press reporter handed a dispatch to Reed's congressional aide, Asher Hinds, with the stunning news that the Vermont Republicans had gone for McKinley. Hinds reluctantly carried the bulletin to his boss, who, upon reading it, showed not a flicker of disappointment. "If I could command my features and feelings like that," his campaign manager, Joseph Manley, later remarked, "I could make my fortune at poker."[58] Next day, the 30th, McKinley took Illinois, pushing aside the favorite son, Senator Shelby Cullom. "That settles it," a Reed manager was quoted as saying; "McKinley will be nominated."[59] For her part, Susan Reed predicted that the bad news settled something else: Her husband, she informed members of the Speaker's staff, would certainly retire from Congress. As for Reed himself, according to Hinds, "I am glad to say that [he] does not seem cast down; and if he is disappointed no one knows it. He told Mr. [Amos] Allen that he felt rather relieved, and that he would not want the office if he had to be tied up with obligations."

IF THE SECTIONAL candidate had lost his section, he still retained a sex; unfortunately, it was the one that couldn't vote. "Among Mr. Reed's callers today," wrote Hinds in a diary entry dated December 7, 1895, "was a lady who wished to shake the hand 'of the next President.' . . . She was an admirer of Sargent, the artist, and told Mr. Reed that she was particularly pleased with the expression 'of benevolence' which Sargent had caught so well in his portrait of Mr. Reed in the House lobby. Mr. Reed was much amused and laughed loudly." On January 28, 1896, the Washington *Post* quoted liberally from Reed's 1884 report on women's suffrage for the House Judiciary Committee. Under the headline "Tom Reed Is For Her," a mostly sympathetic reporter asserted that

"Mr. Reed's strength in his party as a candidate for the Presidency is undeniable. Who can measure the strength which will accrue from the daily growing army of emancipated women when it espouses him as a national chieftain?" It happened that January 28 was the opening day of the meeting of the National Suffrage Association in Washington. "Women Are For Reed," said the next day's headline. The accompanying story reported that Reed's name was cheered to the rafters.*

What Reed lacked—apart from a campaign organization, money and the will to win—was a signature issue. One had expected a cunning silence from McKinley on the currency question. The tariff was his subject, not the dollar. A bimetallic standard negotiated among the leading commercial nations was the Major's expressed preference. So mumbling, he aggravated the gold-standard Hatfields as well as the free-silver McCoys. It was as if, in 1860, Lincoln had ducked the slavery question.

Reed might have filled the monetary vacuum, but no more than McKinley did he seem to appreciate the gravity of the issue in that election year. It was, indeed, the issue of that political era. Early in 1894, with Crisp in the Speaker's chair and the Springer currency measure before the House, Reed had thrown his weight against the administration plan to support the gold standard, as we have seen. The Cleveland Democrats were fit to be tied, and they let Reed know what they thought after the House adjourned for the day.

"You cut a pretty figure today, you great big bluff," Lewis Sperry of Connecticut, in only his second term, accosted the former czar.

"Why didn't you agree to our compromise?" Reed replied.

"Because," Sperry shot back, "a Democratic Congress and a Democratic President have not reached the point where they have to allow a Republican minority to dictate to them."

"In that case," Reed evenly retorted "why didn't you marshal your Democratic majority and pass your bill?"

---

* Two controversial resolutions came up for a vote at the New England Woman Suffrage Association meeting in Boston on May 26. The first, "advising all Republican suffragists to vote for the nomination of Thomas B. Reed for the presidency was finally withdrawn," the Boston *Globe* reported. "The other, declaring that women were better, more temperate, more peaceable and more chaste than men, was lost by a tied vote." See the Boston *Globe*, May 27, 1896.

"You know why!" bellowed Sperry. "It was your opportunity to secure a sound financial law and you fell down. But you cooked your presidential goose. You will never be nominated."[60]

Two years later, however, in the warmth of the springtime presidential-nominating season, Reed's monetary views seemed not so much unsound as inchoate. He regarded himself as a friend of sound money, and he didn't see why he had to defend his record. Had he not taken political risks to beat back free silver? So it was that his public interpreted his silence as they chose, the Massachusetts Republicans pegging him for a gold man, the New Hampshire GOP for an international bimetallist. Which was it? "Mr. Reed says nothing," the New York *Times* complained. "Perhaps he thinks there are some greenback or copper or wampum States yet to select delegates, and is waiting to hear from them before settling the dispute as to his true sentiments."[61]

With a month to go before the convention, a Republican colleague of Reed's, Nehemiah Sperry of Connecticut, brought a friend in to meet the famous Speaker. "Mr. Reed," Sperry's friend addressed him, "you must be under a great strain with things so uncertain about the presidency." "My friend," Reed replied—"fixing on him his penetrating eyes" as Hinds told the story—"it is the uncertainties of life that make it worth living."

But presently, as Reed backers began falling away, there was all too much certainty. "When it comes to political loyalty," said the Washington *Post* on May 12, "New England produces a fine line of coop-flyers." Little did even the *Post* suspect what Reed's own campaign manager would say when presented with the discouraging news that Hanna and McKinley would certainly seat their contested delegates. What Joseph Manley—no poker-face, he—did say was that McKinley would win on the first ballot.

This surprising admission came on June 10, six days before the convention opened. Manley was in St. Louis, holding down the fort until Lodge arrived. Arthur Dunn, the reporter who had put Manley's remarks on the newswire, was eating dinner with some deflated Reed supporters when Manley appeared in front of their table. "Joe," said one of the Reed men, Sam Fessenden of Connecticut, "God Almighty hates a quitter. I have been a soldier in actual war, and am a faithful soldier for Reed now, but my general has deserted."[62]

The next day, Susan Reed tried to brace up Lodge. "I never wrote a letter concerning politics before and probably never shall again, but I do want to say something to you very much," she began.

We are beaten certainly but when this fight is over I want to feel that there is as little as possible to regret. There is nothing to be gained by conceding everything beforehand as Mr. Manley seems to be doing. In justice to the true, loyal friends of ours from New England I hope you will make a brave fight and when you make your nominating speech not allow yourself to be over shadowed by defeat, but make a speech such as you are capable of making—such a one as you will be proud to remember. Presidential Elections do not come often in one's lifetime and I know you will forgive me for saying, not often is such a candidate presented.

It may be hard in these depressing conditions but I know you can do it. There will be time enough in the future to make congratulations and all that but just now something harder is required. Just make a speech worthy of your candidate and of yourself—forgetting defeat.

Of course, Mr. Reed does not know I am writing this and would no doubt object to my doing so, but I am sure you will understand.[63]

Manley was devastated. He had intended no disloyalty, much less treachery. The sight of his own published words (which he did not deny) shocked him as much as they did anyone else. His friends, trying to protect him, set up the story that he was drunk.[64]

Reed, who was in his rooms at the Shoreham with Susan, reminded Lodge that there was to be no question about the vice presidency. He did not want it and would not accept it (the honor went to Garret A. Hobart, a New Jersey lawyer and state legislator). As for Manley, "I hope the thing is a joke, but whether so or not I hope our people will stand up like men and see who they are themselves. The joining the enemy at this time is *too* silly."[65] By telegraph on the 17th, he prodded Lodge to fight the contested delegate cases. Hanna's and McKinley's politicking had been "outrageous."

The next day, Lodge presented Reed's name to the sweltering Republican delegates. He reminded them how low the Democrats had brought the country, how they had stripped the Treasury, lost the gold, shattered the economy and pretended not to notice the Spanish overlords crushing the freedom-loving Cuban people. "The people of a neighboring island," said the Massachusetts senator, "fighting for freedom, look toward us with imploring eyes, and look in vain." There was, however, a way out of this scrape, for the nation and for the party. Concerning his hero, Lodge said all the conventional things but one unconventional thing, and it was the unexpected accolade that perhaps made Hanna smile. "He is," Lodge declared, "a brainy statesman."[66]

When, at long length, the Massachusetts orator uttered the candidate's name, the Reed forces made a brave demonstration, but Manley was a prophet. It was McKinley on the first ballot, taking 661½ votes to Reed's 84½ and remnants for Matthew Quay of Pennsylvania, Levi Morton of New York and William B. Allison of Iowa. The editors of the St. Louis *Globe-Democrat* saw McKinley's triumph for what it was. "There has been no time in the past six months when the best that any human being could do would have defeated Mr. McKinley," they wrote. He was the people's choice.[67]

To the nominee, Reed wired epigrammatic congratulations: "I wish you a happy and prosperous administration, happy for yourself and prosperous for the country." To Lodge, he expressed gratitude for the "cheerless task" the Massachusetts senator had performed so ably. What gratified him most, Reed said, was the fight Lodge had waged and won for the Republican party platform: that is, the money plank pledging the GOP to "maintain inviolable the obligations of the United States, of all our money, whether coin or paper, at the present standard, the standard of the most enlightened nations of the earth."[68]

That Lodge was chiefly responsible for that statement of principle is doubtful. The glory more likely belonged to others, among them H. H. Kohlstaat, a Chicago newspaper publisher and hard-money man so insistent that Hanna called him a "damn crank"; Senator Redfield Proctor of Vermont, who had incurred Reed's loathing in April for steering the Green Mountain State's Republican delegates to McKinley; and Melville E. Stone, general manager of the Associated Press, who was entrusted with writing the final draft because he was "the only man present who could spell the word 'inviolable,'" according to one eyewitness.[69] But far more interesting than what Lodge may or may not have contributed to the gold plank is Reed's belated realization that the party needed it.

As usual, the Speaker confided his innermost thoughts to Gifford. "It does seem," he wrote to his friend in Europe, "as if the office of President was too powerful for any man to hold for himself alone, for his ideas of justice and right. The Speakership has seemed the same and yet I have had the great good fortune to hold it twice without mortgage or even a shadow of a title. Was it not too much to expect the Presidency on the same terms? Nevertheless it was more than known that on no other terms would I have it. I think of an equity of redemption covering this country in the greatest crisis since the war."

Reed would not dare to look into the future—he was then uncertain even whether to run for Congress again. "I only know," he went on,

> that there will never be any place worth my while wherein I shall not be free to do justice as the Higher Powers shall give me light. Office without opportunity is not worth considering.
>
> Of course the world always gets on and you and I can pass away like the summer clouds. Fragile as life is and soon over, do you suppose it will ever cease to be comfort and consolation to have fought your battle without the devil's help? Or—will dyspepsia and the slow-flowing blood of age make all things seem trivial beside hot-water bottles and warm flannel?

Now Reed let fly against McKinley: "To have endorsed paper you could not pay," he wrote in reference to the Walker affair, "to have your debts liquidated by gentlemen who are not charitable, to have exploited for your own benefit 'Industrials' dependent on your public service, to have been and to be now 'Facing-Both-Ways,' to have tried to betray at two conventions and made open failure; who would have thought this was the way to high honor two thousand years after the crucifiction! [sic]"

Reed was punctilious even about paying his own Western Union bills and buying his own train tickets. Was he therefore a fool? "My books," he concluded, "are all away and I have had no time for three years to even read *la belle langue* which I deplore for some of this would have made fine French."[70]

If the Republicans had nominated the man from Maine, Hanna later maintained, William Jennings Bryan, the Democratic party standard-bearer and free-silver romantic, would have won in a walk.[71] Reed didn't understand the country, the kingmaker insisted. He might have been right. But Reed chose to run for Congress after all. *He* won in a walk, 19,029 to 8,800, garnering the most votes, and winning by the fattest margin, of his career. A national figure now as never before, he trailed reporters as he made the rounds of Maine's First Congressional District.[*] "I was obliged to make 15 different speeches," he advised Roosevelt, "or at least to make them look as if they were different, which is very much the same thing."[72]

And what did Reed do after celebrating his own magnificent victory? He went on the stump to assure McKinley's. "California Republicans afterwards asserted that it was Reed's speeches that saved California for McKinley," William A. Robinson relates.[73] Truly, Reed loved the Republican Party.

---

[*] Reed was wont to make light of his new national stature. One day after the election, he passed an irreverent remark about some Democratic politicians. An admiring listener asked why he didn't work the witticism into his speeches. "I would have done so years ago," Reed replied, "but I have gotten into history now and I must be dignified." See Asher Hinds Diary, January 28, 1897. Asher Hinds Collection. Library of Congress.

Chapter 20

"Empire can wait"

I F R EED WAS not the greatest Speaker in the history of the House of Representatives, he was unquestionably the greatest sardonic Speaker. And if he was not the funniest great American statesman, he was certainly among the funniest, not excluding Abraham Lincoln, who had even less to laugh about during his time in Washington than Reed did. The Speaker's lacerating wit cost him friendships and, perhaps, on a net basis, votes. It might even be said that it cost him the Republican nomination for the presidency. "They could do worse—and probably will," he had quipped of his chances around the time of the St. Louis GOP convention. But there was no changing him. He could no more detach himself from his humor than he could from his immense frame.

One Saturday evening late in January 1896, Reed and his wife went to dinner at the Washington residence of Senator Edward O. Wolcott, Republican of Colorado. Theodore Roosevelt was present, as was Joseph Choate, a rich New York lawyer and renowned wit. Choate made the mistake of asserting that he had never been witness either to a poker game or a horse race. "I wish," said the host, "that I could say that." "Why don't you say it," the Speaker piped up. "Choate just did."[1]

Nelson Dingley, Reed's beloved colleague in the Maine congressional delegation, had an opposite makeup. He was literal-minded and famously abstemious. Once, coming upon Dingley seated in the House, the Speaker had fixed him with a stare that caused the author of the 1897 Dingley tariff (a sound, high-protection, Republican measure) to seem to shrink in his seat. "I was merely thinking how respectable you are," Reed drawled. "Actually, Dingley, there are times, as I sit and muse over you, when it seems as if you were respectable to a degree absolutely incompatible with human existence."[2]

Reed saw the world differently than others did. Henry Cabot Lodge and he were sitting down to lunch together one day at a cramped table in the Senate dining room. Edging his way into his seat, Reed over-turned a glass and sent ice cubes scattering. "He picked up the glass," Lodge related, "and, looking at me with his quizzical expression, said: 'I don't care. It isn't my ice.'" A small thing, Lodge allowed, but "the mental process and the angle of reflection were different from those of other people."[3]

Different too was Reed's style of expression. He did not always speak simply, but he invariably spoke clearly. Grandiloquence he found laugh-able or shameful, depending on the cause in which a politician deployed it. He saw red when he heard the words "candor" and "candid." An hon-est man, he seemingly used honest words, not from conscious choice but because he could say no other.

At St. Louis, the McKinley draftsmen were putting the finish-ing touches on the Republican party platform. "The Hawaiian islands should be controlled by the United States," they wrote, "and no foreign power should be permitted to interfere with them; the Nicaragua Canal should be built, owned and operated by the United States, and by the purchase of the Danish islands, we should secure a much needed Naval station in the West Indies."[4]

Cuba, the last relic of Spain's colonial glory days in the New World, presented a more complicated problem, which the platform draftsmen gingerly straddled. The "Ever Faithful Isle" had been in open rebellion against the mother country since February 1895.[5] Or, one might say that some Cuban people, instigated by Cuban-Americans and by American expansionists and financed with American dollars, were in open rebel-lion. It had seemed incongruous even to so improbable an imperialist as Thomas Jefferson that Cuba was a part of Spain and not of the United

States. By 1895, many in America were of that particular Jeffersonian view. Brutality characterized the conduct of the war on both sides, but the American public had picked its favorite before the fighting started. To these friends of the Cuban insurrection, Maximo Gomez, the guerrilla leader, was Sam Adams with a crate of dynamite. The insurrectionists' objective was the destruction of the Cuban economy, in which Americans had sunk between $30 million and $50 million and with which they had conducted $100 million a year in trade before the rebellion.[6] Burn the sugar cane, Gomez reasoned, and American capitalists would pressure the Cleveland administration to act against Spain. Besides, a hungry Cuban peasantry could be more easily prodded to rebel than a fat and happy one. Independence would be a glorious thing for the Cuban people who were lucky enough to survive the revolution. "If innocent persons," said Gomez in defending his policy of destroying railroad trains, "have paid for their imprudence with their lives while traveling, it is not the fault of the revolution, as successive proclamations have ordered all persons not to travel."[7]

Valeriano Weyler, the Spanish governor of Cuba, met force with force. No more sentimental than his enemies, he "reconcentrated" the women and children and aged in towns and cities, where they might more easily be protected but also where they might more easily starve. To the readers of the Hearst or Pulitzer press, "Butcher" Weyler seemed a cutout composite of a Jesuit inquisitor and King George III.

Though Congress was not yet ready to declare war in early 1896, not a few congressmen fairly shouted the word in the House and Senate chambers. Legislation to speed the day of hostilities jammed the hoppers. Advocates of a "large" American foreign policy wanted not only stern measures against Spain but also a muscular stance toward Japan, which was seen to be squinting in the direction of Hawaii. No one banged away more insistently against Cleveland's refusal to begin the assembly of a decent-sized American empire than Henry Cabot Lodge, now a member of the Senate Foreign Relations Committee. In an essay titled "Our Blundering Foreign Policy," the scholar-politician tried to explode the notion that America had ever been an early-to-bed, stay-at-home kind of nation. "We have a record," wrote Lodge, "of conquest, colonization and expansion unequalled by any people of the Nineteenth

Century. We are not to be curbed now by the doctrines of the Manchester School, which . . . as an importation are even more absurdly out of
place than in their native land."[8]

To Lodge and fellow Senate expansionists, Cleveland was a timid
man hiding under the bedclothes with Wall Street shivering next to
him. Of what account was money compared to the suffering of the
Cuban people or the destiny of the United States? To prepare the nation
for policies more glorious than those the Democratic administration
allowed itself to imagine, eight senators, Lodge among them, sponsored
bills to spend as much as $100 million to rebuild the national defenses.[9]

Cleveland, it is true, had refused to annex Hawaii, even when Harrison had left behind a ready-made treaty for that purpose as he closed
the White House door behind him in 1893. Then too, the Democratic
president was a card-carrying member of the very "Manchester" school
of free trade, hard money and nonintervention that Lodge disdained.
Neither did peace suit Theodore Roosevelt. Concerning Roosevelt, one
might object that he spoke from youthful ignorance, never having been
to war. However, one could not say it about Oliver Wendell Holmes,
the Supreme Court–bound jurist and thrice-wounded veteran of the
Union army. "War," Holmes told the Harvard Class of 1895, "when you
are in it, is horrible and dull. It is only when time has passed that you see
that its message was divine. . . . We need it in this time of individualistic
negations. . . . We need it everywhere and at all times. . . . Out of heroism grows faith in the worth of heroism."[10]

There was a swaggering patriotism abroad in the land—some wondered at the sudden outcropping of flagstaffs on school grounds, as if the
children didn't know which country they were in.[11] For their parents,
the international crisis was curiously and safely thrilling. It prompted
imaginings of glories to come as well as memories of battles past. All
these things were in the air that even Grover Cleveland, the Civil War
civilian, breathed. It was, indeed, in Cleveland's second administration
that the United States almost picked a fight with Great Britain.

The crisis erupted over a long-running Venezuelan-British boundary
dispute. Americans, blissfully insulated by geography from the world's
geopolitical strife, did not, in the main, know much about borders,
but they were reasonably sure that Britain was nowhere near Venezu-

ela. However, British Guiana (now Guyana) did border on Venezuela, though the boundary had been in dispute since 1841. When a gold strike in the contested territory elevated a quibble to an international incident, Venezuela called on the United States (as it had done in the past) to represent its interests with its British antagonist. "The United States," Richard Olney, Cleveland's Secretary of State, duly admonished the British Foreign Office in July 1895, "is practically sovereign on this continent and its fiat is law upon the subjects to which it confines its interposition." Not for six months did Whitehall respond to this astonishing impertinence, possibly because it couldn't believe it.[12] At last finding its voice, Her Majesty's Government brushed aside Olney's representations. It would not submit the dispute to arbitration, as Olney had requested. And it refused to accept that the Monroe Doctrine, which the secretary had invoked, was applicable "to the state of things in which we live at the present day."[13]

President Cleveland fired back in a message dated December 17. The Monroe Doctrine, he declared, "can not become obsolete while our Republic endures." He asked Congress for funds with which to establish a commission to find where the contested border lay and that, upon such determination, "to resist by every means in its power as a willful aggression upon its rights and interests the appropriation by Great Britain of any lands or the exercise of governmental jurisdiction over any territory which after investigation we have determined of right belongs to Venezuela." While, said the president, it was "grievous" to contemplate any but friendly relations between the two English-speaking peoples, there was no "worse calamity which a great nation can invite than . . . that which follows a supine submission to wrong and injustice."[14]

Read aloud on the floor of the House, the president's warlike message stirred bipartisan applause and cheers. Next day, in Reed's office, half a dozen Republican congressmen met to map strategy. Reed wanted no debate on the president's request but immediately to vote $100,000 for the boundary commission. Robert Hitt of Illinois, who had, as a youthful stenographer, reported on the Lincoln-Douglas debates, concurred, but William Grout, a stout Vermont infantry veteran of the Civil War, dissented. The House should assert itself and insist on furnishing one of the commissioners, he said.

"Then we assume part of the responsibility, which now belongs to the administration," Reed replied.

"That is what the Republican party and you personally ought to do," returned Grout. "You ought to eclipse Mr. Cleveland in this matter."

"I shall never put myself in competition with Mr. Cleveland," Reed said. "I am not much at the great and good man business."

When Grout insisted, "Reed jocularly told him," as Asher Hinds related, "that if the event should not be favorable he [Grout] would be in the delectable position of the man 'who told you so.'" The commission, in fact, got its appropriation without debate. Happily for the administration, whose navy bore a closer resemblance to Venezuela's than to Britain's, Whitehall had other fires in more urgent need of dousing, and the border dispute was amicably resolved through arbitration in January 1897. Cleveland allowed himself to hope that the example thereby set would mark "the beginning of a new epoch in civilization."[15]

Toward Spain, however, the president refused to give the expansionists the war they craved. The administration rather walked the balance beam of neutrality. It set the navy to intercept vessels trying to supply the rebels from American ports and treated with the colonial authorities on behalf of needy American citizens in Cuba. While maintaining neutrality, however, the administration did not forget to remind Madrid that Cuba lay just 90 miles from American shores and that the United States would not indefinitely tolerate such scenes of human suffering as Spain seemed unable to prevent.[16] By December 1896, when Cleveland delivered his final annual message to Congress, America's neutrality was not absolute but contingent. Madrid was on notice that, barring some satisfactory resolution of the insurgency, Washington would have no choice but to intervene.

Reed was no more inclined than most senior Republicans to succor a Democratic administration, but Cleveland and he were blood brothers in foreign policy. The Senate might threaten to embarrass the administration with resolutions intended to stir up a war. In comparison, the House was a model of restraint. This was not because the majority of the members necessarily shared Reed's deep-seated loathing of war or of American expansionism. Rather, they did what the Speaker bade them.

Not that they always did it cheerfully. One day early in 1897, every representative of the Pacific states converged on Reed to beg and badger him to allow a certain bill to come to the floor. It was the legislation to authorize the outlay of $70 million to $150 million to join the Atlantic and Pacific oceans by a canal cut through Nicaragua. "But the Speaker," reported the *Nation*, "told them it would be impossible to grant their request. Why? Oh, he said that the time had already been assigned to other business. But this, they knew, and he knew, was only another way of saying *Sic volo, sic jubeo*. ['This I will, thus I command, my pleasure stands for reason.'] Thus we have the spectacle of a great majority of the representatives of the freest people on earth forbidden by one man even to speak or vote on a bill which they are extremely desirous of passing." The editors had no objection to his thwarting of the canal project: "The presumption is that the thing Congress wants to do is a bad thing." The trouble lay rather in the fact that there was only one Reed: "If we could only be sure of always having a benevolent tyrant as Speaker, the system would not be a bad one."[17]

Reed's benevolence was in the eye of the beholder. Members of debating clubs, Daughters of the American Revolution chapters and secret societies wrote to him out of the blue seeking answers to knotty parliamentary questions. And when the answers duly arrived in the mail (researched by Hinds, signed by Reed), the Speaker's reputation for kindness and generosity expanded.[18] In Washington, however, many were losing patience with him. His old friend Lodge was increasingly exasperated. The question of the proposed Nicaraguan canal, Lodge believed, was inseparable from that of America's annexation of Cuba, which "lies right athwart the line which leads to the Nicaragua Canal."[19] There was nothing narrow about this "large" policy of Lodge's. It took a world map to explain it.

Because Reed, unlike his Democratic predecessor in the Speaker's chair, refused to take to the floor to debate, the record is largely bare of his opinions on American foreign policy in the months leading up to the war with Spain. However, one can draw easy inferences from his parliamentary maneuvering. Czarlike, he blocked warlike measures from coming to a vote on the House floor. But one day—it was July 7, 1897— Benton McMillin, the federal income tax promoter from Tennessee, innocently asked the chair whether an order to suspend the rules and take up legislation would be in order, "today being a continuation of the legislative day of Monday." Reed, caught flatfooted, said yes, whereupon McMillin moved to suspend the rules and pass a Senate resolution recognizing Cuban belligerency. A failure of timing or of party discipline could have delivered the House into the clutches of the war faction, but Reed, "fumbling with the gavel," according to William A. Robinson, but very much alert, managed to catch the eye of his Maine colleague Nelson Dingley. "[T]he gentleman from Maine is recognized," the Speaker said over the members' knowing laughter. On cue, Dingley moved to adjourn, and Spain was safe for another day.[20]

It seems not to have occurred to Lodge when he nominated Reed for president the year before how much his candidate's views on foreign policy differed from his own. "Great Sire, Noble Prince of Jerusalem, Sublime Prince of the Royal Secret, possible Ex-Bank Cashier," Reed had facetiously addressed his friend and ally before they parted political company.[21] In the summer of 1897 Lodge was accusing Reed of "extreme pro-Spanish prejudices." The Speaker lightly rebutted him on August 27. "Pro-American," Reed admitted to being, not pro-Spanish. "As I have said to you before," the Speaker added, now alluding to a pair of troublesome Silver Republicans, "let us assimilate Pettigrew and Teller before we try something harder." And he prodded Lodge concerning the expansive McKinley foreign policy, in which service Theodore Roosevelt, named Assistant Secretary of the Navy in April, was laboring: "Isn't William trying to make the world better in more spots than he can visit and oversee?"[22]

Let us say, Reed continued the argument on September 13, that administration policy put American and Spanish warships on a course to search one another and that hotheads on one side or the other started shooting. And let us further suppose, Reed continued, that

some man with a real American name, not Sanquilly but Murphy or Schaughnessy, were killed. War would be sure. And our wars cost.

As to their government being like ours in the Revolution, I yield to your superior knowledge but with a slight shake of the head. But that doesn't matter. As for gratitude of nations, that is not worth counting. If we help another people to liberty, we either do it for our own interests or it will seem so when their interests become diverse. In fact, until the federation of the world comes, let each nation look out for itself. . . .

I do not in the least doubt your careful consideration of the case and perhaps I have been too brash in my way. Unfortunately, when I come to a conclusion by a small majority, I sometimes forget the smallness of the majority and think I was unanimous and that everybody else ought to be. So pardon me if I have been unreasonably ironical, for it is my bad habit.[23]

Lodge followed with a blast against Reed's lamentable spelling, which Reed answered with a thrust at Lodge's illegible handwriting. They were still friends.[24]

In October, the Spanish government agreed to recall Weyler, employ a lighter touch against the rebels and give Cuba some measure of self-rule (though not the deed to the island itself). These pacific gestures McKinley welcomed in his annual address to Congress in early December. But this president, like his predecessor, refused to forswear American intervention. He invoked, a little grandly, America's "sovereign prerogative of reserving to itself the determination of its policy and course according to its own high sense of right."[25]

The frank opinion of the Spanish minister to Washington, Enrique Dupuy de Lome, was that the president was a phony and a lightweight and that his speech was an essay in hypocrisy. These thoughts he unwisely committed to a letter, a copy of which came to be plastered on the front page of the February 9 edition of the New York *Journal*.[26] Six days later, the USS *Maine* blew up in Havana harbor.

Dupuy de Lome was wrong about McKinley in one respect, at least: The president did not want war. He had seen quite enough of it at Antietam. And his administration was working earnestly for peace. In the Senate, the rabid war faction met its match in such McKinley allies as Aldrich, Allison, Hale, Hanna (for the president had not failed to remember his campaign strategist and financier), Platt and Spooner. As for the House, there was no contest: It was said that the members didn't even breathe without the Speaker's consent.[27]

The destruction of the *Maine*, along with 266 of her crewmen, set the cause of peace reeling. Strains of "Stars and Stripes Forever," John Philip Sousa's stirring new patriotic march, issued from the nation's parlor pianos.[28] And from the throats of its elected representatives rose demands for justice and vengeance. Who or what had sunk the *Maine*? A navy board of inquiry was set to seek the answer. Interestingly, Fitzhugh Lee, the U.S. consul in Havana, a man almost as hell-bent on intervention as Lodge or Roosevelt, said he believed that the explosion was an accident. In a February speech to the students and faculty of the University of Pennsylvania, a haggard McKinley, always a model of longsuffering, asked his audience to emulate the example of the eternally patient George Washington.[29]

But war fever made its sufferers impulsive. Senator Richard F. Pettigrew, Republican silverite from South Dakota, was one who caught the bug, although his was the calculating, low-intensity strain. Not for him professions of concern for Cuba's suffering masses or dazzling visions of America's geopolitical future. "I don't care anything about Cuba," the senator told Arthur Dunn. "The island would not be worth anything to us unless it was sunk for 24 hours to get rid of its present population, but I want a war with Spain because I believe it will put us on a silver basis."[30]

The more virulent variety of the nervous fever was the one that raged in Assistant Secretary of the Navy Theodore Roosevelt. War was what he wanted: for America's sake, for Hawaii's sake, for Cuba's sake—and for the sake of the Philippines too. At the annual Gridiron Dinner in March, Roosevelt shook his fist under the nose of Senator Hanna, vowing to that peace-loving capitalist, "We will have this war for the freedom of Cuba in spite of the timidity of the commercial interests!"[31]

A month before that encounter, Roosevelt had exhibited one of the greatest displays of impetuous energy in the annals of the federal bureaucracy. Secretary of the Navy John D. Long, his superior, out of the office for a day, had entrusted the workings of the department to his high-strung underling. Returning to the office the next day, the boss discovered that the naval profile of the United States had undergone a marked change. "I find," Long recorded in his diary, "that Roosevelt, in his precipitate way, has come very near causing more of an explosion than happened to the *Maine*." In one unsupervised day at the office, the Rough Rider–to–be had ordered up ammunition, directed ships hither and yon and asked Congress for emergency legislation with which to augment the naval ranks. It was a full-scale, eight-hour, one-man preparedness program—or, if not one-man, then two-, for Lodge was at Roosevelt's elbow.

There was, as well, a strategic element in Roosevelt's busy day at the office. To Admiral George Dewey in Hong Kong, he cabled:

> Secret and confidential. Order the squadron, except Monocracy, to Hong Kong. Keep full of coal. In the event of declaration of war with Spain, your duty will be to see that the Spanish squadron does not leave the Asiatic coast, then offensive operations in Philippine Islands. Keep Olympia until further orders.
> Roosevelt[32]

Preparedness was on McKinley's mind too, though diplomatic niceties stayed his hand. Since the administration was negotiating with the Spanish in good faith, it would be awkward if the president himself were the one to propose $50 million in needed military and naval spending. McKinley, therefore, put the question to Joe Cannon, chairman of the House Appropriations Committee: Would he introduce the bill on his own motion? Indeed he would. The "Fifty Million Dollar Bill," as it was instantly called, passed both the House and the Senate without a dissenting vote.[33] Reed himself didn't stand in its way. "He has set himself against everything that would encourage war," Hinds recorded in his diary, "but did not oppose the preparations when they were considered necessary by the executive."[34]

Asher Hinds, 35 years old, an alumnus of Colby College and an associate editor of the Portland *Daily Press*, served Reed as the "Clerk at the Speaker's table," a position later renamed "Parliamentarian." Hinds was, indeed, a formidable parliamentarian, frequently providing Reed with precedents that the Speaker invoked in controversial rulings—late in March 1898, for instance, in Reed's "very able and convincing argument" (as Hinds put it) against a resolution introduced by the Democratic leader, Joseph Bailey of Texas, calling for recognition of Cuban independence. The Democrats were much impressed by Hinds's erudition. "After the ruling was over," Hinds jotted in his diary, "Mr. Richardson of Texas, their ablest parliamentarian, came up and expressed the wish that I might publish my precedents"—which Hinds did in 1907.

Hinds's wife, Harriet, was herself an observer of the Speaker and an occasional diarist. On March 8, 1898, the day of the passage of the $50 million defense appropriations bill, she wrote, "went to the Speaker's room afterward to get Asher and come home with him. While there a 'newspaper' woman came in to speak to Mr. Reed—a most peculiar woman looking as if she had slipped out of the last decade. But what surprised me was her apparent familiarity with the Speaker. She tried to assist him to put his glasses astride his nose! It never occurred to me that anyone outside his immediate family would dare do such a thing. The Speaker's face was as inscrutable as the Sphinx's during the operation."

REED, THOUGH HE fought to keep his Republican charges united behind the president, was increasingly a party of one. Most regrettable, Lodge confided to his diary long after the fact, was how he had "set himself against the evolution of the country & the forces of the time."[35] More peculiar than even that fact was the cast of characters into which the Speaker's heterodox views now incorporated him. William J. Bryan and Grover Cleveland figured prominently among the opponents of war and annexation, also former president Benjamin Harrison and Finley Peter Dunne, creator of "Mr. Dooley," as well as uncounted pacifists, labor leaders, prohibitionists, social workers, municipal reformers, other shades of Mugwumps and—most alien of all, to Reed—free-traders. It could not have been anything but mortifying to the stalwart Republican to see his name and Carl Schurz's joined in ideological solidarity.[36] On the other hand, there was nothing incongruous about a Republican of Reed's economic views making common cause with organized labor to oppose the annexation of hundreds of thousands of low-wage workers into the American labor force. High domestic wages were, for Reed, the very purpose of the protective tariff system.[37]

It had been six weeks since the unexplained explosion on the *Maine* and still the United States was at peace. Roosevelt, though downcast by the "fear and greed" of his own upper classes, saw better and bolder days ahead. "The President," he observed, "has taken a position from which he cannot back down without ruin to his reputation, ruin to his party, and, above all, lasting dishonor to his country; and I am confident he will not back down."[38]

But McKinley, while preparing for war and praying for peace, committed himself irrevocably to neither position. The fire-eaters, principally Democrats, were beside themselves. On April 11, the House listened to a prolix and thoroughly unmartial presidential message that walked right up to the brink of war but stopped there, as if to rest. On the 13th, name-calling in the House over the substance of a war resolution provoked a near riot after Charles L. Bartlett, Democrat of Georgia, flung a bound edition of the Congressional Record in the direction of Charles N. Brumm, Republican of Pennsylvania, the man who had just called him a liar. Later in the same session, Reed had to order the sergeant-at-arms to return Indiana Republican Henry U. Johnson to his seat. Johnson was raging against the precipitous rush to war, a subject near and dear to the Speaker's heart. Still nearer and dearer, however, were the rules of the House. Johnson hadn't waited to be recognized to speak but had fulminated on his own authority. He spoke to the accompaniment of hissing.[39] To quell these disturbances, Hinds judged, "took all the Speaker's coolness and mastery."[40]

The difference between the parties was not over war and peace, for neither opposed intervention. Rather, the question was whether to wait for the quavering McKinley to lead the way or to drive him to the correct, belligerent posture from the Capitol. Democrats strongly favored the latter course of action. "We had to take you Republicans by the scruff of the neck and drag you into this war," Representative Champ Clark of Missouri later remarked, "and now you are claiming the credit for it." The shrewd Washington State Democrat, James H. Lewis, anticipated Clark in that perception. Arthur Dunn came across Lewis in a corridor outside the House chamber in the midst of the fiery debates over the war resolution. "My dear boy, do you know what we're doing in there, and I mean my party?" Lewis inquired of the newspaperman. "We are forcing a war which will give the Republicans a lease of power for the next 10 years." Actually, the Republican era lasted 14 years.[41]

The Washington *Post* judged that the melee of April 13 was among the greatest embarrassments in the history of the House. Was this the chamber that the supposed omnipotent Speaker held under his thumb? On the 15th, Bailey of Texas, the House minority leader, rose to defend his reputation against press reports that he was the cause of the disturbances. Actually, declared Bailey, it was the Speaker's fault for stifling debate. Until this shameful episode, said the Texan, "I believed that the present Speaker of this House was as partisan as an honest man could be and as honest as a partisan could be." The sordid scenes of the 13th had caused him to change his mind.

"The Chair desires to say, that whatever he has done the other day, or any other day since the commencement of this session, has been done in the presence of the House and of a thousand witnesses," Reed replied. "He does not feel it is necessary for him to make any discussion of his conduct."

The exchange did not end there, however, as the Washington *Post* reported:

> "The gentleman from Texas," continued Mr. Reed, "after two days of deliberation has felt that his situation demanded discussion and explanation." Again the Republicans went into paroxysms of laughter. "With that idea the Chair entirely agrees," continued Mr. Reed placidly, and again the Republicans laughed. "It is not the first time that the gentleman from Texas has assailed me," said Mr. Reed, speaking in the first person.
>
> "And it will not be the last, either," retorted Mr. Bailey hotly.[42]

Reed's unparliamentary lapse into the first person was a sign of the stress under which he was laboring in those days. Hinds feared that the hot-blooded Bailey, having been bested in rhetorical combat with the Speaker, wanted satisfaction of a physical kind.[43] One death threat, at least, did come Reed's way for his perceived obstruction of the McKinley war program. "Speaker Reed is a giant in stature," the District of Columbia detective who was assigned to guard Reed told the Washington *Post*, "and when

I reported for duty I remarked to him that I thought he was better able to take care of me than I of him."[44]*

In the wee hours of Tuesday, April 19, Congress enacted a joint war resolution, the vote in the Senate being 42–35, that in the House, 310–6. McKinley signed it on the 20th. Three of the six holdouts in the House, Samuel W. McCall, Republican of Massachusetts; Charles A. Boutelle, Republican of Maine; and Henry Johnson of Indiana, were the Speaker's personal friends (McCall later wrote a biography of Reed). Willis Brewer, Democrat of Alabama; John J. Gardner, Republican of New Jersey; and Eugene F. Loud, Republican of California, filled out the short list of holdouts.[45] It was at about this time that former New York governor Eli Morton asked Reed if he could not "dissuade" the members from their bellicosity. "Dissuade them! Dissuade them!" Reed laughed in the presence of reporters. "The Governor is too good. He might as well ask me to stand out in the middle of a Kansas waste and dissuade a cyclone."[46]

The legislative prerequisites to American intervention out of the way, the State Department cabled instructions to the U.S. minister to Spain, Stewart L. Woodford. He was to demand that "the Government of Spain at once relinquish its authority and government in the Island of Cuba and withdraw its land and naval forces from Cuba and Cuban waters." But doddering Spain, though it could not hope to win a war with the stripling United States, could at least choose the terms on which the fight would begin. Inasmuch as the congressional resolution was "equivalent to an evident declaration of war," the Spanish authorities informed Woodford, diplomatic relations between the two countries had thereby ceased. The U.S. ultimatum went undelivered, but the war was on.[47]

"I envy you your vote," Reed said to one of the half-dozen House dissenters. "I was where I could not do it." Perhaps none of the patriotic resisters wished the United States harm in the enterprise they dared to

---

* The author of the threat, a discharged employee of the War Department, turned out to be more entrepreneur than assassin. After writing to Reed, he wrote to some New York newspapers to ask if they would be interested in his account of the existence of frightening, secret threats on the Speaker's life.

decry, but it could not have made their lot any easier when Commodore George Dewey led his Asiatic Squadron to a lopsided victory against the Spanish fleet in Manila Bay on May 1. The U.S. navy suffered not one battle fatality. "Dewey done it!" the cheer went up. Proponents of nonintervention had solemnly warned against the "horrors" of war. They had failed to mention the glory. Reed, unwavering in opposition, expressed the wish that Dewey would steam out of Manila as fast as he had steamed in. "It'll make us trouble for all time if he does not," Champ Clark, writing in the New York *World*, quoted him as saying.[48]

Certainly, Dewey's triumph was immediately troublesome to any who would hobble the march of empire. To Lodge, the destruction of the Spanish Pacific fleet made the annexation of Hawaii a project of urgent necessity. Pearl Harbor would be the way station to the Philippines and to American possessions yet unnamed. Reports as late as February had painted Reed as a friend of the Hawaii accession: "He wants to use Hawaiian annexation as one of the great achievements of the Republican Party to go before the country in the coming Congressional campaign," the Washington *Post* claimed.[49] But, before long, the Speaker had changed his mind or—more likely—the reporter had corrected his facts. "Speaker Reed has always been and is now opposed to annexation," the same journal related on May 12, "and if no action is taken in the House it will be due to his powerful and antagonistic influence."[50] It mystified Reed why, in order to whip Spain, America had to have Hawaii. We may as well "annex the moon," he said.[51]

The journalist Ida Tarbell said of Reed that "[h]e believed in doing what the majority wanted done—when he agreed with the majority."[52] In this case, the majority acted as if Reed weren't there. He was in fact out of the chamber on June 15, when the joint resolution permitting annexation came up for a vote. The Speaker, announced John Dalzell of Pennsylvania, was unwell. But had he been present, and had he had a vote, he would have voted nay, Dalzell informed the House. Which hypothetical vote, however, would have made no practical difference. The annexationists had it, 209–91.[53]

The *Nation* now wondered what had become of the omnipotent Speaker of 1897. Reed had fought the teeming majority on every major issue of war and peace. "Mr. Reed's course in all these matters was no doubt deliberately chosen, and has been highly honorable to him," the editors judged. "Courage to oppose a popular mania, above all to go against party, is not so common a political virtue that we can afford not to pay tribute to the man who exhibits it." Virtuous though he was, however, he had lost.[54] That Reed stood virtually alone at this moment, Hinds recorded, "does not disturb him in the least."[55]

On August 2, the Republicans of the First District of Maine nominated the Speaker for a 12th consecutive term. They said nothing about his differences with the administration, and he thanked them for "the large liberty you have always given me in interpreting your wishes." The armistice with Spain was signed 10 days later, thus ending what Reed was wont to call "the War of the Two Skirmishes." "What a curious thing the war has been," he mused. "One hundred days and the poor devils have had no show and not one bit of luck. Now we wake up with their burdens with a joyousness which I hope the future may justify."[56]

AMONG THE OTHER subjects that occupied Reed's thoughts that summer was his bank account. In 1896, he had accepted a lucrative part-time post as a referee for 28 American life insurance companies.[57] Now he was weighing an offer for a full-time position from a New York law firm. He had decided not to oblige the western politicians who were trying to induce him to board a train to make political speeches in the run-up to the November elections. "This last is very distasteful to me," he confided to a friend, "because the course of things as they look now can hardly be defended. Having sown the wind, the whirlwind begins to peep above the weeds. I did not do the sowing and do not want to reap that harvest."[58] In the September Maine balloting, Reed beat his hapless Democratic opponent, 19,029 to 8,800.[59]

Reed seemed to have one foot out the political door even before he returned to Washington in early December for the short session of the 55th Congress. The signing of the Treaty of Paris on December 10 brought the shooting war with Spain to an official conclusion. To the victor went Cuba and Puerto Rico (along with other Spanish possessions in the West Indies), as well as the Philippines, the latter for the consideration of $20 million.[60] But the peace brought no tranquility to

American politics. Cleveland had early predicted that the war would produce, among its other foul consequences, "much demagogy and humbug, great additions to our public burdens and the exposure of scandalous operations."[61] Finley Peter Dunne's fictional Irish-American bartender, Mr. Dooley, was of the same mind as Cleveland.

> "An' so the war is over?" asked Mr. Hennessy.
> "On'y part of it," said Mr. Dooley. "Th' part that ye see in th' pitcher pa-apers is over, but th' tax collector will continyoo his part in th' war with relentless fury. Cav'lry charges are not th' on'y wans in a rale war."[62]

And Reed was of the identical view as Mr. Dooley. The myriad blunders of the War Department were manna for the Democrats in the autumn elections, but the Republicans retained a majority in both the House and Senate. In New York, the nation's most popular war hero, the dashing Colonel Teddy Roosevelt, was elected governor. Thus the people, in whose collective wisdom Reed reposed such great store, gave their blessing to annexationism, expansionism, imperialism and McKinleyism.

"Reed is terribly bitter," Lodge advised Governor-elect Roosevelt on December 20, "saying all sorts of ugly things about the administration and its policy in private talks, so I keep out of the way, for I am fond of him and I confess that his attitude is painful and disappointing to me beyond words."[63] Reed attacked the administration in private because he could say nothing from the Speaker's chair. Besides, though he might see his name connected to the Mugwumps' in the newspapers, he would retire before breaking openly with his own party. Even in retirement he would commit no such disloyalty. So he contented himself with rhetorical guerrilla actions. When, for instance, a member would seek recognition to introduce a private bill for the sake of a constituent's pet project, Reed would refuse. "[T]he money is needed to pay for Malays," he would say. He pretended to be disapproving of a $300,000 appropriation for the Philadelphia Commercial Museum. "This seems like a great waste of money," he said. "We could buy 150,000 naked Sulus with that."[64]

Before the shooting started, McKinley had forsworn "forcible annexation." Such a policy, he declared, could not even be "thought of." It would, indeed, "by our code of morality . . . be criminal aggression."[65] But then came the shooting and, even more dangerous to statecraft than shooting, the cheering, as the great chronicler of the Spanish-American War, Walter Millis, observes. The crowd roaring in his ear, McKinley seemed almost to forget Antietam. A memorandum in the president's hand, written shortly after Dewey's triumph in Manila, read, "While we are conducting war and until its conclusion we must keep all we can get; when the war is over we must keep what we want."[66]

Nelson Dingley died on January 13, 1899, at the age of 66. Reed was deeply attached to him. Congress without Dingley might not have been wholly unimaginable. But Congress without Dingley and *with* the annexation of the Philippines was too much to bear. "Empire can wait," the Speaker had once vainly tried to persuade the readers of the *Illustrated American*.[67] Now, he told Hinds, "I have tried, perhaps not always successfully, to make the acts of my public life accord with my conscience, and I cannot now do this thing."[68]

Reed made what turned out to be the final speech of his political career on the last day of the 55th Congress, March 3, 1899. Except when the opposing parties were too mad at each other to utter a civil word, it was the minority leader who rose on the closing day of the session to express the gratitude of the House to the Speaker for a job well done. Joe Bailey of Texas had the duty on this day. Reed and he had been at each other's throats in the perfervid debates over the war resolution, but the Texan had buried the hatchet. "Mr. Speaker," Bailey began, "we have not always agreed with the distinguished occupant of the chair, and we have taken more than one occasion to emphasize our dissent; but remembering the momentous questions which have confronted us, and remembering, too, the intense excitement which they aroused throughout the country, as well as in this Hall, the wonder is that those occasions were so few; and in this hour of impartial retrospect I do not hesitate to say that he has been more than fair to us and to our side as any one of us, were our positions reversed, would have been to him. [Loud applause.]" Reed replied quite as graciously, venturing that he might, perhaps, be permitted to congratulate himself "upon having had a great opportunity to administer a great office in the fashion indicated by the noble words known to our law, 'without fear, favor or hope of reward.' [Applause.]"[69]*

By the time Reed had set off to Europe that summer, it was nobody's secret that he was going to resign. He made it official on August 23, when he tendered his thanks to the voters of the First District for their unfailing loyalty over no fewer than 23 years.

"Other men have had to look after their districts, but my district has always looked after me," he wrote, nostalgically letting such bygones as the 1884 squeaker be bygones. "Office as a 'ribbon to stick on your coat' is worth nobody's consideration," he closed. "Office as opportunity is worth all consideration. . . . Whatever may happen I am sure the First Maine District will always be true to the principles of liberty, self-government and the rights of man."[70]

Inevitably, it was to Gifford that Reed opened both his mind and his heart. "You are quite right in thinking that money was not the cause of the change," he began, "though some is quite soothing in small families. The position became unendurable. You have little idea what a swarming back to savagery has taken place in this land of liberty." Indeed, Reed went on, he was in a "doubly impossible place. If I was again chosen Speaker and nobody could have prevented that my position would have been a representative one and would not represent me. If I went out on the floor I know all too well I have few followers." So, Reed went on, he did what nobody else had ever done by resigning a great office without exactly saying why. Let the people infer the reason. "[W]hen a man finds out a thing for himself he is prouder of it than if it were told by Shakespeare. Had I stayed I must have been as Speaker always in a false position in aiding and organizing things in which I did not believe or using power against those who gave it to me."[71]

It was time to leave, and he left.

---

* Reed was a facile first-draft writer, but he seemed to struggle in composing these final remarks to the House. "[Y]ou have given me your confidence in all which pertained to my duties here in a manner so full and complete that it will be the solace of my life," he wrote first. On reflection, he crossed out the final phrase and substituted ". . . full and ample that my memory of it will never pass away." See Asher Hinds Collection. Library of Congress.

Coda: Roosevelt Comes
to Portland

Tom Reed made small talk with the other Maine notables who stood waiting for the arrival of the presidential train at Portland's Union Station. It was a bright late August afternoon in the 11th month of the accidental administration of Theodore Roosevelt. William McKinley was dead, shot in Buffalo, New York, on September 14, 1901. "Be easy on him, boys," the mortally wounded president had thought to grunt to his bodyguards as they pummeled the assassin with fists and rifle butts. Now President Roosevelt was making a triumphant tour of the New England states.

Passing the time, Reed might have reflected on the improbable sequence of events that had placed him in the station and Roosevelt on the train, rather than vice versa. It had been only seven years since the then 38-year-old New York City police commissioner was throwing his youthful energy into the nascent Reed-for-president movement. Roosevelt had hung Reed's picture in his Sagamore Hill library; it was, in fact, the largest portrait in the room. Roosevelt would sit in that library reading Reed's occasional essays in the *North American Review*. And, not infrequently, as he put down the article, Roosevelt—himself a successful author—would reach for a pen with which to extol his mentor's wit and intelligence. Reed had told the everlastingly earnest Roosevelt in those days that he was too serious—had ironically commended him on his "original discovery of the Ten Commandments." And the younger man had, of course, respectfully listened.

Reed, because he was living in New York, was the odd man out in the committee to welcome the president. Its members included a pair of judges, the mayor of Portland, an ex-governor of Maine and the famous General Joshua L. Chamberlain, all residents of the Pine Tree State.[1] Upon his retirement from politics, Reed had joined the rising Wall Street law firm of Simpson, Thacher & Barnum. Gone, all at once, was the ex-Speaker's signature House of Representatives ragtag attire. A new Reed, tailored and prosperous—a corporation attorney, a trustee of the New York Life Company and member of the Century Association— inhabited the familiar old hulking form. The New Yorker was earning a minimum of $50,000 a year and was the beneficiary, besides, of top-flight investment counsel. He was bemused, shortly after starting work, to be representing a pair of Standard Oil moguls, William Rockefeller and Henry H. Rogers, in a dispute over the affairs of a Brooklyn gas company. It was a situation ripe for political caricature, and Reed had heard the guffaws. Then again he quipped, in a reference to America's war in the Philippines, that defending the high and the mighty was "preferable to exporting Kentucky civilization to foreign parts."[2]

Now Roosevelt, the hero of San Juan Hill, the very living symbol of the imperialism that had driven Reed from politics, was on the train headed north. The people of Portland would cheer the Rough Rider, just as the people of Lowell, South Lawrence and Haverhill, Massachusetts, and of Dover, New Hampshire, had already done. The young president had won the nation's heart. Reed had yelled for Blaine when the occasion demanded, and he would do his duty with Roosevelt too.[3]

The former Speaker was a believer in progress, and he had done his best to come to terms with the modern world. He had ridden a bicycle and spoken long-distance on a telephone.[4] But he could not reconcile himself to the muscular new American statecraft. The Roosevelt administration's stance of vague hostility toward the "trusts" seemed of a piece with its policy toward the newly colonized peoples of the Pacific. The ex-Speaker's views on the Philippines were well known, or easily inferable. Reed would not directly denounce the policy of his own Republican party. To anyone who wanted to know what he thought, he would rather subversively reply that he believed in the Declaration of Independence, majority rule and the rights of man. And when a friend was musing about the best route to take to visit America's newly acquired possessions, Reed made a suggestion: "Well, if you travel westward you'll reach the Philippines by way of Hawaii, and if you travel eastward you'll reach Hawaii by way of the Philippines. The whole question is whether you prefer to take your plague before your leprosy, or your leprosy before your plague."[5]

Do you remember, Reed had asked Gifford in a letter in the summer of 1900, how, a quarter century earlier, the two of them had opposed Portland's proposed subsidy of the Ogdensburg Railroad? "We were right but we had to suffer and the City as well," Reed recollected. "What a plain case it was and how all the best and all the worst citizens were against us! It drove you out and came near swamping me. I sometimes wonder just how small is the fraction of one percent which in the long run makes honesty the best policy?"

He was now in a similar position, Reed went on: "I do not know if I am right now as I was in the Ogdensburg case but I am almost as lonesome and haven't got the twenty-five years in which to [wait]."[6] This was before the election of 1900, the contest pitting McKinley and Roosevelt against Bryan and Adlai Stevenson.

"For my part," Reed wrote Gifford six months later, "I am in the melancholy condition which led me to remark to an audience, which was sure not to understand; that I was optimistic as to results but pessimistic as to the means the Lord seemed to be using to bring about the results. We praise honesty and straightforwardness but never seem to reward it perhaps for fear that Satan should become discouraged and drop his share of the good work, which share seems by far the largest. It was certainly a hard case when one had to choose between the dishonesty of one and the plain blank foolishness of the other. All things seem to be forcing us in the wrong direction and there seems but little hope of escape."[7]

In May 1901, Reed reported to Gifford that the McKinley people were talking up a third term (and were likely to be successful, Washington rumor had it) and that Joseph Manley, his *bête noire* of the 1896

GOP convention, wanted to be governor of Maine. Reed was making money. Indeed, everybody seemed to be. The depression of the 1890s was a distant sour memory. The dollar, unquestionably, was now as good as gold: With passage of the Gold Standard Act on March 14, 1900, the monetary dispute that had run for as long as Reed served in Congress was finally put to rest.* On Wall Street bulls romped. Reed had led the Billion Dollar Congress. Now, as a moneyed private investor, he was profiting in the excitement kicked up by J. P. Morgan's organization of United States Steel, the first billion-dollar corporation. On April 30, 1901, 3.2 million shares changed hands on the New York Stock Exchange, a record that would stand for 27 years.

Reed's law firm had just moved to sumptuous new offices at 25 Broad Street. "I must say to you notwithstanding your anticipated disgust," Reed wrote to Gifford, "that I have not yet repented coming here." As for national politics, they were still on the skids. "These people," the ex-Speaker went on, "seem to think like [Joseph] Foraker that by giving more power to the government we become a greater nation. We enlarge the 'attributes of sovereignty' and become something greater by taking something from the people and giving it to Congress. . . . I should like to have the luck to live to see this out for I am reluctant to believe that for forty years I could have been talking drivel about liberty and the rights of man."[8]

Reed's parents had both reached the age of 80; he seemed to have the bloodlines for long life. With the help of Turkish baths and fewer fish balls, he had lost some weight. For the most part, he seemed to be enjoying himself, though he toyed with the idea of quitting the law and seeing the world. Would he really live much longer? "Each day," he noted in his diary, "I read speeches about men everywhere whom I have survived. But after all I have great fear of disassociating myself from the industrious life."[9]

Now the senior partner of Reed, Simpson, Thacher & Barnum, he

---

* At the annual dinner of the New York Chamber of Commerce held at Delmonico's in November 1899, Reed made a speech in response to a three-word toast: "The gold standard." The assembled financiers, bankers and businessmen jumped to their feet to give him the loudest ovation of the evening, outdoing even that accorded to the new governor of New York State, Theodore Roosevelt. See the New York *Times*, November 22, 1899.

was conscientiously learning and growing in private practice. At the firm, his reputation for honesty and fair-dealing had literally preceded him. Before reporting for duty, he had taken a vacation in Europe with Susan and Kitty. On the Continent, he interrupted his leisure to take on a legal assignment, and a lucrative one it turned out to be. Rather than accepting this sizable fee for himself, as he was entitled to do, he had it paid into the partnership from which he had not yet drawn a paycheck.[10]

In New York, he had made a new circle of friends, including Mark Twain and H. H. Rogers, his Standard Oil client. He was friendly too, with Nicholas Murray Butler, who saw to it, in 1900, that Reed was made an honorary doctor of laws of Columbia University, the institution Butler headed. It was through her own efforts that Kitty, the same year (she was 25), graduated with a chancellor's certificate from the five-month Woman's Law Class at New York University.[11] In 1901, so rumor had it, the ex-Speaker made a bundle in the Northern Pacific corner. Now, upon plopping into a chair at the Century Association, he was as likely to take up the *Commercial & Financial Chronicle* as he was *Punch*. A public intellectual, he wrote for publications as varied as the *North American Review*, *Saturday Evening Post* and *Youth's Companion*. He contemplated greater achievements—"a book on the human race," perhaps. "Without a doubt I should write a book," he prodded himself in his diary, but he lacked the energy.[12] "Instead of declining," the New York *Sun* appraised Reed's achievements in his adopted city, "his distinction increased, even under the test of the fierce competition of New York."[13]

Nor did Reed turn his back on his native city. He hadn't sold the house on Deering Street. And he returned in the summer of 1900 to give a speech at Portland's Old Home celebration. "Here's to the State of Maine," he closed his remarks at City Hall, "settled mostly by the blood of old England, but always preferring liberty to ancestry; a strong old democratic state, yet among the first to give liberty to the slave. May her future be as noble as her past. Here is to the State of Maine, the land of the bluest skies, the greenest earth, the richest air, the strongest, and, what is better, the sturdiest men, the fairest, and, what is best of all, the truest women under the sun." The applause of his old constituents shook the hall.[14]

When President McKinley passed through Portland that summer,

Reed invited him to visit his home (it was Susan's idea). The two of them had a nice talk. Lodge, whom Reed had not seen in three years, paid a call in September. They too got on in an amicable fashion. "It seems to me," Reed's diary recorded, "that Lodge, Roosevelt and all those men have given to the life of the Republic a rough shaking. But it seems to me also that it would not be possible to give others the impression of ingratitude to the orator who presented my name at the convention in 1896."[15]

So in August 1902, Reed had gone up to Portland to join the delegation to welcome his former protégé, the president of the United States. Shortly after 2 PM, America's most famous teeth were seen to flash as their owner hopped off the train and into the crowd. Hearty handshakes and warm words dispensed with, Roosevelt was led to a speaker's platform by the train shed. During the short walk he spoke with particular animation to General Chamberlain. Then the president turned to the crowd.

"Mr. Mayor, and you, my fellow-citizens, men and women of Maine," he began, "I wish to say a word to you in recognition of a great service rendered, not only to all our country, but to the entire people of democratic government throughout the world, by one of your citizens. The best institutions in the world are no good if they won't work. I do not care how beautiful a theory is. If it won't fit in with the facts, it is no good."

Roosevelt thereupon paid tribute to the author of the Reed rules. He had transformed the House of Representatives from a beautiful theory to something more functional, the president told the crowd. Before Reed had courageously intervened, the minority had seemed to rule in Congress. Now the majority did. Through Congress, now, the country can do well or ill, just as the people demand, said Roosevelt, "but at any rate we can do something. . . . And a great thing for the city, a great thing for any man, to be able to feel that in some crisis he left his mark deeply scored for good in the history of his country, and Tom Reed has the right to that feeling."[16]

Manly action in a time of crisis naturally led the president to the Battle of Gettysburg and to the ineffable deeds of General Chamberlain at Little Round Top. "All honor to the man," the Washington *Post* quoted Roosevelt as saying, "and may we keep ourselves from envying because to whom came the supreme good fortune of winning the Medal of Honor for mighty deeds done in the mightiest battle that the nineteenth century saw—Gettysburg. [Applause.]"

Roosevelt had not found it necessary to caution the people against envying Reed his good fortune in ungumming the works of Congress. Nor did the president choose to compare his elective career with Reed's, though here he was, many long minutes later, indirectly reminding the voters about his exploits in Cuba and comparing them to Chamberlain's at Gettysburg. "Now, General," said the president with a glance at the Medal of Honor recipient, "I was a very little time in my war; you were a long time in yours. I did not see much fighting, but I saw a lot of human nature." And what he had learned from this study of human nature, Roosevelt continued, was that it is the cultivation of commonplace virtues that allows a people to perform great deeds. "I believe," Roosevelt ended up, "that this nation will rise level to any great emergency that may meet it, but it will only be because now, in our ordinary workday life, in the times of peace, in the times when no great crisis is upon us, we school ourselves by constant practice in the commonplace, everyday indispensable duties, so that when the time arrives we shall know that we have learned aright the primary lessons of good citizenship."[17]

Nothing that Reed had ever said in public life resembled this call to collective virtue.* Was the good life now defined as that which fit an individual for service in war? Was Congress made functional only to facilitate the growth in the power of the state? So Roosevelt seemed to suggest. The speech ended, and the president and his party boarded horse-drawn carriages for a tour of the city. Roosevelt was properly awed by the views of Casco Bay (on which the U.S. revenue cutter *Woodbury*, festooned with signal flags, fired a 21-gun salute) and of the distant

---

* At about this time, Reed was writing an essay for the *North American Review* in which he criticized the administration's inchoate hostility toward big business, up to and including proposals to require the disclosure of basic financial information by investor-owned corporations. "I fear," he wrote, concerning these demands for corporate transparency, "we may be going beyond the province of free government, which certainly thus far has left the task of keeping his fingers out of the fire to the citizen whose fingers they were." See "What Shall We Do with the Tariff," *North American Review*, December 1902.

White Mountains. On Deering Street, the president dismounted and strode up to the front door of the Reed home. In he went, and, 10 minutes later, out he came. One was left to wonder if the new Republican party had therein received its benediction from the old.

Then it was on to Blaine's home, the capital of Maine, Augusta, where Roosevelt paid tribute to the late politician for whom Reed had no use. Blaine was, said the president, an exemplar of true Americanism, a believer in America's destiny to "take the lead in the western hemisphere" and, indeed, "a great part among the great nations of the earth." The Monroe Doctrine, which the former Secretary of State had done so much to champion, Roosevelt continued, "is simply a statement of our very firm belief that on this continent the nations now existing here must be left to work out their own destinies among themselves and that the continent is no longer to be regarded as colonizing ground for any European power."[18] The president, however, did not take up the question of why the United States was accumulating colonies in the Pacific.

REED HAD SURVIVED the triumph of Teddy Roosevelt. Perhaps, then, the aging ex-Speaker was indestructible. So it was back to New York and to his Broad Street office. On November 28, he traded witticisms with Mark Twain at the author's 67th birthday dinner, then headed to Washington to transact some business with the Supreme Court.[19] On December 2, he returned to his old haunt, the Ways and Means Committee room, where he regaled his former colleagues with his critique of administration policies. To the New York Republican Sereno E. Payne, he suggested a new constitutional amendment to facilitate and sanction the strong-armed, if vague, campaign against big business that Roosevelt was conducting.

"[A]n indefinable something is to be done," Reed joked, "in a way nobody knows how, at a time nobody knows when, that will accomplish nobody knows what. That, as I understand it, is the program against the trusts. The opportunity is so broad and so long that I wonder that you will not take advantage of it."[20]

*   *   *

IT WAS HIS final recorded epigram. A little later that day, across the Capitol in the Marble Room of the Senate, Reed crumpled in pain. He could barely utter the words that he was sick and must go to bed. The bed to which he was taken was that in his rooms at the Arlington Hotel, and it was there he remained. Doctors diagnosed his condition as Bright's disease, a failure of the kidneys, complicated by an attack of appendicitis. For the next five days Reed was in and out of consciousness, occasionally deliriously expostulating with his physicians in formal parliamentary language. He died at 12:10 AM on December 7, with Susan and Kitty at his bedside. It happened that a Gridiron Club dinner was in full swing at Reed's very hotel on the evening of his death. At news of Reed's passing, the diners rose to drink a silent toast to a man who had so often been among them. Republican Joe Cannon of Illinois, then on the verge of his long and tempestuous career as Speaker (he, not Reed, would have a congressional office building named after him), said a few words of tribute. Later, it struck the men of the club as curiously fitting that, at around midnight, someone had been singing a favorite tune of Reed's, "The Song that Reached My Heart," the melody of which was borrowed from a refrain from "Home Sweet Home."[21]

"A STATESMAN," REED had quipped, "is a successful politician who is dead." The editors of the New York *Times*, no great admirers of the living Reed, took more kindly to him in the hours that followed his passing. He was, they observed, "by far the most scholarly of the men prominent in his time in Congress. . . . He was what is called well-read, and his conversation, as his speeches, even more than his speeches, showed the fine assimilation of his reading. He seemed never to feel the temptation to appear in mental undress. Simple and unpretentious and familiar as he might be in formal or in informal utterance, one felt in the orderly and lucid movement of his thought and in the very inflections of his New England voice the sane culture of a richly endowed mind. He made no show of scholarship. He did not need to, and he would have been entirely above it."[22]

And what had this statesman wrought? Not many pieces of legislation bore his name. Then again, though he had been 22 years in Congress, in only eight of those years had he belonged to the majority party. And in six of the eight he had sat at the head of the House, not himself legislating but directing the course of all legislation.[23] His parliamentary triumph in the 51st Congress had transformed the House from an institution that could not legislate into one that could—for better or worse, as Roosevelt had so recently noted.

And in refashioning the House, Reed had likewise transformed the Speakership, infusing that office with powers that, if they seemed czarlike to some, were derived not from heaven but from the members themselves. And it was the members of Congress, smarting under the arbitrary and worse-than-czarlike Speakership of Joe Cannon, who would reclaim some of those powers in the famous uprising of 1910.

So perfectly honest and incorruptible was Reed that it startled his friends to see that obituary writers seemed to find it necessary to assert that he had never strayed from the true path. Being Reed, what other path could he have trod? He retired from Congress no richer than when he had entered it, just as the newspapers said. And if the newspapers also reported that he had retired from politics in order to build some capital with which to provide for his wife and daughter, that assertion was true, as far as it went. And in this, he had succeeded beyond anything he could have hoped for in the dark days of 1895. Reed himself had died worth $200,000, and that substantial capital, under the management of the executor of his estate, the financier Augustus G. Paine, within four years grew to more than $500,000.[24] As for intellectual capital, Reed had passed along some of that too. Katherine, following her marriage in 1905 to an army officer, Arthur T. Balentine, would go on to found the *Yellow Ribbon*, a San Francisco monthly magazine dedicated to women's suffrage.*

In 1896, Reed had written an introduction to an edition of the collected works of Henry Clay. It was an essay full of understanding of the

---

* They were married in Portland at the Reed home on Deering Street. "The ceremony was as quiet as it was possible to make it," the Washington *Post* reported, "because of the fact that the Reed family is still in mourning." Reed had died two and a half years earlier. See Washington *Post*, June 27, 1905.

plight of the practicing politician. Indeed, in his description of the character, policies and principles of Clay, Reed succeeded in writing a fitting epitaph to himself. Clay had, as Reed related, picked a fight with Andrew Jackson for his conduct during the Seminole War under the administration of James Monroe in 1819. "In point of reason and sound sense," Reed wrote, "Mr. Clay had greatly the advantage, and he entered upon his task from a high sense of duty. But he miscalculated the force of the sentiment which refuses to reason when war is concerned, and only asks which side our country is on."

Clay continued to lead that losing fight for the 12 years that Jackson and his party controlled the White House. And then, in 1840, when the Whigs were finally set to prevail, the party passed over its natural leader in favor of the more electable William Henry Harrison, grandfather of Benjamin Harrison. The nominee won, promptly died and the Whigs lost their only chance to implement the national program that Henry Clay had conceived.

The Speaker happened to be ahead of his time. And after Jackson had passed from the political scene, Reed went on, "Mr. Clay and his party, after a victory up to that time entirely unparalleled, fell into the hands of John Tyler and into the bottomless pit of treachery. Hence one may safely say that the greater part of Mr. Clay's life was spent in defeat and with the vanquished. But his courage never failed. He kept on with his work, listening to no discouragements, and up to the very last moment of his life was doing every day the duty of the hour."[25]

As Reed wrote of Clay, so one might write of Reed. Undaunted, he did his duty.

Acknowledgments

THOMAS B. REED seems to have stayed out of debt. Not so his biographer. I am beholden, first, to my research assistants, Kayleigh George for her work in the early stages of this project and to Adam Rowe for his contributions in all phases. More than a researcher, Mr. Rowe, now a rising young historian, has grown into a full-fledged intellectual collaborator.

I am indebted to my agent, Flip Brophy, for helping to reunite me with Alice Mayhew, my nonpareil editor at Simon & Schuster. Thanks, also, to Bob Castillo, to whose scrupulous copyediting I owe the many errors that will not appear in this book (for all that remain, I claim full credit).

Reed sometimes corresponded in French and he kept a French diary. For allowing us to inspect that portion of the Reed family archive in her possession, I thank Sharon Coop, of San Diego, the Speaker's great granddaughter. Nicole Rudolph and Kate Deimling kindly translated some of Reed's French into English. Earle G. Shettleworth Jr., Maine State Historian, made available the diary of Reed's Portland neighbor, Stephen Berry. Rick Valelly, professor of political science at Swarthmore College, provided insight and encouragement, though he should be held blameless for the consequences of his generosity.

Thanks, as well, to the librarians and archivists at the Library of Congress (an institution that Reed revered), the New York Public Library, the Bowdoin College Library and the Maine Historical Society for their unfailing help and courtesy. And I wish to express my gratitude to a tireless researcher from the 1970s, Robert S. Gallagher, of Plainfield, N.J., who contributed to the Bowdoin library the fruits of his preparation for a biography of Reed that he evidently didn't get around to writing.

To my mentor of so long ago at Indiana University, the historian Robert H. Ferrell, I owe a debt that, like some exploding modern home mortgage, only seems to grow with the passing years.

Notes

Chapter 1   "Oh happy Portlanders"

1. Samuel McCall, *The Life of Thomas Brackett Reed* (Boston: Houghton Miflin Company, 1914), 1.
2. H. Humphrey Read to Thomas Reed, Asher Hinds Collection, Houghton Library, Harvard University.
3. Lewiston *Journal*, July 27, 1901.
4. Constance Carolyn Murray, "Maine and the Growth of Urban Responsibility for Human Welfare, 1830–1860" (Ph.D. diss., Boston University, 1960), 76.
5. McCall, *Reed*, 9.
6. Murray, "Maine," 78.
7. Ibid., 82.
8. Ibid., 84.
9. John K. Moutlon, *The Portland Observatory: The Building, the Builder, the Maritime Scene* (Falmouth, ME, 1916) 85–86.
10. William Willis, *A History of Portland* (Portland: Bailey & Noyes, 1865), 729.
11. Anthony Trollope, *North America* (London: Dawsons, 1968), 1:43.
12. Neal Dow, *The Reminiscences of Neal Dow: Recollections of Eighty Years* (Portland: Evening Express Publishing, 1898), 175.
13. Murray, "Maine," 276.
14. William Hobart Hadley, *First Annual Report of the Minister at Large in Portland* (Portland: F. W. Nichols, 1850), 23.
15. Murray, "Maine," 100.
16. Ibid., 113.
17. Ibid., 192.
18. *Mayor's Report of the Financial Condition of Portland* (Portland: Carter, Gerrish & Co., 1854), 48.

19. John Todd, *John Todd: The Story of His Life Told Mainly by Himself* (New York: Harper, 1876), 142; cited in Murray, "Maine," 197.
20. Willis, *Portland*, 738.
21. Robert H. Babcock, "The Decline of Artisan Republicanism in Portland Maine" *New England Quarterly* vol. 63, no. 1 (March 1990), 120; Willis, *Portland*, 739.
22. Washington *Post*, September 6, 1895; William A. Robinson, Thomas B. Reed: *Parliamentarian* (New York: Dodd, Mead & Company, 1930), 3.
23. Edward H. Elwell, *Portland and Vicinity* (Portland: Greater Portland Landmarks, Inc., 1975), 17.
24. Ibid., 18.
25. Westbrook, Maine School Records, Maine Historical Society.
26. *Mayor's Report*, 44.
27. Thomas Brackkett Reed Diary, May 9, 1887. Thomas B. Reed Collection, George G. Mitchell Department of Special Collections & Archives, Bowdoin College Library. French portions of the diary translated by Nicole Rudolph.

Chapter 2 Acting Assistant Paymaster Reed

1. William Secrest, *California Disasters, 1812–1899* (Sanger, CA: Quill Driver Books, 2005), 93–102.
2. Thomas Reed, "California Essay." Thomas Reed Collection. Bowdoin College.
3. George H. Tinkham, *History of San Joaquin County, California* (Los Angeles: Historical Record Co., 1923), 225–26.
4. Thomas Reed, "California Essay." TBR Collection. Bowdoin College.
5. Sam Fessenden to William Pitt Fessenden, March 20, 1862. William Pitt Fessenden Collection, Bowdoin College.
6. Samuel McCall, *The Life of Thomas Brackett Reed* (Boston: Houghton Mifflin Company, 1914), 34.
7. Thomas Reed, "Speech in California." Asher Hinds Collection on Thomas B. Reed, Houghton Library, Harvard University.
8. Official Records of the Union and Confederate Navies in the War of the Rebellion (Washington, G.P.O. 1894–1922), Series II, Vol.1, 208.
9. Richard S. West Jr., *Mr. Lincoln's Navy* (New York: Longmans, Green, 1957), 60. Cited in James McPherson, *Battle Cry of Freedom* (New York: Oxford University Press, 1988), 358.
10. John D. Mulligan, *Gunboats Down the Mississippi* (Annapolis, MD: U.S. Naval Institute, 1965).
11. Michael Bennett, *Union Jacks: Yankee Sailors in the Civil War* (Chapel Hill: University of North Carolina Press, 2004), 80.
12. Sybil *Log*, December 14, 1864. National Archives.
13. George Williamson, *The White Refugees of Cairo: Their Condition, numbers and wants* (Cairo Relief Organization, 1864), 4.
14. Official Records of the Union and Confederate Navies, Series II, Vol.1, 208.

Chapter 3   "The atrocious crime of being a young man"

1. William A. Robinson, *Thomas B. Reed: Parliamentarian* (New York: Dodd, Mead & Company, 1930), 20.
2. *Rules and Regulations of the Cumberland Bar Association* (Portland: Printed by Stephen Berry, 1864).
3. Robinson, *Parliamentarian*, 25; Samuel McCall, *The Life of Thomas Brackett Reed* (Boston: Houghton Mifflin Company, 1914), 35.
4. Headline, *Kennebec Journal*, March 13, 1868.
5. Headline, *Kennebec Journal*, February 17, 1869.
6. Headline, *Kennebec Journal*, March 13, 1868.
7. Headline, *Kennebec Journal*, March 23, 1870.
8. Headline, *Kennebec Journal*, March 6, 1868.
9. Maine Legislative Records. Forty-Seventh Legislature, No. 126. (Augusta: Stevens & Sayward, February 29, 1868).
10. Headline, *Kennebec Journal*, March 13, 1869.
11. Portland *Daily Press*, February 25, 1869.
12. Portland *Daily Press*, March 4, 1869.
13. Portland *Daily Press*, February 26, 1869.
14. Ibid.
15. Reed to George Gifford, March 5, 1869. Thomas Reed Collection. Bowdoin College.
16. Robinson, *Parliamentarian*, 22–23.
17. Reed to Nathan Webb, January 16, 1869. Nathan Webb Papers. Maine Historical Society. Box 1, Series 2.
18. Reed to Nathan Webb, January 18, 1870. Nathan Webb Papers. Maine Historical Society. Box 1, Series 2.
19. Portland *Daily Press*, October 29, 1869.
20. Ibid.
21. Reed to Susan Reed, May 8, 1871 and May 10, 1871. TBR Collection. Bowdoin College.
22. Reed to George Gifford, May 12, 1872. TBR Collection. Bowdoin College.
23. *Portland Birth and Death Records*. Maine Historical Society.
24. Hendrick Hartog, "Lawyering: Husbands' Rights and the Unwritten Law, in Nineteenth-Century America," *Journal of American History*, June 1997, 79.
25. Hartog, "Lawyering," 88.
26. James Fallon to Nathan Webb, September 20, 1870. Webb Papers. Maine Historical Society; Portland Superior Court Records. Case No. 65. Maine State Archives, Augusta.
27. Kennebec *Journal*, December 7, 1870; December 14, 1870.
28. Kennebec *Journal*, December 14, 1870.
29. Reed's Closing Statements. *Kennebec Journal* Scrapbook. Maine Historical Society.

30. Ibid.
31. *Report of the Attorney General of the State of Maine*. Maine Historical Society (Augusta: Stevens and Sayward, 1872).
32. Ibid.

Chapter 4 With a Flap of the "bloody shirt"

1. "The Centennial Fourth," Portland *Daily Press*, July 6, 1876.
2. Chauncey Depew, "Fourth of July Ovation," in *Life and Later Speeches of Chauncy Depew* (New York: Cassell Publishing Company, 1894) 52.
3. Portland *Daily Press*, June 30, 1876; *Eastern Argus*, September 11, 1876; *Eastern Argus*, July 31, 1876; Reed scrapbook, Thomas Reed Collection, Bowdoin College.
4. Portland *Daily Press*, July 30, 1876.
5. Stephen Berry's Diary. Transcribed and organized by Earle G. Shettleworth, Maine State Historian.
6. Reed Scrapbook. TBR Collection. Bowdoin College.
7. Ibid.
8. Ibid.
9. Samuel Rezneck, "Distress, Relief, and Discontent in the United States during the Depression of 1873–1878," *Journal of Political Economy* vol. 61, no. 6 (December 1950), 494–512.
10. "The Veto Message," *New York Times*, April 23, 1874.
11. Rezneck, "Depression of 1873," 502.
12. Robert G. Ingersoll, *The Political Speeches of Robert G. Ingersoll* (New York: C. P. Farrell, 1914), 115.
13. "The National Campaign," New York *Times*, September 2, 1876, 1; Biography of John M. Goodwin, *Representative Men of Maine* (Portland, ME, 1893).
14. Eastern *Argus*, "Ingersoll, Blaine and Reed," September 5, 1876.
15. Stephen Berry Diary.

Chapter 5 "Make it out of paper"

1. Frank Richardson Kent, *The Democratic Party* (New York: The Century Co., 1928), 251–52.
2. Eric Foner, *Reconstruction: America's Unfinished Revolution* (New York: Harper & Row, 1988), 575.
3. Roy Morris Jr., *Fraud of the Century* (New York: Simon & Schuster, 2003), 176.
4. Ibid., 171.
5. Ibid., 174.
6. Ibid., 227–28.
7. Ibid., 137.
8. Ibid., 171.

9. Ibid., 197.

10. Ibid., 199.

11. Ibid., 206.

12. Ibid., 214.

13. Richard Stanley Offenburg, "The Political Career of Thomas Brackett Reed" (Ph.D. dissertation, New York University, 1963), 22.

14. Investigation by a Select Committee of the House of Representatives Relative to the Causes of the General Depression in Labor and Business. 45th Congress, 3rd Session. Misc. doc. 29 (Washington: GPO, 1879), 565.

15. General Depression, 92.

16. Ibid., 106, 110.

17. Ibid., 14.

18. Ibid., 153.

19. Ibid., 455.

20. Investigation by a Select Committee of the House of Representatives Relative to the Causes of the General Depression in Labor and Business, and as to Chinese Immigration. 46th Congress, 2nd Session. Misc. doc. 5 (Washington: GPO, 1879), 242; 247–48.

21. General Depression, 45th Congress, 182–83.

22. Ibid., 66.

23. Carl R. Osthaus, *Freedmen, Philanthropy and Fraud* (Urbana; University of Illinois Press, 1976), 10.

24. Milton Friedman and Anna Schwartz, *A Monetary History of the United States* (Princeton, NJ: Princeton University Press, 1971), 76.

25. Osthaus, *Freedmen*, 55.

26. Burea of the Census, *Historical Statistics of the United States* (New York: Basic Books, 1976), 1038.

27. Osthaus, *Freedmen*, 145.

28. Ibid., 199; 176.

29. Ibid., 168.

30. Ibid., 197.

31. Ibid., 213.

32. Ibid., 214–18.

33. Bangor *Whig and Courier*, January 3, 1877.

34. Maine *Farmer*, September 8, 1877.

35. Stephen Berry Diary, transcribed and edited by Earle G. Shettleworth.

Chapter 6 The Freshman Makes His Mark

1. Joseph West Moore, *Picturesque Washington* (New York: Hurst, 1884), 120.

2. James Blaine, *Eulogy on James Abram Garfield* (Boston: J. R. Osgood, 1882).

3. Congressional Directory. 45th Congress. First Session (Washington: GPO, 1877).

4. Moore, *Picturesque Washington*, 126.

5. Robert Bruce, *1877: The Year of Violence* (Indianapolis, IN: Bobbs-Merrill), 294.

6. Frank Carpenter, *Carp's Washington* (New York: McGraw-Hill, 1960), 13.

7. Moore, *Picturesque Washington*, 126.

8. Annual Report of the Board of Health of the District of Columbia (Washington, GPO, 1878), 43, 9–10, 7, 26

9. Ibid., 3–5.

10. Fourth Annual Report of the Commissioners of the District of Columbia (Washington: GPO, 1877), 187.

11. Ibid., 185–86.

12. Ibid., 118.

13. Board of Health, 65.

14. Commissioners, 132–33.

15. Ibid., 193, 234.

16. Ibid., 203.

17. Congressional Record. 45th Congress. 1st Session. 717.

18. C.R. 45/2. 470–71.

19. Ibid., 278.

20. Ibid., 1733.

21. Ibid., 1733–34.

22. Ibid., 1222.

23. New York *Times*, April 13, 1878.

24. C.R. 45/2. 2488.

25. Ibid.

26. Ibid., 2489.

27. Ibid., 2490.

28. Ibid.

29. New York *Times*, May 18, 1878.

30. Ibid.

31. Ibid.

32. New York *Times*, May 21, 1878.

Chapter 7 *"Before God and my country"*

1. Testimony Taken by the Select Committee on Alleged Frauds in the Presidential Election of 1876. House Misc. Doc. 31, Part 1, 45th Congress, 3rd Session (Washington: GPO, 1879), 1:16.

2. "Growing Demoralization," New York *Tribune*, May 23, 1878.

3. Testimony, 48–49.

4. Testimony, 1:50.

5. "The Potter-Butler Farce," Chicago *Daily Tribune*, July 5, 1877.

6. Chicago *Daily Tribune*, July 22, 1878.

7. Washington *Post*, July 18, 1878, 2.

8. New York *Tribune*, October 7, 1878.

9. "The Week," *Nation* vol. 27, issue 695 (October 24, 1878).

10. Washington *Post*, December 26, 1878, 1.

11. Election Investigation Testimony, 4:128.

12. Ibid.

13. Ibid., 4:133.

14. Ibid.

15. Ibid., 4:139.

16. Ibid., 4:142.

17. Ibid., 4:197.

18. Ibid., 4:198.

19. Ibid., 4:202.

20. Ibid., 4:203.

21. Ibid., 4:221.

22. Ibid., 4:229.

23. Ibid., 4:234.

24. Ibid., 4:237.

25. Ibid., 4:238.

26. Ibid., 4:247.

27. Ibid., 4:249.

28. Ibid., 4:258.

29. Ibid., 4:266.

30. "Marble's Florida Work," New York *Times*, February 8 1879, 1.

31. John Bigelow, *Life of Samuel J. Tilden* (New York: Harper Brothers, 1895), 2:181.

32. Ibid., 2:168.

33. Ibid., 2:186.

34. Election Investigation Testimony, 4:279.

35. Ibid., 4:280.

36. Ibid., 4:285.

37. Bigelow, *Samuel Tilden*, 2:181.

38. Election Investigation Testimony, 4:286.

39. Ibid., 4:189.

40. Investigation of Alleged Electoral Frauds in the Late Presidential Election, "Committee Report No. 140." 45th Congress, 3rd Session. House of Representatives (Washington: G.P.O., 1879), 102.

41. Ibid., 74.

42. "The Week," *Nation*, March 6, 1879.

Chapter 8 Battling Heresies

1. New York *Times*, August 4, 1878; Eastern *Argus*, August 3, 1878.

2. Eastern *Argus*, August 6, 1878.

3. *Nation*, September 23, 1875.

4. J. H. Randall, *The Political Catechism and Greenback Songbook* (Washington, D.C.: Rufus H. Darby, 1880).

5. New York *Times*, May 6, 1878.

6. Milton Friedman, "The Crime of 1873," *Journal of Political Economy* (December 1990), 1161.
7. Ibid.
8. Wesley Clair Mitchell, *A History of the Greenbacks* (Chicago: The University of Chicago Press, 1903), 41.
9. Ibid., 47.
10. Roscoe Conkling, *The Life and Letters of Roscoe Conkling* (C. L. Webster and Company, 1889), 155.
11. Mitchell, *Greenbacks*, 46.
12. Ibid., 155.
13. Ibid., 55.
14. Ibid., 68.
15. Ibid., 53.
16. Ibid., 56.
17. Ibid., 57–58.
18. Ibid., 59.
19. Conkling, *Life and Letters*, 160.
20. Barton A. Hepburn, *History of Coinage and Currency in the United States* (New York: MacMillan and Co., 1903), 190.
21. Hepburn, *Coinage and Currency*, 183.
22. Ibid., 191.
23. Mitchell, *Greenbacks*, 185.
24. Ibid., 229–30.
25. Ibid., 234.
26. Ibid., 263.
27. Ibid., 397–98.
28. Ibid., 395.
29. Hepburn, *Coinage and Currency*, 208.
30. Ibid., 207.
31. A. T. Huntington and Robert J. Mawhinney, eds. *Laws of The United States Concerning Money, Banking and Loans, 1778–1909* (Washington, G.P.O., 1910).
32. Hepburn, *Coinage and Currency*, 212.
33. Ibid., 213.
34. Money and Banking Laws, 202.
35. Hepburn, *Coinage and Currency*, 215–16.
36. Allen Weinstein, *Prelude to Populism* (New Haven CN: Yale University Press, 1970), 9.
37. Ibid., 10.
38. Irwin Unger, *The Greenback Era* (Princeton, NJ: Princeton University Press, 1964), 331.
39. Weinstein, *Prelude to Populism*, 22.
40. New York *Times*, "The Financial Issue," Aug. 4, 1878.
41. William A. Robinson, *Thomas B. Reed: Parliamentarian* (New York: Dodd, Mead & Company, 1930), 57.
42. Ibid., 58.
43. Eastern *Argus*, August 2, 1878.

44. Bangor *Whig and Courier*, July 30, 1880.
45. Robinson, *Parliamentarian*, 59.

Chapter 9 Maine's Disgrace

1. Richard Stanley Offenburg, "The Political Career of Thomas Brockett Reed" (Ph.D. dissertation, New York University, 1963), 44.
2. Bangor *Whig and Courier*, November 11, 1878.
3. John Sherman, *Recollections of Forty Years in the House, Senate and Cabinet* (Chicago: Werner, 1895), 650.
4. Hartford *Daily Courant*, January 4, 1879.
5. Ibid.
6. Sherman, *Recollections*, 704.
7. Hartford *Daily Courant*, January 3, 1879.
8. Bangor *Whig and Courier*, June 4, 1879.
9. Louis Clinton Hatch, *Maine: A History* (New York: The American Historical Society, 1919), 595–96.
10. Hatch, *Maine*, 596.
11. Ibid., 598.
12. Ibid.
13. Bangor *Whig and Courier*, September 11, 1879.
14. Hatch, *Maine*, 600.
15. Report of the Joint Select Committee to Inquire into Election Returns of September 8, 1879 (Augusta: Sprague & Son, 1880).
16. Ibid., 18.
17. John C. Abbott and Edward H. Elwell, *The History of Maine* (Portland, ME: Brown, Thurston Company, 1892), 562.
18. Chicago *Tribune*, December 17, 1879.
19. Hatch, *Maine*, 602, 604.
20. Ibid., 605.
21. Election Returns, 32.
22. Abbot and Elwell, *History of Maine*, 563.
23. Hatch, *Maine*, 615.
24. C.R. 46/1 257.
25. C.R. 46/1. 1131.
26. Ibid., 113.
27. Ibid., 114.
28. Ari Hoogenboom and Olive Hoogenboom, eds., *The Gilded Age* (Englewood Cliffs, NJ: Prentice-Hall, 1967), 39.
29. C.R. 46/1 1572–1573.
30. Ibid., 1226.
31. Ibid., 1227.
32. Ibid., 1233.
33. Ibid., 1233.
34. C.R. 46/2 575.
35. Ibid., 575–78.

36. Ibid., 578.
37. Ibid., 2417.
38. Ibid., 3306.
39. Ibid., 2361.
40. Ibid., 2660.
41. Ibid.
42. Ibid., 2661.
43. Ellis Paxson Oberholtzer, A History of the United States Since the Civil War (New York: MacMillan, 1917–1937), 4:69.
44. Thomas Collier Platt, Autobiography (New York: B. W. Dodge and Company, 1910), 106, 110.
45. Oberholtzer, History of the United States, 4:71–72.
46. Platt, Autobiography, xix.
47. Platt, Autobiography, 86.
48. Oberholtzer, History of the United States, 4:85; Nation, June 17, 1880.
49. Bangor Whig and Courier, August, 13, 1880.
50. Portland Daily Press, July 17, 1880.
51. Ibid., July 9, 1880.
52. Bangor Whig and Courier, August 30, 1880.

Chapter 10 For Want of a Quorum

1. Reed to George Gifford, March 31, 1882, Thomas Reed Collection. Bowdoin College.
2. Reed to Hannibal Hamlin, July 4, 1881. Hannibal Hamlin Papers. Library of Congress.
3. Reed to Gifford, November 7, 1881. TBR Collection. Bowdoin College.
4. Herbert Bruce Fuller, The Speakers of the House (Boston: Little Brown and Company, 1909), 207.
5. C.R. 47/1 9.
6. Ibid. 2081–95.
7. John Morley, The Life of William Ewart Gladstone (New York: MacMillan Company, 1911), 56.
8. London Times, February 4, 1881.
9. David Herbert Donald, Lincoln (New York: Simon and Schuster, 1995), 77.
10. Testimony in the Contested Election Case of Samuel J. Anderson vs. Thomas B. Reed. 47th Congress, 1st Session. Misc. doc. No. 13 (Washington, G.P.O., 1881), 264.
11. Richard Stanley Offenburg, "The Political Career of Thomas Brackett Reed" (Ph.D. dissertation, New York University, 1963), 63.
12. Walter J. Oleszek, "A Pre-20th Century Look at the House Committee on Rules," U.S. House of Representatives, Committee on Rules (December 1998), 8.
13. Orland Oscar Stealy, Twenty Years in the Press Gallery (New York: Publishers Printing Company, 1906), 402–403.
14. C.R. 47/1 4307.

15. Ibid., 4313.
16. Ibid., 4223.
17. Washington *Post*, May 30, 1882.

Chapter 11 Progress Stops in Washington

1. Garet Garrett, *The American Story* (Chicago: H. Regenery Co., 1955), 136.
2. Report of the Commission of Labor. 48th Congress, 1st Sess. Ex. Doc. 1, part 5 (Washington: G.P.O, 1885), 5:82.
3. Ibid., 5:82.
4. Ibid., 5:84.
5. Ibid., 5:85.
6. Reed to George Gifford, December 30, 1882. Thomas Reed Collection. Bowdoin College.
7. David Ames Wells, *Recent Economic Changes* (New York: D. Appleton and Company, 1899), 349–50.
8. Ibid., 349.
9. Mark Twain, *Notebook*, ed. by Albert Paine (New York: Harper & Bros., 1935), 165.
10. Ibid., 172.
11. C.R. 47/2 1363.
12. Ibid., 2442–43.
13. Ibid., 221.
14. Ibid., 1112.
15. Frank William Taussig, *The Tariff History of the United States* (New York: G. P. Putnam's Sons, 1914), 157.
16. Ida Tarbell, *The Tariff in Our Times* (New York: The MacMillan Company, 1914), 3–5.
17. *Grant's Interest Rate Observer*. October 16, 2009.
18. Tausig, *Tariff History*, 164–67.
19. Tarbell, *Tariff in Our Times*, 27.
20. Ibid.
21. Frederic Bastiat, *Economic Sophisms*, trans. by Arthur Goddard (Princeton, NJ: D. Van Nostrand Press, 1964), 58.
22. Tarbell, *Tariff in Our Times*, 99.
23. Ibid., 107.
24. Ibid., 109.
25. C.R., 47/2 2043.
26. Ibid., 2054–55.
27. Tarbell, *Tariff in Our Times*, 112.
28. CR. 47/2 2660.
29. Ibid., 2055.
30. Ibid., 2582.
31. Ibid., 3348.
32. Washington *Post*, February 27, 1883; New York *Times*, February 27, 1883.
33. Taussig, *Tariff History*, 233.

34. Tarbell, *Tariff in Our Times*, 130.
35. Ibid., 130–31.
36. Reed Diary, 1882. Sharon Coop, Reed's great granddaughter, kindly made this portion of the diary available.

Chapter 12 Votes for Women

1. Elizabeth Cady Stanton, Susan B. Anthony, Matilda Joslyn Gage and Ida Husted Harper eds., *History of Woman Suffrage* (New York: Fowler & Wells, 1881–1922) 4:14.
2. Ibid., 4:18.
3. Ibid., 4:12.
4. Julia Foraker, *I Would Live It Again* (New York: Arno Press, 1932), 41.
5. "The Declaration of Sentiments," Seneca Falls Convention, 1848. Modern History Sourcebook.
6. Frank G. Carpenter, *Carp's Washington* (New York: McGraw-Hill, 1960), 229.
7. House of Representatives. Report on Women's Suffrage. 46th Congress, 2nd Session. Misc. Doc. 20 (Washington, GPO, 1880), 3.
8. *Minor v. Happersett*, 88 U.S. 162.
9. Stanton et al., *Woman Suffrage*, 4:31.
10. Samuel McCall, *The Life of Thomas Brackett Reed* (Boston: Houghton Mifflin Company, 1914), 78
11. C.R. 48/2 316.
12. C.R. 48/2 317.
13. Melanie Susan Gustafson, *Women and the Republican Party* (Urbana: University of Illinois Press, 2001), 56.
14. Ibid., 53–54.
15. House of Representatives, "Woman Suffrage—Arguments before the Committee on the Judiciary," 46th Congress, Misc. Doc. No. 20 (Washington: G.P.O, 1880), 4.
16. Ibid., 6.
17. Ibid., 7–8.
18. Ibid., 22.
19. Reed to George Gifford, April 23, 1884. Thomas Reed Collection. Bowdoin College.
20. Reed to Susan B. Anthony, December 11, 1891; May 26, 1894. Susan B. Anthony Collection. Huntington Library.
21. Eastern *Argus*, February 22, 1887.

Chapter 13 "Monumental liar from the state of Maine"

1. Reed to George Gifford, December 30, 1882. Thomas Reed Collection. Bowdoin College.
2. Arthur Wallace Dunn, *From Harrison to Harding* (New York: G. P. Putnam's Sons, 1922), 5; Samuel McCall, *The Life of Thomas Brackett Reed* (Boston: Houghton Mifflin Company, 1914), 161.

3. McCall, *Reed*, 128.
4. Reed to Gifford, March 31, 1882. TBR Collection. Bowdoin College.
5. David Saville Muzzey, *James G. Blaine* (New York: Dodd, Mead & Company, 1934), 259–60.
6. Reed to a young friend, December 3, 1877. Asher Hinds Collection. Houghton Library. Harvard University.
7. National Bureau of Economic Research, "Business Cycle Expansions and Contractions."
8. New York *Times*, August 6, 1884.
9. Muzzey, *Blaine*, 263.
10. Reed to Gifford, March 31, 1882. TBR Collection. Bowdoin College.
11. Robert McNutt McElroy, *Grover Cleveland* (New York: Harper & Brothers, 1923), 21, 36.
12. Ibid., 20.
13. U.S. Grant to Commodore Daniel Ammen, *The Papers of Ulysses S. Grant*, John Y. Simon, ed. (Carbondale: Southern Illinois University Press, 2005), 28:251.
14. McElroy, *Cleveland*, 87.
15. Ibid., 33.
16. Ibid., 41.
17. Ibid., 48.
18. Ibid., 63–64.
19. Ibid., 53–54.
20. William A. Robinson, *Thomas B. Reed: Parliamentarian* (New York: Dodd, Mead & Company, 1930), 97.
21. Reed to Gifford, December 30, 1882. TBR Collection. Bowdoin College.
22. Reed Diary, November 20, 1886.
23. Reed to Henry L. Chapman, February 8, 1884. TBR Collection. Bowdoin College.
24. Boston *Daily Globe*, August 23, 1884.
25. New York *Times*, August 6, 1884.
26. Washington *Post*, August 27, 1884.
27. Ellis Paxson Oberholtzer, *A History of the United States Since the Civil War* (New York: MacMillan, 1917), 4:412.
28. Ibid., 4:387.
29. Ibid., 4:415.
30. "Report of the Committee of the Senate upon the relations between Labor and Capital and Testimony," 5 vols. (Washington: G.P.O., 1885), 2:1044.
31. "Report and Testimony," 271.
32. Ibid., 104.
33. Ibid., 1100.
34. Allan Nevins, *Grover Cleveland* (New York: Dodd, Mead & Company, 1933), 183.
35. "Report and Testimony," 1067.
36. Ibid., 1068.
37. Ibid., 1084.
38. Ibid., 1085.

39. Ibid., 1085–94.
40. Muzzey, *Blaine*, 75.
41. Ibid., 72.
42. Ibid., 83.
43. Ibid., 79, 81.
44. Ibid., 97.
45. Reed to George Gifford, December 30, 1882. Thomas Reed Collection. Bowdoin College.
46. Robinson, *Parliamentarian*, 97–98.
47. C.R. 48/1, 2049.
48. Reed letter, March 29, 1884. Asher Hinds Collection, Houghton Library, Harvard University.
49. Muzzey, *Blaine*, 233.
50. Reed to George Gifford, March 31, 1882. TBR Collection. Bowdoin College.
51. Reed to Andrew Hawes, June 15, 1884. TBR Collection. Bowdoin College.
52. Robinson, *Parliamentarian*, 111, 109.
53. Ibid., 113.
54. Ibid., 115.
55. Muzzey, *Blaine*, 284.
56. New York *Tribune*, June 6, 1884. Cited in Muzzey, *Blaine*, 282.
57. Julia Foraker, *I Would Live It Again* (New York: Arno Press, 1932), 79.
58. Muzzey, *Blaine*, 294.
59. Frank Richardson Kent, *The Democratic Party* (New York: The Century Co., 1928), 285.
60. Muzzey, *Blaine*, 61.
61. Carl Schurz, *Speeches, Correspondence and Political Papers of Carl Shurz*, ed. by Frederick Bancroft (New York: G. P. Putnam's Sons, 1913), 4:224–25.
62. H. Wayne Morgan, *From Hayes to McKinley: National Party Politics, 1877–1896* (Syracuse, NY: Syracuse University Press, 1969), 215.
63. Muzzey, *Blaine*, 314.
64. Abram S. Hewitt to Reed, September 9, 1884. Asher Hinds Collection. Houghton Library. Harvard University.
65. Muzzey, *Blaine*, 314.
66. Muzzey, *Blaine*, 316–19.
67. Nevins, *Cleveland*, 180.
68. Paul H. Jeffers, *An Honest President* (New York: W. Morrow, 2000), 120.
69. Nevins, *Cleveland*, 186–87.
70. C.R., 48/2 2308.

Chapter 14 Champion of Protection

1. Reed Diary, October 4, 1885.
2. Reed Diary, July 22, 1886.
3. Reed Diary, April 18, 1885.
4. Reed Diary, November 20, 1887.

5. Reed Diary, January 12, 1888.

6. Reed Diary, January 12, 1888.

7. Reed to his attorney (undated). Asher Hinds Collection. Houghton Library, Harvard University.

8. Reed's Attorney to Reed (undated). Asher Hinds Collection. Houghton Library. Harvard University.

9. Reed Diary, February 6, 1886.

10. Reed Diary, January 23, 1888.

11. Reed Diary, September 14, 1883.

12. Samuel McCall, *The Life of Thomas Brachett Reed* (Boston: Houghton Mifflin Company, 1914), 147–48.

13. Reed Diary, March 14, 1886.

14. Reed Diary, Oct. 3, 1886.

15. Reed Diary, April 29, 1886.

16. Reed Diary, Dec. 27, 1886.

17. Reed to George Gifford, April 6, 1886. Thomas Reed Collection. Bowdoin College.

18. William A. Robinson, *Thomas B. Reed: Parliamentarian* (New York: Dodd, Mead & Company, 1930), 119; Reed to Gifford. December 14, 1885. TBR Collection.

19. Reed Diary, April 11, 1886.

20. C.R. 49th Congress, First Session, 3393.

21. Ibid., 3393.

22. Ibid., 3394.

23. Reed Diary, March 19, 1886.

24. C.R. 49/1 3395.

25. McCall, *Thomas Reed*, 24.

26. Reed Diary, November 17, 1887; H.C. Dunham to Reed, July 13, 1886; Reed to Dunham, July 15, 1886. TBR Collection. Bowdoin College.

27. New York *Times*, August 25, 1886.

28. Bangor *Whig and Courier*, August 25, 1886.

29. New York *Times*, September 8, 1886.

30. Congressional Directory, 50th Congress (Washington: GPO, 1888).

31. Reed Diary, October 3, 1886.

32. Reed to George Gifford, October 6, 1886. TBR Collection. Bowdoin College.

33. Murray Rothbard, *A History of Money and Banking in the United States* (Auburn, AL: Ludwig von Mises Institute, 2002), 161.

34. Robert McNutt McElroy, *Grover Cleveland* (New York: Harper & Brothers, 1923), 109–110.

35. National Bureau of Economic Research, "Business Cycle Expansions and Contractions."

36. James Anderson Barnes, *John G. Carlisle: Financial Statesman* (New York: Dodd, Mead and Company, 1967), 138.

37. Davis Rich Dewey, *Financial History of the United States* (New York: Longmans, Green, and Co., 1915), 429.

38. C.R. 50th Congress, First Session, 4447.

39. Grover Cleveland, *Speeches and Writings of Grover Cleveland* (New York: Cassell Publishing Company, 1892), 76.

40. Ibid., 78.

41. Dewey, *Financial History*, 426, 429.

42. Rothbard, *Money and Banking*, 162.

43. Cleveland, *Speeches and Writings*, 80.

44. Ibid., 86.

45. Ida Tarbell, *The Tariff in Our Times* (New York: The MacMillan Company, 1914), 154.

46. Barnes, *Carlisle*, 122–23.

47. Ibid., 128.

48. C.R. 50/1. 80–81.

49. Reed Diary, December 20, 1887.

50. Barnes, *Carlisle*, 132.

51. Tarbell, *Tariff in Our Times*, 155.

52. Ibid., 159.

53. Barnes, *Carlisle*, 132.

54. Allan Nevins, *Grover Cleveland* (New York: Dodd, Mead & Company, 1933), 390.

55. Tarbell, *Tariff in Our Times*, 160–62.

56. Reed Diary, December 15, 1887.

57. Reed Diary, May 4, 1888.

58. Orland Oscar Stealey, *Twenty Years in the Press Gallery* (New York: Publishing Printing Company, 1906), 59.

59. Reed Diary, 1888.

60. Reed Diary, June 4, 1888.

Chapter 15 Great Plains Land Bubble

1. Reed Diary, May 2, 1887.

2. H. Wayne Morgan, *From Hayes to McKinley: National Party Politics, 1877–1896* (Syracuse, NY: Syracuse University Press, Syracuse 1969), 282.

3. Ibid., 281.

4. Ibid.

5. Reed Diary, August 22, 1887.

6. Reed Diary, October 8, 1887.

7. Reed Diary, November 12, 1887.

8. Morgan, *Hayes to McKinley*, 291.

9. Ibid., 295.

10. Ibid., 298.

11. C.R. 50/1 6536.

12. John D. Hicks, *The Populist Revolt* (Minneapolis: The University of Minnesota Press, 1931), 26.

13. George K. Holmes, "A Decade of Mortgages," *Annals of the American Academy of Political and Social Science* vol. 4 (May 1894), 54.

14. James Grant, *Mister Market Miscalculates* (Mount Jackson, VA: Axios Press, 2008), 148.

15. Hicks, *Populist Revolt*, 21.

16. Hallie Farmer, "The Economic Background of Frontier Populism," *Mississippi Valley Historical Review* vol. 10, no. 4 (March 1924), 411.

17. Ibid., 412.

18. Robert Glass Cleland and Frank B. Putnam, *Isaias W. Hallman and the Farmers and Merchants Bank* (San Marino, CA: Huntington Library, 1980), 50.

19. Farmer, "Frontier Populism," 415.

20. Cleland and Putnam, *Isaias Hallman*, 53.

21. Grant, *Mr. Market*, 151.

22. Cited in Grant, *Mr. Market*, 152.

23. Raymond C. Miller, "The Background of Populism in Kansas," *Mississippi Valley Historical Review* vol. 11, no. 4 (March 1925), 478.

24. Cited in Grant, *Mr. Market*, 153.

25. Julia Foraker, *I Would Live It Again* (New York: Arno Press, 1932), 133.

26. Allan Nevins, *Grover Cleveland* (New York: Dodd, Mead & Company, 1933), 434.

27. Ibid., 333.

28. Ibid., 429–31.

29. Chicago Daily *Tribune*, September 7, 1888.

30. Congressional Directory, 50th Congress.

31. Reed Diary, 1888.

32. Nevins, *Cleveland*, 439.

33. H. Wayne Morgan, *From Hayes to McKinley: National Party Politics, 1877–1896* (Syracuse, NY: Syracuse University Press, 1969), 326.

34. William A. Robinson, *Thomas B. Reed: Parliamentarian* (New York: Dodd, Mead & Company, 1930), 182.

35. Robinson, *Parliamentarian*, 183.

36. C.R. 50/1 2722.

37. Robinson, *Parliamentarian*, 184.

38. Thomas B. Reed, "Obstructionists in the House," *North American Review*, October 1889.

39. Ibid.

40. Roger Q. Mills, "Republican Tactics in the House," *North American Review*, December 1889.

41. Ibid.

Chapter 16 To Count a Quorum

1. Reed to Theodore Roosevelt, November, 27, 1888. Theodore Roosevelt Papers. Library of Congress.

2. Reed Diary, April 19, 1889.

3. Reed Diary, February 4, 1887.

4. Reed Diary, January 21, 1889.

5. Reed Diary, February 1889.
6. Reed Diary, January 27, 1889.
7. Reed Diary, January 3, 1889, January 5, 1889.
8. H. Wayne Morgan, *William McKinley and His America* (Syracuse, NY: Syracuse University Press, 1963), 241.
9. Ibid., 21–25.
10. Eric Rauchway, *Murdering McKinley* (New York: Hill and Wang, 2003), 154.
11. Thomas Beer, *Hanna* (New York: Alfred A. Knopf, 1929), 110.
12. Rauchway, *Murdering McKinley*, 153.
13. Reed Diary, February 2, 1889.
14. Reed Diary, January 26, 1889.
15. New York *Times*, December 1, 1889.
16. Mary Parker Follett, *The Speaker of the House of Representatives* (New York: Longmans, Green, and Co., 1896), 112.
17. Ibid., 125.
18. Washington *Post*, December 3, 1889.
19. H. Wayne Morgan, *From Hayes to McKinley: National Party Politics, 1877–1896* (Syracuse, NY: Syracuse University Press, 1969), 333.
20. Washington *Post*, December 3, 1889.
21. Text of President Harrison's message cited in Washington *Post*, December 4, 1889.
22. Morgan, *Hayes to McKinley*, 331.
23. William H. Robinson, *Thomas B. Reed: Parliamentarian* (New York: Dodd, Mead & Company, 1930), 199.
24. Thomas B. Reed, *Reed's Rules* (New York: Rand, McNally and Co., 1894), 213.
25. Washington *Post*, December 3, 1889.
26. Reed to Andrew Hawes, December 9, 1889. TBR Collection. Bowdoin College.
27. Orland Oscar Stealey, *Twenty Years in the Press Gallery* (New York: Dodd, Mead & Company, 1930), 217.
28. C.R. 51/1 433.
29. Ibid. 741.
30. C.R. 51/1. 433–43.
31. Thomas B. Reed, "Contested Election Cases" *North American Review* (July 1890), 114.
32. C.R. 50/1 3491.
33. Reed Diary, April 24, 1888.
34. C.R. 51/1 948–54.
35. Washington *Post*, January 30, 1890.
36. Washington *Post*, January 30, 1890.
37. C.R. 51/1 pg. 977.
38. Washington *Post*, January 31, 1890; C.R. 51/1 974–995.
39. C.R. 51/1 996–1000.
40. Henry St. George Tucker, *Reminiscences*. Tucker Papers, Southern History Collection, University of North Carolina.

41. Ibid.
42. C.R. 51/1 1001.

Chapter 17 "I hope my enemies are satisfied"

1. Thomas B. Reed, *Reed's Rules* (New York: Reed, McNally and Co., 1894), 213.
2. William A. Robinson, *Thomas B. Reed: Parliamentarian* (New York: Dodd, Mead & Company, 1930), 223.
3. C.R. 51/1 1107.
4. House Report No. 23, 51st Congress, First Session; C.R. 51/1 1173.
5. James A. Barnes, *John G. Carlisle: Financial Statesman* (New York: Dodd, Mead & Company, 1967), 152.
6. C.R. 51/1. 1172.
7. C.R. 51/1. 1180.
8. Ibid., 1186.
9. Orland Oscar Stealey, *Twenty Years in the Press Gallery* (New York: Publishers Printing Company, 1906), 319–20.
10. C.R. 51/1. 1210.
11. C.R. 51/1. 1210–1213.
12. C.R. 51/1. 1237.
13. C.R. 51/1. 1236.
14. H. Wayne Morgan, *From Hayes to McKinley: National Party Politics, 1877–1896* (Syracuse, NY: Syracuse University Press, 1969), 331.
15. Fred Wellborn, "The Influence of Silver-Republicans," *Mississippi Valley Historical Review* vol. 14, no. 6 (December 1939), 463.
16. Report of the Director of the Mint, 1897, p. 43.
17. Milton Friedman, "The Crime of 1873," *Journal of Political Economy* (December 1990), 1168.
18. J. Laurence Laughlin, *A History of Bimetallism in the United States, 1896* (New York: Appleton, 1900), 168–69.
19. Ida Tarbell, *The Tariff in Our Times* (New York: The MacMillan Company, 1914), 188.
20. New York *Times*, October 21, 1890.
21. Tarbell, *Tariff in Our Times*, 197.
22. Ibid., 202.
23. William A. Robinson, *Thomas B. Reed: Parliamentarian* (New York: Dodd, Mead & Company, 1930), 237.
24. Thomas B. Reed, "The Federal Control of Elections," *North American Review*, June 1890.
25. Morgan, *Hayes to McKinley*, 341.
26. Arthur Walker Dunn, *From Harrison to Harding* (New York: G. P. Putnam's Sons, 1922), 33.
27. Thomas Adams Upchurch, *Legislating Racism* (Lexington: The University of Kentucky, 2004), 99.

28. C.R. 51/1. 6772.
29. Upchurch, *Legislating Racism*, 105.
30. Ibid., 147.
31. Ibid., 156.
32. Morgan, *Hayes to McKinley*, 342.
33. New York *Times*, July 7, 1890.
34. Robinson, *Parliamentarian*, 243.
35. Wellborn, "Silver-Republicans," 470.
36. Washington *Post*, June 20, 1890.
37. Washington *Post*, June 22, 1890.
38. Allan Nevins, *Grover Cleveland* (New York: Dodd, Mead & Company, 1933), 468.
39. *Wall Street Journal*, June 24, 1890.
40. Davis Rich Dewey, *Financial History of the United States* (New York: Longmans, Green, and Co., 1915), 442.
41. Milton Friedman and Anna Schwartz, A Monetary History of the United States (Princeton, NJ: Princeton University Press, 1971), 132.
42. Wellborn, "Silver-Republicans," 468.
43. Dunn, *Harrison to Harding*, 38.
44. Samuel McCall, *The Life of Thomas Brackett Reed* (Boston: Houghton Mifflin Company, 1914), 178.
45. Bangor *Whig and Courier*, September 9, 1890.
46. Boston *Globe*, September 9, 1890.
47. Chicago *Tribune*, November 11, 1890.
48. McCall, *Reed*, 180.
49. Chicago *Tribune*, August 28, 1890.
50. Robinson, *Parliamentarian*, 241.
51. Cited in Washington *Post*, March 29, 1891.
52. Reed to George Gifford. Thomas Reed Collection. Bowdoin College. Translated from French by Kate Deimling.

Chapter 18 For the Gold Standard

1. Dorsey to Reed, August 14, 1891. Thomas Reed Collection. Bowdoin College.
2. Ibid., October 6, 1892.
3. John D. Hicks, *The Populist Revolt* (Minneapolis: The University of Minnesota Press, 1931), 263–67.
4. H. Wayne Morgan, *From Hayes to McKinley*: National Party Politics, 1877–1896 (Syracuse, NY: Syracuse University Press, 1969), 427–28; James Fords Rhodes, *History of the United States* (New York: Macmillan, 1892–1906), 8:385–88.
5. President Cleveland Repeal Message, August 8, 1893.
6. H. Wayne Morgan, *William McKinley and His America* (Syracuse, NY: Syracuse University Press, 1963), 119.
7. Quoted in *Nation*, August 27, 1891.

8. Alonzo Barton Hepburn, *A History of Coinage and the Currency of the United States* (New York: MacMillan, 1903), 344.

9. Eastern *Argus*, February 24, 1887.

10. David Saville Muzzey, *James G. Blaine* (New York: Dodd, Mead & Company, 1934), 479.

11. Richard Stanley Offenburg, "The Political Career of Thomas Brackett Reed" (Ph.D. dissertation, New York University, 1963), 128.

12. Muzzey, *Blaine*, 490.

13. Reed to Stanley Pullen, February 5, 1893. Stanley Pullen Papers. Maine Historical Society, Portland.

14. C.R. 52/2. 2614.

15. James Anderson Barnes, *John G. Carlisle: Financial Statesman* (New York: Dodd, Mead and Company, 1967), 35.

16. Ibid., 205.

17. Ibid., 202.

18. Robert McNutt McElroy, *Grover Cleveland* (New York: Harper & Brothers, 1923), 2:22.

19. Barnes, *Carlisle*, 235.

20. Ibid., 236–37.

21. McCartney to Reed, May 4, 1893; Elmus Wicker, *Banking Panics of the Gilded Age* (New York: Cambridge University Press, 2000), 59.

22. Populist Platform, 1892.

23. Hepburn, *Coinage and Currency*,

24. Alexander Dana Noyes, *The Marketplace* (Boston: Little, Brown and Company, 1938), 109–110.

25. Hepburn, *Coinage and Currency*, 352.

26. McElroy, *Cleveland*, 2:28.

27. William A. Robinson, *Thomas B. Reed: Parliamentarian* (New York: Dodd, Mead & Company, 1930), 287.

28. Ibid., 295.

29. Barnes, *Carlisle*, 267–68.

30. Ibid., 262.

31. Washington *Post*, August 27, 1893.

32. Ibid.

33. C.R. 53/1 950–55.

34. *Fortnightly Review*, June 1894; July 1894.

35. Robinson, *Parliamentarian*, 316.

36. Davis Rich Dewey, *Financial History of the United States* (New York: Longmans, Green, and Co., 1915), 446.

37. Bureau of the Census, *Historical Statistics of the United States: Colonial Times to 1970* (Washington, G.P.O., 1975) 2:697.

38. Mansow to Stanley Pullen, October 6, 1894. Pullen Papers. Maine Historical Society. Portland, ME.

39. President Cleveland Message to Congress, January 28, 1895.

40. Theodore Roosevelt to Reed, June 8, 1895. TBR Collection.

41. Robinson, *Parliamentarian*, 320.
42. Ron Chernow, *The House of Morgan* (New York: Atlantic Monthly Press, 1990), 77.

Chapter 19   "God Almighty hates a quitter"

1. William A. Robinson, *Thomas B. Reed: Parliamentarian* (New York: Dodd, Mead & Company, 1980), 196.
2. Washington *Post*, April 1, 1892.
3. Walter Martin, "Charles F. Crisp: Speaker of the House, *Georgia Review* (Summer 1954), 167–69.
4. Allan Nevins, *Grover Cleveland* (New York: Dodd, Mead & Company, 1933), 482.
5. C.R. 53/1. 1033.
6. Ibid., 1033.
7. Ibid., 1034.
8. Ibid., 1034–36.
9. Ibid., 3107.
10. *New York Times*, February 25, 1894.
11. C.R. 53/2. 2403.
12. Ibid., 2382.
13. Cleveland *Papers*, 159.
14. C.R. 53/1. 3336.
15. Washington *Post*, March 31, 1894.
16. Robinson, *Parliamentarian*, 301.
17. Ibid., 302.
18. C.R. 53/2 3791.
19. Tucker, *Reminiscences*, 8.
20. Robert McNutt McElroy, *Groves Cleveland* (New York: Harper & Brothers, 1923), 2:107.
21. Ida Tarbell, *The Tariff in Our Times* (New York: The MacMillan Company, 1914), 218.
22. Tarbell, *Tariff in Our Times*, 218; McElroy, *Grover Cleveland*, 109.
23. McElroy, *Grover Cleveland*, 2:107.
24. Nevins, *Cleveland*, 667.
25. McElroy, *Grover Cleveland*, 2:126.
26. James Anderson Barnes, *John G. Carlisle: Financial Statesman* (New York: Dodd, Mead and Company, 1967), 324.
27. House Report, 234. 53rd Congress, 1st Session (Washington: GPO, 1892), 1.
28. Ibid., 2.
29. Ibid., 4.
30. Ibid., 9.
31. Views of the Minority, 16–17.
32. Nevins, *Cleveland*, 565.
33. Tarbell, *Tariff in Our Times*, 228.

34. C.R. 53/1 1781.

35. C.R. 53/1. 1788.

36. Nevins, *Cleveland*, 566.

37. Tarbell, *Tariff in Our Times*, 222, 228.

38. Ibid., 220.

39. Cleveland to William Wilson, June 24, 1894. *Public Papers of President Cleveland* (Washington, G.P.O., 1897), 310.

40. C.R. 53/2. 8475.

41. Orland Oscar Stealey, *Twenty Years in the Press Gallery* (New York: Publishing Printing Company, 1906), 124.

42. Thomas Settle to Reed, September 3, 1894. Thomas Reed Collection. Bowdoin College.

43. H. Wayne Morgan, *William McKinley and His America* (Syracuse, NY: Syracuse University Press, 1963), 127.

44. Charles Sumner Olcott, *The Life of William McKinley* (New York: Houghton Mifflin Company, 1916), 1:269.

45. Morgan, *William McKinley*, 34.

46. Thomas Beer, *Hanna* (New York: Alfred A. Knopf, 1979), 130–31.

47. Julia Foraker, *I Would Live It Again* (New York: Am. Press, 1932), 130.

48. Morgan, *William McKinley*, 141.

49. Ibid., 143.

50. Foraker, *Live It Again*, 106.

51. Joseph Pettigrew to Reed, November 12, 1894. Thomas Reed Collection. Bowdoin College.

52. Morgan, *William McKinley*, 143.

53. Ibid., 145.

54. "Chandler Repeats It," Washington *Post*, March 23, 1896; Asher Hinds Diary. March 16, 1896. Asher Hinds Papers. Library of Congress.

55. Washington *Post*, March 28, 1896.

56. Morgan, *William McKinley*, 152.

57. Robinson, *Parliamentarian*, 334.

58. Asher Hinds Diary, April 29, 1896. Asher Hinds Papers. Library of Congress.

59. Morgan, *William McKinley*, 158.

60. Arthur Wallace Dunn, *From Harrison to Harding* (New York: G. P. Putnam's Sons, 1922), 145.

61. New York *Times*, April 16, 1896.

62. Robinson, *Parliamentarian*, 345.

63. Susan Reed to Lodge, June 11, 1896. TBR Collection. Bowdoin College.

64. Asher Hinds to Reed, June 18, 1896. TBR Collection. Bowdoin College.

65. Reed to Lodge, June 11, 1896. TBR Collection. Bowdoin College.

66. Washington *Post*, June 19, 1896.

67. Robinson, *Parliamentarian*, 347.

68. Reed to Lodge, June 21, 1896. TBR Collection. Bowdoin College.

69. Dunn, *Harrison to Harding*, 174.

70. Reed to George Gifford, June 14, 1896. TBR Collection. Bowdoin College.

71. Beer, *Hanna*, 160.
72. Reed to Theodore Roosevelt, September 19, 1896. TBR Collection. Bowdoin College.
73. Robinson, *Parliamentarian*, 349.

Chapter 20 *"Empire can wait"*

1. Reed Diary, January 26, 1896; William A. Robinson, *Thomas B. Reed: Parliamentarian* (New York: Dodd, Mead & Company, 1930), 134.
2. Robinson, *Parliamentarian*, 134.
3. Henry Cabot Lodge, *The Democracy of the Constitution and Other Essays and Addresses* (New York: C. Scribner, 1915), 205.
4. 1896 Republican Platform.
5. H. Wayne Morgan, *William McKinley and His America* (Syracuse, NY: Syracuse University Press, 1963), 248.
6. Cleveland, *Public Papers*, 123.
7. Walter Millis, *The Martial Spirit* (New York: Houghton Mifflin, 1931), 40.
8. Ibid., 27.
9. Ibid., 45.
10. Oliver Wendell Holmes, "A Soldier's Faith." Cited in David Traxel, *1898: The Birth of the American Century* (New York: Alfred A. Knopf, 1998), 65.
11. Millis, *Martial Spirit*, 35.
12. Ibid., 33.
13. Cleveland, *Public Papers*, 187.
14. Ibid., 187–90.
15. Ibid., 191.
16. Ibid., 127.
17. "Our Ruler the Speaker," *Nation*, January 21, 1897.
18. Asher Hinds Diary, press clipping from January 27, 1897. Asher Hinds Papers. Library of Congress.
19. Millis, *Martial Spirit*, 47.
20. Robinson, *Parliamentarian*, 357.
21. Reed to H. C. Lodge, March 31, 1893. Thomas Reed Collection. Bowdoin College.
22. Reed to Lodge, August 27, 1897. TBR Collection. Bowdoin College.
23. Reed to Lodge, September 13, 1897. TBR Collection. Bowdoin College.
24. Reed to Lodge, September 17, 1897. TBR Collection. Bowdoin College.
25. Morgan, *William McKinley*, 264.
26. Ibid., 268.
27. Ibid., 253.
28. Traxel, *American Century*, 38.
29. Morgan, *William McKinley* 274.
30. Arthur Wallace Dunn, *From Harrison to Harding* (New York: G. P. Putnam's Sons, 1922), 232.

31. Morgan, *William McKinley*, 277.
32. Millis, *Martial Spirit*, 111–12.
33. Ibid., 116–17.
34. Asher Hinds Diary, March 9, 1898. Asher Hinds Papers. Library of Congress.
35. Evan Thomas, *The War Lovers* (New York: Little, Brown, 2010), 190.
36. Fred H. Harrington, "The Anti-Imperialist Movement in the United States, 1898–1900," *Mississippi Valley Historical Review*, vol. 22, no. 2, 217.
37. *Nation*, December 30, 1897.
38. Roosevelt to Elihu Root, April 15, 1898. Root Papers, Library of Congress.
39. C.R. 55/1. 3814; Washington *Post*, April 14, 1898.
40. Hinds Diary, April 13, 1898. Asher Hinds Papers. Library of Congress.
41. Dunn, *Harrison to Harding*, 233.
42. Washington *Post*, April 16, 1898.
43. Hinds Diary, April 19, 1898. Asher Hinds Papers. Library of Congress.
44. Washington *Post*, August 24, 1902.
45. Washington *Post*, April 20, 1898.
46. Traxel, *American Century*, 121.
47. Millis, *Martial Spirit*, 144.
48. Robinson, *Parliamentarian*, 364.
49. Washington *Post*, February 7, 1898.
50. Washington *Post*, May 12, 1898.
51. Millis, *Martial Spirit*, 177.
52. Ida Tarbell, *The Tariff in Our Times* (New York: The MacMillan Company, 1814), 218.
53. Robinson, *Parliamentarian*, 367.
54. *Nation*, June 30, 1898.
55. Hinds Diary, May 29, 1898. Asher Hinds Papers. Library of Congress.
56. Reed to William Crane, August 14, 1898. TBR Collection. Bowdoin College.
57. Robinson, *Parliamentarian*, 377.
58. Reed to William Crane, September 1, 1898. TBR Collection. Bowdoin College.
59. Congressional Directory, 55th Congress.
60. Millis, *Martial Spirit*, 390.
61. Ibid., 161.
62. Finley Peter Dunne, *Mr. Dooley at His Best* (New York: Scribners, 1943), 58.
63. Millis, *Martial Spirit*, 390.
64. Robinson, *Parliamentarian*, 370.
65. Millis, *Martial Spirit*, 173.
66. Ibid., 175.
67. Thomas. B. Reed, "Empire Can Wait," *Illustrated American*, December, 18, 1897.
68. McCall, *Reed*, 238.
69. C.R. 55/2, 2935.
70. McCall, *Reed*, 239.
71. Reed to Gifford, October 18, 1899. TBR Collection. Bowdoin College.

Coda: Roosevelt Comes to Portland

1. "The President at Portland," New York *Times*, August 27, 1902.
2. Reed to Gifford, November 20, 1899, Thomas Reed Collection. Bowdoin College; William A. Robinson, *Thomas B. Reed: Parliamentarian* (New York: Dodd, Mead & Company, 1930), 380–81.
3. Boston *Globe*, August, 27, 1902.
4. Reed to Bourke Cockran, November 26, 1896. Bourke Cockran Papers. New York Public Library.
5. Robinson, *Parliamentarian*, 378.
6. Reed to Gifford, July 16, 1900. TBR Collection. Bowdoin College.
7. Reed to Gifford, January 28, 1901. TBR Collection. Bowdoin College.
8. Reed to Gifford, May 29, 1901. TBR Collection. Bowdoin College.
9. Reed Diary, June 3, 1900.
10. Washington *Post*, December, 7, 1902.
11. Boston *Globe*, March 30, 1900.
12. Reed Diary, July 23, 1902.
13. Robinson, *Parliamentarian*, 382.
14. Samuel McCall, *The Life of Thomas Brackett Reed* (Boston: Houghton Mifflin Company, 1914), 268.
15. Reed Diary, September 3, 1900.
16. Washington *Post*, August 27, 1902.
17. Ibid.
18. Boston *Globe*, August 27, 1902.
19. New York *Times*, November, 30, 1902.
20. Robinson, *Parliamentarian*, 384.
21. Washington *Post*, December 7, 1902.
22. New York *Times*, December 8, 1902.
23. Richard Stanley Offenburg, "The Political Career of Thomas Brackett Reed" (Ph.D. dissertation, New York University, 1963), 184.
24. Chicago *Tribune*, October, 21, 1906.
25. Thomas B. Reed, "Introduction," *Works of Henry Clay*, edited by Calvin Colton (New York: Henry Clay Pub. Co., 1897), 1:16–17.

Bibliography

Archival Sources

Asher C. Hinds Collection on Thomas B. Reed. Houghton Library, Harvard University.
Asher Hinds Collection, Library of Congress.
Fessenden Family Collection, George J. Mitchell Department of Special Collections & Archives, Bowdoin College Library.
George Gifford Papers, Duke University Library. Durham, North Carolina.
Grover Cleveland Papers, Library of Congress.
Hannibal Hamlin Papers, Library of Congress.
James G. Blaine Papers, Library of Congress.
John Steele Henderson Papers, Southern Historical Collection, Wilson Library, University of North Carolina at Chapel Hill.
Nathan Webb Papers. Maine Historical Society. Portland, Maine.
Stanley Thomas Pullen Papers. Maine Historical Society, Portland, Maine.
Thomas Brackett Reed Collection, George J. Mitchell Department of Special Collections & Archives, Bowdoin College Library.
Tucker Family Papers. Southern Historical Collection, Wilson Library, University of North Carolina at Chapel Hill.
U.S.S. Sybil Logbook, National Archives.
William McKinley Papers, Library of Congress.

Periodicals

Alta California, San Francisco, California.
Bangor Whig and Courier, Bangor, Maine.
Eastern Argus, Portland, Maine.
Kennebec Journal, Augusta, Maine.

New York Times, New York, New York.
Portland Daily Press, Portland, Maine.
Wall Street Journal, New York, New York.
Washington Post, Washington, D.C.

Published Sources

Abott, John C. and Edward H. Elwell. *The History of Maine*. Portland, Brown Thurston Company, 1892.

Bastiat, Frederic. *Economic Sophisms* trans. Arthur Goddard. Princeton, NJ: D. Van Nostrand, 1964.

Barnes, James Anderson. *John G. Carlisle: Financial Statesman*. New York: Dodd, Mead & Company, 1931.

Beer, Thomas. *Hanna*. New York: A. A. Knopf, 1929.

Bigelow, John. *Life of Samuel J. Tilden*, 2 vols. New York: Harper & Brothers, 1895.

Blaine, James. *Eulogy of James Abram Garfield*, Boston: J. R. Osgood, 1882.

Bruce, Robert. *1877: The Year of Violence*. Indianapolis: Bobbs-Merrill, 1959.

Cairo Relief Association. *The White Refugees of Cairo: Their Condition, numbers and wants*. Cairo, IL: February 22, 1864.

Carpenter, Frank G. *Carp's Washington*. New York: McGraw-Hill, 1960.

Chernow, Ron. *The House of Morgan*. New York: Atlantic Monthly Press, 1990.

Clark, Champ. *My Quarter Century of American Politics*. New York: Harper & Brothers, 1920.

Clary, Henry. *Works of Henry Clay: Comprising His Life, Correspondence and Speeches*; ed. by Calvin Colton; introduction by Thomas B. Reed and a history of tariff legislation from 1812 to 1896 by William McKinley, 10 vols. New York: Henry Clay Publishing Co., 1897.

Cleland, Robert Glass and Frank B. Putnam. *Isaias W. Hallman and the Farmers and Merchants Bank*. The Huntington Library, San Marino, CA: 1980.

Cleveland, Grover. *The Public Papers of Grover Cleveland*. Washington: Government Printing Office, 1897.

———. *Speeches and Writings of Grover Cleveland*. New York: Cassell Publishing Company, 1892.

Conkling, Roscoe. *The Life Letters of Roscoe Conkling*. C. L. Webster and Company, 1889.

Degler, Carl N. *The Age of the Economic Revolution 1876–1900*. Glenview, IL. Scott, Foresman, 1967.

Depew, Chauncey. *Life and Later Speeches of Chauncey M. Depew*. Joseph Benson Gilder, ed. New York: Cassell Publishing, 1894.

Dewey, Davis Rich. *Financial History of the United States*. New York: Longmans, Green, and Co., 1915.

Dion, Douglas. *Turning the Legislative Thumbscrews: Minority Rights and Procedural Change in Legislative Politics*. Ann Arbor: University of Michigan Press, 1997.

Donald, David Herbert. *Lincoln*. New York: Simon & Schuster, 1995

Dow, Neal. *The Reminiscences of Neal Dow: Recollections of Eighty Years*. Portland, ME, 1898.

Dunn, Arthur Wallace. *From Harrison to Harding: A Personal Narrative, Covering a Third of a Century, 1888–1921*. New York: G. P. Putnam's Sons, 1922.

Dunne, Finley Peter. *Mr. Dooley in Peace and War*. Boston: Small, Maynard & Company, 1899.

———. *Mr. Dooley at His Best*. New York: Scribners, 1943.

Elwell, Edward H. *Portland and Vicinity*. Portland, ME: Greater Portland Landmarks, Inc., 1975.

Faulkner, Harold Underwood. *Politics, Reform and Expansion: 1890–1900*. New York: Harper, 1959.

Follett, Mary Parker. *The Speaker of the House of Representatives*. New York: Longmans, Green, and Co. 1896.

Foner, Eric. *Reconstruction: America's Unfinished Revolution*. New York: HarperCollins, 1989.

Foraker, Julia. *I Would Live It Again*. New York: Arno Press, 1975.

Friedman, Milton. "The Crime of 1873." *Journal of Political Economy*, vol. 98, no. 6 (December, 1990): 1159–1194.

Friedman, Milton and Anna J. Schwartz. *A Monetary History of the United States, 1867–1960*. Princeton: Princeton University Press, 1963.

Fuller, Hubert Bruce. *The Speaker of the House*. Boston: Little Brown and Company, 1909.

Garrett, Garet. *The American Story*. Chicago, H. Regenery Co., 1955.

Graff, Henry F., *Grover Cleveland*. New York: Times Books, 2002.

Grant, James. *Mister Market Miscalculates*. Mount Jackson, VA: Axios Press, 2008.

Gustafson, Melanie Susan. *Women and the Republican Party*. Urbana: University of Illinois Press, 2001.

Hadley, William Hobart. *First Annual Report of the Minister at Large in Portland*. Portland. ME: F. W. Nichols and Co. 1850.

Haley, J. Evetts. *The XIT Ranch and the Early Days of the Llano Estacado*. Norman: University of Oklahoma Press, 1929.

Harrington, Fred H. "The Anti-Imperialist Movement in the United States, 1898–1900." *Mississippi Valley Historical Review*, vol. 22, no. 2 (September 1935).

Hartog, Hendrik. "Lawyering, Husbands' Rights and 'the Unwritten Law' in Nineteenth-Century America." *Journal of American History*, vol. 84, no. 1 (June 1997).

Hatch, Louis Clinton. *Maine: A History*. New York: American Historical Society, 1919.

Hepburn, Alonzo Barton. *A History of Coinage and the Currency of the United States*. New York: Macmillan Company, 1903.

Hicks, John D. *The Populist Revolt: A History of the Farmers' Alliance and the People's Party*. Minneapolis: University of Minnesota Press, 1931.

History of Woman Suffrage, 6 vols. ed. by Elizabeth Cady Stanton, Susan B. Anthony, Matilda Joslyn Gage and Ida Husted Harper. New York: Fowler & Wells, 1881–1922.

Hobsbawm, Eric. *The Age of Capital*. London: Weidenfeld and Nicolson, 1975.

Holmes, George K. "A Decade of Mortgages." *Annals of the American Academy of Political and Social Science* vol. 4 (May 1894).

Hoogenboom, Ari and Olive Hoogenboom, eds. *The Gilded Age*. Englewood Cliffs, NJ: Prentice-Hall. 1967.

Hoyt, Henry Martin. *Protection Versus Free Trade*. New York: D. Appleton and Company, 1886.

Huntington, A.T. and Robert J. Mawhinney, eds. *Laws of the United States Concerning Money, Banking and Loans, 1778–1909*. Washington: G.P.O., 1910.

Ingersoll, Robert G. *The Political Speeches of Robert G. Ingersoll*. New York: C. P. Farrell, 1914.

Jeffers, H. Paul. *An Honest President*. New York: William Morrow, 2000.

Kent, Frank Richardson. *The Democratic Party*. New York: The Century Co., 1928.

Juglar, Clément. *Brief History of Panics and Their Periodical Occurrence in the United States*. New York: Putnam, 1916.

Laughlin, J. Laurence. *A History of Bimetallism in the United States*. New York: Appleton, 1900.

Lipsky, Seth. *The Citizen's Constitution: An Annotated Guide*. New York: Basic Books, 2009.

Lodge, Henry Cabot. *The Democracy of the Constitution and other Essays and Addresses*. New York: C. Scribner, 1915.

McCall, Samuel. *The Life of Thomas Reed*. Boston: Houghton Mifflin Company, 1914.

McElroy, Robert McNutt. *Grover Cleveland*. New York: Harper & Brothers, 1923.

McPherson, James. *Battle Cry of Freedom*. New York: Oxford, 1988.

Mann, Thomas E. and Norman J. Ornstein. *The Broken Branch: How Congress Is Failing America and How to Get It Back on Track*. Oxford: Oxford University Press, 2006.

Martin, Walter. "Charles F. Crisp: Speaker of the House." *Georgia Review* (Summer 1954).

Miller, Raymond C. "The Background of Populism in Kansas." *Mississippi Valley Historical Review* vol. 11, no. 4 (March, 1925).

Milligan, John D., *Gunboats down the Mississippi*. Annapolis, U.S. Naval Institute, 1965.

Millis, Walter. *The Martial Spirit*. New York: Houghton Mifflin, 1931.

Mills, Roger Q. "Republican Tactics in the House." *North American Review* (December 1889).

Mitchell, Wesley Clair. *A History of the Greenbacks*. Chicago: University of Chicago Press. 1903.

Moore, Joseph West. *Picturesque Washington*. New York: Hurst, 1884.

Morgan, H. Wayne. *From Hayes to McKinley: National Party Politics 1877–1896*. Syracuse, NY: Syracuse University Press, 1969.

———. *William McKinley and His America*. Syracuse, NY: Syracuse University Press, 1963.

Morley, John. *The Life of William Ewart Gladstone*. New York: MacMillan Company, 1911.

Morris, Roy Jr. *Fraud of the Century: Rutherford B. Hayes, Samuel Tilden and the Stolen Election of 1876*. NY: Simon and Schuster, 2003.

Moulton, John K. *The Portland Observatory: The Building, the Builder, the Maritime Scene*. Falmouth, ME. 1916.

Murray, Carolyn Constance. *Maine and the Growth of Urban Responsibility for Human Welfare, 1830–1860*. Ph.D. Dissertation, Boston University, 1960.

Muzzey, David S. *James G. Blaine: Political Idol of Other Days*. New York: Dodd, Mead & Company, 1934.

Nevins, Allan. *Grover Cleveland*. New York: Dodd, Mead & Company, 1933.

Noyes, Alexander Dana. *The Marketplace*. Boston, Little, Brown and Company, 1938.

Oberholtzer, Ellis Paxson. *A History of the United States Since the Civil War*, 5 vols. New York: MacMillan Company. 1931.

Offenberg, Richard Stanley. The Political Career of Thomas Brackett Reed. Ph.D. Dissertation, New York University, 1963.

Official Records of the Union and Confederate Navies. Washington, D.C.: G.P.O., 1896–1906.

Olcott, Charles Sumner. *The Life of William McKinley*, 2 vols. New York: Houghton Mifflin Company, 1916.

Osthaus, Carl R. *Freedom, Philanthropy and Fraud: A History of the Freedman's Savings Bank*. Chicago: University of Illinois Press, 1976.

Platt, Thomas Collier. *The Autobiography of Thomas Collier Platt*. New York. B. W. Dodge & Company, 1910.

Poore, Benjamin Perley. *Perley's Reminscences of Sixty Years in the National Metropolis*, 2 vols. A. W. Mills, 1886.

Randall, J. H. *The Political Catechism and Greenback Songbook*. Washington, D.C.: Rufus H. Darby, 1880.

Rauchway, Eric. *Murdering McKinley: The Making of Theodor Roosevelt's America*. New York: Hill and Wang, 2003.

Reed, Thomas B. "Obstructionists in the House." *North American Review* (October 1889).

———. "Contested Election Cases." *North American Review* (July 1890).

———. *Reed's Rules: A Manual of General Parliamentary Law*. Chicago: Rand, McNally & Company. 1898.

———. "Empire Can Wait." *Illustrated American* (December 18, 1897).

———. "What Shall We Do with the Tariff." *North American Review*. (December 1902).

Rezneck, Samuel. "Distress, Relief, and Discontent in the United States during the Depression of 1873–1878." *Journal of Political Economy* vol. 61, no. 6 (December 1950): 494–512.

Robinsion, William A. *Thomas B. Reed: Parliamentarian*. New York: Dodd, Mead & Company, 1930.

Rothbard, Murray. *A History of Money and Banking in the United States*. Auburn, AL: Ludwig Von Mises Institute, 2002.

Secrest, William. *California Disasters, 1812–1899*. Sanger, CA.: Quill Driver Books, 2005.

Schurz, Carl. *Speeches, Correspondence and Political Papers of Carl Schurz*, 6 vols. Frederick Bancroft, ed. New York: G. P. Putnam's Sons, 1913.

Sherman, John. *Recollections of Forty Years in the House, Senate and Cabinet: An Autobiography*. New York: Werner Company, 1895.

Stealy, Orland Oscar. *Twenty Years in the Press Gallery*. New York: Publishers Printing Company, 1906.

Strahan, Randall, *Leading Representatives: The Agency of Leaders in the Politics and Development of the U.S. House*. Baltimore, MD: Johns Hopkins University Press, 2007.

———. "Thomas Brackett Reed and the Rise of Party Government." In Roger H. Davidson, Susan Webb Hammond, and Raymond W. Smock, eds., *Masters of the House*. Boulder, CO: Westview Press, 1998.

Tausig, Frank William. *The Tariff History of the United States*. New York: G. P. Putnam's and Sons, 1892.

Tarbell, Ida M. *The Tariff in Our Times*. New York: Macmillan, 1911.

Thomas, Evan. *The War Lovers*. New York: Little, Brown, 2010.

Tinkham, George H. *History of San Joaquin County, California*. Los Angeles, Historical Records Co., 1923.

Todd, John. *John Todd: The Story of His Life Told Mainly by Himself*. New York: Harper, 1976.

Traxel, David. *1898: The Birth of the American Century*. New York: Vintage Books, 1998.

Trollope, Anthony. *North America*. London: Dawsons. 1968. Originally published in 1862.

Tuchman, Barbara. *The Proud Tower*. New York: Bantam Books, 1966.

Twain, Mark *Notebook*. Albert Paine, ed. Arlington Heights, IL: Mark Twain Company, 1995.

———. *Life on the Mississippi*. New York: Modern Library, 1994.

Unger, Irwin. *The Greenback Era*. Princeton: Princeton University Press, 1964.

Upchurch, Thomas Adams. *Legislating Racism*. Lexington: University of Kentucky, 2004

Valelly, Richard. "The Reed Rules and Republican Party Building: A New Look." *Studies in American Political Development*. October, 2009. 115–42.

Wellborn, Fred. "The Influence of Silver-Republicans." *The Mississippi Valley Historical Review* vol. 14, no. 4 (March, 1928).

Wells, David Ames. *Recent Economic Changes*. New York: D. Appleton and Company, 1899.

Weinstein, Allen. *Prelude to Populism*. New Haven: Yale University Press, 1970.

West, Richard S. Jr. *Mr. Lincoln's Navy*. New York: Longmans, Green, 1957.

Wicker, Elmos, *Banking Panics of the Gilded Age*. Cambridge: Cambridge University Press, 2000.

Willis, William. *A History of Portland*. Portland, ME: Bailey & Noyes, 1863.

Index

About the Author

JAMES GRANT, THE founder and editor of Grant's Interest Rate Observer, is the author of biographies of Bernard Baruch and John Adams as well as *Money of the Mind* and *The Trouble with Prosperity*, among other books on finance and financial history. He and his wife, Patricia Kavanagh, M.D., live in Brooklyn. They have four grown children.